BETWEEN RESISTANCE AND ADAPTATION

Liverpool Latin American Studies

1. Business History in Latin America: The Experience of Seven Countries
   Carlos Dávila and Rory Miller eds

2. Habsburg Peru: Images, Imagination and Memory
   Peter T. Bradley and David Cahill

3. Knowledge and Learning in the Andes: Ethnographic Perspectives
   Henry Stobart and Rosaleen Howard eds

4. Bourbon Peru 1750–1824
   John Fisher

5. Between Resistance and Adaptation: Indigenous Peoples and the Colonisation of the Chocó, 1510–1753
   Caroline A. Williams

Liverpool Latin American Studies, New Series 5

Between Resistance and Adaptation

Indigenous Peoples and the Colonisation of the Chocó, 1510–1753

Caroline A. Williams

LIVERPOOL UNIVERSITY PRESS

First published 2004 by
Liverpool University Press
4 Cambridge Street
Liverpool L69 7ZU

Copyright © 2004 Caroline A. Williams

The right of Caroline A. Williams to be identified as the author
of this work has been asserted by her in accordance
with the Copyright, Designs and Patents Act, 1988

All rights reserved. No part of this book may be reproduced,
stored in a retrieval system, or transmitted, in any form or
by any means, electronic, mechanical, photocopying, recording,
or otherwise, without the prior written permission of the publisher.

British Library Cataloguing-in-Publication data
A British Library CIP record is available

ISBN 0-85323-729-8

Typeset in Plantin by Northern Phototypesetting Co. Ltd, Bolton
Printed and bound in the European Union by
MPG Books Ltd, Bodmin, Cornwall

For Richard

Contents

Abbreviations		viii
Acknowledgements		ix
Introduction		1
1	Discovery, Exploration and First Experiments in Colonisation	10
2	The *Adelantado* Juan Velez de Guevara and the Colonisation of the Chocó, 1638–1643	43
3	New Experiments in Colonisation, 1666–1673	72
4	Conversion and Control: The Franciscans in the Chocó, 1673–1677	94
5	Protest and Rebellion, 1680–1684	127
6	Government and Society on the Frontier	152
7	Resistance and Adaptation under Spanish Rule: The Peoples of Citará, 1700–1750	192
8	Conclusion	220
Appendix: The Chocó: Towns and Mining Camps (c. 1753)		227
Bibliography		233
Index		242

Abbreviations

AGI   Archivo General de Indias, Seville
AGN   Archivo General de la Nación, Bogotá

Acknowledgements

Many former teachers, colleagues and friends have played a part in the writing of this book, which began as a PhD thesis way back in the 1980s, and went through several reincarnations before emerging in its current, and final, shape. At the University of Warwick, Professor Anthony McFarlane, under whose supervision I began work on the Chocó, has been a constant source not only of inspiration, but of practical help and wise counsel over more years (and versions) than I dare remember. I would also like to extend my thanks to Dr Guy Thomson, for inspiration and friendship during, and since, my years at Warwick, and for his willingness to read and comment on an early draft of Chapter 1. My friends and former colleagues at University College London, Dr Christopher Abel and Dr Nicola Miller, have consistently offered support and encouragement, which I have always both appreciated and valued.

Within my own Department of Hispanic, Portuguese and Latin American Studies, at the University of Bristol, I am especially grateful to Professor David Hook, for his unfailing enthusiasm and encouragement, and for his comments on an early version of Chapter 1, and to Dr Sally-Ann Kitts, for the practical assistance she provided in her role as Head of Department, and for her loyalty and friendship. I also wish to thank Dr Christine MacLeod, of Bristol's Department of Historical Studies, for her regular hospitality and generosity towards a fellow historian. For efficiently and professionally turning my amateurish drawings into publishable maps, I'm grateful to Drew Ellis, of the Department of Geographical Sciences. My home institution, in granting me a year-long University Research Fellowship which freed me from teaching and administrative commitments, has enabled me to see this book through to completion more speedily than would otherwise have been the case.

The Archivo General de Indias in Seville is the principal source of documents for this study, and to its staff I am grateful for making research there enjoyable and productive. For access to some of the documents from the Archivo General de la Nación, in Bogotá, which are cited here, I am once again indebted to Professor Anthony McFarlane, who freely made available to me the entire microfilmed collection of 'Caciques e Indios' held at the University of Warwick. To the anonymous readers who read the previous draft of this study on behalf of Liverpool

University Press, I am grateful for their generous comments and helpful recommendations. The final product has undoubtedly benefited from their careful reading and knowledgeable advice.

I would also like to thank Professor John Fisher, of Liverpool University, for recommending this study for publication, and for waiting patiently for its arrival.

These acknowledgements would not be complete without a word of thanks to those family members who, unknown to themselves, have made possible the lengthy task of writing (and re-writing) this study. I am especially grateful to my late father, Erik David Hansen, and my mother, Tricia Hansen, for never wavering in their support, encouragement and belief, and to my husband, Richard Williams, for his calm presence, and for the loving support he has unfailingly offered over the many years that this book has been 'in progress'.

Chapters 3 and 4 of this book are partly based on material published in Caroline A. Williams, 'Resistance and Rebellion on the Spanish Frontier: Native Responses to Colonization in the Colombian Chocó', *Hispanic American Historical Review* (Duke University Press), Vol. 79, No. 3, 1999, pp. 397–424.

Introduction

This is a study of frontier colonisation in Spanish America. It focuses on a remote and inhospitable region of dense rainforest and heavy rainfall situated on the Pacific flank of the colonial territory of the Nuevo Reino de Granada, the New Kingdom of Granada. The region extended across the entire lowland area stretching from the isthmus of Panama in the north to Buenaventura in the south, was separated from the interior by the Cordillera Occidental, and, by the 1560s, had come to be known to the Spaniards as El Chocó.[1] The area was inhabited at first contact by a multiplicity of indigenous groups, a native population that was, at least initially, for the most part fiercely hostile to outsiders. But the Pacific lowlands contained gold as well as hostile Indians, and this ensured that the Chocó was to experience not the neglect associated with other similarly inaccessible regions of the empire, but repeated Spanish incursions. From the beginning of the sixteenth century, armed expeditions of conquest (*entradas*), peaceful penetrations by secular priests and prospective settlers, and Jesuit and Franciscan missionaries all attempted, with varying degrees of success, to extend Spanish control over this extremely desirable gold-producing area.

Colonisation of the Chocó proved, however, to be a complex and lengthy process for Spaniards and Indians alike, a process that in many respects was not complete even as the colonial period drew to a close. Each expedition of exploration and conquest launched from the directions of Urabá/Darién, the Pacific coastal stretch and the New Granadan interior between 1510 and 1570 was violently resisted and successfully repulsed by the indigenous population. More than a century then elapsed between the first sustained experiment in settlement, which took place between the 1570s and 1590s, and effective domination, achieved in the 1690s. Thereafter, the Chocó was converted into a major mining district of the territory that was to become, in 1739, the Viceroyalty of New Granada. But despite the undoubtedly profound transformations that occurred over the centuries of contact between Indians and Europeans in this isolated corner of the empire, colonisation led neither to large-scale Spanish settlement and development, nor to the conversion of native peoples to the Christian faith.

Over the period 1570–1670, the indigenous population of the Chocó suffered severe demographic decline – a result of conquest, disease, enslavement, migration, and the intensification of warfare between native groups to which repeated Spanish incursions gave rise. By the late seventeenth century, all but a handful of these groups had ceased to exist as distinct entities. The development of gold-mining brought European settlers and thousands of slaves to exploit deposits of precious metal across a territory that had formerly supported agriculture, hunting and fishing alone. Spanish colonisation also led to the introduction of an alien system of government, and to the imposition of a new religion. Further changes occurred at the level of indigenous society and culture. Indians, for example, appropriated those elements of European material culture – especially tools, trinkets and cloth – that could usefully be incorporated into native traditions and practices, and, over time, adopted some of the institutions of colonial government to contain the burdens associated with subjection to Spanish rule. Nevertheless, those groups that survived more than two centuries of contact with Europeans also proved remarkably successful at protecting their identities and cultures from encroachment by white or black settlers, and preserving many of the customs and beliefs that gave meaning and purpose to their lives.

This study charts the process whereby the Chocó came to be incorporated into the political and economic life of the colony, and analyses the dynamics of Spanish–Indian interactions over the period stretching from the earliest phase of contact at the beginning of the sixteenth century to the mid-eighteenth century, which marked the beginning of the secularisation of missionary *doctrinas* across the empire, and the partial retreat of the Franciscans from their mission among the Pacific lowlands people. In common with the most recent historiography on frontier experiences elsewhere in Spanish America, it approaches the frontier from the perspective of a 'contested ground' – a zone, in Donna Guy and Thomas Sheridan's definition, 'of constant conflict and negotiation over power – economic, political, and cultural'.[2] It offers an analysis of the development of Spanish policy towards the conquest – later 'pacification' – of frontier populations and the strategies devised to subdue and control native groups, while paying particular attention to the varied, often subtle and pragmatic ways in which indigenous peoples responded to the efforts of Spaniards to reorganise native social, political and economic structures, and to replace native religions and rituals with Christian alternatives.

Central to this history are the peoples of Citará. Inhabitants of a stretch of territory corresponding roughly to the headwaters of the Atrato river, the Citará proved to be among the most resilient of all native groups encountered by Spaniards as they embarked on a succession of campaigns to extend their control over the Pacific lowlands region, and among the most successful at developing strategies that enabled them to preserve many of their social and cultural practices long after the processes of conversion and assimilation should have been completed. Althoug the Citará were protected by distance and terrain from the earliest encounters between Indians and Spaniards in the sixteenth century, by the 1620s, isolation had given way to openness and collaboration, as Indians became increasingly dependent on the products of European technology that could only be procured through contact with outsiders. Despite episodes of rebellion over the years that followed, the desire to trade – to exchange local resources and labour for tools, cloth, and trinkets of various kinds – led Indians into increasingly frequent, and often peaceful and amicable, relationships with Spaniards inside and outside the Chocó frontier. Spanish colonisation, however, was not to be based on a reciprocal exchange of goods and services with the peoples of Citará. As Spaniards gained in numbers and confidence, the balance between natives and Europeans shifted decisively in favour of the latter, and by the end of the seventeenth century, Spanish domination over the Chocó was effectively assured.

Native communities did not readily succumb to European pressures, however, but instead devised new strategies to resist, and at times openly to challenge, the conditions of their subjection to colonial rule. Many Indians capitalised on the existence of large tracts of uninhabited land in the northernmost reaches of the Chocó to reconstitute their communities in territories distant from, and still largely unknown to, Europeans. Where flight was not a viable option, Indians resorted to a whole range of other strategies to resist colonial pressures. Some adopted the now well-known 'weapons of the weak'.[3] Others learned to exploit and manipulate political and economic rivalries between Spanish groups – miners, missionaries, other settlers – and to use Spanish legal channels to defend resources essential to survival, to demand the rights and privileges accorded native peoples under colonial law, and to protect the interests of the indigenous community under the changed conditions of the eighteenth century. Through methods such as these, Indians succeeded in subverting key elements of the colonial project and, on occasion, in obliging the Spanish authorities to adapt colonial requirements to the particular conditions of the frontier itself. 'Spanish conquest was a biological and cultural disaster for many native peoples', Guy and Sheridan remind us, 'but those who survived manipulated the symbols, material items, and even the legal system of the conquerors to protect their communities and pursue their own goals within the empire'.[4]

Such processes of resistance and adaptation among native populations faced with European colonisation have long been articulated by historians of the major Indian societies of Mesoamerica and the Andean region.[5] On the frontiers of empire, however – where Europeans often confronted indigenous groups who, because of the more fragmented nature of their societies and the greater inaccessibility of the territories they inhabited, took far longer to subdue – the strategies developed by native peoples to contain and control colonial domination are only gradually beginning to be charted.[6] It is to this developing field of study that the chapters that follow seek to make a contribution. Three principal aims have guided my research. The first was to identify, insofar as the sources made this possible, the native groups that inhabited the region at contact, to describe the main characteristics of their social and political organisation, and to explain why the fragmented nature of their societies, coupled with the forbidding environment, constituted insurmountable obstacles to early colonisation efforts. My second aim was to look closely at the ways in which

Indians and Spaniards interacted in the Chocó over the 120 years between the 1570s and 1690s, when the two sides contested control over the land and its resources. Those interactions, as we shall see, were neither uniform, consistent, nor unchanging, for Spaniards and Indians related to each other in different ways at different times and in response to different circumstances. By focusing on three distinct phases of colonising activity – 1570s to 1590s, 1630s to 1640s, and 1660s to 1680s – I show that while Indians and Europeans fought each other on numerous occasions, and rebellion was a frequent outcome of unwarranted or excessive demands, the Chocó was not always conflict-ridden. The familiarity that resulted from a long history of contact, for instance, taught Spaniards that peaceful penetrations that relied on gift-giving or barter trade brought better results than did armed expeditions of conquest. Similarly, Indians did not always forcibly reject contact with outsiders, and outright, generalised and unvarying resistance was not the only response to European intrusions. Where contact posed no threat to native groups, and brought benefits to both sides, both sides made efforts to accommodate each other and to coexist.

Moreover, when conflict did occur in the Chocó, it did not always pit the two societies contending for the frontier against each other, for internal struggles within the Spanish and Indian camps were as characteristic of the frontier as was contention between the camps. Starting in the sixteenth century, for example, Spanish incursions disrupted accepted patterns of behaviour between indigenous groups, and in an environment already characterised by competition – warfare between native groups long preceded the arrival of Europeans – some Indians identified early on that access to European weapons could enable them to advance their own goals against those of their neighbours. For the Spanish, expansion onto the gold-rich Chocó provoked competition over pacification and colonisation strategies and, importantly, over spoils: who was to gain jurisdiction over the best deposits, and who was to gain control over native labour? Competing interests, in other words, complicated relationships within as well as between the European and Indian groups, and on occasion, as in the early 1680s, natives and Spaniards could even co-operate to bring about the expulsion of individual settlers – especially missionaries, who, in seeking to congregate and convert indigenous populations, threatened to disrupt peaceful exchanges between both sides.

My third and final aim was to examine the shape and conduct of secular and religious administration on the frontier following the last major episode of rebellion in the mid-1680s, the nature of the society created by the Spanish over the first half of the eighteenth century, and the impact of the region's particular characteristics on the strategies adopted by indigenous peoples to protect their interests, preserve those elements of their culture that continued to serve a purpose in native society, and maintain their way of life. We will see that distance from the main population centres, an insalubrious climate and difficult terrain, and the problems of transport and communication to which these gave rise, all discouraged Spanish settlement. A white population that was limited to mine administrators, overseers, a few officials and a handful of priests, coupled with the corruption, factionalism and 'spirit of animosity' that 'for all time have been the character of the Chocó provinces',[7] permitted indigenous peoples to maintain some distance from Spanish missionaries and settlers alike, and contributed greatly to the persistence of native values and the survival of indigenous practices that were so widely reported in the late colonial Chocó. Acculturation, with all that such a process entailed, cannot here be judged to have been entirely successful: Spanish language, social customs and religion made few inroads into native life.

Accordingly, Chapter 1 discusses early Spanish explorations of the region, establishes the identity of the native groups that inhabited the region at contact, considers the impact of European intrusions on demographic trends and relations between indigenous groups, and analyses the difficulties involved in colonising frontier regions inhabited by distinct groups, further divided into small, dispersed, mobile communities, which retained considerable independence of action from each other. Detailed discussion of political and economic organisation will be left to Chapter 4, where the obstacles posed by native systems of organisation to the Franciscan project of *reducción* and Christian indoctrination will be considered. Chapters 2 to 5 focus on the decades of the 1630s to the 1680s, with specific reference to the development of Spanish policy towards the pacification of frontier groups, the particular strategies adopted in the Chocó – *guerra a sangre y fuego*, gift-giving and trade, military aid, and a missionary-led programme of Christian indoctrination and assimilation – and the responses each of these provoked on the part of indigenous groups. The actions and reactions of the peoples of the Chocó will be seen to have been both closely related to Spanish pacification methods, and central to the success or failure of Spanish colonisation efforts. Finally, Chapters 6 and 7 discuss the social, political and economic transformation of the Chocó during the first half of the eighteenth century, and the continuing challenges that native groups on the frontier, especially the Citará, continued to pose to Spanish efforts to integrate Indian populations into the life of the colony, and to convert them to the Christian faith.

Reference should now be made to the terms that I have adopted in these chapters, and to the strengths and limitations of the sources upon which they are based. I have chosen to entitle this study *Between Resistance and Adaptation* in spite of the particular difficulties posed by the use of such terms to encompass the 'myriad ways' in which indigenous peoples responded to the challenges of colonisation and the outcome thereof. In the Chocó, as in so many regions where native people confronted Spanish settlers, soldiers, administrators and priests over the centuries of colonial rule, indigenous attitudes and actions – resistance, accommodation, collaboration, negotiation, subversion, rebellion, flight, etc. – defy rigid classification.[8] For the purposes of this study, however, resistance should be understood to mean not only outright rebellion, but also all other expressions of non-compliance, including 'failure to adhere to the sacraments, idolatry, fighting, and flight',[9] as well as those more subtle strategies commonly defined as 'resistant adaptation',[10] such as negotiation and manoeuvre, which native peoples devised to exploit divisions between rival Spanish groups, manipulate colonial legal institutions, and further their own goals and interests. As this study will show, however, not every Indian action should be interpreted as an act of defiance, for many Indians willingly appropriated as many European goods as could usefully be incorporated into native practice, swiftly recognised the advantages of trade, settled comfortably into the Spanish names conferred upon them at baptism, and in some cases at least made ever greater concessions to secure the benefits they derived from closer association with the Spaniards.

Two further clarifications are in order. In accordance with current conventions, I have chosen to use the term 'New Granada' to refer to the territory that essentially comprised colonial Colombia, although this was a name that applied to several administrative entities of different size and jurisdictional reach over the centuries of colonial rule. For the sake of clarity, however, no reference will be made here to the shifting boundaries and jurisdictions to which the region was subject during the period of Spanish rule.[11] My decision to make the Citará the main subjects of analysis, rather than the larger 'tribal' or linguistic group known as Emberá, which also included, by the seventeenth century, the Tatama, Poya and Chocó, requires more by way of explanation.[12] Throughout the period covered by this study, Spaniards in closest contact with Indians on the frontier differentiated not between the two large linguistic groups that occupied the Chocó – the Emberá and the Waunana – but between the region's various 'provinces' or 'nations', recognised as such principally by the territories they inhabited and by their relations with their neighbours. No evidence has been found to suggest that the Emberá functioned as a homogeneous group during the colonial period, or that they ever acted in concert against either the Europeans, or their native enemies. Instead, while the sources certainly indicate that the Tatama and the Chocó were traditional allies and, over the course of the seventeenth century, increasingly difficult to distinguish in colonial documents, relations with the Citará were characterised by a deep distrust and hostility that had their roots in age-old conflicts, rather than by an acknowledgement of shared interest in the face of the Spanish advance. Indeed, as late as 1714, Vicente de Aramburu, *oidor* of the Santa Fe *audiencia*, commented of the Tatama that 'although they share one same language with the Chocoes and Citaraes, the province is [a] different one', and that 'they detest the Citaraes'.[13]

Furthermore, because the Citará proved to be among the most resilient of all groups encountered by Spaniards on the Chocó frontier, posing perhaps the greatest challenges to successful colonisation, there exists a fairly full documentary record covering nearly two centuries of contact with Europeans. Indians, of course, left no written documents of their own, and rarely, if ever, did those left by the Spanish record without bias the practices, preferences and interests of native peoples anywhere in the empire.[14] For the historian of the Chocó, these problems are made worse by the characteristics of life on a frontier in which gold was the principal attraction, one that pulled Spaniards to settle a region that would otherwise, given its climate, isolation and difficulties of access and communication, undoubtedly have been ignored. Yet for all the difficulties involved in interpreting documents that, as David Weber has pointed out, 'restrict our vision . . . almost entirely to the hegemonic discourse of the colonisers',[15] the sources relating to the long and difficult process of subjecting the Citará to Spanish colonial rule have proved remarkably rich in the kind of detail that enables us to gain important insights into the perspectives, motivations and interests of this indomitable indigenous group, and of the changes and continuities experienced by their peoples over a long period of contact, peaceful and otherwise, with Europeans within and beyond the boundaries of the colonial Chocó.

Notes

1. Originally the name applied to a tribal territory situated to the west of Anserma, and separated from it by another territory known as 'Sima'. By the late 1560s, the name 'Chocó' began to be used widely to refer to the entire lowland region. See Kathleen Romoli, 'El Alto Chocó en el siglo XVI', *Revista Colombiana de Antropología*, Vol. 19, 1975, p. 12. For a further discussion of the origins of the term 'Chocó', see also S. Henry Wassen, 'Apuntes etnohistóricos chocoanos', *Hombre y Cultura*, Vol. 1, No. 2, 1963, pp. 5–8.
2. Donna J. Guy and Thomas E. Sheridan, 'On Frontiers', in *idem* (eds.), *Contested Ground: Comparative Frontiers on the Northern and Southern Edges of the Spanish Empire*, Tucson, AZ, University of Arizona Press, 1998, p. 4. This is just one definition drawn from the most recent scholarship on the frontier. Elsewhere, we see the frontier defined as a zone 'of transculturation – multiethnic and multiracial'; as a zone 'where political and economic integration is incomplete and unstable, and where no single society . . . holds uncontested sway'; as a zone 'of interaction between two different cultures'; as a 'zone of interpenetration between two previously distinct societies'; and as 'a zone of intercultural penetration'. See, respectively, Jane M. Rausch, *Colombia: Territorial Rule and the Llanos Frontier*, Gainesville, FL, University Press of Florida, 1999, p. x; Thomas E. Sheridan, 'The Limits of Power: The Political Ecology of the Spanish Empire in the Greater Southwest', *Antiquity*, Vol. 66, 1992, p. 154; David J. Weber, *The Spanish Frontier in North America*, New Haven and London, Yale University Press, 1992, p. 10; Howard Lamar and Leonard Thompson, 'Introduction', in *idem* (eds.), *The Frontier in History: North America and Southern Africa Compared*, New Haven and London, Yale University Press, 1981, p. 4; and Jeremy Adelman and Stephen Aron, 'From Borderlands to Borders: Empires, Nation-States, and the Peoples in between in North American History', *American Historical Review*, Vol. 104, 1999, p. 814.
3. These are, in James C. Scott's influential definition, 'the ordinary weapons of relatively powerless groups: foot dragging, dissimulation, desertion, false compliance, pilfering, feigned ignorance, slander, arson, sabotage, and so on'. See *Weapons of the Weak: Everyday Forms of Peasant Resistance*, New Haven and London, Yale University Press, 1985, p. xvi. For a more general exposition of the thesis, centred on the concept of the 'hidden transcript', see James C. Scott, *Domination and the Arts of Resistance: Hidden Transcripts*, New Haven and London, Yale University Press, 1990.
4. Guy and Sheridan, 'On Frontiers', p. 13.
5. Though this is by no means an exhaustive list, the following studies have been particularly influential in changing our understanding of the ways in which native peoples responded to the extension of Spanish colonialism across the empire. For the Andes, see, for example, Karen Spalding, *Huarochirí: An Andean Society under Inca and Spanish Rule*, Stanford, CA, Stanford University Press, 1984; Steve Stern, *Peru's Indian Peoples and the Challenge of Spanish Conquest: Huamanga to 1640*, Madison, WI, and London, University of Wisconsin Press, 1982; and Kenneth Mills, *Idolatry and its Enemies: Colonial Andean Religion and Extirpation, 1640–1750*, Princeton, NJ, Princeton University Press, 1997. For Mesoamerica, see, for example, Nancy Farriss, *Maya Society Under Colonial Rule: The Collective Enterprise of Survival*, Princeton, NJ, Princeton University Press, 1984; James Lockhart, *The Nahuas after the Conquest: A Social and Cultural History*

of the Indians of Central Mexico, Sixteenth through Eighteenth Centuries, Stanford, CA, Stanford University Press, 1992; and Louise Burkhart, *The Slippery Earth: Nahua–Christian Moral Dialogue in Sixteenth-Century Mexico*, Tucson, AZ, University of Arizona Press, 1989.

6 Among historians of frontier regions, the major shift has involved a refocusing of interest away from concern with frontier institutions, best exemplified by Herbert Bolton and the generation of Borderlands historians whom he trained, towards an exploration of the ways in which Indian peoples adapted to the gradual expansion of Spanish domination across the empire. See, for example, Susan M. Deeds, 'Indigenous Responses to Mission Settlement in Nueva Vizcaya', in Erick Langer and Robert H. Jackson (eds.), *The New Latin American Mission History*, Lincoln, NE, and London, University of Nebraska Press, 1995, pp. 77–108; idem, 'Colonial Chihuahua: Peoples and Frontiers in Flux', in Robert H. Jackson (ed.), *New Views of Borderlands History*, Albuquerque, NM, University of New Mexico Press, 1998, pp. 21–40; idem, 'First Generation Rebellions in Seventeenth-Century Nueva Vizcaya', in Susan Schroeder (ed.), *Native Resistance and the Pax Colonial in New Spain*, Lincoln, NE, and London, University of Nebraska Press, 1998, pp. 1–29; William L. Merrill, 'Conversion and Colonialism in Northern Mexico: The Tarahumara Response to the Jesuit Mission Programme, 1601–1767', in Robert W. Hefner (ed.), *Conversion to Christianity: Historical and Anthropological Perspectives on a Great Transformation*, Berkeley and Los Angeles, University of California Press, 1993, pp. 129–63; Cynthia Radding, *Wandering Peoples: Colonialism, Ethnic Spaces, and Ecological Frontiers in Northwestern Mexico, 1700–1850*, Durham, NC, and London, Duke University Press, 1997; David Sweet, 'Misioneros jesuitas e indios "recalcitrantes" en la Amazonia colonial', in M. León Portilla, M. Gutiérrez Estévez, G.H. Gossen and J.J. Klor de Alva (eds.), *De palabra y obra en el Nuevo Mundo*, Vol. I, *Imágenes interétnicas*, Madrid, Siglo XXI de España, 1992, pp. 265–92; Sergio Villalobos R., *La vida fronteriza en Chile*, Madrid, Editorial Mapfre, 1992; Weber, *The Spanish Frontier*; and Neil L. Whitehead, 'Native Peoples Confront Colonial Regimes in Northeastern South America (c.1500–1900)', in Frank Salomon and Stuart B. Schwartz (eds.), *The Cambridge History of the Native Peoples of the Americas*, Vol. III, Part 2: *South America*, Cambridge, Cambridge University Press, 1999, pp. 382–442.

7 Such was the opinion of an unidentified clerical source, writing from Quibdó in 1795, and quoted in Sven-Erik Isacsson, 'The Egalitarian Society in Colonial Retrospect: Emberá Leadership and Conflict Management under the Spanish, 1660–1810', in Harald O. Skar and Frank Salomon (eds.), *Natives and Neighbors in South America: Anthropological Essays*, Gothenburg, Göteborgs Etnografiska Museum, 1987, p. 103.

8 The sheer variety and vitality of indigenous reactions to European conquest and colonisation are increasingly being acknowledged by scholars of colonial America. Writing in 1992, on the occasion of the Columbian quincentenary, Steve Stern, for example, discussed the 'myriad ways' in which 'Amerindians engaged – assisted, resisted, appropriated, subverted, redeployed – European colonial projects, utopias, and relationships', drew attention to the processes of 'alliance, manoeuvre and conflict' that characterised the conquests of Mexico, Peru, and regions across the empire, and argued that in many such regions, indigenous peoples 'remained sufficiently large, socially cohesive, economically endowed, politically engaged, and culturally independent to take colonisers down paths of conflict, frustration, disillusion and struggle'. Susan Deeds, writing specifically of the peoples of northern Mexico, argued that the European presence on this distant frontier resulted not in 'a simple tension between survival and incorporation', but in 'complex processes of resistance, obfuscation, accommodation, appropriation, subversion, revival, and invention'. William Taylor and Franklin Pease, writing of the nature of resistance and survival across the Americas from the fifteenth to the twentieth

centuries, emphasised the importance of doing justice 'simultaneously to complicated local changes as well as continuities', and of seeing 'American history more inclusively, not primarily as the repeated collision of alien worlds in which the only possible outcomes are absolute domination or liberation'. See Steve J. Stern, 'Paradigms of Conquest: History, Historiography, and Politics', *Journal of Latin American Studies*, Vol. 24, Quincentenary Supplement, 1992, pp. 23, 29, 31; Susan M. Deeds, 'Legacies of Resistance, Adaptation, and Tenacity: History of the Native Peoples of Northwestern Mexico', in Richard E.W. Adams and Murdo J. MacLeod (eds.), *The Cambridge History of the Native Peoples of the Americas, Vol. II, Part 2: Mesoamerica*, Cambridge, Cambridge University Press, 2000, p. 45; and William B. Taylor and Franklin Pease (eds.), *Violence, Resistance, and Survival in the Americas: Native Americans and the Legacy of Conquest*, Washington and London, Smithsonian Institution Press, 1994, pp. 10–11.

9   Susan Schroeder, 'Introduction', in *idem* (ed.), *Native Resistance*, p. xiv. For a further discussion of the nature and meaning of resistance, see Radding, *Wandering Peoples*, pp. 264–301. For Radding, 'resistance may encompass individual acts of rebellion or nonconformity', but, she maintains, 'its historical significance points to the mobilization of dispossessed social classes, captives, slaves, or subjugated nations to lessen the burdens imposed on them and to ransom a part of their dignity'.

10 See, for example, Radding, *Wandering Peoples*, pp. 249–50; Deeds, 'Indigenous Responses to Mission Settlement', pp. 77–78; and Nicholas Griffiths, 'Introduction', in *idem* and Fernando Cervantes (eds.), *Spiritual Encounters: Interactions between Christianity and Native Religions in Colonial America*, Birmingham, University of Birmingham Press, 1999, p. 2. See also Stern, *Peru's Indian Peoples*, p. xvii.

11 For a summary of shifting boundaries and jurisdictions, see Anthony McFarlane, *Colombia Before Independence: Economy, Society, and Politics under Bourbon Rule*, Cambridge, Cambridge University Press, 1993, p. 6.

12 For current usage in anthropological research, see, for example, Patricia Vargas Sarmiento's 'Los Emberá, los Waunana y los Cuna: cinco siglos de transformaciones territoriales en la región del Chocó', in Pablo Leyva (ed.), *Colombia Pacífico*, 2 vols., Bogotá, Fondo José Celestino Mutis, FEN, Colombia, 1993, Vol. I, pp. 293–309, and *Los Emberá y los Cuna. Impacto y reacción ante la ocupación española. Siglos XVI y XVII*, Bogotá, Cerec, 1993. See also Isacsson's 'The Egalitarian Society', and 'Emberá: territorio y régimen agrario de una tribu selvática bajo la dominación española', in N.S. Friedemann (ed.), *Tierra, tradición y poder en Colombia. Enfoques Antropológicos*, Bogotá, Biblioteca Básica Colombiana, 1976, pp. 21–38.

13 Documento No. 6, in Victor Zuluaga Gómez (ed.), *Documentos inéditos sobre la historia de Caldas, Chocó y Risaralda*, Pereira, Universidad Tecnológica de Pereira, 1988, p. 40.

14 Many of the documents that will be cited in this study are contained in various 'expedientes', 'testimonios', 'testimonios de autos', 'cuadernos', etc., which are essentially collections of transcripts of letters, petitions, declarations, witness statements, royal *cédulas* and official correspondence, and other miscellaneous papers, selected and copied by an indivual or institution seeking to bring a particular case before the attention of Crown. The biases and interests of the individual, or group of individuals, who forwarded these collections of documents to Spain have, of course, to be borne in mind in assessing the validity of the information they contain.

15 David J. Weber, 'Blood of Martyrs, Blood of Indians: Towards a More Balanced View of Spanish Missions in Seventeenth-Century North America', in David Hurst Thomas (ed.), *Columbian Consequences Vol. 2: Archaeological and Historical Perspectives on the Spanish Borderlands East*, Washington, Smithsonian Institution Press, 1990, p. 433.

CHAPTER ONE

Discovery, Exploration and First Experiments in Colonisation

Early reconnaissance

Native groups of the territory that was to become known as 'El Chocó' were among the first indigenous peoples of the South American mainland to make contact with Spanish explorers searching for gold and booty in the early sixteenth century. Santa María la Antigua de Darién, founded in 1510 on the western side of the Gulf of Urabá, became Spain's first permanent settlement in this part of South America and an important base for further exploration. From Darién, expeditions fanned out in several directions: towards the isthmian region that lay to the north of Santa María; towards the Pacific Ocean that lay to the west of the *serranía* de Darién; and towards the Atrato river, which empties into the Gulf of Urabá and opened access to the Colombian interior and the lands of the Chocó.[1] By settling at Darién, Spaniards gained a 'most favourable position' for reconnaissance – 'a gateway', as Sauer described it, 'to the unknown south and west'.[2] But the principal attraction of the Gulf of Urabá, and the reason it was chosen as a base for Spanish settlement, lay in the early discovery of gold and treasure among the Indian villages of the region.

First contacts were established in 1501, when an expedition conducted by Rodrigo de Bastidas and Juan de la Cosa voyaged along the Colombian coast and penetrated the Gulf of Urabá. No firm attempt at settlement was made on that occasion, but as Spaniards had engaged in peaceful and profitable trade with Indians in Urabá, in 1503 the Crown signalled its intention to found a government in the gulf. In 1504, Juan de la Cosa was selected to lead a new expedition to Urabá where he was authorised to found a settlement. But nothing came of these plans during La Cosa's eighteenth-month stay there. Far from seeking peacefully to colonise, La Cosa's intention was to obtain more treasure, and instead of building a settlement, the members of his expedition looted the town of Urabá, sacked and plundered the town of Darién, on the opposite side of the gulf, and raided the countryside surrounding both settlements in search of food and gold. La Cosa was, as Gonzalo Fernández de Oviedo wrote a decade later, a good example of the kind of discoverer who 'with better reason might be called alterers and destroyers of the land, since their purpose was not so much to serve God and King as to rob'.[3]

La Cosa returned to Spain in 1506, bringing captured treasure in the form of ornaments produced by craftsmen from parts unknown. Two years later, at

Burgos, the decision was made to authorise two concessions for the settlement of the eastern and western sides of the Gulf of Urabá (the latter at Veragua rather than Darién), under the command of Alonso de Hojeda and Diego de Nicuesa respectively. These attempts also proved abortive. Nicuesa's expedition divided, suffered heavy losses, and failed to meet the terms of the concession granted. Hojeda's managed to build a fort and settlement, San Sebastián de Urabá, but it was soon abandoned because of food shortages and attack by Indians whom the Spaniards had repeatedly raided. Spanish fortunes, severely threatened by the actions of Nicuesa and Hojeda, were only saved by the survivors' move to the Indian town of Darién, named Santa María la Antigua, where, under the leadership of Vasco Núñez de Balboa, they prospered. Unlike his predecessors, Balboa avoided provoking the Indian communities upon whom the settlers depended for supplies, and instead made alliances with friendly caciques to the west and northwest of Santa María. These were to provide the food, guides and carriers to enable the Spaniards to begin more systematic reconnaissance.[4]

One important direction taken by Spaniards from Santa María was up the Atrato river, which Balboa named the San Juan. There, he reported, 'I have sure news [that there] are very rich mines on both sides'. By the end of 1512, Spaniards had completed an expedition, gained their first impressions of the Indian inhabitants of parts of the northern Chocó, learned of the existence of gold mines among Indians whose lands lay somewhere to the east (the legendary Dabeiba), and experienced the difficulties of exploring the terrain along the Atrato. 'The manner in which this river must be navigated', Balboa wrote to the king the following year, 'is by canoes of Indians, for there are many small and narrow arms, some closed by trees, and one cannot enter except in canoes three or four palms wide.'[5] Reports indicate that the expedition reached densely inhabited sections of the river – an island of sixty small villages, each consisting of clusters of about ten houses; a settlement of some 500 dispersed houses; and a further settlement, said to be inhabited by 'cannibals' who fled in the face of the Spanish approach. We do not know exactly the route taken or the identity of the groups Balboa's men encountered. However, from the distances and topographical features described, Sauer concluded that Spaniards may have reached the vicinity of Quibdó in 1512.

After completing the Atrato expedition, Balboa turned his attention to the lands that lay to the west of Santa María la Antigua – the *serranía de Darién* and beyond that the Pacific Ocean, sighted for the first time by Europeans on or about 27 September 1513.[6] Not until the summer of 1515 did the Spanish attempt another search for Dabeiba via the Atrato river; this was during Pedrarias Dávila's disastrous tenure as governor and captain general of Castilla del Oro, the name given to the area Balboa occupied for Spain.[7] Two expeditions were sent. The first was led by Balboa; the second by Juan de Tavira, a businessman from Santa María. Neither found the fabled wealth of Dabeiba. Balboa's party suffered attack by Indians along the river, and established that the mines from which the cacique was said to obtain gold lay farther away than had earlier been supposed. Tavira's expedition suffered a worse fate. Indians used 'war canoes' to block the Spaniards' passage: Tavira and many others were drowned;

the remainder of the party, led by Francisco Pizarro, was forced back to Darién. Though later expeditions searched for Dabeiba, these were the last two expeditions to be conducted up the Atrato for several years.[8]

The discovery of the South Sea, however, and the subsequent establishment of a settlement at Panama by Pedrarias Dávila in August 1519, opened up a new base for exploration of the Chocó, which was now conducted down the Pacific rather than up the Atrato (see Map 1).[9] Francisco Pizarro commanded the first expedition to sail south along the tropical coastline of Colombia, which left Panama in November 1524.[10] In January of the following year, he arrived at a small anchorage, soon to be known as Puerto de la Hambre, and in February, he discovered Puerto de la Candelaria, in the Gulf of Cupica, between Cruces Point and the Bay of Solano.[11] Diego de Almagro's expedition of 1525, with Bartolomé Ruiz as pilot, expanded Spanish knowledge of this coastal region far more than that of his partner Pizarro. Taking only a small vessel (45 tons), Almagro and Ruiz navigated for some 1500 km, passing the delta of the San Juan, discovering the Bay of Buenaventura (which he named Bahía de la Cruz), and reaching the San Juan de Micay river, before returning safely to Panama. Almagro returned to the San Juan the following year, accompanied by Pizarro. Attracted, no doubt, by the gold ornaments they found among the local population, their initial intention was to establish a Spanish colony there, but the attempt was soon abandoned.[12]

Spanish interest in this stretch of coastline and what lay beyond it was short-lived. This was partly because the advance down Colombia's Pacific coast resulted in several violent encounters with the inhabitants of coastal settlements. At a palisaded settlement discovered by Pizarro in or near the Bay of Solano in April 1525, for example, serious fighting broke out when Spaniards seized food and gold ornaments; when Almagro arrived at the same site in July, the Indians took the initiative and attacked, for which he retaliated by setting fire to the village, thereafter known as Pueblo Quemado.[13] Spaniards also lost interest in the region because they failed to find evidence of great riches, although Almagro apparently obtained gold from the well-populated area of the Baudó river, and he and Pizarro were reported to have taken a substantial cache of gold from a single Indian community in the vicinity of the San Juan de Micay.[14] Furthermore, all the expeditions faced severe difficulties penetrating the 'impenetrable, rugged or swampy forests of the Chocó'. As Robert Cushman Murphy indicated, the rivers between Darién and the southern Colombian coast were impossible to enter, even by the smallest Spanish vessels utilised in Pacific navigation (40 to 45 tons). 'North of Cape Corrientes', Murphy explained, 'the continental slope is precipitous and the only stream of large volume is the Juradó; farther south the river mouths are blocked by bars and shallows on which heavy surf breaks. Even the San Juan, which has several miles of navigable waters along its inland course, enters the ocean by way of constricted mouths, only two or three of which provide tortuous channels for large launches through the delta.' As Spanish exploration in the 1520s could only take place in canoes or on foot along the river banks, and as the expeditions frequently suffered hunger and disease, Pizarro and others came to accept that the conquest of this region would require

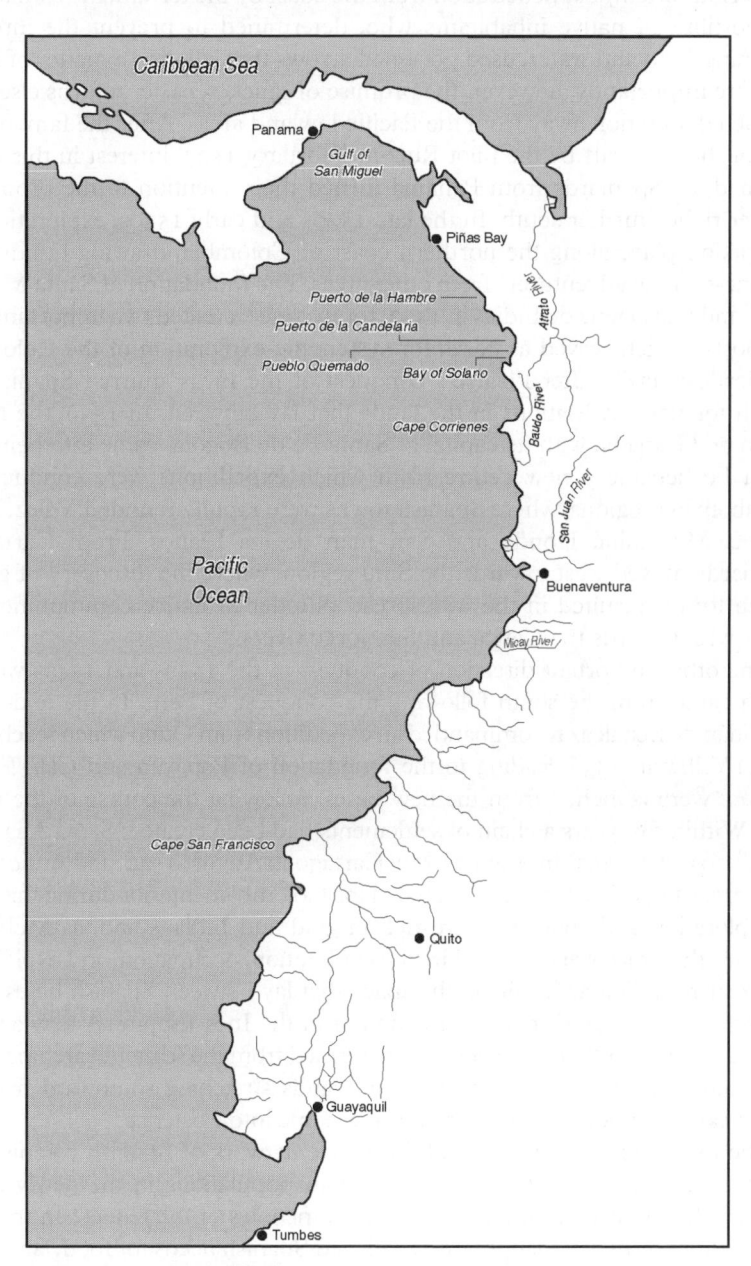

Map 1 *Early Pacific exploration.*

too great an investment of lives.[15] Thus, Spaniards were deterred from making any serious attempt at penetration from the coast by the terrain, the climate, and the hostility of native inhabitants who, determined to prevent the intruders obtaining food and water, used poisoned arrows that killed in a matter of hours.

More importantly, however, the promise of quicker, easier returns elsewhere distracted attention away from the Pacific lowland areas. After the famous capture of the Inca raft by the pilot Ruiz in February 1527, interest in this region declined, as Spaniards from Panama turned their attention to the promise of greater riches further south. In the late 1520s and early 1530s, exploration was also taking place along the northern coast of Colombia, drawing hundreds of fortune-seeking adventurers from other areas. The foundation of Santa Marta in 1526, and Cartagena de Indias in 1533, for instance, created two important frontier posts, which served as bases for systematic exploration of the Colombian interior, especially after Pizarro's conquest of the Incas spurred Spaniards to search for new civilisations in the lands that lay between. In 1539, the Nuevo Reino de Granada, with its capital at Santa Fe de Bogotá, came into being and Santa Fe became a new centre from which expeditions were conducted to neighbouring regions, where Spanish towns were rapidly founded: Vélez, Tunja, Ibagué, Mariquita, Honda and San Juan de los Llanos. From Cartagena, Spaniards moved west towards the Sinú region, where the discovery of gold in Indian tombs resulted in the widespread plunder of native communities, and south-west towards the Cauca and San Jorge rivers.[16]

One other important direction of conquest in the 1530s and 1540s was that which came from the south following the conquest of Peru. In the mid-1530s, Sebastián de Benalcázar commanded an expedition from Quito which reached the Cauca Valley in 1536, leading to the foundation of Popayán and Cali. Further *entradas* were launched from the new bases, following the course of the Cauca river. Within five years a chain of settlements had been created: Santa Ana de los Caballeros (Anserma) in August 1539, Cartago in August 1540, and Antioquia in November 1541. The lands discovered in the Colombian interior during this phase of exploration and conquest were rich in gold and Indians and, as McFarlane explains, their discovery resulted in 'the exploration, occupation, and exploitation of the surrounding areas, filling the space that lay between Spanish bases in the Caribbean and Spanish realms of conquest in the Inca Empire. A new and distinctive network of Spanish colonisation, formed from the scattered archipelago of settlements that Spaniards created in the lands stretching southward from the Caribbean coast deep into the interior now came into existence.'[17]

The formation of this 'new and distinctive network of Spanish colonisation', and the discovery of gold and dense Indian populations in the newly settled territory, had important implications for the peoples of the Chocó. In the short and medium term these lands largely satisfied Spanish needs for food, labour and especially precious metals, and only a few explorers ventured towards the Pacific lowlands over the following decades. One of those who did was Captain Gómez Hernández, who in 1539 led fifty men from Anserma along Indian trails that took them as far as the Andagueda river. The expedition, aimed at extending Spanish control over the lands that lay to the west of the Cauca Valley, was cut short by the stiff resistance offered by the inhabitants of a small settlement near the Andagueda, which left two Spaniards wounded and at least one other dead.[18] This small settlement was inhabited by Indians known by the name Chocó, but as this was also the name by which the entire region from Panama to Buenaventura was known, the 'Chocó' Indians will henceforth be referred to as 'Chocoes'.

Another Spaniard to risk an *entrada* into the Chocó was Pedro de Heredia. Early in 1536 Heredia led a large and well-equipped expedition from San Sebastián de Buenavista (founded near the old site of San Sebastián de Urabá) which once again followed the course of the Atrato in search of Dabeiba, only to be forced back to base by the terrain and insects, which were reported to have caused widespread illness among the men. The poisoned darts used by the Indians and the climate, which, in the words of Franciscan chronicler Fray Pedro Simón, was 'so rainy . . . that they could find no [dry] wood to make a fire', were added deterrents.[19] A third expedition was undertaken by Pascual de Andagoya, who in 1540 led a company of 200 men, on four ships, to take possession of the recently created *gobernación* of San Juan, a vaguely defined stretch of coastal territory extending from Panama to Ecuador.[20] Andagoya did not intend to colonise the hostile environment of the Pacific littoral, but to march inland to Cali and take possession of those parts of the Cauca Valley already occupied by Benalcázar, which he hoped to incorporate into his own *gobernación*. Although Andagoya failed signally to wrest control of the interior from Benalcázar, who had been granted the newly created *gobernación* of Popayán, and although he made no effort to explore inland, the expedition did result in further reconnaissance of the coast. A party of his men penetrated the Chocó's San Juan river, until they were forced back to the coast by 'bellicose Indians'; the estuary of the Raposo river was explored, a small brigantine navigating up-river for a distance of some three leagues; the port of Buenaventura was founded on the right bank of the Anchicayá; and a manageable though dangerous and difficult route between the Cauca Valley and the coast was opened. Buenaventura even survived for a while – some 250 Spaniards were present there for several months after its foundation – but it proved ephemeral. Before the end of 1541, at least 80 men had abandoned the port to make their way south, and 30 more had been killed by Indians from the San Juan river.[21] By 1582, only three men – two soldiers and an *alcalde* – were reported to reside there, and in the years that followed Spaniards repeatedly suffered attack by Indians from the Chocó and from the Raposo region to the south.[22]

Andagoya's *gobernación* of San Juan came to an end partly because of defeat by Benalcázar, and partly because of attack by local Indian groups. But in fact, Andagoya's aims and actions show clearly that by the early 1540s, Spanish interests had shifted to other areas, especially the densely settled Cauca and Magdalena rivers. It was precisely from the Cauca Valley that later movements into the Pacific lowlands were to come. In the mid- to late sixteenth century, for example, Spaniards explored the lowland areas lying to the south of the Chocó and west of Popayán, where they hoped to find a route to connect that town to the Pacific. Because rich deposits of precious metals were discovered, attempts were made to establish permanent Spanish settlements in the region, and before mid-century several *encomiendas* had been granted to *vecinos* of Popayán in the upper reaches of the San Juan de Micay and Saijá rivers.[23] The early colonisation of these southernmost sections of the Pacific littoral meant that the history of the region over the following century would be quite different from that of the Chocó, and for this reason it will not be considered in this study.

The Chocó was, then, the scene of some of the earliest contacts between Spanish explorers and native peoples of the South American mainland, resulting from the establishment of Santa María la Antigua at Darién in 1510, and the discovery of the Pacific in 1513. Exploration of the Chocó up the Atrato and down the Pacific coast, however, was too difficult, and the Indians too hostile, to justify systematic efforts to colonise, especially after the conquest of the Inca empire and the discovery of gold and large sedentary populations in the New Granadan interior. As soon as greater riches became available elsewhere, the Chocó was largely neglected, until such time, that is, as evidence began to circulate of the existence of rich deposits of precious metals in the region, and their possible exploitation seemed to offer a solution to the depletion of the gold-mines and the decimation of Indian populations in the settlements of the interior, most especially the Upper Cauca Valley and the Antioquian region of the Central Cordillera. There is, from about the mid-sixteenth century, a close correlation between recession in the mining industries of those areas and Spanish efforts to occupy and colonise the Chocó frontier.

Colonial gold-mining

By the late 1530s, the quest for gold that had driven Spanish explorers to take part in dangerous expeditions into the unknown interior from Urabá, Santa Marta and Cartagena, as well as from the Inca domains of Peru and Quito, was beginning to yield handsome rewards, and to make possible a form of exploitation that was entirely different from the plunder and grave-robbing that characterised the early years of Spanish occupation of New Granadan territory. Not all regions settled in the 1530s and 1540s proved equally rich in gold, but large sedentary populations capable of supporting groups of settlers were just as important in these early years.[24] Bogotá and Tunja, centres of Chibcha civilisation, had few resources of precious metals, but their conquest gave the Spanish control over a dense and disciplined population supported by intensive sedentary agriculture and trade, which could be redirected to the supply of the Spanish towns and mining settlements that were rapidly emerging to the east and west of the Magdalena river. The Pasto area, in the southern highlands, was also relatively poor in gold, but it was ideal for cultivation of varied crops such as maize, potatoes and cereals. In Popayán and Cali, and in the Antioquian region of the Central Cordillera, on the other hand, Spaniards encountered not only large populations, fertile lands and organised agricultural systems, but also traditions of indigenous gold-mining and gold- and metal-working susceptible to intensive exploitation.[25]

The discovery of large native populations and rich and extensive gold deposits in New Granadan territory marked the end of looting and pillaging and the beginning of more thorough colonisation.[26] Settlements gradually sprang up along the mountain ranges of the Andean cordilleras, and along the banks of the Cauca and Magdalena rivers. Paralleling this, several mining districts developed, as Spaniards searching for new or better rewards expanded their sphere of influence across an increasingly large area. One major mining district was established along the eastern flank of the Cordillera Central, overlooking the Magdalena Valley. This region extended from the mines of Remedios to those of Neiva, discovered in 1543. The gold and silver deposits of Mariquita, exploited after 1543, also formed part of this district. Another mining area, situated close to the city of Pamplona, flourished after 1552. To the south and west, mining districts developed along the banks of the Cauca river and in the Upper Cauca Valley: Popayán, where placers were exploited as early as 1544; Anserma-Cartago, discovered in 1539–40; and Almaguer, founded in 1551. The gold deposits of the Cerro de Buriticá, at the northern end of the Cordillera Central, were exploited after 1541, and from there Spaniards spread out to the placers of Santa Fe de Antioquia. New districts were incorporated in the 1580s and 1590s, including the vein mines of Ibagué and the rich deposits of Cáceres and Zaragoza.[27]

By the mid-sixteenth century, then, Spaniards had occupied the most heavily populated parts of the interior, laid the foundations of a gold-mining industry central to the development of the colonial economy, and opened New Granada's first great mining cycle (see Map 2).[28] For the remainder of the colonial period gold constituted New Granada's principal export to the metropolis, financed the importation of European merchandise (from Spain and, through contrabandists, from other European nations), and fostered the development of other economic sectors.[29] Furthermore, because the mining economy depended for its survival on the continuous incorporation of new deposits to replace exhausted mines, that search for additional sources of gold also fuelled Spanish expansion into inhospitable frontier zones.[30] This was especially notable in the case of the Chocó: only the prospect of discovery of new sources of precious metal could induce the Spaniards to penetrate a region in which heavy rainfall, dense rainforest and hostile Indians served as real deterrents to colonisation. It was in the 1570s, for example, when troubling signs appeared in the mining sector as a result of both the depletion of existing deposits and demographic decline among the indigenous population that supplied the mining enterprises with labour, that the first major expedition of pacification to the Chocó was undertaken, under the command of Melchor Velásquez. Further *entradas* were launched in the 1620s, 1630s and 1640s – a time of acute recession in the mining industry. Despite repeated failures, and an untold number of deaths, new campaigns of pacification took place in the 1660s and 1670s, precipitated once again by recession. From the late sixteenth century onwards, in other words, the fortunes of the peoples of the Chocó came to be inextricably linked with the fortunes of New Granada's mining economy.

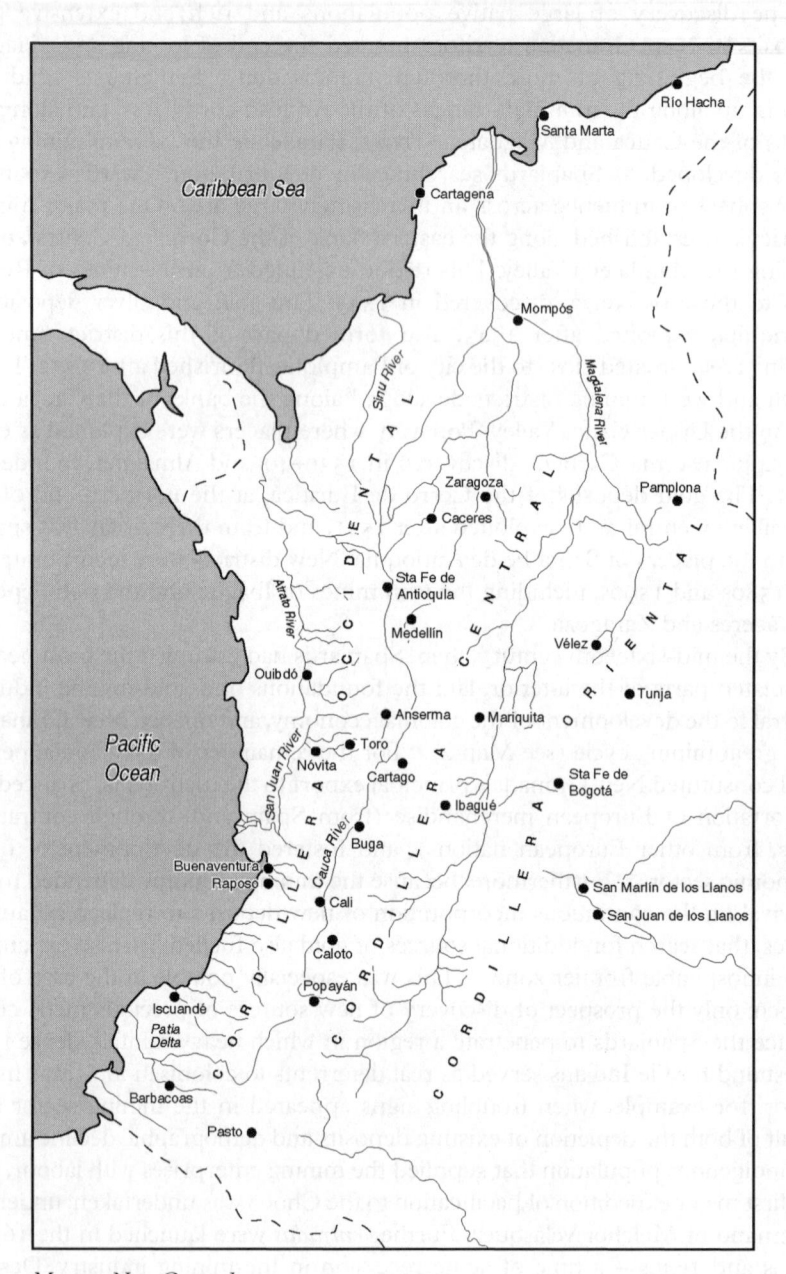

Map 2 *New Granada.*

Sixteenth-century peoples of Urabá and the Pacific

The hostile environment of the Chocó – the difficult terrain and the resistance of the native inhabitants – discouraged extensive exploration of the territory during the first half of the sixteenth century. Contacts between Indians and Spaniards were therefore intermittent, usually violent, and always of short duration. For these reasons, Spanish expeditions gathered little evidence to help us identify the Indian groups they encountered during the early years of reconnaissance, or to estimate their size. Reports of Balboa's first investigations of the Atrato river indicated that the region stretching south from the Gulf of Urabá to somewhere near Quibdó was quite densely populated – an island of sixty small villages, a settlement of 500 dispersed houses, and a settlement of 'cannibals' were all mentioned. These descriptions, however, serve to confuse rather than to clarify the identity of the peoples concerned. As Sauer concluded, the Indians described in 1512 could not be the Indians who occupied this zone in the seventeenth century, because one of the principal characteristics of the indigenous population of the Chocó was their dispersed pattern of settlement. Sauer thus proposed that the Indians encountered by the Balboa expedition were 'cacicazgos of Cuevan character, kinship, and speech'. Romoli's later study of the Cueva peoples of the isthmian region, on the other hand, proposed that the area lying to the south of the Gulf of Urabá was inhabited by the Cuna peoples who, under pressure from enemy groups, migrated northwards in the seventeenth century to colonise lands left vacant by the demographic collapse that befell the Cueva. And in a recent study, Colombian anthropologist Patricia Vargas Sarmiento argues that when Spaniards first penetrated the Atrato in the early sixteenth century, the middle and lower reaches of the river were occupied by groups belonging to the 'Cuna cultural tradition', while the upper reaches were controlled by the Emberá, encompassing several distinct groups of the Chocó region.[31]

Our knowledge of the native peoples who resisted Spanish incursions along the Pacific coast north of Cape Corrientes in the 1520s and 1530s is equally limited. Robert Cushman Murphy's account of Pizarro's and Almagro's operations demonstrates the existence of numerous settlements along that stretch of coastline, but extant sources do not provide sufficient detail to identify the indigenous communities encountered during those years.[32] Vargas Sarmiento proposes that parts of the Pacific coast to the north of Cape Corrientes were occupied by a group she calls Monguinera, which had become extinct by the seventeenth century. This group, like the Burumia (or Burgumia) and the Soruco who were believed to inhabit this area in the second half of the seventeenth century, also belonged, Vargas considers, to the 'Cuna cultural tradition'.[33] Suffice to say that the partial information supplied by early explorers severely hampers our understanding of the population of both the lower Atrato and the Pacific coast when contact with the Spanish first took place.

Patchy information also prevents us from assessing the impact of Spanish exploration on the native population during the first decades of the sixteenth century. It seems unlikely, however, that the first indigenous communities of the

Chocó to make contact with Europeans experienced anything like the appalling consequences suffered by the Cueva peoples of the isthmus, especially after the arrival of Pedrarias Dávila, whose methods of 'pacification' are amply described elsewhere.[34] A pre-conquest Cueva population estimated to have numbered 230,000 had become almost extinct before mid-century, victims not just of European diseases but of 'savage and unpredictable' conquest, as Romoli described it.[35] It was precisely because of their complete devastation within decades of the European arrival that the Cuna, beginning in the early seventeenth century, were able to migrate into and occupy territory which at the time of the conquest had been wholly Cueva-controlled.[36] The effects of Spanish activities in Chocó territory were, therefore, not as destructive as they were in Castilla del Oro, but the extent and the nature of the impact made by European incursions in the first few decades of the sixteenth century remains unclear. There is, for example, no evidence to indicate whether frequent incursions down the Pacific coastline or along the course of the Atrato river resulted in the introduction of the hitherto unknown epidemic diseases that were to prove so destructive of the Chocó population in the late sixteenth and seventeenth centuries.

First experiments in colonisation

Contact between Spaniards and Indians in the Chocó was sporadic before the mid-sixteenth century, and limited to communities located along a stretch of the Atrato river and the Pacific coastal region explored by Pizarro and Almagro. The early 1570s, however, opened a period of more prolonged contact between Spaniards and native groups in the Chocó, only this time expansionary movements were conducted not from Urabá and Panama, but from bases within New Granada itself – especially Popayán, Anserma, Buga, Cali and Cartago.[37] In October 1572, the governor of Popayán, Don Gerónimo de Silva, ordered an expedition of pacification to the region, under the command of Melchor Velásquez, a *vecino* of Buga. It was to be directed towards two areas in particular: that of the Chanco, whose territories extended to the west of Roldanillo, from the slopes of the western cordillera to the headwaters of the Calima river, and that of the Chocoes, inhabitants of a stretch of land lying between the headwaters of the San Juan and Atrato rivers.[38] Both these groups were known to Spaniards. The Chocoes were first identified in 1539, when the Gómez Hernández expedition was repulsed by Indians from a community in the vicinity of the Andagueda River, although no further contact between this group and the Spaniards was to take place before 1573.[39] The Chanco, on the other hand, were known for their attacks against Spanish settlements in the Cauca Valley and against travellers using the trails that linked Cali with Anserma and Cartago. This was not meant to be merely a punitive expedition against the Chanco and Chocoes, however. Velásquez's commission was one of pacification, and in his instructions provision was made for the foundation of two settlements, intended as the first step in the colonisation of the region.[40] Of the several settlements which Velásquez or his fellow Spaniards founded in the heart of the Chocó over the following years, only one – Nuestra Señora de la Consolación de Toro – achieved some permanence. But the importance of the expedition transcended the foundation of a small Spanish city which in its entire existence rarely counted more than a few score residents: first, because it led to the establishment of crucial alliances with Indian groups friendly to the Spanish; secondly, because it marked the beginning of a twenty-year Spanish presence in the region; and thirdly, because it gave Spaniards a far clearer sense of the peoples of the Chocó and of their resources.

The documents relating to this phase of activity in the Chocó are also of particular significance for understanding the consequences of Spanish colonisation efforts. Kathleen Romoli's excellent work on extant sources, for example, enables us to identify nineteen separate Indian groups inhabiting the southern half of the region in the 1570s, and to provide both the first reliable indications of the territories they controlled and the first firm estimates of population size. Hers were particularly valuable contributions to the literature on the Chocó, because by the 1630s, many of the groups she identified had either become extinct, or been absorbed by larger, more resilient neighbours. Romoli's studies, moreover, coupled with Fray Pedro Simón's *Noticias historiales*, allow us to examine the relationships that existed between groups and the way those relationships affected responses towards Spaniards, and to assess the effects of Spanish colonisation methods in this region in the last quarter of the sixteenth century.[41] However, the sources only make possible identification of those Indian groups that inhabited the southern or 'Upper' Chocó – an area then comprising some 18,000 sq km, from Cape Corrientes in the north to just beyond the mouth of the San Juan river in the south, and stretching inland almost as far as the west bank of the Cauca river.[42] Spanish penetrations to the Chocó between the 1570s and 1590s were directed towards this area, rather than towards the 'Lower' Chocó, for which we must rely on the evidence of seventeenth-century penetrations. But before examining the seventeenth-century data, the 1573 expedition will be described, and the impact of this first experiment in colonisation on relations between native peoples in the 'Upper' Chocó in the late sixteenth century will be discussed.

The expedition that left the town of Roldanillo in May 1573 under the command of Melchor Velásquez was composed of 94 armed men, two priests, and two Dominican friars.[43] Clearly unaware of the real nature of the terrain, and the difficulties of crossing it, the Spaniards also took 122 horses, all of which perished, according to one of the participants, the Dominican Fray Martín de Medrano, from hunger and thirst. Between June and November 1573, the Spaniards founded the city of Nuestra Señora de la Consolación de Toro on the banks of the Chancos river, within the jurisdiction of the city of Cartago, and explored the territory of the Yngará and the Tootuma. Meanwhile, a small heavily armed force of approximately 45 men conducted a punitive expedition against the Chanco Indians (and the neighbouring Chiloma), alleged to have been responsible for attacks against Spaniards. And a second armed party launched a surprise attack on a sleeping settlement, inhabited by Chocoes, where they captured over 130 Indians from 'eight houses built on *barbacoas*' and seized gold and 'jewels'.[44]

Medrano's account of the expedition shows that over the months between June and November 1573, the Spaniards learned that a multiplicity of independent groups inhabited the Chocó at this time. In addition to the Chanco and Chocoes, the Spanish encountered the Yngará, Tootuma and Guarra, and heard of many other groups that controlled territory in the region. On the other side of the Darién (Atrato) river, towards Cape Corrientes and northwards towards Panama, Spaniards discovered that there were many more groups, an 'enormous number' according to the Dominican, who were enemies of the Chocoes. Even within the territory the Spaniards explored, the native population was thought to be very dense. The 'province' of Yngará was reported to number 'more than three thousand Indians'; the settlement of the Chocoes attacked by the Pedro Moriones party was said to be surrounded by 'many Indians'; and 'the territory [inhabited by Indians] of the Chocó language' was considered to extend 'over more than fifty leagues without interruption'.[45] These observations should not, of course, be interpreted as accurate estimations of the size of the region's native population, but rather as impressions, which to a great extent reflected the optimism of members of early expeditions who expected a share in the distribution that would follow pacification.[46]

Indian groups who came into contact with the Spanish expedition of 1573 did not react in a uniform way to the presence of the strangers. The Chocoes reacted in a hostile manner to Spanish aggression and the capture of over 130 Indians. Moriones and his men remained in territory controlled by this group for 13 days, hopeful that Indians would submit peacefully, but instead the Spaniards faced armed resistance: 'a large number of Indians fought there with the Spaniards who were unable to sleep by day or by night and [were] in grave danger'. We may be certain that the reaction of the Chanco was equally hostile, given that they and their neighbours the Chiloma faced an armed force intent on revenging repeated assaults on Spanish settlements. The reaction of the Yngará and Tootuma, on the other hand, was entirely different. The Yngará, a large group initially and perhaps over-optimistically estimated at 3000 at contact, not only received the Velásquez party amicably – 'all the caciques of that province, of whom there are seven, came to serve him' – but also placed at the Spaniards' disposal many Indians for the exploration of Tootuma territory. The Tootuma at first reacted with suspicion: only one 'cacique', according to the 1574 testimony, approached the Spanish. But by the end of October, a further 34 caciques 'submitted peacefully . . . to said Captain Melchor Velázquez representing the King Don Felipe'. Thereafter they were said to be peacefully engaged in cultivating lands and building dwellings for the Spaniards living among them.[47] Such co-operation was, however, only short-term, for within a few years the Tootuma rebelled, killing some 80 Spaniards, among whom were four of Velásquez's own sons.[48]

Why the Yngará and the Tootuma reacted amicably to the expedition, providing supplies and Indians for service as well as a safe haven from hostile neighbouring groups, is not entirely clear, especially since the Dominican Martín de Medrano stated that Indians from both provinces 'habitually launched attacks [against the Spanish]', and that they, as well as the Chanco, Chiloma and Guarra, were to be parcelled out to the first settlers, or *vecinos*, in *encomienda*. However, the consequences of Indian co-operation, even in the short term, were to prove to be of great significance both to the Spanish and to the Indians themselves. On 6 December 1573, Nuestra Señora de la Consolación de Toro was transferred to a new site in Tootuma territory. This transfer allowed the Spanish to secure, for the first time, a foothold on the Pacific side of the Western Cordillera and to begin small-scale mining operations. In 1578, a new *gobernación* was formed in Chocó territory, and Melchor Velásquez was appointed its first governor. When Velásquez returned to Toro later that same year, he brought with him more settlers, clearly intended to secure and safeguard the enterprise.

To advance colonisation of the region, however, Spaniards had to expand from their main frontier post in Toro to incorporate surrounding territory and subdue Indian groups determined to resist further incursions. On this front, Spaniards were far less successful, and the resistance of native groups – first the Chocoes, and, from the late 1580s, the Noanama – severely limited their expansion. During Velásquez's tenure as governor, for instance, a new city, Santiago, was founded in territory controlled by the Chocoes, but it apparently met an early and violent end. Further disasters followed, before Velásquez finally resigned his post in 1592. In 1588, a large and well-equipped expedition undertaken against the Chocoes failed to produce lasting results, partly because the Spaniards took as their guides Indian captives from an earlier *entrada*, who deliberately misled them.[49] In 1590, another well-armed force of seventy men, personally commanded by Velásquez, undertook an *entrada* against the Noanama Indians of the San Juan river, a group whom the Spaniards had not yet encountered, but who were rumoured to inhabit territories fantastically rich in gold. This *entrada* left the governor with a severe thigh wound, and resulted in the death of twenty soldiers and a priest in combat, and a further twenty men during the party's retreat to Toro.[50] It was not only the large armed *entradas* that met Indian resistance, moreover. Even small groups of colonists who risked stepping outside of Yngará- or Tootuma-controlled territory to mine in areas controlled by other groups faced instant retribution. In 1592, Captain Luis Franco and two of his colleagues were killed by Chocoes for entering their lands 'inconsiderately to take gold'. That same year, Captain Diego Paredes, a *vecino encomendero* of Toro, was killed, along with nine Indians, for setting up an 'estancia' on the Yarrama (Cajón) river, bordering territory considered to belong to the Noanama, 'and where they disembark and come to rob ... the mines of this city'.[51]

When Melchior de Salazar, a *vecino* of Cartago and Velásquez's successor as governor, arrived in Toro, he ordered the withdrawal of settlers from all outposts and mining camps that could not be defended and concentrated on dispatching expeditions against Indian groups that threatened the survival of the town itself and of the mines then being exploited within its district. In 1593, twelve men, under the command of Captain Simón Sánchez, were sent against the Chocoes.

Twenty men, commanded by Captain García Guerrero, were to defend the mining camps set up along the Cajón and Negro rivers from attack by Noanama Indians. More than thirty soldiers and an unspecified number of Indian 'friends', led by Captain Cristóbal Montaño, conducted an *entrada* that followed the course of the San Juan river as far as its estuary in the Pacific. At least two of these expeditions engaged in combat with Indians. The Sánchez expedition was described as having been 'of great effect'. The Montaño expedition, which traversed the lands of the Noanama, was reported to have met Indians in battle nine times, and to have set fire to twenty native dwellings and a maize crop before returning to Toro with 37 large canoes, five Indian captives, and a booty of gold. This expedition also encountered a new group, the Yacos, about whom little was written except that they 'wore their hair cut differently from that of the Noanama'.[52]

Notwithstanding the reported success of Salazar's operations against the Chocoes and Noanama, and the extensive exploration that resulted from the 1593 *entrada* up the San Juan river, in 1595 his *gobernación* was suppressed: Salazar fell victim not to Indian resistance but to divisions and feuding among Spaniards in Toro, which led to the transfer of that city to the banks of the Cauca River and the incorporation of the *gobernación* of Chocó into that of Popayán. By the mid-1590s, then, the Velásquez/Salazar experiment in colonisation of the Chocó had come to an end. However, the consequences of this twenty-year exercise in frontier colonisation were far-reaching. Between the mid-1570s and the mid-1590s, the Spanish expanded considerably their knowledge of the region, its inhabitants, and most especially its resources. When in 1596 Melchior de Salazar composed his 'Descripción de la Tierra', which he hoped would result in the re-establishment of the *gobernación*, he described in some detail what he had learned about the gold deposits of the region, and where they were to be found. Salazar stated, for example, that the expedition against the Noanama discovered 'many gold mines which the natives exploit'. He also included evidence, obtained from the Indian Aricum, who was captured during the Montaño campaign, to show that the metal from which the Noanama Indians fashioned their 'insignia' (gold jewellery and patens, or breastplates) came from streams in their territory, 'and that they heated it in the fire and that they banged it with stones'. Aricum also informed Salazar 'that heading north is the province of the Botabiraes, and that it consists of many people and that they have much gold in the rivers, and wear jewellery in their noses and ears. Further north ... is the province of the Eripedes Indians to one side of a very large river ... these have much gold'.[53] Salazar was, of course, keen to promote the Chocó and demonstrate its potential, and while he did not succeed in regaining his *gobernación*, the reports of rich gold-bearing streams and rivers that emerged as a result of his and Velasquez's activities there undoubtedly remained in the imagination of colonists in the towns and cities of the Cauca Valley. In the 1620s and 1630s, when recession hit the mining industry of the interior, it was to the Chocó that Spaniards once again turned their attention in search of new deposits to exploit.

Peoples of the 'Upper Chocó'

However unsuccessful Spanish efforts to secure permanent occupation of the Chocó region were in the long term, the effects of their settlement of Toro and of the many *entradas* they conducted into the surrounding areas were decidedly destructive for the indigenous population. Nineteen separate and independent groups are thought to have inhabited the southern or 'Upper' Chocó alone prior to the 1570s, although many of these the Spanish learned of not through direct contact but from Indian 'friends' and captives. Botabirá, Cirambirá, Cobira, Coponama, Chanco, Chiloma, Chocoes, Ebirá, Eripede, Guarra, Morirama, Noanama, Orocubirá, Sima, Tatama, Tatape, Tootuma, Yaco and Yngará: these are the groups that occupied some 18,000 sq km between Cape Corrientes and Buenaventura before the arrival of the Spaniards (see Map 3).[54] Each group was independent and autonomous within a more or less defined and generally

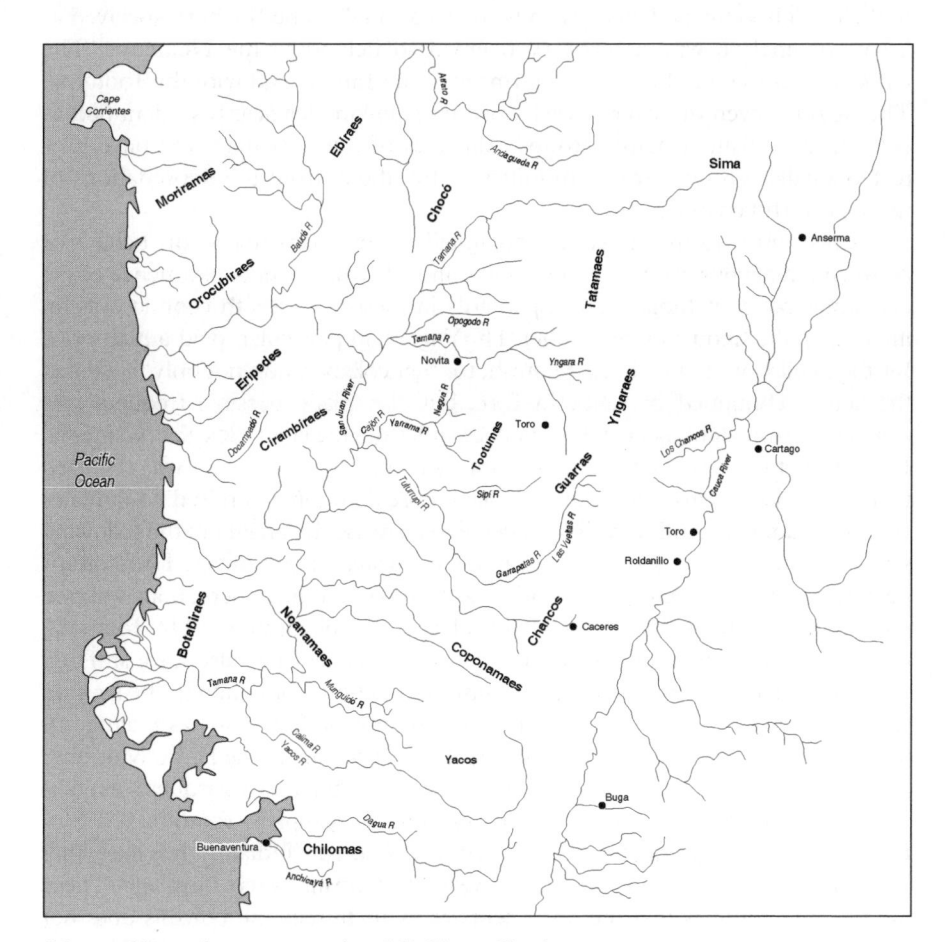

Map 3 *Sixteenth-century peoples of the Upper Chocó.*

recognised area; an uninhabited neutral zone separated each inhabited area from that of its neighbours. The Yngará province of Yaguare, for example, was three leagues distant from the nearest settlement of Chocoes Indians. The northernmost Tootuma groups inhabited an area some two to three days' journey from the closest settlement of Chocoes. A safe distance also separated the southernmost Tootuma settlements from the Noanama communities to the south and west.

Relations between native groups in the Chocó were generally characterised by distrust, a result, no doubt, of the brief but frequent incursions carried out by Indians into neighbouring territories for the purpose of waging war. The Tootuma informed the Spaniards that going to war with the cacique was one of their principal duties, while the Noanama were renowned for the armed flotillas they used for such purposes, and for the fact that their warring expeditions took them to quite distant areas: in the north, they fought the Orocubirá; in the south they conducted expeditions against the Paripeso, whose lands lay beyond Buenaventura. Some, however, were clearly on friendly terms with at least some of their neighbours, and allied with them occasionally. The Botabirá survived as a sort of enclave within territory deemed to belong to the Noanama. The Chocoes were said to be on good terms with the Tatama and with the Tootuma. The Spanish even discovered well-worn trails linking 'cacicazgos' identified as belonging to distinct native groups. Alliances of this sort may well have protected smaller groups, or communities within them, from the depredations of more powerful enemies.

Spanish incursions, however, disrupted accepted patterns of behaviour between indigenous groups in the Chocó, and one important consequence of the encounter between Indians and Spaniards in the late sixteenth century was an increase in the frequency of conflict. The Yngará, in particular, paid a high price for their collaboration with the Spanish, for that collaboration not only facilitated the latter's continued presence in Toro, but also made possible frequent and aggressive campaigns against the Chocoes and, from the late 1580s, the Noanama. In 1576, just three years after the Yngará welcomed the Spanish, it was reported that the Chocoes 'have captured and killed more than three hundred adult males (indios casados)'.[55] And they did not cease to terrorise the Yngará in the following years by means such as surprise assaults on isolated communities. Their disappearance as 'independent tribal entities', as Romoli described them, may well owe more to these actions than to the effects of Spanish colonisation.[56] The Tootuma, despite their long-standing friendship with the Chocoes, may also have suffered the consequences of consenting to Spanish occupation. For although the sources show that in the 1570s one Tootuma community preferred to take refuge in territory belonging to the Chocoes rather than participate in the Pedro Moriones expedition against their neighbours, it was also said that after Velásquez's expedition against the Noanama in 1590, Spanish mining camps in Tootuma territory began experiencing frequent raids by parties of Noanama Indians.[57] It is likely that Tootuma Indians, as well as Spaniards, were killed during raids of this sort. These are the only conflicts that the documents allow us to recount, but this does not mean that conflict and strife did not extend beyond these groups.[58] There is evidence, for example, that in the years following the Gómez Hernández expedition of 1539, and especially after the foundation of Toro, many settlements in territory controlled by the Chocoes were abandoned by their inhabitants. In his 'Descripción de la Tierra', Salazar asserted that 'the province of the Chocó [Chocoes] is today sparsely populated because the many natives it had when discovered have retreated [further] inland, fleeing the Spaniards who are nearby, in the city of Anserma and in Toro'.[59] Significantly, Romoli also pointed out that expeditions conducted to the lands of the Chocoes in the early 1590s were composed of much smaller numbers of soldiers – between nine and 13 – than those undertaken twenty years earlier, which required approximately 45 men.[60] It is therefore possible that migratory movements of this sort among the Chocoes had an impact on relations between native peoples, as Indians moved away from their homelands in search of safer lands to settle and cultivate elsewhere. While the Spanish did not succeed in making permanent their occupation during these years, their actions had an indirect effect on the indigenous population, in the sense that, as Vargas Sarmiento argues, they resulted in cultural and territorial changes among the various native groups.[61]

A second major consequence of the Spanish occupation of Toro was demographic decline. Assessing the extent and causes of the decline suffered by native communities in the Chocó in the late sixteenth century is complicated by the region's character as a frontier zone, which meant that in the early 1570s Spaniards were unable to gauge the size of the indigenous population of the whole area when contact with Europeans first took place. Effective colonisation between the 1570s and the 1590s never expanded beyond the district of Toro; only the Yngará and the Tootuma consented to Spanish occupation; and only over the Chanco, Chiloma and Guarra did Spaniards exert sufficient control to make possible their transfer to Toro and their inclusion in the first *encomiendas*.[62] Spanish contacts with the Chocoes and the Noanama, whom settlers were particularly keen to subdue and incorporate, were invariably violent – circumstances unlikely to produce reliable population counts. Spanish knowledge of other groups, especially on the Pacific side of the Chocó, derived from information supplied by Indian allies and captives rather than from direct contact – such as that provided by Aricum, who informed Salazar that the provinces of the Botabirá and Orocubirá were composed of 'many people'.[63] These early impressions indicating that the population of the Chocó was very large and dense were followed, in the early sixteenth century, by others suggesting that numbers were smaller than initially thought. Fray Pedro Simón, for instance, alluded to the small size of the Noanama and Cirambirá populations. 'Among the other nations that have been encountered in these provinces of the Chocó are those of Noanama and Cirambirá, which although they consist of a small number of people, occupy a large territory', he wrote.[64] The extent to which this reflects a more accurate reassessment, as opposed to severe decline in the intervening years, is not known. And there is one final obstacle to gauging population size in the Chocó region, namely, that in the last quarter of the sixteenth century, Spanish activities were confined to the southern or 'Upper' Chocó. No lasting contact was made until the early seventeenth century with Indian groups inhabiting the northern zone.

Despite the difficulties involved in calculating precisely the size of the indigenous population of the Chocó when Spaniards first founded the city of Toro in Tootuma territory in 1573, Romoli's careful analysis of early estimates of numbers of adult males made by members of the first expeditions (including Velásquez's initial *repartimiento*); of the records of disputes between *encomenderos* in Toro and in a second town, Cáceres, founded in 1575 on the eastern edge of Chanco territory, just outside what might properly be called the Chocó; and of later reports such as those of the *oidor* Guillén Chaparro and the ecclesiastical *visitador* Fray Gerónimo de Escobar, led her to conclude that in the early 1570s, some 35,000 to 40,000 people inhabited the Upper Chocó alone.[65] This is, of course, only an estimate, but in the absence of other data to verify or refine her analysis, Romoli's figures must be seen as plausible.

Assessing the longer-term impact of the Spanish occupation of Toro, and of twenty years of contact with several native groups, however intermittent in the cases of the Chocoes and the Noanama, is equally problematic. Once the *gobernación* was suppressed in 1595, few Spaniards ventured west of the Western Cordillera until the 1620s, and not until the 1670s were more reliable censuses drawn up, by which time Indians and Spaniards had been in contact for over a century, and several failed experiments in colonisation had taken place. Nevertheless, the sources relating to the first experiment in Spanish colonisation of the Chocó enable us to consider some of the causes, if not the extent, of demographic decline in the Upper Chocó in the last quarter of the seventeenth century. As we have seen, the welcome offered to the Velásquez expedition by the Yngará Indians in 1573 provoked the wrath of the neighbouring Chocoes, whose repeated assaults on small isolated communities contributed to the extinction of this group. One particularly poignant manuscript, dating from the mid-1570s, describes how the Indian Sara appealed to Captain Miguel Dávila for assistance when his community came under attack: 'They came ... to request aid ... because the Chocoes Indians had launched an attack against them and surrounded many barbacoas and if they did not receive aid they [the Chocoes] would soon cut them [the barbacoas] down and kill the people who were in them. And the said Miguel Dávila did not want to give the said aid so the Indians left in tears, and when they arrived in their town they found that the said Chocoes had killed or captured twenty three people, men and women'.[66]

Attacks on Indians friendly to the Spanish by defiant neighbouring groups, then, contributed to the extinction of the Yngará, and possibly to that of the Tootuma. However, it is also probable that when Toro was transferred, for the second time, in 1595, many of the Indians whom the first settlers held in *encomienda* were taken out of their homelands and re-settled in the town's new location, thus adding another contributory factor to demographic decline. In 1627, the *visitador* Lesmes de Espinosa recorded the existence of two *encomiendas* of Tootuma Indians in Toro, each of which now consisted of one adult male.[67] The fact that these *encomiendas*, however depleted, were still in existence in 1627 strongly suggests that the Tootuma (and possibly the surviving Yngará, Chanco, Chiloma and Guarra Indians) were transferred out of the Chocó in 1595, and that the demographic decline and eventual extinction of several groups by the early seventeenth century may be attributable at least in part to the effects of *encomienda*.

One other particularly serious effect of two decades of contact between Indians and Spaniards in the Chocó was the introduction of Old World epidemic diseases. Perhaps surprisingly, no evidence has been found to indicate the impact of disease on this population before 1590. But when in that year Melchor Velásquez's son, Melchor 'el Mozo', led an armed force to Noanama territory to avenge the many Spanish soldiers killed by Indians two years before, he found only desolation, the result of smallpox, which the governor's men had unwittingly taken with them. According to Fray Pedro Simón, who was well informed about events in the Chocó in the 1590s, when Melchor 'el Mozo' arrived at the settlement where his father's men were ambushed by the Noanama, 'he found them [the provinces] so empty of people that he could not lay his hands on more than two or three old women and a few sick and miserable men. On asking them about the dissipation of the Indians they replied . . . that they had been swept away by the cruel pestilence which had overcome them the previous year; this was clearly proved when our men saw the fields covered with bones which, there being no one to bury them, had weathered away'.[68] We have no further data to indicate just how far smallpox spread across the region in 1589, how long the epidemic lasted, or how many people succumbed to it. Simón makes no mention of the effects of this outbreak of smallpox in his discussion of the Montaño *entrada* of 1593, when Spaniards once again penetrated Noanama territory and encountered inhabited communities. What is clear, however, is that by the seventeenth century, European diseases had proved as devastating for the indigenous population of the Chocó as they were for native communities throughout Spanish America.

The suppression of the *gobernación* of the Chocó in 1595 and the incorporation of Toro into the *gobernación* of Popayán did not entirely extinguish Spanish interest in the exploration of this region. But whereas expansionary movements into the Chocó in the 1570s, 1580s and 1590s were promoted by successive governors of Popayán, came mainly from cities in that *gobernación* – Buga, Cartago, Anserma and Cali – and were directed because of geographical proximity to the southern sections of the region,[69] the expeditions undertaken just before the turn of the seventeenth century came from Antioquia and Cartagena, and were focused on the northern zone, especially the lands that lay to the south of Urabá. One such *entrada*, commanded by Pedro Martín Dávila, left the city of Santa Fe de Antioquia in June 1596 and headed for the Sinú river and Urabá - the first leg of an expedition that was to follow the course of the Atrato river. This *entrada*, like all previous attempts to penetrate the Chocó from the direction of the Atrato – 'slaughterhouse and graveyard of Spaniards', as Fray Pedro Simón called it – failed to do more than reach the Oromira (Sucio) river and ascertain that the area was well-populated before being forced back by hunger and disease.[70] The second expedition, undertaken in 1598 by order of the governor of Cartagena, Pedro de

Acuña, also followed the course of the Atrato. This time, the *entrada* was aimed not at investigating the potential of the region, but at searching for a tributary of the Atrato rumoured to empty into the Pacific. According to one of the surviving soldiers of the expedition, who was known to Simón, the Cartagena party followed the course of the river for some 130 leagues without incident, fifty leagues beyond the Oromira (Sucio) river. When at this point the expedition, ambushed by Indians, lost six of its members, the remaining soldiers turned back to Cartagena – not, however, before verifying that the Oromira contained alluvial deposits of gold.[71]

Early seventeenth-century colonisation

Aside from the Atrato expeditions of 1596 and 1598, colonising efforts of the kind seen between the 1570s and the 1590s were abandoned until the seventeenth century. But when severe recession hit the gold-mining industry of Antioquia, and to a lesser extent Popayán, in the second and third decades of that century, it was to the Chocó frontier that the search for additional deposits was once again directed. Despite the difficulties and dangers involved in penetrating and occupying the region, the gold-mines exploited during the twenty-year occupation of Toro still served to attract Spanish settlers intent on finding new sources of wealth. In recommending the speedy conquest of the Chocó in 1639, for example, the *alguacil mayor* of Antioquia, Fernando de Toro Zapata, expressed the view that 'it is very important that the said conquest should be achieved . . . because the mineral deposits of both gobernaciones of Popayán and Antioquia have diminished so greatly that if new lands [sources] are not discovered [soon], the king will lose his royal fifths and his subjects will be ruined, for they find themselves with slaves but no mine labour in which to employ them . . . these provinces of Darién and Chocó . . . are the richest we know of in these parts and upon them rest all hopes of . . . [our] recovery'.[72]

By the 1620s, the chances of successful colonisation looked considerably more promising than they had done before. For although the suppression of the *gobernación* of the Chocó in 1595 put an end to the colonising ventures of Salazar, and suspended communication between Indians and Spaniards in the short term, by the 1620s, contacts had been re-established, albeit on an entirely different footing. Whereas in the early 1570s, the encounter between Indians and Spaniards had been a Spanish initiative, promoted by settlers keen to expand colonisation and exploit the region's gold deposits, in the 1620s, communication was initiated by Indians keen to obtain European goods and/or assistance against enemy groups. In 1627, for instance, Lesmes de Espinosa Saravia, *oidor* of the *audiencia* of Santa Fe and visitor general to the district of Anserma, submitted a report, based on information obtained locally, indicating that small parties of Indians 'come frequently to this city . . . and . . . bring gold, maize, flour, hens . . . and fish with which they barter for axes, machetes, knives, and beads'.[73] Neither Lesmes de Espinosa nor his informants identified the Indians concerned, except to state that they inhabited territories close to Anserma itself. Later reports suggest, however, that Indians beyond the vicinity of Anserma may also have begun to make peaceful approaches to Spaniards. In the 1620s, Indians from communities identified as Tatama, Poya, Chocoes and Citará or Citarabirá were all reported to have made overtures for the purpose of trade to settlers in the cities of Popayán, Cartago, Anserma and Antioquia. The Citará, as they will be known in this study, are the most interesting of the four, for this was a large group which inhabited lands to the north of the areas occupied or explored by Spaniards between the 1570s and 1590s, and which remained outside their sphere of activity until the seventeenth century. By the 1620s, however, Citará Indians were said to have attempted to trade with Spaniards in Antioquia on many occasions: 'from the said provinces [Citará] . . . parties of Indians came to this city . . . bringing *pitafloxa trementina*, which are resins that serve as medicine and others which they call *anime*, which serves as perfume, taking [in exchange] knives, beads, and other things'.[74]

Why Indians should have chosen to engage in trade with Spaniards in the 1620s is not clear, but perhaps the experience of close contact with settlers in Toro in the last quarter of the sixteenth century had an unexpected consequence, in making Indians desirous of – perhaps even creating dependence upon – European goods such as metal tools, which they may initially have acquired in confrontations with the Spanish.[75] But there were other incentives, too. For the Poya, the possibility of obtaining protection against larger neighbouring groups was an important consideration. For the Tatama and the Chocoes, traditional allies and by the early seventeenth century virtually indistinguishable in Spanish documents, one particularly attractive advantage to be derived from friendship with Europeans was military assistance against their enemies, the stronger and more powerful Citará. Lesmes de Espinosa's informants in Anserma told of how the Chocoes had recently appealed to two Spanish settlers, Sebastián Guerrero and Jacome Cicerón, for assistance against the Citará, whose territory lay at a distance of three days, and 'with whom they are presently at war'. If the testimony of residents of Anserma is to be believed, hostilities between Chocoes and the Citará broke out because the former attempted to benefit from their recently established communication with the Spanish by exacting 'tribute' for the use of trails linking the region to the Cauca Valley. According to Lesmes de Espinosa, for demanding tribute, and for attempting to prevent the passage of the Citará 'who also came to this city on three or four occasions, they are presently at war'. Whatever the causes of conflict between Indians, Spanish firepower seems to have motivated the Chocoes' request for aid, for Spanish weapons made it possible for a numerically smaller group to defend itself from attack by a larger or in other ways more powerful enemy. As the *oidor*'s informants stated, 'said Indians greatly fear [our] harquebuses'.[76]

It seems, then, from testimony presented to Lesmes de Espinosa, that in the mid- to late 1620s, Chocoes and Tatama Indians, probably depleted in their numbers by the effects of European diseases and Spanish aggression in the closing decades of the previous century, requested of the Spaniards military aid to enable them to survive in an environment in which they were vulnerable to the depredations of a stronger neighbouring group. Gonzalo Gortisdiente further reported that some Chocoes went so far as to offer services in return for assistance, promising 'they would go to the lands of the said Citarabiraes [Citará] and they would bring [back] much gold and pearls, the shells of which they showed them, broken to pieces and used as necklaces'.[77] It was precisely one such offer of assistance against the Citará, made by the Tatama/Chocoes, that made possible the first seventeenth-century expedition to reach the headwaters of the Atrato and locate the territory controlled by the Citará.

The expedition that left Anserma in 1628 under the command of Martín Bueno de Sancho, a *vecino* of Cartago, was composed of 12 soldiers and 22 Indian carriers. The bulk of the expeditionary force, however, consisted of Chocoes and Tatama 'friends', who guided the Spanish party across Indian territory to the province of Citará – a journey that took nine days to complete. The records do not indicate whether any attempt was made to enter into dialogue with the Citará on this occasion, but the testimony of the *alférez* Diego Ruiz de Alarcón suggests that, perhaps because of the nature of the agreement between the Spaniards and their Tatama/Chocoes allies, the party attacked, rather than approached peacefully, the first Indian settlement it reached. On arrival in the province, Alarcón recalled, the Spaniards 'discovered ... one hundred Indian *barbacoas*, in each of which according to their custom lived twenty or thirty Indians with their families, in which province one hundred children and adults were either captured or killed'.[78] The number of *barbacoas* attacked was undoubtedly exaggerated, since large settlements of this kind were not characteristic of the region, but the Spaniards' action, coupled with their policy of gift-giving, guaranteed Martín Bueno de Sancho the respect and future co-operation of his Poya, Tatama and Chocoes allies. When, some ten years later, Bueno was killed in Citará territory, it was said that the Tatama and the Poya had 'considered him a friend'.[79]

Thus, in the early decades of the seventeenth century, as had been the case in the 1570s and 1580s, Spanish advances in the Chocó were entirely dependent on the co-operation offered by indigenous groups who, either through military necessity or because of a desire to obtain European goods, chose to permit and even assist the activities of Spanish expeditionary leaders in Indian territory. As Chapter 2 will show, however, in the longer term Bueno de Sancho's strategy of capitalising on divisions between the Chocoes/Tatama and the Citará to advance Spanish colonisation in the region had the opposite of the intended effect. Far from leading to permanent occupation of the Chocó, and to the exploitation of its much-needed precious metal, this strategy brought upon Bueno de Sancho and Spaniards more generally the wrath of the Citará, the most powerful and most resilient of all Indian groups of the seventeenth-century Chocó.

Seventeenth-century peoples of the Chocó

The long gap in the documentary record that resulted from the Spaniards' withdrawal from Toro in the mid-1590s makes it impossible to track the demographic consequences for the indigenous population of the first Spanish attempt to colonise the Chocó. We have seen, however, that Spanish sources dating from the last quarter of the sixteenth century identify a total of nineteen groups in the Upper Chocó alone – the region stretching approximately from Cape Corrientes to Buenaventura – and that Kathleen Romoli estimated for those groups a total population of between 35,000 and 40,000 at the beginning of the 1570s. The accounts of participants in late-sixteenth-century expeditions also show that Spaniards were well aware that many other groups occupied territories to the north of Cape Corrientes and east and west of the Atrato river, and considered the area to be densely populated. There is, unfortunately, no evidence to enable us to verify such impressions, for as we have seen, early contacts between Spaniards and Indians along the Pacific coast north of Cape Corrientes were invariably violent and of short duration, while expeditions from Urabá were repeatedly repulsed by unidentified Indians south of the Oromira (Sucio) river. Given the nature of the sporadic encounters between Indians and Europeans in this part of the Chocó in the sixteenth century, it is also impossible to assess the demographic consequences of Spanish incursions along the Pacific coast and up the Atrato river before the seventeenth century.

Any analysis of the consequences for the indigenous population of Spanish exploration and occupation of the Chocó in the sixteenth century is, therefore, severely limited by lack of information regarding the identity and size of the native groups that occupied a large section of the region when contact with Europeans first took place, and the territories each inhabited. What is clear, however, is that by the mid-seventeenth century, many of the peoples identified by Spaniards in the late sixteenth century had either entirely disappeared, or had united with or been absorbed by larger neighbouring groups. The evidence supports both possibilities. The Yngará, Tootuma, Guarra, Chanco and Chiloma, for example, cease to figure in documents after the 1590s. This, as explained above, was a consequence of the creation of *encomiendas* in Toro after 1573, the transfer of many Indians to the Cauca Valley when the *gobernación* of the Chocó was suppressed in 1595, and, in the case of the Yngará and perhaps also the Tootuma, of attack by Chocoes and Noanama intent on revenging collaboration with the Spanish. The effects of disease on these groups are unrecorded, as no evidence has emerged of epidemics striking the indigenous population of the Chocó before 1589, and even the impact of that epidemic is unclear. The Tatama and Chocoes, traditional allies since at least the 1570s, seem, on the other hand, to have survived the encounter with Spaniards, but to have become virtually indistinguishable by the early seventeenth century. In fact, from the late 1620s, Spanish documents use without distinction the names Tatama, Chocó, and sometimes even Poya, a much smaller group not encountered in the 1570s– 1590s, to refer to Indians who inhabited the area lying between the headwaters of the San Juan and Atrato rivers.

Despite a serious shortage of evidence, there can be no doubt that for all these groups, the effects of Spanish attempts to occupy the Chocó were devastating. For by the second half of the seventeenth century, the Spanish could identify a total of only five groups in the entire Chocó region; a sixth, the Membocana, appears briefly in documents of the late 1630s to mid-1640s, only to disappear again thereafter. Of the five groups that consistently figure in the documents after mid-century, one, the Soruco, was known to the Spanish mainly by reputation. Believed to inhabit an ill-defined stretch of territory on the eastern flank of the Serranía de Baudó, they were said to be in a permanent state of war with other groups. In May 1672, the Spaniard Lorenzo de Salamanca informed Governor Díaz de la Cuesta, of Popayán, that the Soruco were 'such warlike Indians that they never let go of their arms. They continuously and without pause organise wars attacking the . . . peaceful Indians [who are] reduced to the Royal Crown . . . on several occasions they have set fire to many dwellings and caused the death of many Indians'.[80] Writing from the Chocó in 1676, *corregidor* Jorge López García reported a recent outbreak of violence between the Chocoes and the Soruco, resulting in 'many deaths and injuries on both sides'.[81] Much else that was said about the Soruco was mere speculation, however. In April 1669, for instance, when the possibility of conquering these 'nations' was discussed in Popayán, Governor Díaz de la Cuesta estimated that the Soruco population comprised 5000 adult men, plus women and *chusma* (the young and the elderly).[82] Three months later, he revised his estimate to 3000 adult men.[83] The lands the Soruco inhabited were also said to be exceptionally rich in mineral wealth, which the 'warlike' nature of the Indians prevented the Spanish from exploiting.[84] Even less was known about the Burgumia (also known as Boromea and Poromea). This group – described as 'brave' – was said to inhabit lands beyond those of the Soruco, between the Bojaya river and the Panamanian border, and by the mid-1670s, their pacification was reported to be in the hands of Dominican and Mercedarian friars based in Panama. Some Burgumia prisoners captured by the Citará and encountered among them later that decade apparently knew a few prayers in Spanish.[85]

Of the other three groups – Noanama, Tatama/Chocoes and Citará – much more became known as the seventeenth century progressed. More continuous contact from the 1630s allowed Spanish settlers, missionaries and officials to record the extent of the territories they inhabited, their resources, and the principal features of their social and political organisation. In the Chocó region, this was not for the purpose of understanding indigenous peoples *per se*, but for the sake of facilitating their pacification and advancing the exploitation of mineral resources, a feature of colonisation here that limits the ethnological value of colonial documents. Nevertheless, between the 1630s and the 1670s, the Spaniards learned a great deal about the peoples of the Chocó. They learned, for instance, that the three principal surviving indigenous 'provinces' or 'nations', as the Spanish described them, belonged to two separate language groups.[86] The Tatama/Chocoes (henceforth Tatama) and the Citará – Indians of the upper reaches of the Atrato, San Juan, and eastern tributaries of the lower Baudó – belonged to the Emberá language group.[87] The Noanama – peoples who inhabited the middle and lower San Juan drainage, the area around Buenaventura, and the lower courses of the Dagua, Anchicayá and Raposo rivers – formed part of another group, known by the name Waunana.[88]

It was also during these decades that the Spaniards became aware of the particular difficulties posed to the process of pacification and settlement by the social and political organisation of the peoples of the Chocó – most especially the dispersal and mobility of Indian settlement, and the weak and decentralised nature of political leadership.[89] The characteristics of native society in the Chocó will be discussed fully in due course. Suffice to say for now that an indigenous population organised into small, scattered, temporary riverine communities capable of swift dispersal was to prove a serious hindrance to Spanish efforts to establish control over this frontier, while the absence of a strong, central authority was to prevent the Spanish either apprehending, or establishing alliances with, the political leaders, which in other areas had enabled them almost at once to command the obedience of large Indian populations.[90] As Sven-Erik Isacsson pointed out, everywhere the Spaniards went, they 'followed the norms elaborated during a century and more among the Andean cultures. This system presupposed [the existence] of some form of social stratification and political organisation that could be used to the Spaniards' own advantage.' In the Chocó, however, they came upon 'a special case, where the conditions [necessary] for the introduction of this system did not exist'.[91]

Yet notwithstanding the particular advantages that the peoples of the Chocó enjoyed over Spanish expeditionary forces – advantages that were repeatedly to frustrate attempts to dominate them – none of the groups that survived a century of contact with Europeans, however intermittent, emerged from the experience unscathed. As we have seen, the people of the Upper Chocó alone have been estimated to have numbered between 35,000 and 40,000 in the 1570s. By 1678, according to a report compiled by Jesuit Antonio Marzal on the outcome of several years of missionary activity in this region, the combined populations of three of five surviving groups – Noanama (650), Tatama/Chocoes (1600) and Citará (1600) – totalled no more than 3850.[92] While it is possible that at least a proportion of Noanama, Tatama and Citará peoples remained unaccounted for at the end of the 1670s – many communities continued to seek refuge in distant and inaccessible stretches of the territory – it is evident that the native population underwent severe demographic decline over the century spanning the 1570s to 1670s, and that the rate of decline was comparable with that which occurred in other parts of Spain's American empire.

The exceptionally small size of the Noanama group in 1678 must be attributable at least in part to the fact that this group succumbed to Spanish domination decades before the Emberá peoples of Tatama and Citará. Indeed, the evidence indicates that the Noanama were subjected to the Spanish in the 1630s, though the process whereby that subjection was achieved remains unclear. It is possible, however, that the pacification of the Noanama occurred as an extension of Spanish campaigns against Indians who inhabited the more southerly sectors of the Pacific lowlands (see Map 4) – namely, Barbacoas, and especially the Raposo-Iscuandé regions. Little is known about the native population of these areas when contact with Europeans took place, or about early Spanish explorations there, but the records show that an *entrada* was conducted to

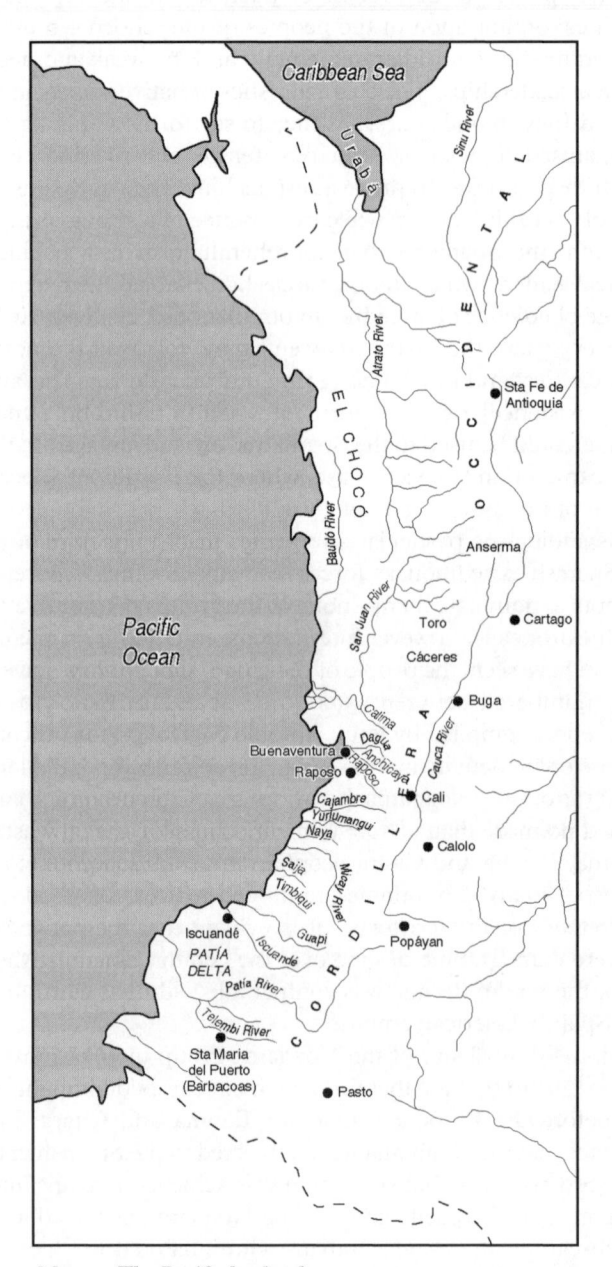

Map 4 *The Pacific lowlands.*

the Barbacoas region in 1600, which reached the Telembí river and founded the settlement of Santa María del Puerto. Because of the hostility of the Indian inhabitants and the difficulties involved in obtaining food supplies, mining activities on a large scale did not begin until the last quarter of the seventeenth century.[93] However, small-scale mining was certainly taking place there and in the Iscuandé region long before mid-century. In 1610, for example, Francisco Ramírez de la Serna led a punitive expedition against the Timbas, Piles, Cacajambres and Paripesos of the upper and middle sections of the Saija and Micay rivers, who were said to have raided the port of Buenaventura and gold mines in its vicinity. On that occasion, Ramírez de la Serna was also reported to have encountered and defeated a small 'armada' of Noanama Indians on their way to Buenaventura. Reports dating from the 1630s also show that Spaniards were by now well aware that the rivers Patía, Micay, Timbiquí and Iscuandé were rich in gold deposits. By 1640, plans were afoot to open trails to connect the ports of Santa María and Santa Bárbara (in the vicinity of the Timbiquí, where mines were being exploited by 1646) to Pasto and Popayán. And in 1647, the governor of Popayán complained that a Jesuit priest, Francisco Ruje, employed Indians to extract gold from placers along the Tilimbí. By 1665, mining camps just south of Buenaventura were fully operational, as was the entire zone known as 'minas de la Montaña de Raposo'. This zone encompassed the Calima river and streams just to the south of Buenaventura, an area inhabited by the Noanama.[94]

Unlike the Noanama, the Emberá peoples of Tatama and Citará continued to resist subjection to the Spanish for another four decades. Even the small-scale contacts established with Spaniards in the 1620s came to an end in the late 1630s, following the massacre, in 1639, of a colonising expedition dispatched by the newly appointed *adelantado* and governor of Antioquia, Don Juan Vélez de Guevara. The events surrounding the attack on that colonising expedition, and the impact of the subsequent declaration of a *guerra a sangre y fuego* against Indians in the Chocó, will be discussed in the next chapter. Before assessing the implications for Indians and Spaniards of the colonising ventures of the 1620s and 1630s, however, Chapter 2 will consider how and why Vélez de Guevara came to be in charge of the Crown's newest effort to colonise territory inhabited by the Emberá. What considerations led the Crown to appoint Vélez to lead the enterprise? What conditions were laid down to govern the conduct of this latest enterprise in the region? To what extent were such conditions observed? And what effect did the Crown's decision to entrust the exercise to Juan Vélez have on Spanish objectives in this region?

Notes

1 The following account of early Spanish activity on the northern coast of South America is based on Carl Ortwin Sauer, *The Early Spanish Main*, Berkeley and Los Angeles, University of California Press, 1992, pp. 108–19, 161–77, 218–37 and 247–65. A further useful source for this early period of exploration is Jorge Orlando Melo, *Historia de Colombia: El establecimiento de la dominación española*, Bogotá, La Carreta 1978, pp. 73–86.
2 Sauer, *Spanish Main*, p. 175.

38   BETWEEN RESISTANCE AND ADAPTATION

3   Quoted in Sauer, *Spanish Main*, p. 225.
4   Balboa's record is not, however, entirely clean. Some Indian communities and their caciques were threatened and attacked by Balboa and his men as they expanded their operations westwards towards the Pacific in 1513. See Sauer, *Spanish Main*, pp. 231–37.
5   Quoted in Sauer, *Spanish Main*, p. 225.
6   Sauer, *Spanish Main*, pp. 231–32.
7   For an account of Spanish activities – and atrocities – in this region following the arrival of Pedrarias Dávila, see Sauer, *Spanish Main*, pp. 247–57.
8   Sauer, *Spanish Main*, pp. 257–58.
9   Sauer, *Spanish Main*, p. 280.
10 My discussion of early Spanish explorations along the Pacific coast of the Chocó is based on Robert Cushman Murphy, 'The Earliest Spanish Advances Southward from Panama along the West Coast of South America', *Hispanic American Historical Review*, Vol. 21, 1941, pp. 2–28; and Kathleen Romoli, 'El descubrimiento y la primera fundación de Buenaventura', *Boletín de Historia y Antigüedades*, Vol. 49, 1962, pp. 113–22. Romoli's article, published twenty years after Murphy's, clarifies the extent of Spanish discoveries and rectifies misapprehensions in the record of Spanish exploration along this stretch of the Pacific coast between the 1520s and the 1540s. For a geographer's description of the coast between Darién and the Gulf of Guayaquil – topography, precipitation, winds and temperatures – see Robert Cushman Murphy, 'The Littoral of Pacific Colombia and Ecuador', *The Geographical Review*, Vol. 29, 1939, pp. 1–33.
11 Murphy, 'Earliest Spanish Advances', pp. 20–21.
12 Romoli, 'El descubrimiento ... de Buenaventura', pp. 114–15. See also *idem*, 'Apuntes sobre los pueblos autóctonos del litoral colombiano del Pacífico en la época de la conquista española', *Revista Colombiana de Antropología*, Vol. 12, 1964, pp. 261–62 and 266–67. Romoli insists that the river discovered by Almagro in 1525 was the San Juan de Micay, which empties into the sea south of Buenaventura, rather than the better known San Juan of the Chocó, as is usually stated.
13 Murphy, 'Earliest Spanish Advances', pp. 22–23.
14 Murphy, 'Earliest Spanish Advances', pp. 12–13; and Romoli, 'Apuntes sobre los pueblos autóctonos', p. 266.
15 Murphy, 'Earliest Spanish Advances', pp. 13, 15.
16 McFarlane, *Colombia*, pp. 7–9, 17–18.
17 McFarlane, *Colombia*, p. 9.
18 Romoli, 'El Alto Chocó', p. 14; and Fray Pedro Simón, *Noticias historiales de las conquistas de Tierra Firme en las Indians Occidentales*, 6 vols., Bogotá, Banco Popular, 1981, Vol. V, Noticia 3, Chapter 1, pp. 279–80.
19 Simón, *Noticias historiales*, Vol. V, Noticia 2, Chapter 1, p. 169.
20 The *gobernación* of San Juan was created in 1537, and it was to extend from the San Juan de Micay river, located to the south of Buenaventura, to the Santiago river, at the border with Peru. Gaspar de Espinosa was the Crown's first appointee, but he died before taking possession. Andagoya received his appointment in December 1538. Under the terms of his appointment he was granted jurisdiction, for a period of three years, of the coastal region to the north, stretching to the southern limits of Castilla del Oro. Romoli, 'El descubrimiento ... de Buenaventura', pp. 114–16.
21 Andagoya was defeated and detained by Benalcázar and in September 1541 left the New World to plead his case in Spain. Romoli, 'El descubrimiento ... de Buenaventura', pp. 116–18.
22 Fray Géronimo Escobar, 'Relación de Fray Gerónimo Descobar, de la orden de San Agustín, sobrel carácter e costumbres de los indios de la provincia de Popayán', in Jacinto

Jijón y Caamaño, *Sebastián de Benalcázar*, 2 vols., Quito, Editorial Ecuatoriana, 1936–38, Vol. II, pp. 150–51; and Romoli, 'El descubrimiento ... de Buenaventura', p. 119.
23 Romoli, 'Apuntes sobre los pueblos autóctonos', pp. 268–69.
24 Germán Colmenares, *Historia económica y social de Colombia, 1537–1719*, Medellín, Editorial La Carreta, 1975, pp. 32, 269–70.
25 McFarlane, *Colombia*, pp. 12–13, 16–17.
26 Colmenares, *Historia económica*, pp. 21–22.
27 On the development of Colombia's mining districts, see Robert C. West, *Colonial Placer Mining in Colombia*, Baton Rouge, LA, Louisiana State University Press, 1952, pp. 9–34.
28 For a discussion of mining cycles, see Colmenares, *Historia económica*, pp. 257–76. For a summary, see *idem*, 'La formación de la economía colonial (1500–1740)', in José Antonio Ocampo (ed.), *Historia económica de Colombia*, Bogotá, Siglo Veintiuno Editores, 1988, pp. 35–37.
29 Jaime Jaramillo Uribe, 'La economía del virreinato (1740–1810)', in Ocampo (ed.), *Historia económica*, p. 49.
30 See Colmenares, *Historia económica*, pp. 29, 259–60, 262–64.
31 Sauer, *Spanish Main*, pp. 225–26, 268–69, 288–89; Kathleen Romoli, *Los de la lengua de Cueva. Los grupos indígenas del istmo oriental en la época de la conquista española*, Bogotá, Ediciones Tercer Mundo, 1987, pp. 50–55, and 91–92; Vargas Sarmiento, *Los Emberá y los Cuna*, pp. 19, 41. See also Robert C. West, *The Pacific Lowlands of Colombia: A Negroid Area of the American Tropics*, Baton Rouge, LA, Louisiana State University Press, 1957, pp. 88–90.
32 Murphy, 'Earliest Spanish Advances', pp. 21–23.
33 Vargas Sarmiento, *Los Emberá y los Cuna*, pp. 31, 35, and p. 108 n. 13. See also West, *The Pacific Lowlands*, pp. 88–89, and p. 222 n. 17.
34 These included the systematic theft of Indian crops, enslavement and forced migrations. For a discussion of the devastating consequences of Spanish colonisation on the Cuevan peoples of the isthmus, see Alfredo Castillero Calvo, *Conquista, evangelización y resistencia. ¿Triunfo o fracaso de la política indigenista?*, Panama, Editorial Mariano Arosemena, 1995, pp. 37–48; and Romoli, *Los de la lengua de Cueva*, pp. 27–50.
35 Romoli, *Los de la lengua de Cueva*, p. 40.
36 This study of the Cueva and Cuna peoples sets out to demonstrate the impossibility of affinity between the two groups: through a meticulous comparison of linguistic patterns, she shows that the Cuna were latecomers to the isthmian region, beginning their occupation of territory formerly controlled by the Cueva in the eastern sections of the isthmus only some seventy years after the continuous demographic decline provoked by the Spanish conquest led to the virtual disappearance of the former. Romoli, *Los de la lengua de Cueva*, pp. 50–69.
37 My discussion of the expedition of 1573 relies heavily on Romoli, 'El Alto Chocó', and *idem*, 'El Alto Chocó en el siglo XVI. Parte II: Las gentes', *Revista Colombiana de Antropología*, Vol. 20, 1976, pp. 25–67. Romoli's are the only studies so far to examine the nature and consequences of this phase of colonisation on the indigenous peoples of the Chocó. Based on sixteenth-century sources, several of which are transcribed in full in the appendices, and others cited extensively in the text, Romoli's studies are also the first to identify the native groups that inhabited the region at contact and to estimate their size.
38 'Comisión de Don Jerónimo de Silva ... al Capitán Melchor Velásquez de Valdenebro ... para la pacificación de la Provincia de los Chancos, población y evangelización de las del Chocó y Dabeiba', 15 October 1572, in Enrique Ortega Ricaurte (ed.), *Historia documental del Chocó*, Bogotá, Departmento de Biblioteca y Archivos Nacionales, 1954, pp. 45–53.

39 Romoli, 'El Alto Chocó', p. 14.
40 'Comisión de Don Gerónimo de Silva', in Ortega Ricaurte (ed.), *Historia documental*, p. 48.
41 Although Fray Pedro Simón did not arrive in the New Kingdom until 1597, when he came as a member of a contingent of seven Franciscan missionaries, he was particularly well informed about events in the Chocó during the 1590s, not least because he was acquainted with many Spaniards who took part in expeditions to the region, including Melchior Salazar, who had conducted an *entrada* to Noanama territory in 1593. See Luis Carlos Mantilla Ruiz OFM, *Actividad misionera de los Franciscanos en Colombia durante los siglos XVII y XVIII. Fuentes documentales*, Bogotá, Editorial Kelly, 1980, p. 25; and Romoli, 'El Alto Chocó', pp. 11, 21.
42 Romoli, 'El Alto Chocó', p. 10.
43 This account of the expedition is based on the testimony of Fray Martín de Medrano, contained in the *probanza de servicios* which Melchor Velásquez had compiled in Buga in 1574. For a transcript of the *probanza*, see Romoli, 'El Alto Chocó', pp. 16–18.
44 See Fray Martín de Medrano's testimony, in Romoli, 'El Alto Chocó', p. 17. See also Simón, *Noticias historiales*, Vol. 6, Noticia 7, Chapter 1, p. 235; and Romoli, 'Las gentes', p. 34.
45 Fray Martín de Medrano, in Romoli, 'El Alto Chocó', pp. 17–18.
46 'Comisión de Don Gerónimo de Silva', in Ortega Ricaurte (ed.), *Historia documental*, pp. 51–53.
47 Fray Martín de Medrano, in Romoli, 'El Alto Chocó', p. 17.
48 Vargas Sarmiento, *Los Emberá y los Cuna*, p. 89.
49 Simón, *Noticias historiales*, Vol. 6, Noticia 7, Chapter 2, pp. 237–38.
50 Simón, *Noticias historiales*, Vol. 6, Noticia 7, Chapter 2, p. 239.
51 See the testimony submitted by Cristóbal García et al. to the *audiencia* of Santa Fe, Toro, 16 July 1593. The main sections of this document are transcribed in Romoli, 'El Alto Chocó', pp. 22–23.
52 Cristóbal García et al., in Romoli, 'El Alto Chocó', pp. 22–23; and Simón, *Noticias historiales*, Vol. 6, Noticia 7, Chapter 3, pp. 242–44, and Vol. 6, Noticia 7, Chapter 4, pp. 246–47.
53 Melchior Salazar, 'Descripción de la Tierra', 15 April 1596, transcribed in Romoli, 'El Alto Chocó', pp. 28–31.
54 The discussion of the demographic data that follows is based on Romoli, 'Las gentes', pp. 27–67.
55 Romoli, 'Las gentes', p. 33.
56 Romoli, 'Las gentes', pp. 32–33, 41.
57 See the testimony of Cristóbal García et al., in Romoli, 'El Alto Chocó', p. 23. See also Romoli, 'Las gentes', p. 36.
58 For a further discussion of the reasons why European colonialism exacerbated intra-Indian conflict, in the context of native groups in North America, see Adelman and Aron, 'From Borderlands to Borders', p. 818.
59 Salazar, 'Descripción', in Romoli, 'El Alto Chocó', p. 30.
60 Romoli, 'Las gentes', p. 36.
61 On this point see also Vargas Sarmiento, *Los Emberá y los Cuna*, pp. 17, 19.
62 The Spaniards seem in any case not to have concerned themselves with drawing up reliable population censuses even for these groups. See Romoli, 'Las gentes', p. 37.
63 Salazar, 'Descripción', in Romoli, 'El Alto Chocó', p. 29.
64 Simón, *Noticias historiales*, Vol. 6, Noticia 7, Chapter 1, p. 234.
65 For a discussion of the evidence available to Romoli, and her interpretation of it, see 'Las gentes', pp. 37–48.

DISCOVERY, EXPLORATION AND FIRST EXPERIMENTS   41

66   Quoted in Romoli, 'Las gentes', p. 36.
67   Romoli, 'Las gentes', p. 47.
68   Simón, *Noticias historiales*, Vol. 6, Noticia 7, Chapter 2, p. 240.
69   Melchor Velásquez was a *vecino* of Buga. His successor Melchior de Salazar was a wealthy *encomendero*, mine-owner and slave-holder in Cartago. Francisco Redondo, founder of the city of Cáceres on the edge of Chanco territory, had connections in Cali (from where he originated and where his father, one of the first discoverers, was a wealthy *encomendero*) and Anserma (where his father-in-law, Captain Lucas Dávila, was a respected and wealthy *vecino*). See 'Capitulación del Capitán Francisco Redondo ... para la jornada, pacificación y población de las provincias del Chocó, Chancos y otras a ellas comarcanas', 16 April 1576, in Ortega Ricaurte (ed.), *Historia documental*, p. 77; Simón, *Noticias historiales*, Vol. 6, Noticia 7, Chapter 1, p. 235, and Chapter 3, p. 241; and Romoli, 'El Alto Chocó', pp. 15, 20–21.
70   Simón, *Noticias historiales*, Vol. 6, Noticia 7, Chapters 5, 6, 7 and 59, pp. 249–60, 483.
71   Simón, *Noticias historiales*, Vol. 5, Noticia 2, Chapter 4, p. 181.
72   Antioquia, 14 December 1639, AGN, Caciques e indios, 68, fol. 411.
73   'Información hecha por mandado del doctor Lesmes de Espinosa Saravia ... sobre los indios chocoes que salen de paz a esta ciudad de Anserma', Anserma, 4 March 1627, AGN, Caciques e indios, 68, fol. 925.
74   See, for example, the testimony of Francisco Guzmán, Antioquia, 8 July 1639, AGN, Caciques e indios, 68, fols. 240–41.
75   Historians of other frontier regions – Chile and northern Mexico, for example – have identified similar processes. In Chile, it was reported at the end of the sixteenth century that Araucanian Indians looked forward to the campaigns the Spaniards launched against them because it was during those campaigns that Indians replenished their stores of horses and stirrups, swords, knives, machetes, and especially axes. It was also reported that in order to obtain prized European goods, Indians exploited the food shortages that Spanish soldiers manning frontier posts often suffered, to exchange local food products for iron and even, in many cases, Spanish weapons. The Tepehuanes peoples of northwestern Mexico also became dependent on the food, clothing, weapons and horses initially acquired through raids on Spaniards, and their increased reliance on such items eventually facilitated their pacification through what is known as the 'peace-by-purchase plan'. See Louis de Armond, 'Frontier Warfare in Colonial Chile', *Pacific Historical Review*, Vol. 23, 1954, p. 131; Villalobos, *La vida fronteriza*, pp. 298–306; and Charlotte Gradie, *The Tepehuan Revolt of 1616: Militarism, Evangelism, and Colonialism in Seventeenth-Century Nueva Vizcaya*, Salt Lake City, UT, University of Utah Press, 2000, p. 142.
76   'Información hecha por ... Lesmes de Espinosa', Anserma, 4 March 1627, AGN, Caciques e indios, 68, fol. 927.
77   'Información hecha por ... Lesmes de Espinosa', Anserma, 4 March 1627, AGN, Caciques e indios, 68, fol. 927.
78   For a summary of the 1628 Bueno de Sancho expedition to Citará territory, see Sven-Erik Isacsson, 'Fray Matías Abad y su diario de viaje por el río Atrato en 1649', *Boletín de Historia y Antigüedades*, Vol. 61, 1974, p. 458.
79   See the statements of Francisco Martín and Pedro Fernández Gómez, dated Cartago, 28 and 29 January 1640, in AGN, Caciques e indios, 68, fols. 449–50, 452–53.
80   AGI Quito 67, Declaración, Popayán, 9 May 1672. See also West, *The Pacific Lowlands*, p. 89.
81   Tadó, 4 December 1676, in AGI Santa Fe 204, Ramo 2, fol. 48.
82   AGI Quito 67, Gabriel Díaz de la Cuesta to Crown, Popayán, 8 April 1669, and 24 April 1669.

83 AGI Quito 67, Gabriel Díaz de la Cuesta to Crown, Popayán, 28 July 1669.
84 AGI Quito 16, Miguel García to Crown, Popayán, 22 November 1674.
85 See the report of Don Juan Bueso de Valdés to Antioquia's Governor Miguel de Aguinaga, Antioquia, 30 June 1677, in AGI Santa Fe 204, Ramo 1, fol. 190. On the Soruco and the Burgumia, see also Antonio de Guzmán, 'Descubrimiento y pacificación de la provincia del Chocó', 31 January 1671, in Ortega Ricaurte (ed.), *Historia documental*, pp. 123–24. For a recent Emberá narrative of ancient conflicts between the Burgumia (Burumia) and the Tatama/Citará (Emberá), see Vargas Sarmiento, *Los Emberá y los Cuna*, pp. 27–31. This is an anthropological study of the Emberá and Cuna peoples, based partly on archival sources and partly on the oral history of the communities concerned, much of which is reproduced in the book.
86 Isacsson, 'The Egalitarian Society', p. 100. See also Melo, *Historia de Colombia*, p. 48.
87 Vargas Sarmiento, *Los Emberá y los Cuna*, p. 35.
88 West, *The Pacific Lowlands*, p. 93. One hypothesis, cited by Vargas Sarmiento, is that the Waunana and Emberá initially formed part of the same linguistic group, and that a split occurred, in pre-conquest times, when the Emberá occupied the upper reaches of the San Juan river, and the Noanama or Waunana, the lower. See Vargas Sarmiento, *Los Emberá y los Cuna*, pp. 46, 53.
89 Although in the late 1620s Spanish expeditionary leaders continued to seek out caciques with whom they could communicate, Fray Pedro Simón had noted in the 1620s that 'they have no leaders, as each wishes to be one'. See Simón, *Noticias historiales*, Vol. 6, Noticia 7, Chapter 1, p. 234. For later assessments of indigenous social and political organisation, see, for example, Fray Matías Abad's reflections on the Citará, dated San Francisco de Atrato, 5 October 1648, in AGI Santa Fe 199; AGI Quito 16, Miguel García to Crown, Popayán, 22 November 1674; and Antonio Marzal, 'Informe sobre el Chocó', in Juan Manuel Pacheco, *Los Jesuitas en Colombia*, 3 vols., Bogotá, Editorial San Juan Eudes, 1959–89, Vol. II, p. 494.
90 'Decentralized societies', as James Saeger has pointed out in writing of the peoples of the Gran Chaco, 'prevented Spanish forces from apprehending a commanding chief, as they had done in the Mexican and Peruvian conquests'. James Schofield Saeger, *The Chaco Mission Frontier: The Guaycuruan Experience*, Tucson, AZ, University of Arizona Press, 2000, p. 9.
91 Isacsson, 'Emberá', p. 25.
92 Marzal, 'Informe', in Pacheco, *Los Jesuitas*, II, pp. 494–95.
93 According to Kris Lane, indigenous people in the area that came to be known as the Province of Barbacoas 'were among the most effective at military resistance of any encountered by the Spanish in South America. Like the Mapuche of South Central Chile they succeeded in driving out scores of would-be conquistadors from the 1520s to the early to mid-seventeenth century, when unfamiliar Old World diseases seem to have taken a firm hold in their communities.' By the 1680s, high levels of gold production were being registered in Santa María del Puerto. See Kris Lane, 'Taming the Master: *Brujería*, Slavery, and the *Encomienda* in Barbacoas at the Turn of the Eighteenth Century', *Ethnohistory*, Vol. 45, No. 3, 1998, pp. 480–81.
94 West, *The Pacific Lowlands*, pp. 93–96; Colmenares, *Historia económica*, pp. 267, 274.

CHAPTER TWO

The *Adelantado* Juan Velez de Guevara and the Colonisation of the Chocó, 1638–1643

The Crown and Spanish colonisation

From the earliest years after the discovery of the New World, the exploration, conquest and settlement of the vast territories that were to fall under the dominion of the Spanish Crown were left largely to private initiative. Rather than investing directly in the incorporation of new territories, the Spanish Crown limited its role, with few exceptions, to that of sanctioning privately financed expeditions and setting down the conditions within which the conquest and settlement of unexplored regions were to take place. These conditions were laid down in a contract, or licence, called the *capitulación* – a document that stipulated the duties and obligations of the leaders of expeditions as well as the political and economic privileges that they would receive in the newly acquired territories following conquest.[1] The concept of the *capitulación*, whereby the Crown or its agents commissioned an individual to take charge of a particular military enterprise or other public service, existed in Spanish law long before the discovery of America.[2] After the discovery, however, the number of *capitulaciones* issued increased enormously, while their principal objective now became the occupation of a new continent. Early in the sixteenth century, the Crown delegated the right to issue licences for new discoveries to Spanish institutions such as the Casa de Contratación in Seville. Later, Spanish officials in the colonies were also authorised to negotiate such agreements provisionally, though always subject to the final approval of the Council of the Indies.[3]

Capitulaciones had two principal purposes. On the one hand, they were intended to stimulate the exploration and occupation of vast new territories. On the other, they sought to ensure, through the granting of an array of political and military privileges or *mercedes* to expeditionary leaders, that newly conquered and settled areas should become and remain possessions of the Spanish Crown. The contracts followed a fairly standard pattern. The expeditionary leader pledged himself to undertake and finance the campaigns that would result in the securing of new territorial possessions for the Crown. In exchange for his efforts, he could expect political, military and economic privileges: among others, the title of *adelantado*, the governorship of the territory concerned, and the right to distribute the booty and resources deriving from the subjugation of a new region. The *adelantado* was granted, for instance, the right to conduct a *repartimiento* of

Indians to the members of the expedition in accordance with their status. Control over the resources of the newly subjugated area was thus the principal reward that the expeditionary leader received in exchange for his contribution to the incorporation of territory to the dominion of the Spanish Crown.[4]

The use of *capitulaciones* as a tool for encouraging further exploration and settlement was, then, of great significance to the Crown, in that it promoted the speedy occupation of the territories of the Spanish empire. During the early decades of the sixteenth century, bands of *conquistadores*, motivated partly by the promise and expectation of reward for their efforts and partly by the spirit of adventure, formed, as Góngora described it, 'the spearhead of Spanish settlement and colonisation'.[5] But after the first phase of conquest (1510–1550) had passed, and the occupation of the most densely inhabited parts of the continent had been completed, a period of consolidation followed. Evidence of the brutality and ruthlessness of the early conquest period, and of the ineffectiveness of early decrees aimed at protecting Indian populations, forced the Crown to reconsider its methods and, at the end of 1549, temporarily to halt the process of further expansion altogether.[6] Then, on 13 July 1573, Philip II promulgated the *Ordenanzas para Descubrimientos* (Ordinances for New Discoveries), which famously substituted for the word 'conquest' the word 'pacification'. This was no mere change in terminology, for Philip's aim was to introduce new methods for the colonisation of border regions.[7] Stringent conditions were laid down for the granting of new licences to discover; armed and unauthorised *entradas* were henceforth forbidden; where possible, the task of exploration was to be entrusted to missionaries. And even where explorers, rather than missionaries, took charge of new discoveries, they were entreated to approach Indians peaceably. 'Explorers . . . are not to engage in any form of war or conquest', the document specified, 'nor support one group of Indians against another, nor become involved in contention with the local people, nor do them any harm, nor take any of their property, unless it be in the way of barter'.[8] The use of force was not absolutely forbidden. As a last resort Spaniards were authorised to use forcible methods, but only in cases where Indians, after all peaceful means had been tried, continued to resist Spanish settlement and the preaching of Christianity.[9] Despite this proviso, the *Ordenanzas* clearly reflected a 'royal preference' for persuasion over force in extending Spanish domination over unpacified regions of the empire.[10]

One important consequence of the promulgation of the *Ordenanzas* was that they marked the beginning of the so-called 'golden age' of the frontier mission in Spanish America.[11] From the late sixteenth century onwards, large parts of Spanish America from northern Mexico to southern Chile became mission territories administered by Franciscans, Jesuits, Dominicans and Augustinians, among others.[12] Missionaries were usually sent, however, to frontier areas that were of little interest to Spanish colonists because they had little in the way of natural resources of immediate value to Europeans, and were occupied by Indian groups who were often both difficult to subdue and extremely hostile to outsiders.[13] The Chocó frontier was of an altogether different nature. In spite of the difficult terrain, the great distances that separated the region from the centres of Spanish settlement in New Granada, and a long history of hostility towards Europeans on the part of many local indigenous groups, the Chocó's gold deposits acted as a magnet that drew expedition after expedition to the area. In the 1570s and 1580s, and again in the 1620s and 1630s, wealthy individuals in cities neighbouring the region put before the Crown or its officials in New Granada proposals for *capitulaciones* aimed at the pacification of the Chocó.[14] One hopeful contender in the late 1620s was Don Antonio Maldonado de Mendoza, who proposed to carry out an *entrada* aimed at pacifying the Indians of the region within six years of taking up the governorship of the Chocó (this being one of the privileges he requested from the Crown in return for his efforts). He proposed to resettle the mines of Toro, to found three Spanish cities, and to lead an annual expedition, consisting of 140 men, until such time as the region was fully pacified. In addition to the governorship of the Chocó, Maldonado de Mendoza requested several other privileges traditionally bestowed on leaders of expeditions of this sort: the title of *adelantado*, the governorship of Popayán, and the right to a *repartimiento* in each of the cities founded.[15] A similar proposal was made, in 1630, by the governor of Popayán, Bermúdez de Castro.[16] Well into the seventeenth century, therefore, the Spanish Crown, or its representatives in the colony, continued to depend on privately financed *entradas* to bring about colonisation in the Chocó, appointing 'entrepreneurs' to carry out the task which in other areas was beginning to be entrusted to missionaries.[17] This does not mean, of course, that the Crown ignored the notion of peaceful pacification that it keenly promoted elsewhere, in that it always required expeditionary leaders to avoid the use of force and to include priests in all expeditions.[18] But, until the second half of the seventeenth century, it was the *entrada*, rather than the mission, that was the favoured method for bringing this frontier under Spanish control.

Thus, in the early 1630s, when news reached Spain that 'parties' of Indians from the provinces of Poya, Tatama and Citará had begun to make overtures for the purpose of trade and/or military aid to Spanish settlers in the cities of the Cauca Valley, the Crown saw this as an excellent opportunity finally to extend domination over this extremely desirable frontier region. To advance colonisation, in 1634 the Crown negotiated a new *capitulación* with Don Juan Vélez de Guevara, as a result of which four major *entradas* to the Chocó were undertaken between 1639 and 1640. Under the terms of the *capitulación*, Vélez, who originated from the Spanish city of Burgos, pledged himself to travel to New Granada, to organise and lead however many *entradas* were required to bring about the pacification of the peoples of the Chocó, and to found three Spanish cities in the region, each with a population of at least 50 *vecinos*. Vélez also pledged himself to complete the enterprise within three years, and to finance the exercise to the tune of 30,000 pesos, which he was to deposit in the Royal Treasury on arrival in Santa Fe de Bogotá. This investment was to cover the cost of supplies, weapons, munitions, and the wages of the soldiers he was to recruit for service.

In exchange for services rendered, Don Juan Vélez, much like other Spaniards charged with carrying out important tasks for the Crown, could expect to receive a whole series of privileges and rewards, in addition to those benefits that would in any case accrue from successful pacification of a gold-rich region such as this. Some of the privileges conferred on Vélez went into effect on his arrival in New Granada. Others were dependent on the success of his enterprise. Vélez was automatically awarded the title of *adelantado*, for example, as well as the governorship of the neighbouring province of Antioquia for a period of five years. This appointment was made specifically to facilitate the *adelantado*'s operations and to prevent a clash with a sitting governor. Should pacification be successful, Vélez could also expect, among other rewards, the title of marquis, the governorship of the newly created *gobernación* of Chocó, an Indian *repartimiento* in each newly founded city, and a reduction of the mining tax, or *quinto*, from 20 per cent to 10 per cent.[19] The rewards of successful pacification were indeed considerable.

While granting the *adelantado* wide powers to meet the obligations with which he was entrusted, the Spanish Crown also sought to ensure that the pacification of the Chocó's indigenous populations and their subsequent conversion to Christianity should be conducted peacefully and with a minimum of violence. Clearly following the provisions contained in the 1573 *Ordenanzas*, which Vélez was instructed to observe to the letter, Clause V of the 1634 *capitulación* instructed him 'that you will not apply the term conquest to the said entrada, pacification, and conversion: because my intention is that the Indians . . . should not be vexed or disturbed, or brought into our Holy Catholic Faith and Christian Religion . . . by force of arms, but by . . . word and example'. The *capitulación* did not, however, entirely prohibit the use of force. Notwithstanding the Crown's peaceful intentions, the contract did authorise Vélez to resort to force in certain cases. Thus, while Clause V urged him to use peaceful methods, Clause VI specified that forcible methods might be used in such cases where Spaniards were required to defend themselves from hostile natives, or where Indians impeded their passage to neighbouring regions for the purpose of preaching and pacification, or prevented the exploitation of 'the said mines of Toro, which form part of my Royal Patrimony'. In cases of 'uprising' or 'rebellion' on the part of Indians previously pacified and baptised, the document further clarified, Vélez was authorised to resort to war, to achieve his objectives 'by means of war' or 'by means of arms'. And while the Crown recommended that, prior to making war against Indians, Vélez should seek the consensus of the priests and other 'prominent persons' taking part in the expeditions, the prior agreement of the *audiencia* of Santa Fe need only be sought in such cases where 'no harm shall result from delay'.[20]

How, then, did Juan Vélez de Guevara, armed with his *capitulación*, conduct his campaign of pacification of the Chocó between 1638 and 1640? His approach was to mark a fresh stage in Spanish activity, reverting to methods of occupation that were reminiscent of the 'heroic' age of Spanish conquests in the early sixteenth century. While during the previous ten to fifteen years Spaniards had employed a gradual approach, which had brought them their first successes in the region since the 1570s, the new governor of Antioquia favoured harsher and more violent methods. Vélez soon took advantage of the provisions contained in his *capitulación* with the Crown – that force might be used in cases of uprising or rebellion, and that only the advice of the religious and 'prominent persons' need be sought – and, on meeting resistance in Citará territory in 1638, declared a total war, or 'guerra a sangre y fuego'. Between July 1639 and March 1640, Vélez dispatched three punitive expeditions to the Chocó, all with clear instructions to use any means necessary to achieve the ultimate purpose of eliminating further opposition to Spanish colonisation. To explain why he resorted to violence and how he justified making war on the Indians, and to weigh the repercussions of his actions for relations with the peoples of the Chocó, these *entradas* will now be examined in detail.

Spanish–Indian interactions: the 1620s and 1630s

Contacts between small groups of native peoples from the Chocó and Spaniards in Anserma, Cartago and Antioquia had been growing for some years before Vélez took up his governorship in 1638. Indians identified as Poyaes, Tatamaes (or Chocoes) and Citaraes (or Citarabiraes) were all reported to have made overtures to Spanish settlers for the purpose of obtaining gifts, engaging in barter trade, or, in some instances, requesting military assistance. Because they inhabited territories said to lie relatively close to Anserma, Indians from the provinces of Tatama and Poya made contact with settlers in that city and in neighbouring Cartago. The Citará, who occupied territory further north, established communication with settlers in Antioquia, and it was even said that some Citará resided permanently in that city. Giving evidence in 1639, General Alfonso Rodas Carvajal described how on several occasions over the previous year, one Captain Fernando Docio Salazar, appointed as Juan Vélez's second in command, 'dispatched . . . Indians from the said province who, having come to this city, remained here and became *ladinos* to invite . . . their captains and caciques to this city'.[21] The number of Indians living in Antioquia in the late 1630s was probably very small, however. Docio himself mentioned only 'an Indian in [my] service named Antonio who some seven or eight years ago left that province and is a native of it', and another named Andrés Sorrito, 'who for many years now has been married in this city'.[22]

For the Citará, as for the Tatama and the Poya, the opportunity to obtain European goods, either through barter or by receiving these as gifts, was the main incentive for seeking out Spanish settlers in cities neighbouring the Chocó. Native peoples here, as indeed throughout the Americas, were eager to obtain European goods, and tools that facilitated agricultural activities, as well as clothing, beads and trinkets of various sorts, were particularly prized.[23] The *oidor* Lesmes de Espinosa, we have seen, discovered on a tour of inspection of the *gobernación* of Popayán that Indians came to Anserma 'frequently . . . and . . . bring gold, maize, flour, hens . . . and fish with which they barter for axes, machetes, knives, and beads'.[44] In Antioquia, Alfonso Rodas Carvajal, commenting on Fernando Docio's attempts to develop a relationship with the Citará, indicated that tools were particularly important inducements, for he had witnessed 'parties [of Indians] arrive on different occasions to whom the said captain . . . gave maize and meat for them to eat . . . [and] tools . . . axes, machetes, and knives, [and] reinforced those which they brought with them with iron and steel'.[25] The bishop of Popayán, Diego de Montoya, who was directly involved in promoting the pacification of the Poya during the 1630s, also used gifts of tools, cloth and other goods as a means of befriending Indians. According to Don Gaspar de Borja, Bishop Montoya gave 'large numbers of axes, machetes, knives, blankets, [items of] clothing, [and] iron'.[26]

All Indians who sought out Spanish settlers in the cities of Anserma, Cartago and Antioquia did so, then, to obtain European goods. Only in some cases, however, did trade lead to closer contact. For the Poya Indians, a small group estimated to number no more than 230 in 1640,[27] contacts begun for the purpose of trade became sufficiently advantageous to make possible permanent Spanish settlement, leading, by the mid-1630s, to the reopening of the old mining district of Toro. The move to reopen the mines and establish a permanent Spanish presence in Poya territory took place under the auspices of the Montoya family – Bishop Don Diego, his brother Francisco, and his cousin Ventura de Montoya. Thanks to the family's activities there, a new Spanish settlement was also founded, La Sed de Cristo, at a site which, according to the bishop, was much more suitable for the exploitation of the mines than the old city of Toro. In 1638, the district's gold deposits were reported to be in operation, employing as many as two hundred slaves.[28] Among this small group, therefore, contacts went well beyond occasional exchanges of goods, and Poya Indians were even reported to sell their labour to local miners and settlers. Giving evidence in 1640, Don Pedro Carrillo de Mendoza, *procurador general* of the city of Cartago, described how, from about the mid-1620s, the Poya had, 'for very moderate rates', provided a variety of services to the Spanish, including providing assistance 'against the warlike Indians that infest said mines [the Noanama]', maintaining the trails into the district, carrying supplies, introducing the livestock that sustained miners and settlers, and paddling canoes along the many rivers that constituted the primary means of communication in the Chocó.[29] Juan Leyva Zavala, also of Cartago, described how the Poya 'gave of their own maize supplies and other foodstuffs, without which it would not be possible to penetrate [the region]'.[30]

Among the Tatama, the Spanish advanced more slowly, but this group also sought to exploit the important advantages, apart from trade, that could result from contact with Spaniards – most especially the assistance and/or protection they could offer against their enemies, the Citará. Knowledge of the Citará and the Tatama was extremely limited in the 1620s, and Spaniards could not properly explain the reasons for the long-standing enmity between the two groups. Some reports did suggest, however, that the Citará were the larger and more powerful group at that time. Juan Gómez Fernández, for example, who claimed to have entered the Chocó on seven different occasions, informed Lesmes de

Espinosa in 1627 that whereas the Tatama numbered 'maybe five hundred Indians', the Citará numbered many thousands. According to the Spaniard's informant, the Tatama 'cacique' Paparra, the Citará were so large a group that two of their *parcialidades* alone comprised 4000 Indians, and beyond these there was a third *parcialidad* that consisted of so many Indians that he 'could not count them'.[31] These figures cannot, of course, be read as sound estimates of the size of either group – by the 1670s the two populations were said to be roughly equal in size – but they surely indicate that, in the late 1620s, the Tatama were vulnerable in a contest with the Citará, and that this was why, in 1628, they accepted Martín Bueno's aid in their conflict with their northern neighbours. That year, as we have seen, a small armed force of twelve Spanish soldiers, commanded by Bueno but backed up by a far larger force of native 'friends' and allies, advanced on a Citará settlement, killing or capturing many of its inhabitants before returning to Anserma. But however advantageous to the Tatama the assistance offered in 1628 may have been, it did not lead to permanent Spanish occupation. Martín Bueno carried out three or four more *entradas* to the region after that year, explored territories hitherto unknown to Spaniards, and prospected for gold in the vicinity of the old city of Toro and beyond, but the settlement he founded, San Juan de Castro, did not achieve permanence.[32] Nevertheless, by the late 1630s, peaceful contacts with the Tatama, mostly for the purpose of trade, had lasted for some twenty years, during which time no 'uprising or treachery' against Spaniards took place.[33]

Developments among the Citará were not as advanced in the 1620s, but by the 1630s small groups of Indians from that region, too, established communication with Spanish settlers, and a few even took up residence in Antioquia. Attracted, perhaps, by the opportunity to acquire European tools, others agreed to allow Spaniards into their territory, and apparently even 'embraced' the offer of baptism and conversion. According to Martín Delgado Jurado, a *vecino* of Antioquia, Indians came in large groups on their frequent visits to the city: 'six, seven and eight and eighteen and other times twenty Indians', he said.[34] But documents dating from the late 1630s and early 1640s suggest that contacts with Spaniards were far more limited than this, perhaps involving only a handful of communities clustered in a small area close to the Pani Pani river, especially those known to Spaniards as Comita and Buenavista. There, contacts were sufficiently long-standing for some Indians to be known by names given to them by the Spanish – Omanbita, known as El Sarco, and Churucupita, known as Gaspar de Luna – and to feel sufficiently secure to seek out Spaniards in the city of Antioquia itself, where, it was said, they enjoyed lavish hospitality. Fernando Docio, for instance, described how he 'gave them food, sat the capitanes and principales at his own table, provided accommodation in his own home, and gave them supplies for their return'.[35] Beyond Comita and Buenavista, we know little about the reactions of Indian communities. But the events that followed the arrival in Antioquia of the new governor Don Juan Vélez de Guevara – almost the entire membership of an *entrada* meeting a violent end at the hands of Indians – indicate that the Citará may have been divided in their attitudes towards Europeans. When the Indian Tocama was interrogated in Antioquia in 1640, he stated that 'the Indians of the Atrato River are enemies of those of Buenavista and Comita and Taita . . . because *those of the Atrato River* killed Captain Martín Bueno and now [all] are being pursued by the Spaniards'.[36]

Nevertheless, considerable progress had been made by the late 1630s in the pacification of the peoples of the Chocó. Poya, Tatama and Citará Indians all showed that they were not averse to entering into dialogue with Spaniards, exchanging foodstuffs for European tools, or even, in the case of the Tatama, requesting military aid when this enabled them to shift the balance of power in their favour. These relationships were, however, still very fragile. Among the Citará, interactions with Spaniards were recent, and probably limited to a handful of communities in the vicinity of the Pani Pani river. Among the Tatama, contacts were of longer duration but this did not necessarily signify acceptance of Spanish occupation: several *entradas* had taken place, but these had not yet led to permanent settlement. Even among the Poya, where Spaniards had settled and begun mining by the mid-1630s, Spanish occupation was considered precarious. Indeed, when Juan Vélez de Guevara arrived in Antioquia in 1638, Bishop Montoya, now appointed to the See of Trujillo but still conscious of the threat that future operations might constitute to his family's activities in the Toro region, pleaded with the *adelantado* not to enter or even bypass La Sed de Cristo 'making gestures of war that might agitate or stir up its inhabitants'.[37] It was this fine balance that was disrupted by the arrival in Antioquia of Juan Vélez de Guevara in 1638.

Martín Bueno de Sancho and the 1638 expedition

Don Juan Vélez arrived in New Granada in 1637.[38] In May 1638, he deposited 30,000 pesos in the Royal Treasury in Bogotá and in September of that year he left the capital for Antioquia, there to take up his post as governor.[39] As Bishop Montoya feared, Vélez's arrival in the city signalled the beginning of a phase of more intense Spanish involvement in the Chocó, but this time it was conducted from Antioquia, rather than, as in the late sixteenth and early seventeenth centuries, from the cities of the *gobernación* of Popayán. The *adelantado* quickly set about implementing his plans to colonise the Chocó, and before the end of the year he chose Martín Bueno de Sancho, with Diego de Andrade as his second in command, to undertake a new expedition to the region, where he was to realise the main provisions of the 1634 *capitulación*. Accompanied by approximately 44 officers and men, two priests, Fray Lucas de la Candelaria and Fray Nicolás de San Juan Bautista, as well as several women and children, Martín Bueno left Anserma late in 1638 and made his way towards Tatama territory. There a new settlement, Salamanca de los Reyes, was founded and left in the care of a handful of soldiers under the command of Mateo de Cifuentes, and the Augustinian Fray Nicolás de San Juan Bautista. At least one woman was also left in Salamanca. The remainder of the party, accompanied by an estimated two hundred Tatama Indians, moved on to Citará territory, where, it seems, a second settlement was founded before the party moved on once again, heading now towards territory said to be controlled by the Membocana.[40]

Little more is known about Bueno de Sancho's activities in the Chocó in late 1638, for in February 1639 the expedition was ambushed by Indians somewhere along the Atrato river, and all but the women and children were killed.[41] No account was ever given by Spaniards present at the event, for although the women and children were spared, being captured rather than killed, they were never rescued. All our information relating to the incident comes, then, from Indian sources, as recorded by Spaniards, and from these four different versions of events emerged over the following months. The first version is that given by a Tatama Indian, Arrogoma, who in May 1639 appeared before the governor of Popayán, Don Juan de Borja, to inform him of the events that had occurred, and to assure him that this act of aggression had been the work of the Citará, acting independently from other Indian groups in the region. According to Arrogoma's version, the Citará deliberately lured the Spanish onto canoes, with promises to guide them to the lands of the Membocana, only to launch a surprise attack, killing the men and taking their weapons, which were then broken up and used to make axes and other tools.[42] The second version, based on confessions obtained from Citará Indians captured during the first punitive campaign that followed the incident, placed responsibility for the assault on a coalition of Citará and Tatama. According to testimony taken from Indians, admittedly under threat of torture, the arrival of Martín Bueno in the Chocó, with plans that now involved pacifying Tatamaes and Citaraes alike rather than supporting one against the other, resulted in these erstwhile enemies forming an alliance to organise an ambush upon the company when it was deep in Indian territory and unable to defend itself or escape. For their participation, the Tatama obtained an equal share of the Spaniards' belongings – the clothing, tools and weapons that were taken after their deaths.[43] A third version, based on confessions obtained during an expedition conducted in 1640 against the Poya, spread the net of responsibility ever wider, and involved this group in the affair as well. In the words of the commander of that expedition, Juan Antonio Pereira, 'an Indian interpreter whom I brought with me told me . . . that he had heard it said during one of their drinking parties [*borracheras*] and other gatherings . . . that they had been present at the deaths of Martín Bueno and his soldiers'.[44] And the fourth version, derived from evidence obtained during the final campaign, suggests that far from resulting from a broad alliance of Citará, Tatama and Poya, the attack on the company was carried out by the Citará who occupied that part of the Atrato through which the expedition passed en route to the Membocana, aided and abetted by the Tatama who accompanied Bueno. In this version, then, this was not a generalised attack on the part of the Citará peoples against the Spanish colonisers. According to the Indians Tocama and Guapama, interrogated by Juan Vélez in Antioquia in mid-1640, it was perpetrated only by 'those of the Atrato River', and no Indians from the communities of Buenavista, Taita or Comita were present when it occurred.[45] That Indians were divided rather than united by the massacre was also the opinion of the Spanish captain Gregorio Céspedes y

Guzmán. Back in Antioquia after completing his expedition, Céspedes informed the *adelantado* that the Indians of the Chocó 'are in conflict and it is thought that wars . . . [have broken out] between them over who advised that said killings be carried out'.[46] Another member of that expedition, Joseph Lescano, confirmed Céspedes' assessment, reporting 'the discord which it is now known exists among Indians over the death of . . . Martín Bueno'.[47]

Given the absence of reliable first-hand accounts, the contradictory nature of the evidence that is available, and the fact that much of it was obtained by violent means, it is not possible to determine the reasons for the attack, the sequence of events that brought it about, or the identity of the Indians who carried it out. We cannot be certain whether this action was the work of a single Indian group, or of one or more communities within it, or whether it resulted from a coalition of Indians determined to repel this latest Spanish incursion. All we do know is that throughout 1639 no reports reached the Spanish of a threat to their activities in Toro or Sed de Cristo from the Poya; that the settlement of Salamanca which Bueno founded in Tatama territory at the end of 1638 was still intact in mid-1639; and that in May 1639 Mateo de Cifuentes, back in Anserma in search of reinforcements, informed Popayán's governor, Don Juan de Borja, that he had no fears that any harm would come to the Spanish from the Tatama. These Indians, according to Cifuentes, 'have always sought the protection of the Spaniards for their survival, due to . . . ancient rivalries . . . with the . . . Citarabirá [Citará]'.[48] We also know that rarely, if ever, did the Citará and Tatama ally to wage war on Spaniards, and that it was the former who had good cause to target Martín Bueno, for it was he who led the assault on one of their settlements in 1628.[49] There is, moreover, a suggestion that he conducted slaving expeditions to the Chocó after that year, although we do not know which group or groups were affected. In 1636, the governor of Popayán, Don Lorenzo de Villaquirán, complained of Bueno that he had done little to advance colonisation in the region, and that he had merely occupied himself in seizing women and children 'to people his estate'.[50]

Our purpose, however, is not to judge the truthfulness of the versions of events presented, or the validity of the evidence that the Spanish gathered to justify their response to Bueno's death. It is instead to explain what the Spanish response was, and the ways in which their actions affected relations with Indians on the frontier. The more important point is, therefore, that before a proper investigation was carried out to establish the causes of the events of February 1639, or the identity of the Indians responsible for them, Juan Vélez, supported by 'prominent persons' in Antioquia, declared an offensive war – a 'guerra a sangre y fuego' – against the Indians of the Chocó. In the process, he overturned the strategy of gradual advance based on trade, gift-giving and occasional assistance which had brought the Spanish slow but significant progress over the previous fifteen to twenty years – indeed, in the case of the Poya, actual settlement for the first time in half a century. On 18 July 1639, at a meeting of prominent *vecinos* called to discuss the events surrounding Bueno's death, Vélez launched the 'guerra a sangre y fuego', and announced that Indians captured during the forthcoming campaigns would be distributed in compensation for service – as slaves for the first ten years, and thereafter in *encomienda*.[51] While the 'guerra a sangre y fuego' was directed initially against the Citará, within months the *adelantado*, arguing now that Bueno met his death at the hands of a broad coalition that included Citará, Tatama and Poya Indians, extended the war to the latter two groups as well.

'Guerra a sangre y fuego'

The attack on Martín Bueno was a serious blow to Juan Vélez. Not only did it put an end to his hopes of rapidly fulfilling his duties to the Crown, and being handsomely rewarded for his efforts, but it also represented a great financial loss, a substantial sum of money having been invested in supplying and provisioning the men and women participating in that expedition. As he ruefully observed in early July 1639, 'not only has the loss of these people ensued . . . but of the large sums of money laid out to place [them] there, and all the equipment, munitions, weapons and provisions and other supplies necessary for new settlements have also been lost'.[52] By July, moreover, over a year had passed since the enterprise began, and he was bound by the terms of a *capitulación* which specified that 'within three years', counted from the day he deposited 30,000 pesos in the offices of the Royal Treasury, 'you must have established and populated the city and mines of Toro, to serve as provincial capital, and two other sufragan cities, each with at least 50 Spanish vecinos'.[53] The pressure of time clearly weighed heavily on Vélez, for he was unwilling to defer even for a short time a final decision on the response to be made, if this meant delaying action against the Indians of the Chocó: it was imperative, he informed the meeting of 18 July, that a decision should be made immediately.[54] Furthermore, the option of withdrawing from the exercise was not open to him, for as the *capitulación* specified, should Vélez fail in his attempt – however 'fortuitous' the reason – none of the money that remained unspent would be returned.[55]

The *adelantado* had other problems, too, which endangered the success of his enterprise, not least of which was that of recruitment of rank and file soldiers to serve on expeditions to the frontier. In fact, difficulties of recruitment were so severe that even the expected duration of the first expedition had to be kept secret from all below officer rank.[56] The Chocó was simply not a good proposition for the average soldier, and the massacre of an entire Spanish expedition made it even less so. Too many *entradas* had ended in disaster, the climate was unpleasant, the terrain was difficult, distances were long, and pay was bad.[57] Most provisions had to be carried across long distances by the soldiers or their Indian carriers, which severely limited their supplies, especially of food. This was particularly problematic during times of hostility, when Indians destroyed their own fields to prevent Spaniards seizing their crops, rendering local provisioning extremely difficult.[58] In commenting in 1642 on the many obstacles to colonisation of this territory, Vélez indicated that 'shortage of food [is] our greatest enemy', for over the thirty days required to penetrate the rough and swampy terrain of the Chocó, soldiers and Indian carriers had consumed what supplies they had not lost to the fast-flowing waters of the region's main rivers.[59] While the Chocó drew many entrepreneurs expectant of both reward from the Crown and great wealth from its rich gold deposits, for poorer colonists, the attractions were far less obvious, and other inducements had to be offered.

In accordance with the terms of his *capitulación*, moreover, Juan Vélez was also required to account for the circumstances that justified war against the indigenous population of the Chocó – to report on 'the causes', that is, 'which [have] obliged [you] to resort to said force of arms'.[60] For as Patricia Seed has indicated, from the very beginning of the sixteenth century the Spanish Crown had insisted on proper procedures being followed prior to engaging Indians in combat. Even the infamous *Requerimiento* of 1512, which 'required' newly encountered Indians 'to acknowledge the superiority of Christianity and submit to the political dominion of the Spanish', had to be read to, and be rejected by, Indians before war could legitimately be launched against them. And while this particular 'political ritual' for legitimising war proved to be short-lived, successive monarchs and their advisers nevertheless continued to debate and formulate policies to restrict the use of force as a method of pacification. When the Crown issued new instructions in 1573 which are reflected in Vélez's 1634 licence, it authorised war only against 'apostates and rebels' – Indians who had previously submitted and received the faith – and against those who persisted in refusing to acknowledge the superiority of the Christian faith, and to admit Catholic priests for preaching and conversion.[61]

Juan Vélez thus justified his decision to declare 'guerra a sangre y fuego' on the grounds that Indians would not be peaceably 'reduced', that their offers of peace and friendship, made solely in order to obtain prized European tools, could not be trusted, and that gentle and peaceful methods were inappropriate for the peoples of the Chocó, who were, in the end, 'irreducible' except by force.[62] In reality, however, the 'guerra a sangre y fuego' also served several other purposes. First, in including a provision to the effect that Indians could be enslaved, it served as an incentive to recruitment. When, in late 1639, recruitment began for Gregorio Céspedes' *entrada*, it was publicly announced that, as remuneration for the task ahead, Indian captives would be distributed among the soldiers.[63] Many of the men who signed up for that and the previous expedition under Fernando Docio's command were attracted only by the expectation of such reward. Francisco Díaz, one of the members of the Docio *entrada*, was to state later that it was precisely the prospect of obtaining slaves of his own that enticed him and his fellow soldiers to participate in the expedition.[64] Secondly, an all-out war served the purposes of comprehensively defeating the enemy, asserting Spanish military supremacy and underlining the futility of further resistance,[65] hence Vélez's specific instructions that these campaigns were to spare only those too young to represent a future threat of uprising or rebellion.[66] And thirdly, the 'guerra a sangre y fuego' also served as a means of enslaving Indians for service elsewhere, and perhaps in this way even to enable the *adelantado* to recoup some of his losses. Thus, Vélez also explicitly directed Juan

Antonio Pereira that 'should you consider it convenient to bring out the said chusma, endeavour to bring [the most suitable] ... so that they may serve His Majesty ... and one quarter of which I will reserve for distribution'.[67]

The 'guerra a sangre y fuego' launched by the governor of Antioquia against the Indians of the Chocó in July 1639, then, changed completely the nature of the enterprise upon which Vélez had embarked just a few months earlier. By August 1640, three separate punitive expeditions had been dispatched against the Citará, the Tatama and the Poya, though none of these, perhaps unusually, was personally conducted by the *adelantado*. Two *entradas* were directed against the Citará. The first, consisting of some 60 men and one Augustinian friar, left Antioquia at the end of July 1639, and was commanded by Fernando Docio.[68] The second, consisting of approximately 72 soldiers and led by Gregorio Céspedes y Guzmán, left the same city in March of the following year.[69] No priest took part in that expedition. Only one *entrada* was sent against the Tatama and Poya. It left Anserma, under the command of Juan Antonio Pereira, before July 1640.[70]

The consequences of Vélez's decision to turn the pacification into a 'guerra a sangre y fuego' were, however, disastrous for Indians and Spaniards alike. For many Indians – especially the Poya and Citará – the punitive expeditions of late 1639 and early 1640 brought death or enslavement. For those who evaded capture, they brought migration. Forced to flee their settlements, Indians destroyed crops, burned stores of food, and, it was said, suffered hunger and strife. As for the Spaniards, the ferocity of the 'guerra a sangre y fuego' brought an equally ferocious response from Indians. Some time during August 1639, the settlement of Salamanca de los Reyes was wiped out by Indians. Thereafter, the settlement of La Sed de Cristo was abandoned, all mining operations in the district of Toro ceased, and more than a decade of co-operation between Indians and Spaniards in this region came to an end.[71] Even outside the Chocó, Spaniards felt the consequences of war. In Anserma and Cartago, the violence with which Juan Antonio Pereira proceeded against the Poya provoked real fears that Indians would seek revenge by targeting these cities. More generally, of course, the *entradas* of late 1639 and early 1640 halted all further Spanish advances in the pacification and settlement of the Chocó. It is, therefore, to the ways in which these campaigns were conducted, and their impact on the native peoples each encountered, that we now turn.

The Docio expedition
The dispatch of the first punitive expedition in July 1639 provoked deep suspicion among the Citará: many communities, clearly informed in advance of Fernando Docio's progress across the territory, were abandoned by Indians as the Spaniards drew near. All Indians – including those of Comita and Buenavista, who had long-standing links with settlers in Antioquia – were apprehensive about Docio's intentions. Thus, when on 17 August 1639 the expedition arrived at Comita, said to be the residence of the Indian Baquirura, all it discovered was 'one large abandoned Indian dwelling and fresh Indian tracks'.[72] Over the following days and weeks, as Spaniards advanced across the region, this pattern was repeated in place after

place. At the Pani Pani river, the company again found nothing but 'one dwelling which they heard was abandoned by the Indians who lived there, [who] made off . . . for the Darién [river], towards which they were all retreating'.[73] And, on arriving at Buenavista, 'on a ridge they found six large abandoned dwellings . . . which the Indians had deserted'.[74]

Indians had a great advantage over Spanish forces in the Chocó, however well armed these might be. Forewarned of the Spanish advance by spies and scouts, knowledgeable of the terrain and its rivers, proficient in the use of canoes which allowed them to make a rapid escape, and small enough numerically to disperse quickly and efficiently, the many small communities that dotted the landscape of the Chocó could successfully evade the expeditions by withdrawing to more distant regions. Only children and the elderly – the *chusma*, as the Spanish called them – were vulnerable to capture, sometimes being left behind to make their way as best they could. But rarely did the able-bodied fall into Spanish hands. When, on 18 August 1639, 29 or 30 members of the community of the octogenarian 'El Sarco' were seized by a small force of twelve men under the command of Juan de Rodas, not a single *gandul* (able-bodied adult male) was to be found among them.[75] As Fernando Docio recorded, 'Juan de Rodas . . . brought captive the said Sarco and his wives and sons and daughters plus another old Indian with his wife and three small children amounting in total to thirty individuals, and not a gandul among them'.[76] At the settlement of Los Organos, the soldier Francisco Díaz later informed *fiscal* Herrera, the Spaniards were likewise told that 'there were two households [consisting of] chusma . . . of whom there were a large number and among the chusma there were no more than five gandules and these were old and disabled because the rest of the . . . gandules from that . . . [community] were to be found in [the region of] the Darién River'.[77]

Aware that Spanish weaponry alone was insufficient to achieve the aims of the *entrada*, Fernando Docio understood that other, more underhand ways had to be found if he was to comply with his instructions to eradicate further opposition, 'leaving only those too young to represent a threat of uprising or confederation with others'.[78] His objective thus became to deceive the Citará of Comita, Buenavista and other communities beyond into believing that they had nothing to fear from the Spanish, and that the Spanish had come in a spirit of friendship rather than in war. Docio believed that only if he could persuade the Indians of his peaceful intentions would they return to their settlements, and that this was crucial to the success of his *entrada*, for the nature of the terrain and its many rivers, combined with the Indians' knowledge of their own territory, rendered futile any attempt at pursuit: 'they cannot be . . . caught', he said. It was in view of these considerations that the captain made the decision to take no immediate action against El Sarco, and to continue to provide Indians with gifts of European goods: 'by giving gifts to those who come [of their own volition] we will assemble enough people on whom to inflict punishment'. If, on the other hand, Spaniards made any show of force, 'they will flee'.[79]

Three main tactics thus underpinned Docio's actions in the early days of the *entrada*. First, as noted, he took no action against his Indian prisoners and made no attempt to ascertain from them the whereabouts of the Citará population that had fled. This ensured that the initial hostility that El Sarco's capture provoked – there were reports of Indians approaching the camp 'parading with their bows and arrows and . . . darts [as is their] custom when at war'[80] – soon abated, and that within days Indians felt secure enough to approach the Spanish at their camp. Secondly, Docio made determined efforts to ensure that his men abstained from ill-treating the Citará. Not only were *salidas* in search of Indians to seize and enslave forbidden, but the men were also entreated not to remove maize crops or other foodstuffs from Indian fields. As the captain recorded in his log, 'I have bought [from the Indians] supplies for our camp in the hope that such treatment would . . . attract them [to it].' And thirdly, to further convince Indians of his peaceful intentions, he offered gifts of tools, trinkets and clothing. In Buenavista, for example, Docio described how, instead of resorting to force, 'I gave them axes and machetes and knives . . . and beads and needles and told them to invite [to our camp] the caciques from the river and not to flee, for when they went to Antioquia . . . they received tools, clothing and other things'.[81] These methods were confirmed by other members of the expedition. According to Francisco Díaz, the most informative of all the soldiers who took part in this *entrada*, and also the most critical of Docio's methods, many Indians came to the Spanish at Buenavista 'with foodstuffs that they sold to the soldiers and even the general in exchange for knives, machetes, needles, and fishhooks, and the said Indians then left the camp with what they had obtained'.[82]

Initially at least, Docio's tactics seemed to be successful. While the Spanish were based at Comita, the Indians Esteba (El Sarco's son-in-law) and Churucupita, also known as Gaspar de Luna, both visited the camp and had discussions with the captain. While based at Buenavista in early September, as many as 70 Citará Indians, including several *indios principales* from communities of the Atrato river area – the most prominent of whom were Tego and Tebue – were said not only to have come to the camp, but even to have lodged there.[83] But by early September, less than three weeks after the Spanish first arrived at Comita, and more than three months before the entrada was due to end, Fernando Docio abandoned his gradual but deliberate approach, and the expedition entered a new phase. Capitalising on the presence at Buenavista of El Sarco, Esteba, Tego and Tebue, among others, and citing as justification the discovery of a roll of rope alleged to have come from Martín Bueno's supplies, Docio ordered the arrest and imprisonment of all Indians then at the camp. Surprised, no doubt, by this turn of events, the Indians resisted capture, and in the resulting affray, seven were killed. As Docio explained the incident, 'I ordered their capture and they resisted as a result of which seven were killed and the rest were placed in . . . irons.'[84]

Docio did not explain the reasons for this change of heart so soon into his four-month assignment. Probably he acted under pressure from his men, who, according to reports submitted to the Santa Fe *audiencia*, repeatedly advised Docio in the early stages of this campaign that Indians, too, were playing a game of deception, and that in this game it was they who held the upper hand. Francisco Díaz, for example, insisted that the Indians' apparent willingness to communicate and trade with the Spanish had more to do with buying time to enable them to 'move their people and the food they had', a fact that was obvious to all except Fernando Docio. In describing one occasion when camp was set up along the banks of the Pani Pani river, Díaz related how 'some of the Indians of the vicinity came with some fruits and the general allowed them to leave, deceived by the Indians who said that later they would all go to Buenavista', where they would again meet the Spaniards. Because of the captain's refusal to accept, despite all the evidence, that it was he who was being duped, Indians gained time to make good their escape. Thus, by the time the company arrived at Buenavista all it found were six deserted dwellings, all 'due to the delay . . . in arriving at said place, for which reason the soldiers were unable to launch an attack or take any prisoners, as the Indians had had time to retreat'.[85] Similar movements, it was said, were occurring throughout Indian territory. More and more settlements were being abandoned, and hundreds of Indians were gradually migrating north and west, towards the lower reaches of the Atrato river.[86]

Whether Docio acted under pressure from his men, whether he concluded that his methods were failing, or whether he simply feared Vélez (Díaz also accused his captain of deceiving the *adelantado* about the numbers of Indians executed), once he made the decision to take action, he acted quickly and decisively.[87] Torture was now used freely to obtain information relating to the attack on Martín Bueno. When the Indian El Sarco claimed to be too old and too blind to know what had happened to Bueno, he was warned 'that he would be tortured unless he told the truth, [that he would be] tied to a pole and that the noose would be tightened until he died or told the truth'. When El Sarco refused to be intimidated, Docio, true to his word, had him tied to a makeshift wooden frame, complete with twisted rope, whereupon the Indian, 'seeing himself so tied . . . asked to be released [and said] that he wanted to tell the truth'.[88] Through means such as these, Docio gathered the necessary evidence to 'prove' the participation in Bueno's death of all the *indios principales* being held prisoners at Buenavista. Indeed, the cacique Tebue allegedly confessed that Bueno 'was killed on the Atrato River by this prisoner and the cacique Tego and the cacique Chucurrupi [Churucupita] . . . and the vast majority of the caciques of this province and all the Indians . . . and also all the Tatamaes'.[89] Armed with improbable confessions of this kind, Docio proceeded to act in accordance with instructions, condemning all *gandules* being held prisoner to be impaled alive, 'as punishment to themselves and as an example to others'.[90]

Despite the execution of ten Citará Indians – more if Docio is to be believed – and the capture of a further thirteen *chusma*, the *entrada* of the summer of 1639 was not a great success. Indians, as we have seen, were far more knowledgeable of the terrain and far more proficient in river navigation than the Spanish. Living in settlements that were invariably located on or very near the river banks, Indians used the rivers as means of escape, and this allowed entire communities easily to avoid capture by retreating to distant regions where they could not be followed by Spaniards. But this does not mean that native peoples suffered no ill-effects from the events of late 1639. As we shall, in forcing Indians to leave behind their communities – their fields, their homes, and their stores of food, which were usually destroyed by burning before departure – the Docío expedition brought great turmoil and anguish upon the peoples of Citará province.

The Pereira expedition

By the time Juan Antonio Pereira's expedition left Anserma in early July 1640, the 'guerra a sangre y fuego', limited at first to the Citará, had been extended to include the Tatama. For in the months that preceded the *entrada*, more evidence was gathered – some of it by Fernando Docío – to 'confirm' that Martín Bueno and his companions met their deaths at the hands of a coalition that included both Tatama and Citará. Further incidences of violence against Spaniards in and out of the Chocó had also taken place, reportedly perpetrated now by the former rather than the latter. In August 1639, the settlement of Salamanca, founded in Tatama territory, was destroyed. That same month the Spaniard Gabriel de Guevara was decapitated at his *hato* or estate, some three leagues distant from Anserma, by Tatama who had come to the city to trade.[91] These acts of aggression, which took place in a context of increasing violence between Indians and Spaniards, provided the *adelantado* Vélez with the necessary justification to dispatch a punitive expedition against the Tatama (the first since the attack on Bueno more than a year before), for as he argued before the *cabildo* of Anserma, evidence of an act of rebellion ('traición a Su Magestad') was necessary to enable him to extend the war to this group as well.[92] No such justification existed to include the Poya in the war declared against the people of the Chocó, since no reports ever reached the Spanish either of their participation in the attack on Martín Bueno, or of any uprising or rebellion against miners and settlers in the Toro district. Many Spaniards in cities neighbouring the Chocó, moreover, insisted that the Poya were entirely loyal to Spaniards. The *procurador* of Cartago, Don Pedro Carrillo de Mendoza, described the Indians as 'peaceful'.[93] Gaspar de Borja, *teniente general* of Anserma, used the words 'greatly loyal'.[94] The documents also show that by 1640, many Poya Indians had adopted Spanish names, and were described as acculturated or partially acculturated – *ladinos, ladinos cristianos, medio ladinos*.[95] Notwithstanding the lack of evidence to suggest that the loyalty of this small group was anything but genuine, Juan Antonio Pereira was nevertheless given wide powers to investigate the extent of Poya participation in recent events and, should their involvement be proven, to act accordingly.[96]

All that was required, therefore, for Juan Antonio Pereira to extend the 'guerra a sangre y fuego' was proof of participation in acts of rebellion on the part of Poya Indians. And no sooner had he arrived in Poya territory, where, by all accounts, he was peacefully received, than that evidence presented itself in the shape of a statement by one of the captain's own Indian *lenguas*, or interpreters, who claimed to have overheard 'in a drinking party . . . how they had been present at the death of Captain Martín Bueno . . . and had been responsible for other attacks on the trail into La Sed de Cristo and in Tatama against Captain Mateo de Cifuentes and that they were to do the same to me'.[97] Armed with this information, Pereira turned on the Indians and, capitalising on the surprise he provoked, seized some 130 people, including 34 *gandules*.[98] Unlike Fernando Docio, however, who adopted extreme measures to punish Indians found guilty of actions against Spaniards, Pereira did not intend to sentence the Poya to death, but to transfer them from the Chocó to the city of Anserma, there to be sold into slavery. To obtain the information that would enable him to justify fully this course of action, the captain proceeded to conduct wide-ranging interrogations of his Indian prisoners, not infrequently assisted by means of torture.

The testimony taken in the days that followed the seizure of some 130 Poya did more than merely prove widespread involvement in the Bueno and Cifuentes affairs. It also raised the spectre of an Indian population proficient in the use of captured Spanish weapons, prohibited under colonial law,[99] of a confederation of tribes withdrawing completely from communication with Spaniards, of future attacks on the settlement of La Sed de Cristo and neighbouring mining camps, and indeed of planned offensives on Spanish settlements outside the Chocó. For example, the Indian Adoata's interrogation provided evidence that 'the three parcialidades [Poya, Tatama and Citará] went for . . . Cifuentes because he had put them to work building a corral and a hut', and that a total of 20 Citará caciques were present when the attack occurred. Gaspar Sangarra's statement suggested that Pereira himself was under similar threat from the Poya acting in concert with their neighbours: 'it was for this reason that Chuagarra, Teguerre, [and] Guatagoma went to inform the province of Tatama, and the said Guatagoma [then] went on to the province of Citarabirá [Citará] with other Tatama Indians for a general meeting [to plan] to kill us [which they were to do] in a convenient place [and] on a rainy night so that . . . [our weapons] would not fire'. Bauri's testimony showed that involvement in attacks against the Spanish was not limited to a select group of individuals, since 'no gandul remains at home when they carry out a killing . . . and when they do so all Indians throw a dart [at the body] even if [already] dead'. Porras's statement indicated that Indians not only seized Spanish firearms, but were also learning to use them: 'the Indians . . . teach each other to shoot'. To this, Yarrami added that the Tatama possessed firearms and gunpowder, and that they used them to hunt. And Gaspar Sangarra described how, after the Spaniards had been killed, the three provinces (Citará, Tatama and Poya) would unite with the Noanama (who belonged to a different language group) to launch attacks against the Spanish both inside and outside the Chocó. When asked if any plans had been made to attack the city of Anserma, Sangarra answered that all places would be targeted.[100] Concluding, on the basis of these 'confessions', that the role of the Poya was to serve as spies for their fellow Indians, the captain made the decision, on 21 August 1640, to bring his *entrada* to a close, and to return, with his prisoners, to Anserma.[101]

However carefully Juan Antonio Pereira constructed his case, it did not convince everyone of the guilt of the Poya. Indeed, some Spaniards in Anserma and Cartago remained deeply suspicious of the Indian confessions, and of Pereira's motives for taking them. The fact that none of the prisoners was put to death, but that they were all instead taken to Anserma for distribution among the members of the expedition, only served to heighten those suspicions. Don Gaspar de Borja made no secret of his conviction that from the very start Juan Antonio Pereira intended this *entrada* to be neither more nor less than a slaving expedition, to acquire live captives for his own *repartimiento* and for sale in 'various places'. Nor did he make any secret of his belief that Pereira had fabricated evidence to justify the enslavement of Indians and the theft of their possessions. Only by submitting them to 'exquisite' torture, Borja reported to the *audiencia*, did he succeed in extracting the confessions needed to carry out his objective – namely, to enslave them and take their possessions, 'which they had acquired *by serving as carriers and selling maize to the mines of Toro and Sed de Cristo*'.[102] These actions, of course, did little to assist the pacification in the longer term, for the price the Spaniards paid for the capture of 130 unsuspecting Poya Indians was the immediate destruction of La Sed de Cristo, the death of several of its Spanish residents, and the cessation of all mining operations in the Toro district. The carefully constructed relationships built up by the Montoya family over several years in Toro and La Sed de Cristo came to an abrupt and ignominious end.

The Céspedes y Guzmán expedition
The second punitive expedition against the Citará, commanded by Gregorio Céspedes y Guzmán and consisting of approximately 72 men, was the least successful of the three undertaken under the auspices of the governor and *adelantado* Juan Vélez de Guevara.[103] When the company left Antioquia at the end of March 1640, the effects of the Docio *entrada* were still in evidence in this part of the Chocó. Indians had not returned to their settlements and now made even more determined efforts to conceal themselves from Spaniards. A month-long exploration of a wide area extending from the Pani Pani river to Taita failed to discover a single inhabited settlement, or any evidence of recent occupation. At the Sitio de Ocumita, Céspedes y Guzmán recorded in his log, 'I came upon three dwellings ... which appear to have been abandoned some six months ago'. Investigations in the surrounding area uncovered no more than 'two empty dwellings, abandoned a long time ago'. Nor were there any traces of Indians in the vicinity – neither 'old nor fresh tracks', as the captain put it. At the site of Gaspar de Luna's settlement on the Pani Pani river, another empty dwelling was found, 'apparently abandoned over four months ago'. Along the Bebarama river, where the Spanish discovered two further households, the *alférez* Joseph Ruiz de la Cámara recorded that he 'found no one in said dwellings'.[104] Unlike in August and September 1639, moreover, in April 1640 no Indians made contact – peaceful or otherwise – with the intruders, and none approached the Spanish encampments.

This made the Céspedes expedition an entirely different one from that which had preceded it. Instead of establishing a base to attract Indians with gifts of tools and promises of trade, as Docio had done at Comita and then at Buenavista, Gregorio Céspedes had to traverse Citará province in search of inhabited settlements to attack and Indians to seize. Different tactics, tailored to meet the new circumstances, failed, however, to make more than minimal impact on the population of Citará province. For throughout the weeks of the *entrada*, as the Céspedes company headed north from the Pani Pani towards Taita, repeated Spanish 'ambushes' intended to 'capture the . . . spies that the Citarabirá [Citará] commonly employ along their trails' netted the expedition no more than thirty Indians in total: two at the Pani Pani river; ten more, including two gandules, at the Baberama; a further eighteen between the Baberama and Taita.[105] Furthermore, though the seizure of Indians did provide the expedition with information leading them to Indian retreats in the Taita area, all the Spanish discovered was that these settlements, too, had been deserted by Indians forewarned of the Spanish advance. On arrival in Taita, after two weeks of travel, Céspedes recorded that the six dwellings in this community had been abandoned some four or five days earlier, 'undoubtedly because they were warned [of our approach]'. Four days beyond Taita, another large settlement, consisting of eight dwellings, was not only deserted but had also been burned down: 'when the Citará became aware of our approach they . . . set fire to them'.[106]

The Céspedes y Guzmán expedition achieved little of utility to the Spanish. After a month or more of long and arduous journeying through the region, as well as severe shortages of food,[107] Céspedes returned to Antioquia, in June 1640, with no more than thirty prisoners, many of them women, for distribution among his men.[108] This tour of the region did, however, serve to show that the kind of war declared by the *adelantado* Vélez on the native peoples of the Chocó was never likely to lead to the defeat of the Citará, or not, at least, unless overwhelming force was deployed against them. For even under severe pressure, Indians could still exploit the advantages of their terrain and the hundreds of rivers that criss-crossed the region to make a swift escape to places where Spaniards, whose knowledge of the Chocó region was still very limited in 1640, could not follow. Writing in Taita in May 1640, Céspedes y Guzmán summed up the obstacles he encountered in the following way: 'as the Taita River flows alongside their homes . . . and as they were equipped with canoes they quickly got on board, and although I wanted to follow on foot, the guide said that we would [surely] lose our way and die'.[109]

Another failure of Spanish colonisation

If the main objective of the 'guerra a sangre y fuego' was to eradicate opposition to Spanish colonisation of the Chocó and to enable the *adelantado* to implement the provisions contained in his 1634 *capitulación*, it proved, despite the seizure of approximately two hundred Indians in three expeditions, entirely counter-productive. Pereira's actions among the Poya – described as 'excessive and cruel' – were particularly damaging to Spanish interests.[110] As Don Pedro Carrillo de Mendoza argued in the aftermath of that *entrada*, these peoples had not only sustained peaceful relations with Spaniards for fifteen years, but were also central to the continuance of Spanish mining in the Toro district. It was they, after all, who served the Spanish, maintained the trails into the district, and paddled the canoes upon which supplies were carried into the Chocó.[111] The Poya were also, as Juan Leyva Zavala pointed out, crucial to the well-being of cities outside the Chocó, for in making possible the exploitation of gold deposits, they had enabled those cities to 'recover from the hardships of the past'.[112] Many Spaniards inside and outside the Chocó, therefore, paid the price for the ruthless way in which Juan Antonio Pereira conducted his *entrada* against this small group. In the Chocó, retaliatory attacks started immediately. According to Gaspar de Borja, the priest of La Sed de Cristo, Pedro García de Salamanca, as well as one Captain Francisco Redondo, three or four Spanish soldiers, and several black slaves were all killed by the Poya in revenge for Pereira's actions.[113] Outside the region, these events provoked real fears that Indians would also target the cities of Anserma and Cartago. As Carrillo de Mendoza admitted, not only were La Sed de Cristo and Toro vulnerable to attack, but all Spanish estates neighbouring the Chocó and even the city of Anserma were now at risk.[114] And these fears were not entirely unfounded. In April 1641 Juan Leyva Zavala reported that three Indian spies had recently been detained in Anserma, apparently assessing the likelihood of a successful attack on the city during the forthcoming celebrations for Holy Week.[115]

Elsewhere in the Chocó, the impact of the punitive expedition of 1639–40 was less dramatic for Spaniards, if not for Indians, but it was equally counterproductive. Fernando Docio's actions among the Citará succeeded only in alienating the native population and promoting the migration of Indians away from their communities and settlements. By April 1640, entire communities had abandoned their traditional homelands and moved northwards and westwards, towards Taita and the lower reaches of the Atrato river. The second expedition, headed by Gregorio Céspedes, made some inroads into these areas, but all this provoked was a further retreat. As Spaniards discovered, weaponry alone could not lead to the defeat of hundreds of small, dispersed, largely autonomous native communities, because, in the end, they were ideally suited to making a quick escape as news spread of Spanish incursions.[116] As Gregorio Céspedes recorded in Taita, the native population had the advantage of 'so many . . . rivers and such a large expanse of land, being as it is . . . [both] harsh and hostile'.[117]

This is not to say, of course, that the Citará were unaffected by this phase of contact. The punishments meted out to those captured were extreme. Some met violent deaths. Others were transported out of the Chocó, separated from their relatives and distributed among Spaniards or sold into slavery.[118] Even for Indians who evaded capture, the consequences were severe. In order to protect themselves, communities were forced to abandon settlements and cultivated fields. Where possible, they cut down their crops and set their dwellings alight, all in order to prevent the Spanish plundering maize stocks and obtaining shelter. And, as Tocama reported to the *adelantado* in June 1640, the Indians 'are now being pursued by the Spanish . . . who have captured many Indian women and boys and some adult males, and many have died, and as they [have had to] flee and suffered hunger, many people have died, about . . . 400, the majority from the Atrato River'.[119] For his part, Céspedes y Guzmán informed Vélez that 'it is thought that wars [have broken out] between them over who advised that said killings be carried out'.[120] The impact of events on relations with other native groups is not known, however, nor is it clear by what means the communities of the region reformed and reconstituted themselves on returning to their traditional territory in the aftermath of the Vélez campaigns.

Although the punitive expeditions dispatched by the *adelantado* in response to Martín Bueno's death failed to meet their stated objectives, Spaniards drew different conclusions from the obstacles they faced in 1639–40. For some, especially Don Juan Vélez, the real reason for the failure to advance colonisation lay in the nature of the terrain and the peoples who inhabited it, 'for the Indians inhabit [settlements spread across] more than 200 leagues of territory, divided one from the other and with canoes [at the ready] . . . so that on hearing [any] disturbance they warn each other and escape leaving no traces [for us to follow]'.[121] The governor's supporters in Antioquia, including the expedition leaders, put forward other explanations, focusing particularly on the small size of the forces available to the Spanish to carry out this forbidding task. Writing from Taita in May 1640, for example, Gregorio Céspedes concluded that 'it is as impossible to conquer and pacify the said provinces with the people of Antioquia alone as it is to chuck all the water of the sea into a puddle'.[122]

At no point, it seems, did the realisation of the futility of war against the indigenous peoples of the Chocó lead Vélez or his supporters to consider the kind of peaceful approach proposed by Spanish officials in other frontier territories to overcome the impediments to successful colonisation posed by native populations with a similar capacity for rapid dispersal. Rodrigo Río de la Losa, for instance, who spent many years on Mexico's northern frontier during the Chichimeca War and became governor of Nueva Vizcaya in 1590, 'learned firsthand', as Charlotte Gradie has shown, 'the shortcomings of the Spanish policy of total war against . . . Indians . . . who always outnumbered the Spanish, enjoyed the further advantage of fighting on their home territory, and could vanish into the desert or sierras, where they could not easily be pursued'. But whereas Río de Losa, after experimenting with various strategies, came eventually to believe that only peace with Indians would secure Nueva Vizcaya for the Spanish, in Antioquia, the conclusion drawn was that only overwhelming force, in the shape of military expeditions introduced from several directions, could overcome the resistance of the native population to Spanish colonisation.[123] Gregorio Céspedes, for instance, considered it imperative that future campaigns should consist of a minimum of 200 men, and that they should be undertaken from two directions at once: from Cartagena (via the Atrato), and from Antioquia itself. Failing this, matters 'will forever remain as they have thus far'.[124] Captain Fernando de Toro Zapata, *alguacil mayor* of Antioquia, arrived at a similar conclusion. His view was that this 'conquest' – the term 'pacification' had, significantly, been discarded – could only be achieved by forces penetrating the Chocó from the directions of Cartagena, Panama, Popayán and Antioquia.[125] Captain Francisco de Guzmán, *alcalde ordinario* of Antioquia, proposed even more extreme measures to subject the Citará, namely, a campaign of extermination aimed at putting to death all able-bodied males, leaving only the *chusma* to begin settlement.[126]

This was not, however, the interpretation of Crown officials in Santa Fe, who considered that the real reasons for the failure of this latest attempt at pacification and settlement actually lay in a policy that relied on privately negotiated *capitulaciones* to extend colonisation. For Don Jorge de Herrera y Castillo, *fiscal* of the *audiencia*, *capitulaciones* that authorised the use of force had always brought 'severe problems' in their wake, served merely to enable wealthy individuals to 'maximise their profits under the pretext of religion', had rarely achieved significant results, and should not therefore be relied on in future as a method for pacifying frontier populations.[127] As Chapter 3 will show, over the following years the Crown took seriously the advice of officials such as *fiscal* Herrera. For not only did Vélez prove to be the last Spaniard to be awarded a *capitulación* for the pacification of the Chocó, but, in the late 1660s, a campaign began to recruit Franciscan missionaries who were finally to take charge, here as in other regions of the empire, of the task of colonisation and conversion.[128] However, while the Crown was persuaded to reassess the efficacy of the *capitulación* as a method for extending Spanish domination over this frontier region, it also accepted some of the arguments put forward by Vélez and his supporters in Antioquia. Indeed, the opinions of all concerned in this failed experiment of 1639–40 were reflected in later royal instructions for the pacification of the Chocó.

Notes

1 Colmenares, 'La formación de la economía colonial', pp. 23–25. Mario Góngora has explained that this notion of reward for services rendered originated in the Reconquista, which led 'to the formulation of a system of political justice which placed great emphasis on concepts derived from the royal duty of rewarding and granting favours to men who had distinguished themselves in war'. When 'the great overseas expansion' to the Atlantic coast of Africa and the Canaries began, 'there was no modification of the traditional notion that the participants in an enterprise of conquest had a right to be rewarded for their personal efforts and the expenses they had incurred'. See Mario Góngora, *Studies in the Colonial History of Latin America*, Cambridge, Cambridge University Press, 1975, pp. 3–5.
2 In 1480, for example, Pedro de Vera obtained a *capitulación* for the conquest of Gran Canary. Originally, the term 'capitulación' denoted the privileges granted to Muslim and Jewish groups who lived under Christian rule. See Góngora, *Studies*, pp. 4–5.
3 Silvio Zavala, *Las instituciones jurídicas en la conquista de América*, 2nd edition, Mexico City, Editorial Porrúa, 1971, p. 101.
4 Colmenares, 'La formación de la economía colonial', pp. 23–25.
5 Góngora, *Studies*, p. 30.
6 The decision to halt further expansion was made thanks to the pressure exerted by Las Casas. The prohibition was to remain in force until such time as a meeting of jurists and theologians debated and concluded on the justice of further conquest. See Lewis Hanke, 'The Development of Regulations for Conquistadores', in *Contribuciones para el Estudio de la Historia de América. Homenaje al Dr. Emilio Ravignani*, Buenos Aires, Editorial Peuser, 1941, pp. 80–81. At least in some areas, however, royal approval for new expeditions was being granted by the 1550s. See Gradie, *The Tepehuan Revolt*, p. 96.

7 The laws did, however, prohibit even the use of the term 'conquest' in the context of new campaigns of colonisation. See Andrew L. Knaut, *The Pueblo Revolt of 1680: Conquest and Resistance in Seventeenth Century New Mexico*, Norman, OK, and London, University of Oklahoma Press, 1995, p. 24.
8 J.H. Parry, *The Spanish Seaborne Empire*, Berkeley and Los Angeles, University of California Press, 1990, pp. 150–51. See also Góngora, *Studies*, p. 42. For the edited and translated version of the text of the *Ordenanzas*, which is cited here, see John H. Parry and Robert G. Keith (eds.), *New Iberian World: A Documentary History of the Discovery and Settlement of Latin America to the Early 17th Century*, 5 vols., New York, Times Books, 1984, Vol. I, pp. 366–71 (quotation on p. 368). An edited Spanish version of the text may be found in Richard Konetzke, *Colección de documentos para la historia de la formación social de Hispanoamérica, 1493–1810*, 5 vols., Madrid, Consejo Superior de Investigaciones Científicas, 1953–1962, Vol. I, pp. 471–78.
9 Hanke, 'The Development of Regulations', p. 84, and Patricia Seed, *Ceremonies of Possession in Europe's Conquest of the New World, 1492–1640*, Cambridge, Cambridge University Press, 1995, pp. 95–96.
10 Parry, *The Spanish Seaborne Empire*, pp. 150–51. As this and other studies show, however, the conditions laid down in the *Ordenanzas* were frequently ignored, or at best loosely interpreted. Writing of the Cañacure and Canesi people of Moxos (in modern Bolivia), David Block, for example, states that in the seventeenth century, both groups 'were decimated in a "just war" when Spaniards entered the savanna in support of these peoples' traditional enemies'. David Block, *Mission Culture on the Upper Amazon: Native Tradition, Jesuit Enterprise, and Secular Policy in Moxos, 1660–1880*, Lincoln, NE, and London, University of Nebraska Press, 1994, pp. 19, 30–31.
11 C.R. Boxer, *The Church Militant and Iberian Expansion, 1440–1770*, Baltimore, Johns Hopkins University Press, 1978, pp. 71–72.
12 David Sweet, 'The Ibero-American Frontier Mission in Native American History', in Langer and Jackson (eds.), *The New Latin American Mission History*, pp. 9–10.
13 As Lockhart and Schwartz have pointed out, 'Spaniards rushed into feverish founding activity where there were sedentary Indians and mineral wealth; elsewhere their territories languished in neglect'. See James Lockhart and Stuart B. Schwartz, *Early Latin America: A History of Colonial Spanish America and Brazil*, Cambridge, Cambridge University Press, 1983, p. 60.
14 For an example of a sixteenth-century *capitulación* for the pacification of the Chocó, see 'Solicitud del Capitán D. Lucas de Avila para que, por veinte años, se le encomiende la Gobernación de las Provincias del Chocó. Cosas que ofrece hacer en servicio de Su Majestad', 14 July 1574, in Ortega Ricaurte (ed.), *Historia documental*, pp. 55–60.
15 'Papel Original de don Antonio Maldonado de Mendoza, sobre la pacificación de los indios Chocoes, Noanamas, Cirambiraes y población de las minas de Toro', n.p., n.d., in British Library, Additional 13,992, No. 45, fols. 357–59. This document, though undated, was clearly submitted some time before 1630, for in April 1669, the governor of Popayán, Don Gabriel Díaz de la Cuesta, made reference to a royal *cédula* of 7 March 1630 which instructed the *cabildo* of Popayán to report on Don Antonio Maldonado's proposed *capitulación*. See AGI Quito 67, Gabriel Díaz de la Cuesta to Crown, Popayán, 24 April 1669.
16 Germán Colmenares, *Cali: Terratenientes, mineros y comerciantes, siglo XVIII*, Cali, Universidad del Valle, 1975, pp. 133–34.
17 This is not to suggest, however, that the Chocó was the only frontier territory subject to privately financed *entradas* in the seventeenth century, or that the search for precious metals was the only factor that motivated Spaniards to undertake such expeditions. The region of La Pimienta, for example, which was located along the southeasternmost stretches of the Yucatán peninsula, and became a haven for runaways from areas settled by Spaniards to the north, was seen to constitute an ongoing threat of rebellion in the

peninsula, and was for this reason also subject to successive *entradas* that bear a strong resemblance to those undertaken in the Chocó. See Grant D. Jones, *Maya Resistance to Spanish Rule: Time and History on a Colonial Frontier*, Albuquerque, NM, University of New Mexico Press, 1989, pp. 155–87.

18 The requirement that every expedition should include at least two priests to instruct Indians in Christianity and protect them 'from the rapacity and cruelty of the Spaniards' dated from 1526, when it was included in the 'Ordinances on discoveries and good treatment of the Indians'. See Hanke, 'The Development of Regulations', pp. 75–76. For an example of the difficulties that could arise in expeditions that combined religious and military purposes, see Jones, *Maya Resistance*, pp. 155–87.

19 Madrid, 27 September 1634, AGN, Caciques e indios, 68, fols. 38–44. The *capitulación* may also be found in AGI Santa Fe 357. For comparison with the 1573 *Ordenanzas*, see Parry and Keith (eds.), *New Iberian World*, pp. 366–71.

20 Madrid, 27 September 1634, AGN, Caciques e indios, 68, fol. 39.

21 Antioquia, 8 July 1639, AGN, Caciques e indios, 68, fol. 237.

22 Antioquia, n.d., AGN, Caciques e indios, 68, fol. 253. Sorrito was later to serve as Fernando Docio's interpreter in the Chocó. See, for example, Sitio de Buenavista, 8 September 1639, fol. 376.

23 There was nothing unusual in this response, for native peoples everywhere in the Americas entered into trade with European colonists – not just the Spanish, but also the Portuguese, English and French. See, for example, Mary Karasch, 'Interethnic Conflict and Resistance on the Brazilian Frontier of Goiás, 1750–1890', in Guy and Sheridan (eds.), *Contested Ground*, pp. 130–31; James Axtell, *The Indians' New South: Cultural Change in the Colonial Southeast*, Baton Rouge, LA, Louisiana State University Press, 1997, pp. 47, 53, 61, and *After Columbus: Essays in the Ethnohistory of Colonial North America*, Oxford and New York, Oxford University Press, 1988, pp. 167–77. In some cases, as has already been noted for the cases of Chile and northern Mexico, the economies of native groups underwent significant and substantial transformations as a result of trade with Europeans. This was also the case elsewhere, however. Writing of the Guaycuruans of the Chaco region, for example, James Saeger has shown how their subsistence-based economy gradually became an economy based on barter trade with the Spaniards. Not only were Spanish animals and horses, in addition to Spanish captives, honey, wax and skins bartered for Guaycuruan captives, knives, fishhooks, iron, hatchets, beads and clothing, but even their traditional diet of game, fish and wild plants began to be supplemented with horsemeat and beef. See Saeger, *The Chaco Mission Frontier*, pp. 7–8, 59–62, and 'Another View of the Mission as a Frontier Institution: The Guaycuruan Missions of Santa Fe, 1743–1810', *Hispanic American Historical Review*, Vol. 65, 1985, p. 496.

24 Anserma, 4 March 1627, AGN, Caciques e indios, 68, fol. 925. According to the *oidor*, Indians and Spaniards had been trading in this manner since 1620.

25 Antioquia, 8 July 1639, AGN, Caciques e indios, 68, fol. 237.

26 'Información que hace al Sr Fiscal de la Audiencia el teniente general de la ciudad de Anserma', AGN, Caciques e indios, 68, fol. 815.

27 This was Juan Antonio Pereira's estimate. Auto, Sitio de Poya, 21 August 1640, AGN, Caciques e indios, 68, fol. 554.

28 Cartago, 16 November 1638, AGN, Caciques e indios, 68, fol. 258.

29 Cartago, 30 August 1640, AGN, Caciques e indios, 68, fol. 508.

30 Cartago, 19 April 1641, AGN, Caciques e indios, 68, fol. 902.

31 Anserma, 4 March 1627, AGN, Caciques e indios, 68, fol. 930.

32 See, for example, the testimony of Don Pedro Carrillo de Mendoza, Francisco Martín and Pedro Fernández Gómez, Cartago, 28 and 29 January 1640, AGN, Caciques e indios, 68, fols. 445–47, 449–50, 452–53. For a brief discussion of the 1628 expedition, see Isacsson, 'Fray Matías Abad', p. 458.

33 See the response of the *cabildo* of Anserma to Vélez's proposal to extend the 'guerra a sangre y fuego' to the Tatama. Anserma, n.d., AGN, Caciques e indios, 68, fol. 340. See also the statement of Francisco Martín, Cartago, 28 January 1640, fols. 449–50.
34 Antioquia, 8 July 1639, in AGN, Caciques e indios, 68, fol. 239.
35 Antioquia, n.d., AGN, Caciques e indios, 68, fol. 254.
36 Antioquia, 6 June 1640, AGN, Caciques e indios, 68, fol. 835.
37 Cartago, n.d., AGN, Caciques e indios, 68, fols. 257–58.
38 Antioquia, 30 July 1639, AGN, Caciques e indios, 68, fol. 263.
39 Santa Fe, 1 May 1642, AGN, Caciques e indios, 68, fol. 910.
40 This summary of the expedition is based on documents dated 5 and 17 May, 7 July and 14 September 1639, and 17 May 1640, in AGN, Caciques e indios, 68, fols. 235, 236, 350, 439, 827. For the membership of the Bueno expedition, see Certificación, n.p., n.d., fols. 441–42.
41 Buga, 27 August 1639, AGN, Caciques e indios, 68, fol. 346.
42 Anserma, 1 May 1639, AGN, Caciques e indios, 68, fols. 235–36.
43 30 July 1639, AGN, Caciques e indios, 68, fol. 266. See also the testimony of the Indians Tego and Tebue, Buenavista, 8 September 1639, fols. 375–77.
44 Toro, 4 September 1640, AGN, Caciques e indios, 68, fol. 522.
45 Antioquia, 6 June 1640, AGN, Caciques e indios, 68, fols. 835–36.
46 Antioquia, 5 June 1640, AGN, Caciques e indios, 68, fol. 833.
47 Antioquia, 5 and 6 June 1640, AGN, Caciques e indios, 68, fols. 833–35.
48 See Acuerdo, 17 May 1639, AGN, Caciques e indios, 68, fol. 440.
49 Isacsson, 'Fray Matías Abad', p. 458.
50 16 October 1636, AGN, Caciques e indios, 68, fol. 6.
51 19 July 1639, AGN, Caciques e indios, 68, fol. 261.
52 Antioquia, 7 July 1639, AGN, Caciques e indios, 68, fol. 236.
53 Madrid, 27 September 1634, AGN, Caciques e indios, 68, fol. 38.
54 Antioquia, 18 July 1639, AGN, Caciques e indios, 68, fol. 260.
55 Madrid, 27 September 1634, AGN, Caciques e indios, 68, fol. 39.
56 See, for example, the instructions to Fernando Docio, dated San Agustín de Urrao, 31 July 1639, AGN, Caciques e indios, 68, fol. 392.
57 For an excellent account of the difficulties of traversing the territory, see Charles Stuart Cochrane, *Journal of a Residence and Travel in Colombia during the Years 1823 and 1824*, 2 vols., London, 1825, reprinted New York, AMS Press, 1971, especially Vol. II, pp. 393–433.
58 Antioquia, 13 October 1639, AGN, Caciques e indios, 68, fol. 382. Here, Vélez commented that Indians commonly cut down their own crops 'on sensing the advance of the Spaniards'. See also the petition submitted by soldiers of the Docio expedition, Buenavista, 10 November 1639, fol. 390.
59 Antioquia, 11 August 1642, AGN, Caciques e indios, 68, fol. 917.
60 Madrid, 27 September 1634, AGN, Caciques e indios, 68, fol. 39.
61 For an analysis of the origins and meaning of the Requerimiento, and the evolution of procedures for making war on indigenous populations, see Seed, *Ceremonies of Possession*, pp. 69–99. It is also in this context that Seed interprets the use of the term 'cannibalism' to justify the capture and enslavement of nomadic groups that successfully resisted submission to Spanish rule. For this discussion, see Patricia Seed, *American Pentimento: The Invention of Indians and the Pursuit of Riches*, Minneapolis and London, University of Minnesota Press, 2001, pp. 103–105, 122, 133. For a further discussion of the debates surrounding the justice of 'guerra a sangre y fuego', in this case against the Chichimecas in late-sixteenth-century Mexico, see Stafford Poole, '"War by Fire and Blood": The Church and the Chichimecas', *The Americas*, Vol. 22, No. 2, 1965, pp. 115–37.
62 Juan Vélez to Juan de Borja, 12 September 1639, AGN, Caciques e indios, 68, fols. 348–49.

63 Antioquia, 16 December 1639, AGN, Caciques e indios, 68, fol. 414.
64 See the statement of Francisco Díaz, n.d., AGN, Caciques e indios, 68, fol. 285
65 Robert Padden's work on the Araucanian (Mapuche) peoples of central Chile suggests that Spaniards may have considered such a strategy – the assertion of military superiority – particularly appropriate for establishing control over those native groups that owed no allegiance, or obedience, to a central political authority. 'From past experience', Padden argued, 'the invaders knew that peace would follow the defeat and usurpation of a central authority. In the absence of a central Araucanian authority the only alternative was to instill fear by demonstration of military supremacy, and so the Spaniards constantly sought a definitive battle which, when won, would convince the Araucanians of the futility of resistance.' Robert Charles Padden, 'Cultural Adaptation and Militant Autonomy among the Araucanians of Chile', in John E. Kicza (ed.), *The Indian in Latin American History: Resistance, Resilience, and Acculturation*, Wilmington, DE, Scholarly Resources, 1993, p. 76.
66 San Agustín de Urrao, 31 July 1639, Anserma, 22 September 1639, and Antioquia, 23 March 1640, AGN, Caciques e indios, 68, fols. 392, 361–62, 493.
67 Anserma, 22 September 1639, AGN, Caciques e indios, 68, fol. 362.
68 According to a 'Certificación' dated 1 August 1639, the expedition consisted of 106 men, including 'mestizos, mulatos, and Indians', and an Augustinian friar. AGN, Caciques e indios, 68, fol. 267.
69 Antioquia, 23 March 1640, AGN, Caciques e indios, 68, fols. 489–90.
70 The exact date of departure is unknown.
71 In May 1639, three months after the massacre took place, Mateo de Cifuentes was back in Anserma requesting reinforcements from the governor of Popayán. AGN, Caciques e indios, 68, fol. 439.
72 See Francisco Díaz's statement, AGN, Caciques e indios, 68, fol. 285.
73 Francisco Díaz's statement, AGN, Caciques e indios, 68, fols. 287–88.
74 Francisco Díaz's statement, AGN, Caciques e indios, 68, fol. 288. See also Fernando Docio's declaration, dated Buenavista, 3 September 1639, fol. 374.
75 Francisco Díaz's statement, AGN, Caciques e indios, 68, fols. 285–86.
76 Sitio de Comita, 18 August 1639, AGN, Caciques e indios, 68, fol. 373.
77 Francisco Díaz's statement, AGN, Caciques e indios, 68, fol. 293.
78 Valle de Urrao, 31 July 1639, AGN, Caciques e indios, 68, fol. 392.
79 Sitio de Comita, 18 August 1639, AGN, Caciques e indios, 68, fol. 373.
80 Francisco Díaz's statement, AGN, Caciques e indios, 68, fol. 286.
81 Sitio de Buenavista, 7 September 1639, AGN, Caciques e indios, 68, fol. 374.
82 Francisco Díaz's statement, AGN, Caciques e indios, 68, fol. 288.
83 Francisco Díaz's statement, AGN, Caciques e indios, 68, fols. 286–88. See also Docio's own evidence, dated 12 September 1639, fol. 380.
84 Sitio de Buenavista, 7 September 1639, AGN, Caciques e indios, 68, fols. 374–75.
85 Francisco Díaz's statement, AGN, Caciques e indios, 68, fols. 286–88. See also Gaspar Francisco de Ledesma's statement, Santa Fe, 9 March 1640, fol. 301.
86 Francisco Díaz's statement, AGN, Caciques e indios, 68, fol. 293.
87 Francisco Díaz's statement, AGN, Caciques e indios, 68, fol. 290, and Docio's account, Buenavista, 9 September 1639, fol. 379.
88 Omanbita's statement, 8 September 1639, AGN, Caciques e indios, 68, fol. 378.
89 Tebue's statement, Buenavista, 8 September 1639, AGN, Caciques e indios, 68, fol. 377.
90 Sitio de Buenavista, 9 September 1639, AGN, Caciques e indios, 68, fol. 379.
91 See the petition of Francisco Benítez et al., Anserma, 24 August 1639, AGN, Caciques e indios, 68, fol. 227; Auto, Anserma, 12 September 1639, fol. 341; and Auto, Buga, 27 August 1639, fol. 346.
92 See Anserma, n.d., AGN, Caciques e indios, 68, fol. 339.

93 Cartago, 30 August 1640, AGN, Caciques e indios, 68, fol. 508. See also Miguel de la Yuste's statement, which referred to the Poya as 'friends', Cartago, 30 August 1640, fol. 506.
94 'Informe que hace al Sr. Fiscal de la Audiencia de Santa Fe el teniente general de la ciudad de Anserma', AGN, Caciques e indios, 68, fol. 816.
95 Gaspar Sangarra, for example, was referred to as 'indio ladino cristiano de nación chocó'; Juanico as 'indio ladino de nación chocó ... llamado en su lengua Bauri'; Singuiboga went by the name of Lázaro; Andrés Budagama was referred to as 'ladino' but not 'muy ladino'. See the 'confessions' of Indians taken in Poya province between 29 July and 16 August 1640, AGN, Caciques e indios, 68, fols. 532, 535, 537 and 538.
96 Anserma, 22 September 1639, AGN, Caciques e indios, 68, fols. 361–62.
97 Toro, 4 September 1640, AGN, Caciques e indios, 68, fol. 522.
98 Pereira claimed he had captured 170 Indians in this encounter, including 34 *gandules*. Toro, 4 September 1640, AGN, Caciques e indios, 68, fols. 522–23. See also Sitio de Poya, 21 August 1640, fol. 554.
99 It is difficult to escape the conclusion that such allegations were deliberately intended to create fear and panic among Spaniards, who traditionally prohibited the use, by native peoples, of firearms and gunpowder weaponry. On such prohibitions, see Seed, *American Pentimento*, pp. 82, 89, 133.
100 See the statements taken between 10 and 15 August, in AGN, Caciques e indios, 68, fols. 529–49, especially fols. 530, 531, 535, 537, 540.
101 In order 'to proceed with the said punishment and distribute the captives between the soldiers ... reserving those that are due to me'. Sitio de Poya, 21 August, 1640, AGN, Caciques e indios, 68, fols. 554–55.
102 'Informe que hace ... el teniente general de la ciudad de Anserma', AGN, Caciques e indios, 68, fol. 816. See also Guzmán's report to the effect that Pereira 'not only took their property but their wives and children [whom he] sold as slaves in other provinces'. Cartago, 19 April 1641, fol. 900.
103 Certificación, Antioquia, 23 March 1640, AGN, Caciques e indios, 68, fols. 489–90; Valle de Urrao, 23 March 1640, fol. 820. Included in the company were 42 officers and soldiers, 15 Indians, among them the two interpreters Andrés Sorrito and Cristóbal, a Chocó Indian, and an unknown number of blacks and mulattos. According to Céspedes, Cristóbal had been 'for many years a prisoner of the said Citarabiraes'.
104 See, in particular, Céspedes' reports of 20, 22 and 24 April 1640, AGN, Caciques e indios, 68, fols. 821, 822, 823–25.
105 Quebrada de Biramiarda, 24 April 1640, AGN, Caciques e indios, 68, fols. 823–24.
106 Sitio de Taita, 12 and 16 May 1640, AGN, Caciques e indios, 68, fol. 826.
107 Within weeks of the arrival of the expedition, supplies had run out, and four men deserted the camp. See the reports of 20, 22 and 24 April 1640, AGN, Caciques e indios, 68, fols. 821, 822, 823–25.
108 Antioquia, 1 June 1640, AGN, Caciques e indios, 68, fol. 831.
109 Sitio de Taita, 12 May 1640, AGN, Caciques e indios, 68, fol. 826.
110 Cartago, 19 April 1641, AGN, Caciques e indios, 68, fol. 902.
111 Cartago, 30 August 1640, AGN, Caciques e indios, 68, fol. 508.
112 Cartago, 19 April 1641, AGN, Caciques e indios, 68, fol. 902.
113 'Informe que hace ... el teniente general de la ciudad de Anserma', AGN, Caciques e indios, 68, fol. 816.
114 Cartago, 30 August 1640, AGN, Caciques e indios, 68, fol. 508.
115 Cartago, 19 April 1641, AGN, Caciques e indios, 68, fol. 902.
116 Writing on the Reches (Mapuches) of south-central Chile, Guillaume Boccara has also noted the crucial importance of dispersed patterns of settlement – 'atomismo residencial' – to the ability of Indian groups to resist Spanish conquest. The dispersal of the

population constituted in that case, he argues, 'a "natural" defense against the enterprise of conquest'. James Saeger, writing on the Guaycuruans of the Gran Chaco, considered that the small size of native bands, combined with the absence of a central authority among the Guaycuruan peoples, also constituted their greatest advantage vis-à-vis the Spanish, in that intruders 'only infrequently encountered large numbers of Guaycuruans'. See Guillaume Boccara, 'Etnogénesis mapuche: resistencia y restructuración entre los indígenas del centro-sur de Chile (siglos xvi–xviii)', *Hispanic American Historical Review*, Vol. 79, No. 3, 1999, pp. 428–29; and Saeger, *The Chaco Mission Frontier*, p. 11.

117 Sitio de Taita, 16 May 1640, AGN, Caciques e indios, 68, fol. 826.
118 Antioquia, 31 December 1639, and Sitio de Taita, 17 May 1640, AGN, Caciques e indios, 68, fols. 432, 830–31.
119 Antioquia, 6 June 1640, AGN, Caciques e indios, 68, fol. 835.
120 Antioquia, 5 June 1640, AGN, Caciques e indios, 68, fol. 833.
121 Antioquia, 11 August 1642, AGN, Caciques e indios, 68, fol. 917.
122 Sitio de Taita, 16 May 1640, AGN, Caciques e indios, 68, fol. 827.
123 Gradie, *The Tepehuan Revolt*, pp. 109–11.
124 Sitio de Taita, 16 May 1640, AGN, Caciques e indios, 68, fol. 827.
125 Antioquia, 14 December 1639, AGN, Caciques e indios, 68, fol. 411.
126 Antioquia, 25 June 1640, AGN, Caciques e indios, 68, fol. 836.
127 Santa Fe, 19 September 1640, AGN, Caciques e indios, 68, fol. 515.
128 Proposals for *capitulaciones* aimed at the pacification of the Chocó did, however, continue to be put to the Crown until at least the 1720s. While these no longer received authorisation, the Crown did authorise similar contracts, at least until 1760, for the reduction and pacification of Indians in the Guajira peninsula. For one such *capitulación*, see Eduardo Barrera Monroy, *Mestizaje, comercio y resistencia: La Guajira durante la segunda mitad del siglo XVIII*, Bogotá, Instituto Colombiano de Antropología e Historia, 2000, p. 185.

CHAPTER THREE

New Experiments in Colonisation, 1666–1673

New strategies for colonisation

The failure of the expeditions of 1638–40 to bring about the pacification and settlement of the Chocó frontier led to a reassessment, in Antioquia and Santa Fe, of the methods employed to colonise this frontier region. There was, however, no agreement on the lessons to be learned from the disasters of those years. The *audiencia* of Santa Fe, always deeply suspicious of the methods and motives of the *adelantado* Vélez,[1] argued that the real reason for the failure to advance colonisation lay in a system that gave wealthy individuals the freedom to act in a manner that furthered their personal interests rather than those of the Crown, and concluded that *capitulaciones* should no longer be relied on for the purpose of colonising frontier regions.[2] Don Juan Vélez, his lieutenant Gregorio Céspedes, and the *alguacil mayor* Fernando de Toro Zapata interpreted the failure to advance colonisation in an entirely different way. Apportioning no blame to the manner in which the campaigns were conducted, they focused instead on the difficulties involved in subjugating Indians who lived dispersed along the rivers that intersected this extensive and largely unknown terrain. Only a war of conquest, undertaken by far larger forces than any hitherto employed for this purpose, could secure victory over the peoples of the Chocó. For Gregorio Céspedes, two armed Spanish companies of 100 men apiece, dispatched from the directions of Cartagena and Antioquia, would be required to achieve their conquest.[3] Fernando de Toro Zapata considered that at least twice that number would be needed: four expeditions of 100 men apiece, he argued, should penetrate the region from the directions of Cartagena, Panama, Popayán and Antioquia.[4]

For more than two decades, however, the Crown made no attempt to develop a new strategy for subduing the indigenous population of the Chocó, perhaps because it was unwilling to commit to the proposed expeditions of conquest and wary of supporting new *capitulaciones* like that of Vélez de Guevara, which its own officials in Santa Fe opposed. This is not to say, of course, that all communication between Indians and Spaniards ceased following the departure of the *adelantado*, for successive governors in Popayán and Antioquia soon resumed efforts to pacify the indigenous population of this extremely important frontier region. But it was not until the mid-1660s that the Crown once again involved itself in the colonisation of the Chocó. This time, it acted on the advice of Don Diego de Egües y Beaumont, the new president of the *audiencia* of Santa Fe, who in November 1664, drawing on the experience of earlier failed experiments in colonisation, recommended the speedy conquest of the region and the incorporation of its 'great riches'. Like his predecessors in the *audiencia* in the early 1640s, Egües was of the opinion that *capitulaciones* should no longer be relied on to extend Spanish rule over this frontier, but, unlike his predecessors, he was persuaded that only by 'war or conquest', undertaken jointly by the governments of the surrounding provinces, could Spanish domination of the peoples of the Chocó finally be achieved.[5]

This was a notable departure from the frontier policy normally pursued by this *audiencia* president. Egües, who governed New Granada between 1662 and 1664, generally favoured peaceful methods, preferably led by missionaries, for bringing unpacified Indians under Spanish rule. Considering the Indians of New Granada's frontier territories to be 'the most neglected and backward of his subjects', he did much to foster the missions, particularly in the Llanos region. In 1662, he established the Junta de Propaganda Fide, composed of the senior *oidor* of the *audiencia* and several senior clerics, including the archbishop of Santa Fe and the prelates of every religious order represented in the New Kingdom. Egües was also one of its members. The Junta met once a week to discuss the work of the church in New Granada, and it was as a result of their deliberations that the Llanos was divided into five large territories, each of which was assigned to the religious orders for the purpose of evangelisation and administration. To ensure that this task should be conducted peacefully, he also prohibited any further armed *entradas* to the Llanos, and placed all Christianised Indians under royal protection.[6]

Egües was not, therefore, generally in favour of force as a method for subduing unpacified Indians. It was not his wish, he stated in 1664, that 'new conquests should be undertaken in the Indies or that the reduction of Indians to our Catholic religion should be attempted by military force'. But he was convinced that the Chocó was an altogether special case. First, there was a long history of violent resistance to Spanish colonisation efforts, which made it possible to argue that since native peoples would not be reduced peacefully, and were more fiercely resistant than Indians elsewhere in the empire, military conquest was fully justified. Secondly, and perhaps more importantly, the region was also far richer in natural resources than other frontier territories such as the Llanos.[7] At a time – the mid-1660s – when New Granada had not yet recovered from the economic decline that it had entered at the beginning of the century, the *audiencia* president was no doubt acutely aware of the importance of the Chocó and of the revenue that would accrue to the Royal Treasury following its conquest.[8] Indeed he, like officials elsewhere, had come to regard the Chocó as the key to the economic recovery of the entire Nuevo Reino. The governor of Popayán, Don Gabriel Díaz de la Cuesta, went so far as to state, in 1668, that the exploitation of its deposits of precious metal would lead to the economic recovery of all the provinces of the kingdom.[9] The potential of the Chocó, then, contrasted markedly with official expectations of other unpacified areas such as the Llanos, and it is this crucial difference that accounts for the *audiencia* president recommending a different strategy towards the former territory and the conquest of its native peoples.

The Crown took seriously the advice of its officials in the New Kingdom, and the recommendations of Diego de Egües y Beaumont certainly influenced, though they did not entirely shape, Spanish policy towards this frontier over the following years. While a royal *cédula* of 27 November 1666 instructed the governors of Antioquia, Popayán and Cartagena, and the president of the *audiencia* of Panama, to involve themselves directly in the reduction of those sections of the Chocó bordering their own territories, over which they would subsequently gain jurisdiction, it stopped short of authorising military conquest. This was to be a campaign of pacification, and it was to be entrusted not to soldiers, but to missionaries (*ministros evangélicos*). Consistent with Crown policy towards indigenous peoples elsewhere in the empire, the *cédula* further specified that newly pacified Indians should not be distributed in *encomienda*, but should come under the protection of the Crown, and be exempted from tributes for the first ten years of their subjection to the Spanish, unless, by rebellion, they forfeited this privilege.[10] And, perhaps in an effort to prevent the kind of unrestrained behaviour that had characterised earlier *entradas* to the region, the Crown further directed that the *audiencia* of Santa Fe should take charge of the organisation and co-ordination of the enterprise, which it was to assist in all possible ways, except, that is, financially. Treasury funds were not to finance the pacification of the Chocó.[11] The interests that guided Spanish policy towards the colonisation of this frontier territory were reflected in the words of the fiscal of the Council of the Indies, who stated in 1669 that while the crown expected to benefit from the exploitation of the gold deposits that would surely follow its incorporation, the principal objective remained the conversion of the native population.[12] In the Chocó from the mid-1660s, colonisation and conversion were to go hand in hand.

The main thrust to occupy the Chocó came from Antioquia and Popayán rather than from the north, for neither the governor of Cartagena nor the president of the *audiencia* of Panama complied with the provisions of the 1666 *cédula*. Indeed, the governor of Cartagena, Don Benito de Figueroa y Barrantes, considered that it was simply too dangerous to dispatch priests and soldiers via the Gulf of Urabá and Darién, the area that bordered his *gobernación*, because it was known to be inhabited by 'wild Indians'.[13] This was, of course, Cuna territory. No such reservations were expressed in Antioquia or Popayán, however. There, successive governors, keen to lay claim to those parts of the region richest in precious metals, turned their attention to the pacification of those areas over which each government claimed a 'natural' right of jurisdiction, based on geographical proximity and/or participation in earlier colonisation campaigns. Antioquia staked a claim only to the nearby province of Citará. Popayán sought to extend its jurisdiction over the entire area comprising Noanama, Tatama and Citará provinces. The Poya Indians, most seriously affected by the Pereira *entrada* of 1640, were no longer considered a distinct group in the mid-1660s, their peoples seemingly confined to a small settlement within territory now deemed to be Tatama-controlled.[14]

The Crown's directive of 1666, then, opened a new and distinct phase of colonising activity in the Chocó. Between 1668 and 1673, when the Franciscans took charge of the mission, frontier officials, secular priests, Jesuit missionaries, and even an *adelantado* appointed by the governor of Popayán all initiated efforts to pacify and 'reduce' its indigenous population. The varied approaches and methods employed to advance the project of colonisation, and the different outcomes thereof, form the subject of this chapter, which focuses particularly on the peoples of Citará. Indian reactions to a greatly increased Spanish presence in the Chocó show that, notwithstanding the *audiencia* president's insistence on the 'ferocity' of the region's inhabitants, and the suspicion, even hostility, that had long characterised inter-ethnic relations on the frontier, native responses to Spanish penetrations during these years were determined more by the nature of contact than by a generalised desire to reject Europeans outright. Where contacts were to their advantage – especially where they provided the opportunity to exchange gold, foodstuffs and even labour for iron tools and other sought-after European goods – and where, crucially, they posed no threat to the interests of the communities themselves, Indians were prepared not only to tolerate, but to accommodate and assist Spanish operations, even when these included gold-mining.

The secular priest Antonio de Guzmán, for instance, appointed by Governor Luis de Berrio to take charge of Antioquia's pacification efforts among the Citará, befriended indigenous communities across the territory through such methods as proffering gifts, extending hospitality at his estate in the Urrao Valley, and trade. These alliances enabled the Spaniard to conduct repeated *entradas* to the province, and to establish a chain of mining camps, worked by his slaves and those of relatives, for which he depended on the material support of Indians in the vicinity. Similar methods underpinned the activities of Juan López García, a *vecino* of Cali, among the Tatama and Noanama over more than a decade beginning in the late 1650s. Conversely, because they were perceived as a threat to the interests of the native communities, the activities of *adelantado* Don Francisco de Quevedo, selected by Popayán's governor Díaz de la Cuesta to lead an armed *entrada* to the Chocó in 1669, and those of the Jesuits who followed him there to take up the task of congregation and evangelisation, were decisively and at times violently rejected by indigenous peoples across the region. Before considering the effects of these latest campaigns to extend Spanish rule over the Chocó and its peoples, however, we shall first examine the character and extent of contact there in the years following the departure of Don Juan Vélez. Although no major expeditions were launched against Indian groups of the Chocó in the aftermath of the failed *entradas* of 1638–41, miners and missionaries from Popayán and Antioquia continued to penetrate the region to preach, prospect for gold, and trade. These movements were on a much smaller scale than hitherto, involving small numbers and posing no immediate danger to the security of native groups, but they began soon after Vélez's term of office came to an end, and in some cases led to contacts being established that were both amicable and of long duration.

Spanish incursions into the Chocó, 1645-1668

Spanish pushes into the Chocó resumed soon after Vélez's departure. According to Patricia Vargas, the new governor, Antonio Portocarrero, attempted to re-establish contact with Indian groups in Citará province as early as 1645. That year, Portocarrero sent two Citará, probably prisoners captured during earlier campaigns, to assure Indians of his peaceful intentions. No further armed expeditions were dispatched against this group from Antioquia thereafter. Spanish penetrations were now made by small bands whose tactics were broadly similar to those which had brought the Spaniards some success in earlier decades – namely, a combination of gifts (especially of tools and beads), trade and military aid. One expedition of 1645, led by Santiago Garcés, was reportedly conducted in response to a request from the Citará for military assistance against the Membocana, with whom they were then at war.[15] Three years later, in 1648, two missionaries – Fray Matías Abad, a Franciscan, and Fray Miguel Romero, of the order of San Juan de Dios – left Antioquia for the Chocó with the aim of taking Christianity to the Citará.[16] Early reports were enthusiastic. Accorded a warm reception by Indians in the vicinity of the Arquía river, and in the more densely inhabited area of the Atrato, where the friars founded the settlement of San Francisco de Atrato, Fray Matías asked for more missionaries to join him.[17] Fray Bernardo de Lira and Fray Jacinto Hurtado, and the lay brother, Fray Juan Troyano, responded to the call, and made their way to the Chocó to join the evangelisation effort, but the plans for the mission were cut short by the deaths of Abad and Romero in January 1649, apparently at the hands of the Cuna.[18] All three newcomers were said to have left the region thereafter, but at least one of their number – Jacinto Hurtado – remained after Abad's death, for in the late 1650s he was to submit to the Crown a report on seven years of missionary work among the peoples of the Chocó.[19]

By the 1650s, Spaniards had established a more stable and durable presence elsewhere in the Chocó – namely, in Noanama province. Contact with this group, which occupied territory along the San Juan, Tamaná, Sipí, Garrapatas and Negro rivers, as well as smaller enclaves along the banks of the Anchicayá, Raposo and Dagua, grew out of the efforts of Spaniards in the *gobernación* of Popayán, especially in Cali, to extend Spanish domination over the southernmost sections of the Pacific lowlands.[20] The way in which the subjugation of the Noanama was achieved is imperfectly understood, but the indications are that once entrenched in Barbacoas and Raposo-Iscuandé, Spanish influence gradually extended northwards. At the end of the 1650s, a permanent official presence was established among the Noanama, with the appointment of the miner and *maestro de campo* Diego Ramón as *teniente*, *corregidor* and *alcalde mayor de minas* in a vaguely defined region encompassing the province of Noanama, the mines of Raposo, and the area surrounding the port of Buenaventura.²¹ As Ramón died soon after his appointment, in November 1659, Governor Luis Antonio de Guzmán y Toledo appointed a new *teniente* and *corregidor*, Juan López García, whose activities were to bring the *gobernación* important advances here. From 1663, frequent though irregular tribute payments were returned to Popayán.²² By the end of the decade, Spaniards were sufficiently secure to exploit gold deposits in Nóvita, along the banks of the Negro, Garrapatas and Iró rivers, and at the old sites of Toro and La Sed de Cristo.²³ In September 1666, Governor Guzmán y Toledo extended López García's appointment (with his son Jorge as deputy) to include Tatama province, and in 1668, Governor Díaz de la Cuesta further extended his jurisdiction, with a new appointment as *corregidor, justicia mayor* and *capitán a guerra* 'of all said provinces'.²⁴

This latest appointment, made by a governor keen to extend Popayán's influence, at the expense of Antioquia, over the province of Citará, brought Juan and Jorge López García into serious conflict with the priest Antonio de Guzmán in the early 1670s. But their activities are of interest to us more because of their duration and peaceful nature than because of the competition that they engendered between the two *gobernaciones* for control of the area. The López Garcías' presence in the Chocó spanned some fifteen or so years, during which they not only explored the region extensively, but also sustained several mining camps in Noanama and Tatama provinces, leading to the gradual introduction of several slave gangs.²⁵ At least two *doctrineros* also began missionary activities during these years. In 1664, Simón Amigo was appointed *doctrinero* of the Poya and of the mining camps of Nóvita and La Sed de Cristo, which were then already operational. Two years later Luis Antonio de la Cueva joined the evangelisation effort; his duties were to extend across Noanama and Tatama provinces. Both were to claim to have safely undertaken missionary work in communities throughout the region. In addition to his duties among the Noanama and Tatama, Simón Amigo erected a chapel for the Citará, celebrated Mass, and preached Christian doctrine over a period of four months. Luis Antonio de la Cueva reported even greater achievements, and claimed to have baptised more than 500 Indians in Tatama and Citará provinces alone.²⁶

The accounts of frontier officials and clergy active in the Chocó in the 1660s strongly suggest, therefore, that native communities displayed no inclination to resist Spanish penetrations into their territory during these years, perhaps because they had nothing to fear, and much to gain, from allowing these incursions to take place. Not only were the activities of López García, his fellow miners, and the priests Amigo and Cueva entirely peaceful, but the Spaniards also constituted the only source of supply of the iron tools, cloth and other items now considered essential by native peoples. All reports concur on the fact that López García understood and capitalised on this need. While Luis Antonio de la Cueva indicated that his approach was based on gift-giving, the *audiencia* of Santa Fe reported that in addition to proffering gifts, he traded machetes, axes and 'other things they desire' for Indian gold.²⁷ Peaceful methods, then, were central to this family's contacts with indigenous communities throughout the region.

Such had, of course, also been the experience of Spaniards from Anserma and Cartago in the late 1620s and 1630s, and of the Franciscans who came to Citará province in the late 1640s. When, in 1648, Fray Matías Abad wrote to his Father Provincial from the Chocó, he requested stocks of needles, knives, fishhooks and beads, because such items not only enabled the missionaries to obtain food, but also greatly facilitated their evangelical work, in that they made Indians far more inclined to hear the Christian message.[28] And in the late 1650s, when Fray Jacinto Hurtado reported on his experiences, he described how Indians, when they were offered Spanish goods, could be baptised by the thousands. This was not a sign of true conversion, Hurtado was at pains to point out, so much as an indication of how desirable European goods had become to the indigenous peoples of the Chocó: their willingness to accept the presence of missionaries was entirely dependent on what gifts they were offered in return.[29] The experiences of Simón Amigo and Luis Antonio de la Cueva in the 1660s confirm that the work of the missionaries was greatly facilitated by gifts of tools and other items.[30] Even the Jesuit Antonio Marzal, whose approach to the task of conversion was quite different from that of his secular colleagues, recognised the crucial role played by European goods in arousing the interest in matters Christian of the indigenous population.[31]

By the late 1660s, then, when the Crown's newest instructions on the pacification and reduction of the native peoples of the Chocó arrived in the New Kingdom, important advances had already been made in this region. Mining operations were expanding. Several slave gangs had been transferred from Anserma to Tatama and Noanama provinces. Indians peacefully exchanged gold, food and/or labour for European products. At least two *doctrineros* were safely engaged in preaching and baptising Indians across the Chocó, and no violent confrontations appear to have taken place for at least a decade. No progress had been made, however, on that other crucial prerequisite of Spanish colonisation – namely, reducción or *congregación*. This was the principle that guided Spanish policy towards non-sedentary and semi-sedentary native groups in all marginal areas of the empire. The congregation of small, dispersed, often mobile, communities into larger permanent village units was seen as a prerequisite to their instruction in Christianity, which the Crown was determined to promote, and as a means of facilitating the task of civil administration. Non-sedentary and semi-sedentary groups were to be required to conform to the sedentary, village-dwelling existence that was both more familiar and more useful to Europeans.[32] These principles were embodied in the duties conferred on all Spaniards, lay and religious, who received official appointments to the Chocó. Thus, as *teniente* and *corregidor*, López García was entrusted with the task of furthering the establishment of permanent Indian settlements, and with attending to the Christianisation of native peoples under his jurisdiction.[33] Despite later claims to the contrary – a petition presented on his behalf stated that, by means of a strategy of peaceful and voluntary resettlement, he had succeeded in reducing several prominent 'caciques' and their 'parcialidades' – no major resettlement of native communities occurred before the end of the

1660s.[34] In 1669, the settlement of La Sed de Cristo was reported to consist of no more than two dwellings, while that of San Joseph, on the banks of the San Juan river, contained five dwellings, none of which was inhabited by Indians, and a derelict chapel.[35] Such a state of affairs suggests that while Indians throughout the Chocó were not averse to interacting with Spaniards, their willingness to enter into relationships beneficial to both sides did not signify an equal willingness to conform to the other requirements of European colonisation, especially where these involved abandoning traditional community life for the large nucleated settlements favoured by the Spanish.

Incursions into the Chocó from Antioquia: 1669-1673

The arrival in the New Kingdom of the 1666 *cédula* initiated a race between the *gobernaciones* of Popayán and Antioquia to occupy Citará province. Although the *audiencia* of Santa Fe was granted overall control of the enterprise, and was strongly urged to lend its assistance, no financial resources were available to it to play an active role in this new campaign of colonisation. Without capital to invest the *audiencia* could do little to support the endeavour and was left with no alternative but to leave the initiative to the governors concerned. Luis de Berrio, governor of Antioquia, followed his instructions to the letter, and in 1668 appointed the secular priest Antonio de Guzmán to undertake a new *entrada* to Citará territory.[36] The indications are that the governor's selection of Guzmán to lead this latest drive into the Chocó was not a chance decision, but was based on the long-standing 'friendships' that this priest, who was also the owner of a livestock estate in the Urrao Valley, enjoyed with prominent *capitanes* in Citará province. Contacts between Guzmán and the peoples of the Chocó were initiated not by the Spaniard, but by one Don Pedro Daza, *capitán* or 'cacique' of the settlement of Taita. We have no details to indicate when or why Daza's relationship with Spaniards began, or why he was known as Don Pedro, but in 1676 he was described as a 'ladino who understands and speaks well enough our Castilian language', and he was also said to have been baptised in the city of Antioquia.[37] In the late 1660s and early 1670s, Daza served as a crucial link between Guzmán and the Indians of Citará. Thanks to their friendship, he and other *capitanes* made frequent visits to the Spaniard's estate, where they obtained European goods and enjoyed generous hospitality.[38] One other Indian served as a bridge between Guzmán and the peoples of the province during these years. This was Don Pedro de Bolívar, who was described in 1671 as a 'ladino who grew up in the city of Antioquia . . . and [later] returned to his province'. Bolívar served as the priest's guide and interpreter, and remained on friendly terms with Spaniards until the 1680s.[39]

From these small beginnings, Antonio de Guzmán succeeded in developing long and amicable relationships with Indians across Citará territory (see Map 5), which enabled him not only to conduct repeated *entradas*, but to rely, during long periods of residence in the region, on the guidance and assistance offered by prominent *capitanes* within the province itself. Reporting on his first *entrada*

BETWEEN RESISTANCE AND ADAPTATION

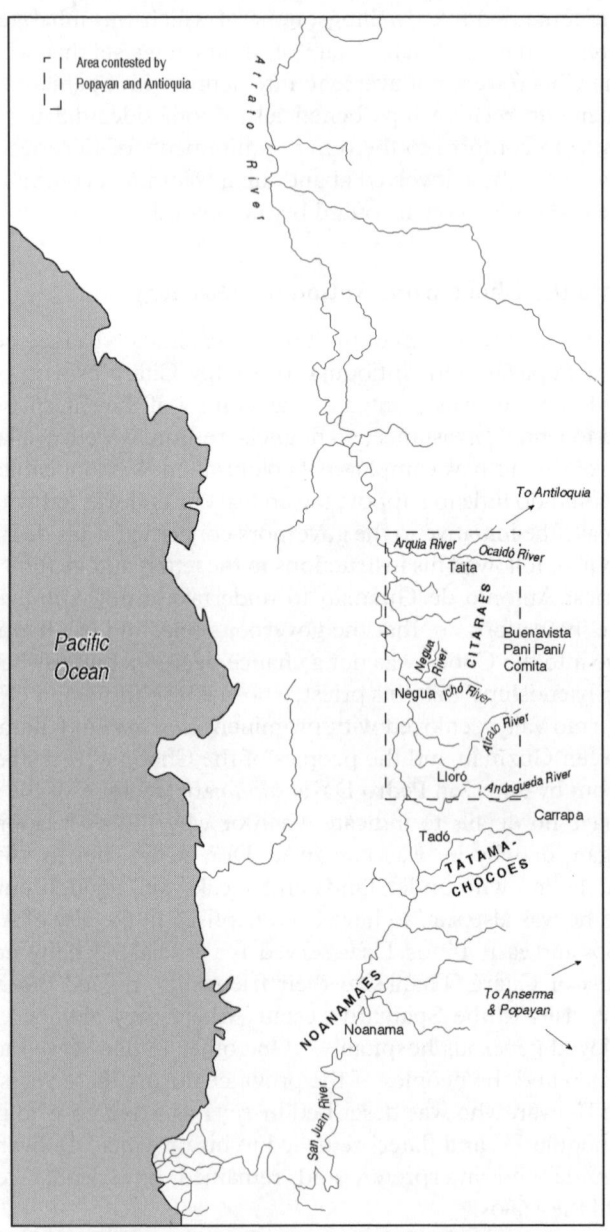

Map 5 *Citará territory: main area of exploration and settlement, 1669–1676.*

of 1669, during which he undertook extensive explorations to the east of the Atrato river, Guzmán indicated that what he had described 'I discovered on . . . [my] first journey . . . to this province . . . accompanied by four Indian capitanes, named Tequia, Pancha and Siguma and Cupamay'.[40] Following his second *entrada* of 1670, apparently conducted at the request of one Capitán Coabra, Guzmán reported that the Citará served as carriers for himself and his six companions. Thereafter, he gradually developed contacts with Indians across the province, and by the early 1670s he was engaged in mining there as well. In 1673, Guzmán was said to be the owner of a mine, Santo Domingo, in the vicinity of the Negua river, which he worked with his own slave gang.[41] His activities, however, were probably not limited to that camp alone, for as he informed the governor of Antioquia, he was engaged 'in the discovery of gold mines which I have achieved in the said province with my own black slaves [that] I brought to it'.[42] By 1674, moreover, several relatives – his brother Ignacio and their nephews Juan de Guzmán Jaramillo, Gregorio de Guzmán, and Juan Nuño de Sotomayor – were reported to have introduced an additional 40 slaves, as well as more than 60 others employed as trackers and carriers.[43]

Several elements underpinned Guzmán's growing relationship with the Indians of Citará. First, he extended hospitality to all Indian visitors to his home, gave them gifts, and provided supplies for the return journey. Capitán Coabra, for example, was hospitably received when he visited the estate in 1671: 'I regaled him . . . [when he came to] my home'.[44] Such hospitality was generously reciprocated by Indians in the Chocó. The Indian Icapá, for instance, guided the Spaniards Miguel Ruiz and Francisco Benítez to a ravine rich in placer gold, in gratitude, according to Guzmán, for the hospitality he received in Antioquia.[45] Secondly, Guzmán invariably travelled to the Chocó laden with goods to trade, to exchange for labour, or to offer as gifts to the communities through which he passed: 'of these goods alone [knives, fishhooks, and trinkets such as beads and bells]', he wrote in 1671, 'I took two hundred pesos [worth] to distribute and please them'.[46] Indian guides and carriers, as well as influential native leaders who offered assistance, always received generous compensation in the form of tools or other items. Capitán Coabra was given two axes and an adze when he promised to explore the area surrounding his Bebará river settlement for deposits of gold that could be exploited by the Spanish.[47]

By means such as these, Guzmán succeeded in developing alliances that were to prove pivotal to Antioquia's colonising activities in Citará province over the years that followed, and they were further cemented by the governor of Antioquia himself, who conferred on co-operative *capitanes* appointments to positions of authority within their own communities. Thus, Guzmán related how, having completed his second *entrada* to the Chocó, 'of the Indians who came out with me, said Governor . . . named as governor of this province an Indian named Santiago, brother of the cacique Tegue, who had come out . . . with 30 Indians, captains and gandules to . . . offer themselves as tributaries of the . . . crown'.[48] In societies such as that of the Chocó, where, as we shall see, leadership was dispersed rather than centralised, it is unlikely that the men appointed as Indian governors gained any permanent political authority over the region's native communities. Indeed, following moves to confer on Don Pedro Tegue the title of cacique of Citará province, one missionary was to remark in the mid-1670s that 'he only enjoys the title of cacique ... for he has no following, nor is he acknowledged as such by the Indians'.[49] Subsequent attempts to impose on the province a paramount authority were similarly rejected, 'hence each one', the Jesuit Antonio Marzal commented, 'does as he pleases'.[50] Nevertheless, such tactics may well have had an important effect in enhancing the prestige of prominent individuals, promoting their goodwill, and reinforcing alliances central to the progress of Spanish colonisation of this territory.[51]

Indian goodwill towards Spanish activities was conditional rather than guaranteed, however, and remained dependent on Spaniards respecting the reciprocal character of their relationships with the indigenous population and exercising restraint on the twin requirements of congregation and evangelisation. Native peoples did not object to the preaching of Christianity, nor did they necessarily reject baptism or resist the erection of Christian chapels in Indian territory. Simón Amigo and Luis Antonio de la Cueva, we have seen, safely undertook missionary work in Citará province from the mid-1660s, and Amigo was permitted to erect a small chapel, where Mass was celebrated. Many Indians, attracted, perhaps, by the promise of tools and trinkets, apparently accepted baptism.[52] Under Guzmán's direction, moreover, at least two further chapels were erected between 1669 and 1670. One of these, dedicated to San Juan Bautista, was erected in Negua, where, Guzmán recorded, 'I congregated all the [Indians], men and women, adults and children ... and I preached Christian Doctrine and I named Don Pedro de Bolivar as *fiscal*'.[53] Yet as subsequent experience was to show, Indian tolerance of, even co-operation with, the Spanish clergy was closely linked to the regularity and rigour with which they carried out their evangelising activities, and the wider impact of those activities on native life.

These conditions provide the final key to explaining the willingness, widely documented in our sources, with which the Indians of Citará accommodated the activities of Antonio de Guzmán, his brother Ignacio, and their many associates. For rather than seeking systematically to carry forward Spain's programme of evangelisation and congregation, Guzmán's methods of pacification were aimed at creating the conditions that would make possible the exploitation of the gold deposits of a region he considered to be 'the richest that has ever been discovered in the entire gobernación of Antioquia'.[54] As miners, the Guzmáns were not only acutely aware that their carefully constructed alliances, based on the exchange of goods and 'favours' with the indigenous population, would be severely undermined by any show of force or coercion, but that strict implementation of the policy of *congregación* ran counter to the interests of a developing mining industry. Thus, while in 1674 Ignacio de Guzmán sought to persuade Franciscan *comisario* Fray Miguel de Castro that the Citará were simply 'too recently [pacified] for us to ... oblige them ... to settle [in the *reducciones*]', and that successful congregation would only be achieved 'over the long run' through 'gentleness and love',[55] his brother Antonio tried to convince his missionary colleagues that the provisioning of the mining camps that were beginning to multiply rapidly across Citará province depended on the Indians' continued access to their fields and crops. Indeed, notwithstanding claims that he had successfully brought about the congregation of 1153 Indians (326 tributaries) by 1672, Guzmán's own reflections on the question indicate that he favoured a more gradual approach,[56] that was to lead, in time, to the congregation of Indians in not one but several *reducciones*, comprising the surrounding territory, and convenient to missionaries, miners and Indians alike.[57] As he was to inform Jesuit Antonio Marzal, 'it would not be convenient to reduce the Indians to one settlement, nor would be it be possible to exploit the gold mines . . . because in the absence of Indians in the vicinity [of the mines], those who come to work them will lack [the manpower] to paddle canoes, and . . . the maize and other supplies and assistance provided by said Indians'.[58]

In the early 1670s, Guzmán's detractors in Citará province – secular and religious – were repeatedly to claim that the peoples of those areas 'most frequented by said priest' knew little of Christian doctrine, and that he showed greater concern for '[developing] his mining interests' than for converting native peoples to the Christian faith.[59] Yet the stability of the alliances he developed with Indians across the region – his prestige was such that even the *audiencia* recognised the importance of his remaining there after the Franciscans took control of the mission, a decision that was not overturned until 1677[60] – suggests that the interests of the miner/priest from Antioquia coincided with those of the indigenous community. Guzmán's presence in the region was tolerated – indeed welcomed – because it provided Indians with the opportunity peacefully to exchange local products and labour for the tools and other goods they most desired from contact with Europeans, while forcing no immediate and unwelcome changes on native life. Contacts for the purpose of trade did not imply a willingness to convert to Christianity, or to comply with a resettlement programme that compromised the integrity and well-being of the region's existing communities. Where efforts were made to impose such norms, as during Francisco de Quevedo's *entrada*, Indian responses were entirely different.

Incursions into the Chocó from Popayán, 1669–1673

The royal *cédula* of November 1666, which initiated a new drive finally to occupy the Chocó, specifically stated that this latest campaign of colonisation was to be led by missionaries rather than soldiers. Privately financed *entradas* were to play no part in the subjugation of indigenous peoples after 1666. Whereas the governor of Antioquia, Luis de Berrio, selected a secular priest with a long record of interactions with the Citará to take charge of that *gobernación*'s latest colonising efforts, the governor of Popayán, Don Gabriel Díaz de la Cuesta, completely disregarded the clear instructions contained in the Crown's directive, and in 1669 authorised an armed, privately financed *entrada* to be commanded by his nephew, Don Francisco de Quevedo.[61] The governor's selection of his nephew as the new *adelantado* of the Chocó undoubtedly had as much to do with family connections and the potential profits both expected to derive from the *entrada* as it did with his determination to stamp Popayán's authority over those parts of a gold-rich region claimed by a rival *gobernación*. Our interest in the expedition, however, lies not in the governor's long-term objectives in the Chocó, but in the responses his decision to entrust the venture to his nephew provoked on the part of indigenous peoples across Tatama and, especially, Citará territory. For Don Francisco de Quevedo's *entrada* was considerably more aggressive than recent incursions. Quevedo's force consisted of 40 Spanish officers and men, all armed, and one priest, Don Pedro Gómez del Valle, the *adelantado*'s cousin. Forty Indians also took part in the campaign.[62] Quevedo's was, in other words, the first large, armed expedition for many years, and in this regard it bore greater similarities to those conducted under the auspices of Juan Vélez than to the peaceful incursions promoted by Juan López García and Antonio de Guzmán. For this reason, its effect on Spanish–Indians relations in the Chocó was decidedly counter-productive, hindering, rather than furthering, Popayán's efforts to extend its jurisdiction over the region.

Writing from Tulua in March 1669, prior to his departure, the *adelantado* Quevedo stated that the principal purpose of his forthcoming expedition was to reduce the populations of the Chocó's dispersed communities to large, permanent settlements, and to leave those new settlements in the charge of Spanish priests. 'I will not leave that territory. . .', he declared, 'until such time as I have settled them [in *reducciones*] and [provided them] with doctrineros'.[63] With this ultimate objective in mind, Quevedo travelled directly to San Joseph de Noanama, where, assisted (albeit with strong reservations) by *corregidor* López García, he met representatives of the Noanama, Tatama and Citará peoples. At the meeting, Quevedo demanded the Indians' immediate compliance with the following four demands: they were to convert to Catholicism and receive a missionary; they were to recognise the king as sovereign; they were to pay tributes (despite the Crown's express instructions to the contrary); and finally, they were to abandon their traditional way of life in favour of the new settlements to be founded by Quevedo himself. In exchange for their co-operation, Indians received the *adelantado*'s assurance that they should not be parcelled out in *encomiendas*, and that, when required, they would receive military aid against their enemies. According to Don Francisco, the Indians offered only a modicum of resistance, and soon agreed to his terms – fearful, perhaps, of his warning that 'I would not leave . . . before pacifying them or conquering them *a fuego y sangre*'.[64]

Unfortunately, insufficient detail emerges from the documents to enable us to provide more than an outline of the course of this *entrada* following Francisco de Quevedo's arrival in Noanama province. Moreover, the information we have comes not from the *adelantado* himself, but from sources in Popayán, and from Spaniards who witnessed the effects of the expedition in the Chocó itself. Nevertheless, from these we know that after bringing about a major resettlement of Noanama in San Joseph, on the banks of the San Juan river, Quevedo made his way to Tatama and Citará provinces, in each of which he founded five new settlements, all with their own chapels, and obtained the 'voluntary' agreement of the indigenous inhabitants annually to contribute two gold pesos, in tribute, to the Crown.[65] The *adelantado* remained in Citará province for approximately a year, during which he founded San Sebastián de Negua, on the banks of the Negua river; San Francisco de Atrato, at the confluence of the Atrato and Andagueda rivers; San Miguel and San Gabriel, both of which were located on the Andagueda; and San Pedro de Tacoda, the location of which is unclear.[66] On leaving the Chocó, two Spaniards – Lorenzo de Salamanca and Domingo de Veitia y Gamboa – were appointed to serve as *corregidores*, and at least one hundred slaves – possibly twice that number – were transferred into the region from other cities of the *gobernación*.[67] Thereafter, following a request to the Jesuit order, Benito de Carvajal and Antonio Marzal began missionary work among its native population.[68]

These developments led Governor Díaz de la Cuesta to inform the Crown that the Quevedo expedition, whose legality had been questioned by the *audiencia*,[69] was a great success.[70] However, other evidence indicates that the *entrada* of 1669–70 failed to achieve its objectives even in the short term, and that far from advancing colonisation of this extremely important frontier region, it actually threatened once again to bring to an end all communication between Indians and Spaniards in the Chocó. *Corregidor* López García, for example, claimed that because it brought great turmoil to the peoples of the region, its effects had been destructive. Secular priest Luis Antonio de la Cueva wrote of the disturbances and *tumultos* that it provoked: 'this province and all the others were agitated', he reported from La Sed de Cristo.[71] Even Miguel García, Díaz de la Cuesta's successor as governor of Popayán, considered the expedition counter-productive, as it had brought the population to the verge of rebellion.[72] None of the new settlements of Citará or Tatama provinces achieved permanence, moreover. All were abandoned by Indians on Quevedo's departure, and some were destroyed by burning. According to Spaniard Joseph de Salamanca, San Pedro de Tacoda, which consisted of 19 dwellings at the end of the *entrada*, was quickly deserted; San Juan de Negua 'was destroyed . . . and set alight'; one of the settlements on the Andagueda 'was also burned down by the Indians'.[73] Efforts to collect tributes met similar defiance: 'they resisted the payment that was asked of them', Antonio de Guzmán reported, 'the province was in rebellion, and they said that bows and arrows would be their tribute'.[74] One *corregidor*, Lorenzo de Salamanca, was also to comment on the difficulties that had arisen in procuring supplies locally in the aftermath of Quevedo's *entrada*, 'for in coming down towards Negua . . . neither plantains nor chickens did they want to sell me, whereas before the natives of Lloró [always willingly] did so'.[75]

The dispatch of the Jesuits Antonio Marzal and Benito de Carvajal coincided with these developments, and added a further source of friction to already tense and uneasy relations between Indians and Spaniards on the frontier. Increasingly accustomed to the peaceful – and piecemeal – methods of Antonio de Guzmán, the Citará were to perceive the Jesuits' arrival as a threat to the mutually beneficial relationships to which his activities had given rise, and they rejected them outright: 'not only do they ignore me', Marzal lamented, 'but make no effort to come [to this settlement] so that I can indoctrinate them, as I am unable to go to them for lack of canoe and people [to assist] me; rather they claim to be Father Guzmán's people'. Misunderstanding, at this early stage of activity, the bases upon which the co-operation of the Citará peoples rested, and unwilling to acknowledge that Spanish colonisation could not progress without the support of the indigenous population in this region where whites were so vastly outnumbered, Antonio Marzal was repeatedly to insist that his efforts were deliberately undermined by Antonio de Guzmán, and that the Indians' repudiation of his own authority was attributable directly to the influence that his rival exercised upon them. Only by promising 'such and such a thing', he stated, did Guzmán gain the Indians' loyalty and favour.[76]

It is entirely plausible that Antonio de Guzmán, his brother Ignacio and their many associates contrived to retain their influence over the peoples of Citará by fostering attitudes detrimental to the work of the Jesuits. As historians of other frontier areas have shown, Spanish settlers who competed with missionaries for control over Indians commonly, and often successfully, encouraged indigenous populations to disavow their Catholic ministers. William Merrill, for example, has argued that, in the case of the Lower Tarahumara peoples of northern Mexico, many Indians 'assimilated the antimissionary attitudes of the non-Indian settlers with whom they came into contact, an animosity that derived from the settlers' competition with the priests for land and the Indians' labor'.[77] Writing of a different case, the Pueblos of New Mexico, Andrew Knaut similarly discussed the unscrupulous ways in which two seventeenth-century governors – Juan de Eulate (1618–25) and Luis de Rosas (1637–41) – set out to undermine the missionaries' authority and assure their own control over native labour. While Eulate sought to 'drive a wedge' between Indians and Franciscans by allowing the former to continue their traditional religious ceremonies, and encouraging them to neither attend Mass and prayers, nor obey their ministers, Rosas came to an agreement with the Tano inhabitants of Peco whereby they provided labour in exchange for a pledge that the governor would not interfere in their traditional ceremonies.[78]

The evidence from the Chocó not only supports the findings from the northern frontiers, but also accounts in large part for the subsequent decision of the Jesuits to withdraw their missionaries from the Chocó,[79] thus depriving this frontier of the funding, manpower and experience that enabled the order to establish successful missions among such diverse peoples as the Guaraní, the Guaycuruans and the Moxos.[80] In 1674, for example, *corregidor* Veitia y Gamboa claimed that Don Pedro de Bolivar and one Don Gonzalo, both of whom participated in the destruction of Quevedo's *reducciones*, had been encouraged to take action by 'people from Antioquia', on the grounds that, as his informants stated, the Spanish Crown required only 'that we should pay tributes and remain in our *estancias*, with our children'.[81] Fellow Spaniard Sebatián García likewise alleged that Ignacio de Guzmán sought to persuade Indians 'not to obey the friars but [rather] his brother and . . . that they would protect [the Indians]'.[82] Even the Franciscans, who came to the Chocó as part of a much larger team of operatives, were to be forced to confront the consequences of anti-missionary attitudes fomented by the miners from Antioquia. According to *comisario* Fray Miguel de Castro, the Guzmán family engaged in a deliberate campaign of misinformation against his missionaries, claiming that since the friars had not been sent by the king, they should not be obeyed.[83] The Franciscan *procurador general*, Fray Lucas de Villa Veces, similarly accused the Guzmáns of encouraging Indians 'not to provide any Spaniard, whether lay or religious, with food supplies . . . plantains . . . [or] maize unless they see the gold first . . . [advice] which they loyally follow'.[84]

These are just a few examples of many such accusations levelled against the Guzmáns and their supporters during the early years of Jesuit and Franciscan activity among the peoples of the Chocó. However, this family's record of interactions with Indians in Citará province suggests that rather than being the outcome of a deliberate ploy on the part of one or more individuals to 'drive a wedge' between Indians and missionaries, indigenous attitudes were the result of a gradual awakening to the rivalries emerging among Spaniards over access to the resources, human and material, of the Chocó. Over the course of the 1660s and 1670s, the Indians of Citará gradually learned to identify potential allies, and to exploit clashes between missionaries and miners over control of Indians, and competition between the *gobernaciones* of Antioquia and Popayán over jurisdiction, to their own advantage. By the 1670s, the Indians' 'natural antipathy' towards the agents of Popayán began to be reported with greater and greater frequency, and over the course of that decade, dozens of Citará were to appear before the governor of Antioquia to appeal for protection.[85] Such was the case in 1673, for instance, when Indians appeared before Governor Francisco de Montoya y Salazar to request assistance in their dispute with *corregidor* Salamanca, a Popayán appointee, who sought to collect from their people not only a two-peso tribute, but an additional one-peso charge for his services as *corregidor*. According to Montoya y Salazar, the Indians explicitly stated that 'they did not wish to appeal to Popayán because . . . of their aversion towards its people', and that, should they fail to obtain protection, 'they will retreat to their ancient settlements'.[86] The ways in which the Indians of Citará used the knowledge gained during this phase of interaction, and its impact on the activities of Franciscan missionaries, will be considered in the chapter that follows.

Notes

1. It is to be noted that in spite of his failures, the *audiencia* of Santa Fe said of Vélez in 1671 that 'hoy es marqués de Quintana'. AGI Quito 67, Audiencia of Santa Fe to Crown, Santa Fe, 18 June 1672.
2. Santa Fe, 19 September 1640, AGN, Caciques e indios, 68, fol. 515.
3. Sitio de Taita, 16 May 1640, AGN, Caciques e indios, 68, fol. 827.
4. Antioquia, 14 December 1639, AGN, Caciques e indios, 68, fol. 411.
5. AGI Quito 67, Diego de Egües y Beaumont to Crown, Santa Fe, 25 November 1664.
6. Jane M. Rausch, *A Tropical Plains Frontier: The Llanos of Colombia, 1531–1831*, Albuquerque, NM, University of New Mexico Press, 1984, pp. 52, 60–61. See also Pacheco, *Los Jesuitas*, Vol. II, pp. 187–88, and Mantilla Ruiz, *Actividad misionera*, p. 32.

7 AGI Quito 67, Diego de Egües y Beaumont to Crown, Santa Fe, 25 November 1664.
8 Figures on gold production in Popayán, for example, show that levels of production registered in the four-year period between 1656 and 1659 were the lowest for over a century. Production figures for the district of Antioquia – which included the mines of Antioquia, Zaragoza and Cáceres – show a similar downward trend. Figures on gold minted in the Casa de Moneda in Santa Fe also show the same signs of crisis: less gold was minted between 1660 and 1664 than in any other single quinquennium during the entire century between 1635 and 1739. See Colmenares, *Historia económica*, Tables 22, 23 and 25, pp. 316–17, 323.
9 AGI Quito 67, 'Testimonio de Autos' (Franciscans), Popayán, 7 May 1668, fol. 130. This chapter and the next draw heavily on transcripts of documents collected in two 'Testimonios de Autos', both of which may be found in Quito 67. One of these relates to the Franciscan mission established in the 1670s, and will thus be referred to throughout as 'Testimonio de Autos (Franciscans)'. The other, apparently compiled by the Santa Fe *audiencia* for forwarding to Spain, will be referred to as 'Testimonio de Autos (Audiencia)'.
10 During the seventeenth century, unpacified indigenous groups were commonly offered a ten-year exemption from tributes as reward for submission, as well as a promise that they would not be distributed in *encomienda*. See, for example, Seed, *Ceremonies of Possession*, p. 86 n. 72, and Jones, *Maya Resistance*, pp. 162, 172.
11 Only in exceptional circumstances – 'in extreme circumstances and no other form of defense being possible' – was force to be used against indigenous peoples after 1666. AGI Santa Fe 204, Ramo 1, Royal Cédula, Madrid, 27 November 1666, inserted in Royal Cédula, Madrid, 6 June 1674, fols. 1–4. This *cédula* contrasted markedly with the Vélez *capitulación* of 1634, but, as noted, its provisions regarding exemption from tribute and *encomienda* were standard practice for Indians gathered in missionary *reducciones*. See C.H. Haring, *The Spanish Empire in America*, New York, Harcourt, Brace and Company, 1975, p. 65 n. 65.
12 These remarks, dated Madrid, 24 May 1669, were appended to a letter from the governor of Cartagena. See AGI Quito 67, Benito de Figueroa to Crown, Cartagena, 2 July 1668.
13 AGI Quito 67, Benito de Figueroa to Crown, Cartagena, 2 July 1668. In 1672, the *audiencia* of Santa Fe reported that the governor of Cartagena had withdrawn from the enterprise completely. AGI Quito 67, Audiencia of Santa Fe to Crown, 18 June 1672.
14 See, for example, Marzal, 'Informe', in Pacheco, *Los Jesuitas*, II, p. 505.
15 Patricia Vargas Sarmiento, 'La fundación de pueblos en la cuenca alta del Atrato. Siglo XVII', *Revista de Antropología*, Vol. 1, 1985, pp. 63–65.
16 Fray Matías Abad was once a silver miner in Mariquita. See AGI Quito 67, Audiencia of Santa Fe to Crown, Santa Fe, 18 June 1672. By 1648, according to Abad, some Indians from the Chocó had begun to make frequent 'salidas' to the city of Antioquia, apparently for the purpose of making peace with the Spaniards. Matías Abad to Juan Ortíz Nieto, Antioquia, 21 July 1648, in Mantilla Ruiz, *Actividad misionera*, p. 117.
17 Isacsson, 'Fray Matías Abad', pp. 463–64. For Abad's report on activities in the region, see AGI Santa Fe 199, San Francisco de Atrato, 6 October 1648.
18 Abad and Romero, accompanied by 22 Indians, left San Francisco de Atrato to journey down the Atrato river, only to be killed by Cuna Indians on the coast of Urabá. See Isacsson, 'Fray Matías Abad', pp. 465–66. See also Juan Manuel Pacheco, *Historia eclesiástica, vol. 2: La consolidación de la iglesia, siglo XVII*, Bogotá, Ediciones Lerner, 1975, pp. 670–71.
19 Biblioteca Nacional (Madrid) Ms 19699[31], 'Declaración que hizo el Padre Fray Jacinto Hurtado, estando por morir, de algunos puntos tocantes a la conversión de los indios de la provincia del Chocó', n.p., n.d.. Although Hurtado's report is not dated, it is safe to

assume that it was submitted to the Crown not long before 1658. When, in 1672, the *audiencia* of Santa Fe mentioned Fray Jacinto in a letter to the Crown, it noted that the report the friar presented in Spain resulted in a royal *cédula* dated 1 November 1658. See AGI Quito 67, Audiencia of Santa Fe to Crown, Santa Fe, 18 June 1672. Fray Bernardo de Lira and Fray Juan Troyano were later to take part in the pacification of the Paez Indians, also within the New Kingdom. See Fray Juan Doblado's 'Misiones de la Santa Provincia de Santa Fe o del Nuevo Reino de Granada de la Orden de nuestro Padre San Francisco', in Mantilla Ruiz, *Actividad misionera*, pp. 49–53.

20 Marzal, 'Informe', in Pacheco, *Los Jesuitas*, II, p. 494. For a discussion of early Spanish incursions in this part of the Pacific lowlands, see West, *The Pacific Lowlands*, pp. 93–94, and *idem, Colonial Placer Mining*, pp. 18–20.
21 Popayán, 29 November 1659, AGI Quito 67, 'Testimonio de Autos (Audiencia)', fol. 8. According to Antonio Marzal, writing in the late 1670s, Ramón's contacts were with the Noanama, where his mining operations were based, and where he took refuge during the violence that followed the Vélez-sponsored *entradas* of the late 1630s and early 1640s. See Marzal, 'Informe', in Pacheco, *Los Jesuitas*, II, pp. 495–96.
22 AGI Quito 13, Luis Antonio de Guzmán y Toledo to Crown, Quito, 26 April 1669. See also AGI Quito 67, 'Testimonio de Autos (Audiencia)', Popayán, 5 May 1668, fol. 12.
23 Petición (Bartolomé Benítez), n.p., n.d., AGI Quito 67, 'Testimonio de Autos (Audiencia)', fols. 1–2. See also Luis Antonio de la Cueva's declaration, La Sed de Cristo, 16 December 1670, in AGI Quito 67, 'Testimonio de Autos (Franciscans)', fols. 137-38, and Marzal, 'Informe', in Pacheco, *Los Jesuitas*, II, pp. 496–97.
24 Pasto, 7 September 1666, AGI Quito 67, 'Testimonio de Autos (Audiencia)', fol. 27, and Popayán, 7 May 1668, 'Testimonio de Autos (Franciscans)', fols. 130–32.
25 Describing the activities of the *corregidor*, Luis Antonio de la Cueva, for example, referred to the numerous gold deposits discovered and put into operation by Juan López García, and his sons Jorge and Juan, in Toro, La Sed de Cristo, Nóvita, and the Negro, Garrapatas and Iró rivers, among other places. Then, during the 1660s, the miners Lorenzo Benítez de la Serna, Francisco Díaz de la Serna, Francisco Ramírez de la Serna, Diego Manzano, Bartolomé de Espinosa and Simón Luis Moreno de la Cruz were all reported to have transferred their slaves from Anserma to the Chocó, where they were also said to be engaged in mining for gold. AGI Quito 67, 'Testimonio de Autos (Franciscans)', La Sed de Cristo, 16 December 1670, fols. 137–38.
26 See the declarations of Juan López García, Luis Antonio de la Cueva and Simón Amigo, dated San Joseph de Noanama, 28 May 1669, and La Sed de Cristo, 29 May 1669, in AGI Quito 67, 'Testimonio de Autos (Audiencia)', fols. 12–15. See also a further declaration of Luis Antonio de la Cueva, dated La Sed de Cristo, 16 December 1670, in 'Testimonio de Autos (Franciscans)', fols. 138–39.
27 AGI Quito 67, 'Testimonio de Autos (Franciscans)', fol. 138, and Audiencia of Santa Fe to Crown, Santa Fe, 18 June 1672.
28 AGI Santa Fe 199, San Francisco de Atrato, 6 October 1648, and Isacsson, 'Fray Matías Abad', p. 472.
29 Biblioteca Nacional (Madrid) Ms 19699[31], 'Declaración que hizo el Padre Fray Jacinto Hurtado'.
30 AGI Quito 67, Audiencia de Santa Fe to Crown, Santa Fe, 18 July 1672.
31 Marzal, 'Informe', in Pacheco, *Los Jesuitas*, II, p. 497. Such willingness to hear the Christian message in exchange for European goods was reported by missionaries working among other frontier groups. To give one example, as late as 1792 it was said that the Yaaucanigas – Abipones peoples of the Gran Chaco – 'attended Mass and lessons in doctrine for presents, and ... sent their children to the priest for instruction and baptism because the youngsters received gifts of clothing'. Saeger, *The Chaco Mission Frontier*, p. 164.

32 Robert H. Jackson, 'Introduction', in Langer and Jackson (eds.), *The New Latin American Mission History*, p. vii.
33 Popayán, 29 November 1659, AGI Quito 67, 'Testimonio de Autos (Audiencia)', fols. 8–9.
34 Petición (Bartolomé Benítez), n.p., n.d., AGI Quito 67, 'Testimonio de Autos (Audiencia)', fols. 1–2.
35 AGI Quito 67, Don Francisco de Quevedo, San Joseph de Noanama, 15 May 1669, fols. 6–7.
36 Bishop Melchor Liñán de Cisneros further conferred on Guzmán the title of *misionero apostólico*. Antonio de Guzmán to Miguel de Castro Rivadeneyra, Antioquia, 29 April 1674, AGI Quito 67, 'Testimonio de Autos (Franciscans)', fol. 90.
37 Taita, 18 September 1676, in AGI Santa Fe 204, Ramo 1, fols. 63–64. In 1672, Antonio de Guzmán also described him as an acculturated and Christian Indian who was 'very friendly towards the Spaniard[s]'. Río de Atrato, 20 December 1672, AGI Quito 67, 'Testimonio de Autos (Franciscans)', fol. 105.
38 Antonio de Guzmán, 'Descubrimiento', in Ortega Ricaurte (ed.), *Historia documental*, p. 110.
39 Antonio de Guzmán, 'Descubrimiento', in Ortega Ricaurte (ed.), *Historia documental*, pp. 114–15.
40 Antonio de Guzmán, 'Descripción del río Atrato y de sus afluentes', 23 July 1669, in Ortega Ricaurte (ed.), *Historia documental*, p. 104.
41 See, for example, Real de Santo Domingo, 16 September 1673, AGI Quito 67, 'Testimonio de Autos (Franciscans)', fols. 66–67.
42 Antonio de Guzmán to Francisco de Montoya y Salazar, n.p., n.d., AGI Quito 67, 'Testimonio de Autos (Franciscans)', fol. 94.
43 Petición (Don Francisco Mayoral de Olivos, Don Carlos de Molina y Toledo, Don Diego Beltrán de Castillo, Doctor Luis Jaramillo and Juan Jaramillo), Valle de Aburra, 28 August 1674, AGI Quito 67, 'Testimonio de Autos (Franciscans)', fol. 33. According to Antonio del Pino Villapadierna, 80 people, apart from the 40 slaves, had moved into the province since Guzmán discovered the new mines. Antonio del Pino had himself sent in seven slaves with a miner-manager. Petición, n.p., n.d., fols. 36–37.
44 Guzmán, 'Descubrimiento', in Ortega Ricaurte (ed.), *Historia documental*, p. 112.
45 Guzmán, 'Descubrimiento', in Ortega Ricaurte (ed.), *Historia documental*, pp. 115–16.
46 Guzmán, 'Descubrimiento', in Ortega Ricaurte (ed.), *Historia documental*, p. 109.
47 Guzmán, 'Descubrimiento', in Ortega Ricaurte (ed.), *Historia documental*, p. 113.
48 San José, 28 September 1672, Documento No. 3, in Zuluaga Gómez (ed.), *Documentos inéditos*, p. 19. Governor Montoya y Salazar also conferred on Don Juan Chigri the title of governor of Citará province, for in June 1674, he instructed the Franciscans to return his staff of office, which they had confiscated, for reasons he did not explain. AGI Quito 67, 'Testimonio de Autos (Franciscans)', 6 June 1674, fols. 95–97.
49 Quoted in Isacsson, 'Emberá', p. 26.
50 Marzal, 'Informe', in Pacheco, *Los Jesuitas*, II, p. 501.
51 In discussing a similar move on the part of the Spanish in Río de la Hacha in 1730 to confer upon Caporinche, the most powerful Guajiro cacique, the Spanish title of 'capitán', complete with staff of office, Eduardo Barrera Monroy considered that such titles were welcomed by Indians, perhaps because they interpreted them as an acknowledgement of their power and authority. Barrera Monroy, *Mestizaje, comercio y resistencia*, p. 177.
52 According to Domingo de Veitia y Gamboa, a member of Don Francisco de Quevedo's expedition of 1669–70, and subsequently *corregidor* of Citará, most of the indigenous population of that province had received baptism prior to this *entrada*, thanks to the efforts of Luis Antonio de la Cueva and Simón Amigo. AGI Quito 67, 'Testimonio de

NEW EXPERIMENTS IN COLONISATION, 1666–1673   91

Autos (Franciscans)', Sitio y Real de Minas de Nuestra Señora de Belén, 28 July 1674, fol. 61.
53 Guzmán, 'Descubrimiento', in Ortega Ricaurte (ed.), *Historia documental*, p. 113. Between 1669 and 1670, at least one chapel was erected, in Taita, where, according to Don Pedro Daza, Guzmán always stopped for a day, on passing through, to celebrate Mass. See AGI Santa Fe 204, Ramo 1, Nuestra Señora de la Candelaria de Taita, 18 September 1676, fol. 65.
54 Guzmán, 'Descubrimiento', in Ortega Ricaurte (ed.), *Historia documental*, p. 116.
55 Ignacio de Guzmán to Castro Rivadeneyra, Mina del Señor Santo Domingo, 30 April 1674, AGI Quito 67, 'Testimonio de Autos (Franciscans)', fol. 70.
56 In 1674, Domingo de Veitia y Gamboa gave evidence that Guzmán had made no progress in founding *reducciones* or resettling indigenous populations. AGI Quito 67, 'Testimonio de Autos (Franciscans)', Sitio y Real de Minas de Nuestra Señora de Belén, 28 July 1674, fol. 62.
57 It was imperative, he informed Castro Rivadeneyra, that no measures should be taken that would 'exasperate' the local population, and thereby lead to rebellion. Antonio de Guzmán to Castro Rivadeneyra, Antioquia, 29 April 1674, in AGI Quito 67, 'Testimonio de Autos (Franciscans)', fols. 90–91.
58 San José, 28 September 1672, Documento No. 3, in Zuluaga Gómez (ed.), *Documentos inéditos*, p. 20.
59 These allegations were made by Fray Lucas de Villa Veces, Franciscan *procurador general* for the mission of the Chocó. AGI Quito 67, 'Testimonio de Autos (Franciscans)', n.p., n.d., fols. 14–15.
60 In June 1673, for example, the *fiscal* of the *audiencia* of Santa Fe advised that, while the Franciscans had, by royal *cédula*, been placed in charge of the Chocó mission, he considered Guzmán's continuing presence in the region advantageous, due to the relationships he had developed with local Indians. The *audiencia* did not overturn this decision until 24 January 1677, when orders were issued to the effect that Antonio and Ignacio de Guzmán should leave the Chocó region. Documento No. 3, Santa Fe, 13 June 1673, in Zuluaga Gómez (ed.), *Documentos inéditos*, pp. 22–23.
61 When, in 1672, the *audiencia* protested that the governor had no authority to negotiate such a contract, or *capitulación*, and that in so doing the authority of that body had been undermined, Díaz de la Cuesta argued that his decision had not been made lightly. Only because he had found it impossible to obtain any assistance from either the *audiencia* of Santa Fe or that of Quito had he felt it necessary to agree to a *capitulación*. Indeed, he complained, the *audiencia* of Santa Fe turned down his request for 100 men to take part in a new expedition; when these were not forthcoming, he asked for 50; when even this request could not be met, he requested just 50 arquebuses; but these were not supplied either. His request to the *audiencia* of Quito for ammunition was simply ignored. In view of these obstacles, the governor insisted, he had no option but to take up Quevedo's offer to invest 18,000 pesos in the enterprise – in exchange for the traditional privileges – and to contribute a further 4000 pesos of his own. AGI Quito 67, Audiencia of Santa Fe to Crown, Santa Fe, 18 June 1672; Gabriel Díaz de la Cuesta to Audiencia of Santa Fe, Popayán, 20 July 1672; Gabriel Díaz de la Cuesta to Crown, 8 April 1669; Gabriel Díaz de la Cuesta to Crown, Popayán, 28 July 1669; and Gabriel Díaz de la Cuesta to Crown, Popayán, 20 July 1672.
62 See AGI Quito 67, Don Francisco de Quevedo's report, San Joseph de Noanama, 15 May 1669, fol. 1.
63 Francisco de Quevedo to Juan López García, Tulua, 15 March 1669, in AGI Quito 67, 'Testimonio de Autos (Audiencia)', fol. 16.
64 AGI Quito 67, Don Francisco de Quevedo, San Joseph de Noanama, 15 May 1669, fols. 4–7.

65 AGI Quito 67, Gabriel Díaz de la Cuesta to Audiencia, Popayán, 20 July 1672, and Gabriel Díaz de la Cuesta to Crown, 28 July 1669.
66 This evidence was provided by the Spaniards Nicolás de Castro and Sebastián García Benítez, in Sitio y Real de Minas de Nuestra Señora de Belén de Nemota, 24 and 27 July 1674, in AGI Quito 67, 'Testimonio de Autos (Franciscans)', fols. 52, 54.
67 In July 1669, Governor Díaz de la Cuesta reported that one hundred slaves had already been transferred into the Chocó, and that preparations were being made to transfer a further hundred from Popayán. AGI Quito 67, Gabriel Díaz de la Cuesta to Crown, Popayán, 28 July 1669.
68 Benito de Carvajal had a short spell in the region in 1669, and then returned, accompanied by Marzal, in 1672. See Pacheco, *Los Jesuitas*, II, pp. 449–50. On the appointment of Lorenzo de Salamanca as *corregidor*, see Juan Bueso de Valdés, San Sebastián de Negua, 9 November 1676, in AGI Santa Fe 204, Ramo 1, fol. 171.
69 AGI Quito 67, Audiencia of Santa Fe to Crown, Santa Fe, 18 June 1672.
70 AGI Quito 67, Gabriel Díaz de la Cuesta to Crown, Popayán, 20 July 1672.
71 AGI Quito 67, 'Testimonio de Autos (Franciscans)', La Sed de Cristo, 16 December 1670, fol. 139.
72 AGI Quito 16, Miguel García to Crown, Popayán, 22 November 1674.
73 Negua, 25 October 1676, in AGI Santa Fe 204, Ramo 1, fol. 170. Marzal reported that the settlements founded in Tatama province met the same end, being abandoned by Indians after Quevedo's departure. See Marzal, 'Informe', in Pacheco, *Los Jesuitas*, II, p. 498. See also Domingo de Veitia y Gamboa's declaration, dated Sitio y Real de Minas de Nuestra Señora de Belén, 28 July 1674, in AGI Quito 67, 'Testimonio (Franciscans)', fol. 62.
74 San José, 28 September 1672, Documento No. 3, in Zuluaga Gómez (ed.), *Documentos inéditos*, p. 21.
75 AGI Quito 67, 'Testimonio de Autos (Franciscans)', Lloró, 20 August 1674, fol. 125.
76 San Francisco de Atrato, 23 November 1672, Documento No. 3, in Zuluaga Gómez (ed.), *Documentos inéditos*, p. 15.
77 Merrill, 'Conversion and Colonialism', pp. 148–49.
78 Knaut, *The Pueblo Revolt*, pp. 94–102.
79 The reported resistance of the indigenous population to the evangelising activities of the Jesuits is unlikely to have brought about the withdrawal of the order. Over a period of almost 200 years between 1598 and 1767, for example, Jesuits persisted in their efforts to evangelise among the Mapuche peoples of south-central Chile, although the Mapuche remained resistant to, and beyond the boundaries of, Spanish colonial rule throughout those years. See Kristine L. Jones, 'Warfare, Reorganization, and Readaptation at the Margins of Spanish Rule: The Southern Margin (1573–1882)', in Frank Salomon and Stuart B. Schwartz (eds.), *The Cambridge History of the Native Peoples of the Americas, Volume III: South America, Part 2*, Cambridge and New York, Cambridge University Press, 1999, p. 148. For a further discussion of Jesuit endeavour, see Alistair Hennessy, *The Frontier in Latin American History*, Albuquerque, NM, University of New Mexico Press, 1978, pp. 57–60.
80 For recent analyses of the Jesuit missions among the Guaycuruans of the Argentine Chaco, the Moxos of the Bolivian Amazon, and the Guaraní, see Saeger, *The Chaco Mission Frontier*; Block, *Mission Culture*; and Frederick J. Reiter, *They Built Utopia: The Jesuit Missions in Paraguay, 1610–1768*, Potomac, MD, Scripta Humanistica, 1995.
81 AGI Quito 67, 'Testimonio de Autos (Franciscans)', Sitio y Real de Minas de Nuestra Señora de Belén, 28 July 1674, fol. 60.
82 This accusation was made by Sebastián García, giving evidence in 1676. Negua, 20 October 1676, in AGI Santa Fe 204, Ramo 2, fol. 34.

83 Petición, n.p., n.d., AGI Quito 67, 'Testimonio de Autos (Franciscans)', fol. 44. See also AGI Santa Fe 204, Ramo 1, Real Provisión, Santa Fe, 1 April 1675, fols. 53–54.
84 AGI Quito 67, 'Testimonio de Autos (Franciscans)', n.p., n.d., fol. 15.
85 'I have learned that they feel what seems like a natural antipathy towards the people of Popayán', Guzmán observed, 'due to the oppression and threats [they experience] therefrom'. San José, 28 September 1672, Documento No. 3, in Zuluaga Gómez (ed.), *Documentos inéditos*, p. 17.
86 Governor Francisco de Montoya y Salazar, n.p., 4 September 1673, Documento No. 3, in Zuluaga Gómez (ed.), *Documentos inéditos*, p. 24.

CHAPTER FOUR

Conversion and Control: The Franciscans in the Chocó, 1673–1677

Early evangelisation efforts

When the Spanish Crown issued its royal *cédula* of 27 November 1666, instructing the governors of Popayán, Antioquia and Cartagena, and the president of the *audiencia* of Panama, to take part in a new effort to colonise the Chocó, it stressed that missionaries – *ministros evangélicos* – were to lead the pacification campaign, and that the conversion of Indians to the Christian faith was to be achieved without recourse to force. There was, of course, nothing new or unusual in the type of pacification advocated in this royal instruction. The term 'pacification' replaced the word 'conquest' in official documents as early as 1573, when Philip II promulgated the *Ordenanzas para Descubrimientos*. It was also at this time that the mission, supported where necessary by a small military escort, became the favoured method for colonising frontier regions. From the late sixteenth century onwards, large parts of Spanish America from northern Mexico to southern Chile, inhabited by an as yet unknown number of distinct native societies, became mission territories administered by Franciscans, Jesuits, Dominicans, Augustinians, Capuchins, Mercedarians and Calced Carmelites.[1] Usually, however, missionaries were sent to frontier areas that were unappealing to other colonists, either because they contained little in the way of resources of immediate value to Europeans, or because they were occupied by non-sedentary or semi-sedentary Indian groups that were hostile and difficult to subdue. These were the regions that normally fell to the missionary orders. They were given responsibility for opening and holding new territory, and for pacifying Indian populations numbering millions, before disease and the other effects of contact with the Spanish took their toll.[2]

The Chocó frontier was of a different nature. In spite of the difficult terrain, the long distances that separated the region from the centres of Spanish settlement in New Granada, and a long history of hostility on the part of indigenous groups, the Chocó's gold deposits repeatedly drew colonists from other parts of the New Kingdom to attempt pacification and settlement. Well into the seventeenth century, therefore, the Spanish Crown continued to rely on privately financed *entradas* to undertake the task that in other areas it was beginning to entrust to the regular orders. This does not mean, however, that a religious purpose was entirely absent from campaigns to subjugate the peoples of the Chocó, for the Crown did not ignore its obligation to take Christianity to the Indians and always required *entrada* commanders to include priests in their expeditions.[3] The expedition organised and led by Melchor Velásquez in 1573 counted two priests and two Dominican friars among its members.[4] Two priests, Fray Lucas de la Candelaria and Fray Nicolás de San Juan Bautista, were recruited to serve on the ill-fated Martín Bueno expedition of 1638.[5] But it was quite unrealistic to expect that evangelisation could take place in the context of an armed *entrada*, and when confrontations between Indians and Spaniards took place, even the most rudimentary preaching was abandoned. Following the attack on Martín Bueno in 1639, for instance, *adelantado* Juan Vélez dispensed altogether with the services of priests, on the grounds that the presence of clergy slowed the troops' advance, giving the advantage to Indians who, 'in sensing [the approach of] the Spaniard[s], flee [their settlements], forsaking their homes'.[6]

Far more promising, because they were less threatening to indigenous people, were the activities of priests who penetrated the Chocó without the backing of an armed force in the aftermath of the Vélez-sponsored *entradas*. Apart from Fray Matías Abad and his fellow friar Miguel Romero, both of whom met their deaths at the hands of the Cuna in 1649, at least one Franciscan, Fray Jacinto Hurtado, and two Jesuits, Pedro de Cáceres and Juan de Santa Cruz, made efforts to preach to the Indians, though results were meagre.[7] In the mid-1660s, a time when relations between Spaniards and Indians were far less antagonistic than ever before, the priests Simón Amigo and Luis Antonio de la Cueva made a new attempt to take Christianity to the peoples of the Chocó. Neither *doctrinero* seems to have encountered resistance from the native population, and by the end of the decade, Cueva was reporting that the Holy Faith was spreading rapidly across the communities of the region.[8] Then, in 1668, Antonio de Guzmán, the secular priest and estate owner from Antioquia, became *misionero apostólico* for the province of Citará, where he began his activities in 1669.[9] That same year, another secular, Pedro Gómez del Valle, joined the evangelisation effort, coming into the region as a member of the Francisco de Quevedo expedition and remaining there, according to Bishop Liñán y Cisneros, for over two and a half years.[10]

Brave though these attempts to evangelise among a population long accustomed to repel unwanted intrusions may have been, they did not constitute a serious threat to indigenous society in the Chocó, and it is perhaps for this reason that Spanish clergy were allowed to remain there in safety. Contemporary reports suggest that while they often stayed in the region for long stretches of time, and travelled widely across it – preaching, celebrating Mass, conferring baptism – the peripatetic nature of their activities had little impact on indigenous beliefs or practices. Indeed, even where efforts were made to erect small chapels, however basic, these were turned over to other purposes as soon as Indians were left to their own devices. According to Fray Miguel de Castro Rivadeneyra, who came to the Chocó in 1673, the chapels erected under Guzmán's direction were by this time used as hencoops, or as workshops for making arrows and building canoes.[11] Spaniard Esteban Fernández de Rivera, giving evidence in 1676, similarly said of the chapel of Lloró that it had no altar and that in it 'the Indians built canoes'.[12]

Because they were few in number, and because they were required to preach to a large population divided into small settlements dispersed across a vast area, the secular priests who took on the duty to evangelise in the Chocó in the late 1660s and early 1670s made no more than minimal impact on the indigenous population. The Jesuit Antonio Marzal, whose reflections on the potential of Indians to become Christian will be discussed later, proved no more successful in his efforts to convert the peoples of Citará than his secular colleagues.[13] It was for this reason that the *audiencia* of Santa Fe, mindful of the difficulties involved in a task of this magnitude, and arguing that there were too few missionaries in the New Kingdom to cover its many frontiers, asked the Spanish Crown to send additional missionaries for the specific purpose of converting the Indians of the Chocó.[14] Following consultation with the Franciscan order, the Crown instructed the Casa de Contratación in Seville, by royal *cédula* of 30 October 1671, to pay the travel and maintenance costs of twelve Franciscan friars, one lay brother and two servants, who were to be sent to take charge of 'the conversion of the Indians of the provinces of Chocó, Dorado and Darién'.[15] With the arrival of the friars, in 1673, the Chocó formally came under Franciscan control.

Two principal aims underpinned the activities of missionaries in frontier areas occupied by semi-sedentary groups such as the Citará. The first aim was to convert indigenous populations to Christianity as a first step in their assimilation of the basic elements of European civilisation. The second aim was to change the social and economic structures of native peoples in order to make them 'conform more closely to that of the sedentary, town-dwelling agricultural communities that the Spanish successfully dominated and exploited in Mesoamerica and the Andean region'.[16] Over time, mission villages were also expected to become 'economically viable units' which, on transfer to the secular clergy, would become tax-paying parishes.[17] The job of the missionary sent to the frontiers of the Spanish empire, therefore, unlike that of the friars who first took on the duty to evangelise in the core areas, had to begin with the task of 'reducing' Indians to life in large, permanent, mission settlements, where the teaching of Christian doctrine could then take place. The social and spiritual aspects of the policy of *congregación* or *reducción* were explicitly stated in the *Recopilación de las Leyes de Indias*: 'the Indians should be reduced to villages, and not be allowed to live divided and separated in mountains and wildernesses, where they are deprived of all spiritual and temporal comforts, the aid of our ministers, and those other things which human necessities oblige men to give one another'.[18] As Alfredo Castillero Calvo argues, for the case of Panama rather than the Chocó, this was 'one of the most important stages in the process whereby Indians were integrated into the colony'.[19]

All Spanish missionaries sent to the frontiers of the Spanish empire went to the task with the same final objectives in view. The Chocó was no exception. The small team of Franciscans who came to this region directly from Spain were entrusted with the duty to reduce dispersed populations to permanent village settlements, to instruct Indians in the Christian faith, and to convert them to Catholicism. Once the task was accomplished, they were to repeat the process among unpacified Indians in that part of the territory known as Darién. The means whereby they set out to achieve those ends, the obstacles they encountered, the ways in which they responded to the hostility of native peoples, and the extent to which their efforts were successful, are the questions that I shall aim to answer in the following pages, which once again focus on the Citará. We shall see that the principal characteristics of indigenous society in the Chocó in themselves constituted insurmountable obstacles to the process of *reducción*, and, when combined with general and widespread resistance both to the missionaries' efforts to instruct Indians in the faith, and to the requirement that native peoples contribute to the upkeep of the mission, rendered the work of the friars unrealisable.

Obstacles to *reducción*: the social, economic and political organisation of the Citará

Spanish documents of the seventeenth century furnish ample evidence to show that the social and economic bases of Indian life in the Chocó were ideally adapted to the environment native groups inhabited. One major feature, to which Fray Matías Abad drew attention in 1648, was the dispersed nature of Indian settlement. Travelling across the region from Taita to the Atrato river, Abad described the landscape as inhabited by widely scattered communities, 'a league, and two, and three leagues' distant from their nearest neighbours.[20] Indian communities varied in size, but, by the seventeenth century, rarely consisted of more than six dwellings. In August 1639, Francisco Díaz, back from an expedition to the Chocó, described how he and his fellow soldiers came upon 'one large Indian dwelling' at Comita, in Citará province, 'one dwelling' on the banks of the Pani Pani river, but 'six large dwellings' at Buenavista.[21] Díaz provided no details to indicate how many families inhabited each of these, but in 1627 the Indian Don Pascual testified that, on a recent incursion to the Chocó, he had seen four Indian settlements, separated by distances of approximately half a league, in each of which he had seen eight large dwellings containing four hearths. With this evidence, Colombian anthropologist Patricia Vargas Sarmiento concluded that each hearth represented one nuclear family, that several nuclear families – between four and seven – inhabited each dwelling, and that each community was composed of eight dwellings.[22] Other evidence indicates, however, that by the 1670s – by which time the Chocó had suffered severe demographic decline – large settlements were rare, and Indian households never comprised more than four families. Antonio de Guzmán's account of his activities in 1670 suggests that settlement was extremely dispersed in the Chocó. Arriving at the Ocaidó river, to which he travelled from Taita, the Spaniard came upon a single household inhabited by a few adult males with their wives and children; the *sitio* of Chichiridó similarly consisted of a single household inhabited by three nuclear families.[23] In 1674, the young Spaniard Joseph de Salamanca said of the Indians of San Francisco de Atrato that 'according to the style and custom of the natives of this said province each dwelling is composed . . . of two families.'[24] And in 1677, following an *entrada* by Antioquia's former governor, Juan Bueso de Valdés, Franciscan Bernardo Ramírez said of the Indian dwellings recently erected in the settlement of Lloró that 'in each one . . . live two and three families'.[25] Bueso de Valdés' own report indicated that 'three and four families inhabit each one [as is the] custom in this nation'.[26]

A second feature of social organisation noted by contemporary observers was the temporary nature of Indian settlement. This, and the small size of the communities, were adaptations to the topographical and climatic conditions of the territory they inhabited. Sven-Erik Isacsson has shown that the 'rain-soaked environment' of the Chocó and the consequent absence of a sufficiently long dry period gave rise to 'a unique mode of cultivation rarely found outside this lowland area'. Slash-mulch, rather than slash-burn, was the only appropriate method of cultivation in the wet and humid climate of the Chocó: since longer fallow periods were required, as well as more extensive lands for cultivation, settlement sites shifted frequently.[27] Spaniards repeatedly reported this aspect of the organisation of Indian communities in the Chocó. In 1674, for example, Governor Miguel García, of Popayán, described how Indians relocated their communities and built new dwellings after each harvest, when they went in search of new lands to cultivate.[28] And in 1678, the Jesuit Marzal confirmed that settlement patterns were closely linked to agricultural practices in the Chocó. In discussing obstacles to congregating the Noanama, Marzal explained that Indians absented themselves from the settlements for long periods of time, for 'where they have cultivated [maize] once they cannot cultivate it again immediately after'.[29]

The scattered and temporary nature of Indian settlement was, then, determined by the agricultural needs of the communities, which necessitated extensive lands and rotating plots. Food requirements also gave rise to a third important feature of social organisation: a riverine pattern of settlement. As Robert West argued, the river banks not only offered the best soils for cultivation, but also provided the additional foodstuffs – fish, molluscs, crustaceans, and so on – that supplemented a basic diet of maize and plantains.[30] Antonio de Guzmán's account of 1670 shows how the availability of supplementary foodstuffs determined the location of Indian settlements across the province of Citará. In reporting his discussions with Capitán Lloró regarding a possible location for a new settlement, he explained that the site chosen was well provided with plantain groves, good land for maize cultivation, 'and the Atrato River exceptionally rich in all types of fish'.[31] Bueso de Valdés, writing from the Chocó in September 1676, also drew attention to the importance of supplementary foodstuffs in determining the location of Indian settlement. He described the small 'sitio' of Taita as well provided with maize and plantains and 'some fish yielded by the river on the banks of which the town is situated'.[32] In addition to providing a secondary source of food, however, the rivers also constituted the quickest and sometimes the only means of communication through the region's difficult environment. In the heavily forested Chocó, where the terrain was often swampy and rugged, and always hard to traverse, the rivers served as 'highways' connecting each part of the region to the others.³³ The location of that same *sitio* of Taita, Guzmán's account shows, was also chosen with a view to ease of communication, the river, which flowed into the Atrato, navigable throughout its course by Indian canoes.³⁴ Finally, the river served one further purpose. As Isacsson pointed out, it not only afforded the 'prerequisites for physical survival' but also set 'the frame for social identity'.³⁵

One further important feature, with implications for the effectiveness of missionary endeavour in the region, relates to the political organisation of Citará society. Unlike the core areas of Spanish settlement, such as Mexico and Peru, where highly centralised political systems fell to the Spanish with relative ease following victory over the Aztecs and the Incas, in the Chocó political authority was dispersed and diffuse. Spanish documents of the seventeenth century repeatedly refer to the fact that the absence of a centralised political system constituted one of the principal obstacles to the *reducción* process in all three provinces of Noanama, Tatama and Citará. In 1648, Fray Matías Abad reported the absence of Indian leaders who could command obedience in Citará province: 'there are only some capitanes', Abad remarked, 'and these are little respected'.³⁶ Thirty years later, in 1678, Antonio Marzal likewise wrote of the Indians that they 'are a people without leaders, who do not obey or respect anyone even in war, and if they have capitanes it is not because they obey them in anything, but because they have a reputation for being brave'.³⁷ Fellow Jesuit Benito de Carvajal, in discussing what he perceived as the benefits Indians derived from subjection to Spanish rule, stated that 'because said Indians have no government . . . they were greatly in need of subjection to the Spaniard [in order] to be indoctrinated'.³⁸ All attempts on the part of Spaniards to create such a leadership structure, moreover, failed.³⁹ As we have seen, when in the mid-1670s the Spanish conferred on Don Pedro Tegue the title of cacique of the province, one Franciscan remarked that 'he only enjoys the title of cacique . . . for he has no following, nor is he acknowledged as such by the Indians'.⁴⁰

The Spanish here came up against one other crucial difference between colonising the core and colonising the semi-sedentary frontier: the absence of a centralised political leadership that could be co-opted or coerced to implement European commands.⁴¹ This does not mean, however, that Spaniards grasped fully the political organisation of native groups in the Chocó. The documents show that they frequently misunderstood the nature and extent of the authority enjoyed by those prominent individuals upon whom they conferred the titles of 'cacique' and 'capitán', terms that they never specifically defined, but applied according to the apparent importance of the individual concerned, and perhaps the extent to which he seemed to fulfil the role of spokesman for the community. Reporting on his expedition to Citará province in late 1639, for instance, Fernando Docio described the Indians Tego, Tebue, El Sarco (Omanbita) and Oycomea as 'the principal caciques of the whole territory'.⁴² The sources suggest, however, that there was no overarching authority anywhere in the Chocó, that the influence of those men whom Spaniards addressed as 'cacique' was limited, and that, as Isacsson pointed out, the authority of 'capitanes' did not extend beyond periods of war, and even then was limited to very small followings of 10 to 15 men.[43] At best, bravery and success in war conferred on some members of Indian society a prestige that extended beyond war, although this carried no authority across the group as a whole.

Spanish missionaries in this part of the Spanish empire, then, had a difficult job to undertake. And, as noted, it was the Jesuits, rather than the Franciscans, who were the first to experience the obstacles that the characteristics of indigenous society posed to the establishment of a mission in the territory. In 1672, Antonio Marzal came to Citará province with the expectation that the establishment of a missionary base, at San Francisco de Atrato, would suffice to persuade the population of the surrounding area to abandon their own settlements in favour of life in a larger, permanent community that would reflect 'European conceptions of orderly society', transform Indians 'from gentiles into neophytes', and make possible their eventual conversion to the Christian faith.[44] The Jesuit soon discovered, however, that he was not only unable to persuade the population of the vicinity to congregate in San Francisco de Atrato, but that on his arrival, Indians who already inhabited the settlement abandoned it: 'the Indians are far from [willing] to live in the houses of this town, [to the extent that] they have not only allowed the houses they had begun [to erect] to go to rack and ruin, but also those that they had finished [erecting]'. Marzal was to attribute his failures to induce Indians to accede to their *reducción*, or to hear the preaching of Christian doctrine, to the influence wielded by Antonio de Guzmán. Thus he exhorted his rival, on pain of excommunication, to 'leave this town on this very day, and the Chocó and Citará region within fifteen days, taking your relatives, belongings, and the slaves in your care'.[45] For reasons that have already been discussed, the Guzmán family may well have used its influence with its Citará allies to obstruct the work of the Jesuit, but the real roots of the problems faced by Spanish missionaries in the Chocó lay elsewhere. As the following section will show, Marzal's experiences among the Citará paralleled those of the Franciscans who came to take charge of the mission the following year. Contact with Spaniards for the purpose of trade did not imply wholesale acceptance of European norms more generally, especially Christianity.

'Reducción y conversión': Franciscans take over the Chocó mission

The arrival of the Franciscans towards the end of 1673 was to change completely, in the short and the long term, the nature of the demands made by Spaniards of the indigenous peoples of the Chocó. Not only did the missionaries come to the task with expectations that were entirely different from those of the secular colleagues who preceded them, but they were expected to achieve the Crown's ultimate objectives of reduction and conversion at minimum cost. The royal *cédula* of 30 October 1671, which ordered the Casa de Contratación to pay the costs of sending twelve missionaries, one lay brother and two servants to the Chocó, Dorado and Darién, shows the extent of the contribution that the Crown made to the new mission. Each member of the Franciscan team was to be provided with sufficient funding to cover the cost of travel and maintenance from his place of residence to his port of embarkation – Sanlúcar de Barrameda or Cádiz – and from there to Cartagena. The costs of travel and maintenance from Cartagena to Honda were to be met by royal officials in the New Kingdom. Likewise, the governor of Antioquia, Don Francisco de Montoya y Salazar, was instructed to pay the costs of sending the members of the expedition on to the mission, and to provide them with chalices, missals and church ornaments. No further provision was made in this *cédula* for financial support beyond the funds required to buy supplies for the missionaries.[46] The Crown, then, made no more than a minimal investment in the Franciscan mission in the Chocó.[47] Moreover, keen as it was to promote peaceful colonisation, it also exempted Indians from tributes, and from the payment of stipends to the clergy, for the first ten years of their subjection to Spanish rule.[48] The only proviso was that Indians were expected to maintain the friars from 'los frutos de la tierra' – to provision the missionaries, that is, with a portion of their own crops. Unless additional support, in the form of charitable contributions from the laity, could be procured, this was to be their only source of maintenance.[49] Thus, as Robert Jackson has pointed out, missions were supposed to be a particularly cost-effective method of colonisation. In exchange for a very small investment, missionaries were expected to run 'the evangelisation and assimilation programs that pacified many frontier Indian groups and contributed to the economic development of frontier regions'.[50]

It seems that the Franciscan contingent that eventually came to the Chocó comprised eleven, rather than twelve, missionaries.[51] Three of the twelve initially recruited never made it to the region, though two who were not on the original list – Joseph de Córdoba and Esteban de Iruñela – did accompany the group.[52] Upon arrival, each of the members of the team was assigned to cover a specific section of Tatamá and Citará territory. No Franciscan was to be sent to Noanamá province, where the Jesuits had already established a temporary presence. There were, of course, no fully-fledged settlements in either province, for in spite of claims to the contrary, all efforts to advance *reducción* among the peoples of the Chocó proved ineffective before 1673. Nevertheless, the new missionaries made their way towards those places where Spaniards had recently attempted to found permanent villages, and which now became bases for the missionaries' own activities. Three Franciscans were sent to Tatamá; five more were sent to Citará.[53] Franciscan *comisario* Fray Miguel de Castro Rivadeneyra was to act as a kind of peripatetic overseer of the mission.

Despite having arrived from Spain very recently, and despite being unfamiliar with, and inexperienced in, the kind of environment in which they were now to operate, the young friars were expected to implement procedures leading to the congregation of the population dispersed across the assigned area to the settlements that were to become their missionary bases. The ideal, according to Fray Juan Tabuenca, was to create villages of some 200 inhabitants (a number considered sufficient to support a *doctrinero*[54]), but in Citará province, a total of only three settlements, apart from the 'sitio' of Taita, were thought sufficient to incorporate a population estimated to number 1663 in 1676–77.[55] Each missionary was to persuade his Indian charges to live in the new village, to supply him with provisions, and to attend instruction in Christian doctrine and be converted to Catholicism. Not surprisingly, some friars encountered difficulties from the very beginning of their activities: Fray Pablo Ruiz, for instance, discovered on arrival at Nuestra Señora de la Paz de Pureto, in Tatama province, that it had been deserted by the Indians who lived there. Others found Indians to be more fearful than hostile, and willing, at least initially, to accommodate them. Juan Tabuenca, assigned to Nuestra Señora del Pilar de Zaragoza, on the Negua river, reported that on reaching the area 'I found the Indians [to be] very fearful, but nevertheless they attended Mass and prayers and brought me some food, although meagre, as the land yields no other'.[56]

The *comisario*'s own early experiences among the Citará were entirely different. Castro Rivadeneyra described how, arriving at the Atrato river in the company of Juan López García, Antonio Marzal and Ignacio de Guzmán, he informed the Indians of the area that he had come in the name of the king of Spain to teach them to pray, to celebrate Mass and to give them instruction in the Holy Faith, and that in exchange for this they should choose a place for a new settlement within one day, and clear a site for its chapel. For reasons that are not clear, but may have had to do with the Indians' prior experience of Spanish clergy, they showed no unwillingness to comply with his request. According to Castro, 'all the Indians of the Samugrado River, the Andagueda River and the Atrato willingly set themselves to the task'. That obliging attitude did not last, however, for Indians soon understood that Castro, unlike his predecessors, fully intended to enforce permanent settlement there. The *comisario* indicated that no sooner had the new chapel been completed, than 'the Indians began to retreat', and that all attempts to coax them to remain were to no avail, for the Indians insisted that 'they will be assigned priests in their [own] homes'.[57] Though Castro gave no further details of the incident, the evidence of Spaniard Bartolomé de Alaraz shows that the Indians' refusal to congregate in the newly founded settlement, also, confusingly, named San Francisco de Atrato, reflected not so much a complete rejection of the missionary himself, whom Indians seemed prepared to appease at this early stage, but of the requirement that the inhabitants of communities dispersed across the territory should live together in a village selected for them by the Spanish priest. In a statement of 1674, Alaraz described how Indians, sufficiently alarmed to have met the Franciscan armed with bows and arrows, told him 'that their town would be separate, and that they would build a separate church and settlement'.[58]

Indian resistance to the Franciscans' *reducción* programme is attributable to several factors. One factor, to which Fray Juan Tabuenca drew attention in May 1674, was hostility among the various *capitanes* who were to be congregated in the new mission villages. Details are scarce, but in discussing attempts to attract the inhabitants of the communities of the Bebará river to a settlement on the Negua river, the friar explained that 'those of the Bebará River will soon be coming here, because one has promised me, and the other says that he will not come because of enmity towards this cacique, and now I am waiting for . . .

[both] to come, so that I can reconcile them'.[59] Of far greater significance to the Indians, however, was the question of how they were to survive in the few large villages envisaged for them by their Franciscan priests.[60] Thus, according to Juan de León Castellanos, when moves were made to concentrate the population of the Atrato into a single settlement under Franciscan administration, Indians became 'upset and agitated'.[61] Ignacio de Guzmán made the same point in April 1674, when he informed Castro Rivadeneyra that three Citará Indians – Aucavira, and the *capitanes* Chaguera and Cupamay – had recently appealed to him to be allowed to remain in their own communities rather than be forced to join that of Don Pedro Tegue (San Francisco de Atrato), because there 'they had no way of sustaining themselves'.[62] The Franciscans, it seems, failed to grasp the difficulties that would result from congregating in a small number of mission villages populations that depended for their livelihoods on small, temporary plots of land scattered across the length and breadth of Citará territory.

At no point in 1673–74 did the Spanish missionaries detail precisely which Indian communities were to be congregated in the new settlements, or the criteria they applied to determine the composition of each of these. For this we must turn to the statements made by the friars Ramírez, Iruñela and Córdoba during the *entrada* conducted by Antioquia's former governor, Juan Bueso de Valdés, in 1676–77. Questioned about their failure to advance *reducción* among the Citará, Ramírez explained that the Indians who theoretically formed part of Nuestra Señora de la Concepción de Lloró continued to live alongside plots of land that could be as far as four and five leagues distant from that settlement. The same applied to San Francisco de Atrato. Many of the Indians who formed part of this settlement lived in communities that were often two and three days distant from it.[63] As for San Juan de Negua, it comprised the inhabitants of communities dispersed along several of the region's rivers: many lived in small groups along the Bebarama river, at a distance of three days' travel from Negua; more than 50 lived along the Ichó river; others, who lived along the Tutunendo, had not yet even had contact with Spaniards.[64] Another proportion of San Juan's population inhabited communities along the Naurita river and the Negua river itself.[65] Great distances, in other words, were to separate Indians from the lands they traditionally occupied and farmed, and upon which they would continue to depend for their livelihoods following resettlement.[66]

A second and equally fundamental obstacle faced by missionaries was the Indians' refusal to receive Christian instruction in the formal environment of the mission settlement. For while Indians, as we have seen, had proved themselves open to the kind of informal evangelising activity in which secular clerics had engaged in Citará territory over several years, especially where such activity made possible the acquisition of a variety of European goods, they were far less inclined to accommodate the more thorough and systematic indoctrination promoted by the missionaries. Even in Taita, where the friars Miguel de Vera and Bernardo Ramírez were charged with the religious instruction of the community of the acculturated and otherwise co-operative Don Pedro Daza, Indians reacted with defiance. Thus, while Vera, who was soon to abandon the Chocó, indicated that Indians resisted all forms of subjection to the missionaries, preferring to flee their settlements than to attend Christian instruction, Ramírez argued that 'no progress . . . will be made until a way is found to oblige Indians to obey the religious . . . [and to] attend [instruction in] Christian Doctrine'.[67]

The friars' experience in this regard paralleled that of the Franciscan Jacinto Hurtado, who lived among the Indians of the Chocó in the late 1640s and early 1650s, and of the Jesuit Marzal, who undertook missionary labour among the peoples of Citará over a 17-month period at the beginning of the 1670s. Despite their different methods, both men were to acknowledge that their efforts to bring the indigenous population into the Christian church had been in vain. Hurtado came to the realisation that the mass baptism of Indians, achieved through gifts of Spanish goods, did not equate to conversion, and this experience was to lead him to advocate a strategy that combined preaching and armed force, for 'it has been seen by the experience of all the conquests carried out throughout the Indies [that] . . . not even the smallest town has been reduced through . . . preaching, unless supported by force'.[68] Marzal, as a member of an order that favoured thorough instruction prior to baptism, reflected on the difficulties he had encountered in instructing native children in the Christian faith.[69] Because of 'the resistance of the parents', he reported in 1678, 'no such education can be provided', and it was, therefore, 'not licit to baptise the children given the present state of said provinces'. The Jesuit's experiences in San Joseph de Noanama, to which he was sent in late 1673, served merely to confirm his negative assessment of the entire Christianisation process in the Chocó. In discussing indigenous responses to his activities along the Raposo river and in the mining camp of San Agustín, Marzal stated not only that 'if they are spoken to of God they mock us, if of . . . hell they don't believe it, if of vices these are what they most love', but that he could see no further purpose in 'endeavouring to ensure that the children . . . learn to be Christians, for when the meetings of elders or drinking parties take place, they speak the exact opposite'.[70]

A third obstacle to missionary endeavour among the Citará in the middle years of the 1670s concerned the requirement that Indians maintain the friars from 'los frutos de la tierra'. We know that when the Franciscans first came to the Chocó region, they brought with them sufficient supplies of European goods to enable them to barter for food, at least for the short period while the mission became established.[71] Many of the friars, therefore, found that initially they encountered no difficulties procuring supplies. Fray Juan Tabuenca, writing from Negua in November 1673, indicated that Indians would exchange food for quite specific items, especially metal tools such as machetes, knives, axes, scissors and needles. Indians would also accept beads, he said, although 'they have to be coaxed to accept them', but only so long as they weren't made of glass.[72] Yet Indian willingness to barter with the missionaries could not be guaranteed. Miguel de Vera and Pascual Ramírez, both of whom reported determined resistance to their evangelising activities in Taita, also claimed to have been unable to obtain food supplies from Indians there, despite the 'needles, beads, bells, and other things' they offered in exchange. Indeed, according to

Franciscan *procurador general* Fray Lucas de Villa Veces, not only did indigenous peoples 'give them nothing', but they 'said that those [goods] were owed to them for . . . [allowing the friars] to live in their lands'.[73] The Indians' expectation, it seems, was that reciprocity should govern all interactions between themselves and Spaniards, lay and religious.

To understand the response of indigenous peoples to the presence of Franciscans, we must bear in mind the particular circumstances in which their mission was established. The existence of gold and the long history of contact between native communities and European settlers in the Chocó gave the encounter between Indians and missionaries a character quite different from that in other frontier regions of the empire. Whereas in some areas, according to recent research, Indians accepted missionaries because of the goods they brought with them to exchange, because of the protection mission villages offered against slave raids and/or exploitation by other settlers, or even because the European friars were better equipped to explain and cure disease, in the Chocó none of these conditions applied.[74] Not only had Indians encountered the diseases that were to prove so devastating and disorientating to the native population long before the establishment of the mission, but the very arrival of the friars threatened to disrupt existing and mutually beneficial alliances which already provided indigenous peoples with access to European goods on acceptable terms. The requirement that Indians maintain missionaries from 'los frutos de la tierra' – a means whereby the Crown minimised the cost of running its evangelisation programme – meant that far from representing a source of European artefacts, friars actually represented a drain on the resources of the communities. Indians did not normally object to trading with Franciscans, notwithstanding Vera's and Ramírez's experience in Taita, but when their supplies of European goods ran out, the problem of procuring food became acute. In September 1674, Fray Pablo Ruiz was obliged to leave Tatama for Citará territory, due to the impossibility of obtaining supplies from Indians in the former province.[75] But in Citará province, the problems were just as serious. As Fray Joseph de Córdoba bitterly complained, Indians demanded payment even for a bunch of plantains: 'and if they give us something', he said, 'however small it may be, they expect us to give them something [in return] . . . which is impossible because of our poverty'.[76] Indeed, the situation of the friars became a source of increasing concern for *comisario* Miguel de Castro, and for *procurador* Lucas de Villa Veces, both of whom came to regard Indian exemption from the payment of stipends as unsustainable, and to advocate the collection of an annual one-peso stipend.[77]

There was one further obstacle to the task of reduction and conversion, which had more to do with the nature of this frontier territory and the interests of the Spaniards who settled it than it did with the characteristics of indigenous society. For the *corregidores* and other officials appointed to administer and bring order to the Chocó, as for the miners who gradually began to penetrate the region in the wake of López García and Antonio de Guzmán, only the prospect of growing rich from the exploitation of the gold deposits that littered the territory served as sufficient incentive to settle a region that one Franciscan was to describe as 'worse than that of hell itself'.[78] The interests of all these men were at odds with those of the missionaries. Whereas the Franciscans sought to concentrate populations in mission settlements where instruction in Christian doctrine could most effectively be carried out, miners wished the population to remain widely dispersed, 'because in the absence of Indians in the vicinity [of the mines]', as Guzmán pointed out in 1672, 'those who come to work them will lack [the manpower] to paddle canoes, and . . . the maize and other supplies and assistance provided by said Indians'.[79] Many, of course, were also conscious of the possible consequences, for themselves and their slaves, of enforcing a *reducción* policy that Indians clearly rejected.

The extent to which such conflicts of interest obstructed their work was repeatedly spelled out by missionaries active in the Chocó throughout the decade of the 1670s. Antonio Marzal, for example, argued that, far from supporting the efforts of the friars by obliging Indians to remain in the mission villages and attend religious instruction, it was the *corregidores* themselves who were responsible for the Indians' long absences from them. Aware that any attempt on the part of the priest to prevent native peoples leaving the settlements to work on distant fields would result in severe food shortages for the mines, it was they who sent the Indians away for the ten months of every year that were required to cultivate and harvest maize sufficient to meet their needs and those of the miners, and encouraged them to spend the other two months of the year making the canoes that were vital to the transportation of goods across the province.[80] The problems faced by the friars lay not only, however, in the fact that secular officials refused to assist the mission and encouraged Indians to remain apart from it, but also in the fact that Indians themselves gradually became aware that they, too, could exploit Spanish struggles for control to their own advantage. As Fray Juan Tabuenca reported in May 1674, Indians had 'so much freedom' that if any attempt was made to reduce them, they appealed to López García, or to Joseph de Salamanca, or to Domingo de Veitia, or to Luis de los Ríos – all of whom served as officials in the Chocó. 'I do not believe', the friar remonstrated, 'that this is the [correct] . . . method for indoctrinating them, but for them to do with us what they please'.[81] For Fray Joseph de Córdoba, it was precisely because of the reluctance of *corregidores*, of whom 'there are many', to assist the missionaries, that Indians, when called upon to attend prayers, 'respond very rudely'.[82]

Conflict between missionaries and royal officials was, of course, a common feature of the colonisation of remote frontier regions that offered little in the way of reward for royal service except the opportunity for economic gain – legal or illegal.[83] But unlike many such regions where missionaries spearheaded the establishment of a Spanish presence, allowing them to claim lands, resources and native labour for the upkeep of the mission community, in the Chocó of the 1670s it was the friars who were the newcomers and who had to carve out a role for themselves, establish their authority, and secure the resources to feed and maintain themselves with dignity.[84] The apparent indifference of frontier officials to their plight, and the disrespect, even contempt, in which they were seemingly held by many fellow Spaniards, were to render the task of the friars exceptionally difficult, as well as diminishing their authority and prestige in the eyes of the native population.[85] And these difficulties were made all the worse by their inability to communicate with peoples whose languages they neither spoke nor understood. As Fray Juan Tabuenca despondently reported from Negua in November 1673, no good could come of further effort to make Christians out of 'these barbarians', for he could find no way of teaching people who could not understand him.[86]

In this final sense, then, as in so many others, the record of the Franciscans in the Chocó stands in sharp contrast to that of missionaries on colonial frontiers elsewhere in Spanish America. The ability to communicate in one or more native languages had long been recognised as crucial to the ways in which Indians reacted to the presence of Spanish missionaries.[87] Jesuit Gerónimo Ramírez, for example, who spoke Nahuatl, Tarascan and Tepehuan, was said to have been greeted 'with demonstrations of great joy and happiness, both young and old, men and women' when he visited a small Tepehuan settlement in 1596 and preached to them in their own language.[88] Similarly, the success of the earliest Franciscan missions among the Guaraní, which predated the more famous Jesuit *reducciones* by some 30 years, has been explained by the fact that the missionaries, who came to that region in the 1580s, 'were the first to understand that a thorough knowledge of Guaraní language and customs was indispensable'.[89] Even the otherwise hostile population of the Itza-Maya centre of Tah Itza (in the central Petén) accorded the Franciscan Fray Bartolomé de Fuensalida a stunned reception when he arrived, in 1618, and 'broke into a long and impassioned sermon in fluent Mayan'.[90] Nor was this simply a feature of early missionary endeavour among the native peoples of the Americas,[91] for in the seventeenth and eighteenth centuries, Jesuits active among the Moxos peoples of the upper Amazon showed equal dedication to learning the great variety of native languages spoken in that region, and to compiling grammars, dictionaries and even religious tracts written in the vernacular.[92] No similar evidence has emerged, however, to suggest that the Franciscans of the Chocó, already disadvantaged by their status as *chapetones*, or newcomers, threw themselves into the learning of the languages of the indigenous peoples whose conversion they sought.

For a variety of reasons, then, the team of young Franciscans who came to the Chocó in 1673 encountered serious impediments to their efforts to bring about *reducción* and obtain material support for the mission, and without these, the process of converting Indians to Christianity could not properly begin. Faced with obstacles that they could not overcome without assistance from other sources, some of the missionaries gave up on the enterprise within weeks of their arrival.[93] Fray Joseph Marton apparently left within six weeks, making his way to Antioquia and then to Cartagena.[94] The lay brother Miguel de Vera, assigned to Taita, left soon after.[95] Others deserted within the first year, such as Bernardo Ramírez, who had abandoned Taita by July 1674.[96] And at least one of the original group, Fray Juan Tabuenca, even sought to persuade his order that it should withdraw completely from the Chocó, for as he advised Miguel de Castro in May 1674, it would be to the greater credit of the Franciscans to retreat from the mission at that stage, than to be forced to leave years later without having accomplished the task they had been set.[97] But while Marton, Vera, Ramírez, Tabuenca and a few others left the Chocó, a handful of Franciscans chose to remain. How they adapted to their situation, the methods they adopted to overcome the hostility and resistance of their native charges, and the consequences of their actions for Spanish relations with Indians will now be discussed.

'Mientras no reine el castigo': changing strategies for *reducción* and conversion

The departure of approximately half the members of the Franciscan mission within the first year of its establishment rendered the task of reduction and conversion more difficult for the remaining friars. As their situation became increasingly desperate, and as they became increasingly familiar with the environment in which they found themselves, alarming reports began to reach the cities of Santa Fe and Antioquia that the Franciscans had begun to resort to coercion both to accomplish the aims of the mission and to secure the means to maintain themselves in the region. In 1674, Ignacio de Guzmán reported that one friar, whose identity he did not reveal, had recently beaten and severely injured the Indian Cupamay – a well respected *capitán* from Citará province – for his refusal to pay the friar a stipend.[98] This was just one instance of aggression on the part of one individual friar, but it reflected a more general trend among missionaries – Franciscans and others – who came to see the use of force as the only appropriate method for dealing with Indians.[99] By September 1674, Fray Joseph de Córdoba, whose relationship with native people was to become particularly fraught over the following years, claimed to have lost all patience, and threatened to leave the mission on the grounds that Indians 'do nothing' except 'by force'.[100] The Jesuit Marzal also regarded corporal punishment as the only means likely to bring about the conversion of Indians: 'because they are so barbarous', he stated in May 1674, no good could be expected of them 'mientras no reine el castigo' – unless force ruled supreme, that is. It was a grave mistake, he argued, to think that Indians would 'understand the truth through . . . spiritual means', for they were both 'lacking in reason' and characterised by excessive 'malice'.[101]

We have no evidence to indicate whether Marzal adopted such methods in Noanama province after 1673, but we do know that it was the actions of the Franciscans, rather than those of the Jesuit, that provoked the gravest concern outside the Chocó. In December 1674, Don Pedro Salazar Betancur reported that the friars Joseph de Córdoba and Pablo Ruiz ill-treated the Indians.[102] Antonio de Guzmán reported conflicts between missionaries and Indians provoked by the former demanding 300 pesos in payment of stipends.[103] In May 1675, the *cabildo* of Anserma also complained about the behaviour of Joseph de Córdoba and Pablo Ruiz, both of whom it accused of intercepting correspondence between the Chocó and neighbouring cities – presumably to forestall the arrival in those cities of adverse reports on their activities.[104] Even the *audiencia* of Santa

Fe grew concerned about these friars, and requested that the Franciscan Provincial, Pedro de Soto, should recall both to Santa Fe.[105]

Apprehension in cities neighbouring the Chocó about the consequences of such desperate measures was not misplaced. For as the Franciscans increasingly came to rely on corporal punishment in their dealings with Indians, the tolerance that the latter had showed in the early days of the mission gradually wore thin. The relationship between Indians and Spaniards had probably never been entirely free of tension – Fray Juan Tabuenca had reported minor 'rebellions' and 'uprisings' as early as September 1673 – but after 1674 reports of Indian unrest, mostly directed against the missionaries, began to reach the authorities with greater and greater frequency.[106] In May 1674, Antonio Marzal reported that the Indians of Lloró had taken up arms against the Franciscan *comisario*, Miguel de Castro.[107] In September of that year, Fray Joseph de Córdoba wrote from Lloró that the Indians had *again* attempted to kill the Spanish.[108] In January 1676, reports reached Antioquia that Fray Francisco García and Joseph de Córdoba had both been assaulted: the former by an Indian he had called to prayer; the latter apparently suffered an ambush, and the burning down of the house in which he lived.[109] The Franciscans were not the only Spaniards who lived under threat of attack – in 1674, Domingo de Veitia y Gamboa reported from Lloró that 'the Indians . . . everyday say they want to kill us' - but they were the principal targets of the Indians' wrath.[110] Indeed, in 1676, Fray Francisco Caro, of Antioquia, stated that the Franciscans experienced outrages on a daily basis, and were justifiably distrustful and fearful.[111]

Within a very short time after the establishment of the Franciscan mission in the Chocó, therefore, the relationship between Indians and Spaniards which had been carefully nurtured over many years by Juan and Jorge López García, Antonio and Ignacio de Guzmán, and their many collaborators, was in danger of breaking down once again. There was, however, much confusion inside and outside the Chocó regarding the causes of tension and the best methods for dealing with a situation that appeared to threaten Spanish occupation of the region. Franciscans blamed the intractable nature of the Indians and the lack of assistance offered by secular officials whose duty it was to support the mission.[112] But for many Spaniards engaged in mining in the Chocó, it was the Franciscans themselves who posed the gravest threat to Spanish interests. When, in 1674, a group of miners presented a joint petition to the governor of Antioquia in protest at missionary treatment of Indians in Citará, they emphasised that the missionaries were all *chapetones* who had no experience of dealing with or even understanding Indians whose language they did not speak, and with whom they could communicate only by means of interpreters, of whom there were but a handful.[113] Antonio del Pino Villapadierna likewise protested about the missionaries' ignorance of the peoples with whose conversion they were entrusted, for 'they are chapetones recently arrived from . . . Spain'.[114] This is not to say, of course, that the attitudes of Spanish colonists were any different from those of the missionaries. The petitioners themselves called Indians 'rustic', 'vengeful' and 'bellicose'.[115] Villapadierna described them as 'barbarians incapable of reason . . . a people recently reduced after having been accustomed to treacherous [acts]'.[116] But, like Antonio de Guzmán, who tried unsuccessfully to persuade Castro Rivadeneyra that 'affection and flattery . . . are the magnets that attract them',[117] these Spaniards regarded the missionaries as impediments to the development of a mining economy that depended on Indian co-operation.

Outside the Chocó, opinions were equally divided. In Antioquia, Fray Francisco Caro, of the Franciscan *hospicio*, or friary, was sympathetic to the missionaries' plight, and justified the decision of many to leave the Chocó on the grounds of Indian defiance.[118] Fray Lucas de Villa Veces considered that the missionary effort was doomed to failure unless backed up by an armed force. At least thirty men, he said, should be sent without delay, for otherwise the lives of all Spaniards would be at risk: 'unless they [the Indians] recognise some authority in their own lands they will return to live in those places where they lived previously and nobody's life will be safe . . . [neither those] of the religious nor the rest'.[119] Even the General of the Order, Fray Juan Luengo, entered the debate in defence of the friars. While he accepted that the Chocó missionaries were perhaps too young and inexperienced for the task they had been assigned, it was also the case, he stated in 1676, that they faced a particularly difficult terrain, were unable to procure food for themselves and suffered hunger, and had to deal with intractable *cimarrones* (fugitives) who did not even live in fixed residences. Luengo added, moreover, that the mission was accepted against the better judgement of the Franciscan Province of Santa Fe, which had once before unsuccessfully attempted the reduction of the Chocó (he was, perhaps, referring to Abad and Hurtado), and contrasted the Franciscan record there with the activities of friars in the Llanos, where the number of Indians was greater, but where progress was being made.[120]

The Franciscans also enjoyed some support among senior officials in the New Kingdom. The governor of Popayán, Miguel García, for example, stated in November 1674 that the influence of *doctrineros* alone was never likely to lead to the reduction of the indigenous population of the Chocó, and that assigning missionaries for the purpose was tantamount to 'placing gates on an open field'.[121] The governor of Antioquia, Juan Bueso de Valdés, focused instead on the difficulties that had arisen in the region as a result of competition between missionaries and secular clergy over control of Indians.[122] But voices sympathetic to the friars were few and far between, and the general view was that the Franciscans' actions were threatening to undermine the advances that had already been made on the frontier. The Bishop of Popayán, Melchor Liñán y Cisneros, for example, harboured doubts about their effectiveness, and advised them to leave the region to their secular colleagues and proceed instead to Darién.[123] The *audiencia* of Santa Fe also expressed severe reservations regarding the mission. When, by *cédula* of August 1674, this body was asked to report on the number of additional missionaries that would be required for the Chocó, it responded that, for the moment at least, no more were required, for those already in the field lacked the necessary 'wisdom', and the results expected of them had not so far materialised.[124]

While a wide variety of opinions regarding the causes of growing tension in the Chocó were expressed in the mid-1670s, there was general agreement that the problem required an immediate solution, for by 1676 the reduction of the peoples of the Chocó had come to a virtual standstill. All but three of the original group of Franciscans sent to establish the mission had left, and those who remained could see no reason to persevere in their duty to convert Indians while the latter displayed such resistance to their efforts, refused to provide food supplies unless compensated, and threatened the physical safety of the friars.[125] The withdrawal of the Franciscans could not easily be ignored in Popayán or Antioquia, moreover, not least because in the mid-1670s both *gobernaciones* remained in the grip of mining recession, and neither expected that a major improvement in fortunes could take place without the incorporation of the gold deposits of the Chocó.[126] Indeed, far from contemplating a withdrawal, the respective governors sought to strengthen Spanish domination over native peoples, and planned to extend their influence over those parts of the Pacific lowlands inhabited by still unpacified Indian groups – the Cuna, the Burgumia, and especially the Soruco, who were believed not only to occupy lands exceptionally rich in gold, which the 'warlike' nature of the native inhabitants prevented Spaniards exploiting, but were also considered to represent a threat to Spanish activities among the Tatama and Citará.[127] As the governor of Popayán, Gabriel Díaz de la Cuesta, explained, the Soruco repeatedly 'infested' the territories of neighbouring Indian groups, 'killing their people and destroying their maize fields in ambushes'.[128] The departure of the Franciscans, then, was a serious blow to the interests of both *gobernaciones* in the Chocó. Not only did it signal the demise of a mission that was intended to lead to the congregation and conversion of the Indian population of Citará and Tatama, and thus facilitate the subsequent exploitation of the mineral resources they controlled, but also rendered less likely Spanish expansion beyond the area inhabited by these groups.

Despite the fears expressed in the cities of the *gobernaciones* of Antioquia and Popayán, however, the chances of successful occupation and settlement in the Chocó were greater in the mid-1670s than they had ever been before. Greater familiarity with Spanish ways, increasing dependence on items of European manufacture, and a growing awareness of the benefits that might accrue from commerce with outsiders meant that Indians were willing to allow Spaniards to remain in their territory without fear of attack. Some Spaniards, aside from missionaries, did express fears of Indian violence during these years – such was the case of Veitia y Gamboa, who came to the Chocó with Francisco de Quevedo – but there is remarkably little evidence to indicate any desire on the part of the indigenous population to sever their links with the Spanish. Outbreaks of violence were directed at individuals – missionaries in particular – and were not manifestations of general and widespread resistance to European activities there. By 1677, many Spaniards lived, and mined, in the Chocó. Several small slave gangs were engaged in mining along the Mungarra river, in the vicinity of Tadó; other slave gangs were employed in extracting gold from the river beds in the vicinity of Negua.[129] Antonio and Ignacio de Guzmán, and their many relatives and associates, remained actively engaged in mining in Citará province at least until that year. Indeed, when Bueso de Valdés returned to Antioquia from his expedition of 1676–77, he reported that many slave gangs had recently been withdrawn from the region – not, however, due to any threat of Indian violence, but for fear that he might investigate why *quintos* were not being paid on the output of the mines.[130] It is also to be noted that the petitions submitted by miners during these years complained not of fear of violence, or even of their inability to procure supplies, but of the high prices charged by Indians for the foodstuffs needed to maintain their operations. Bartolomé de Borja, Juan Nuño de Sotomayor, Jacinto Roque de Espinosa and Luis de Acevedo Redes all informed Bueso de Valdés of the high and arbitrary prices charged by Indians for their produce – 5 to 6 pesos for a *fanega* of maize; 6 *tomines* to 1 peso for a bunch of plantains – which diminished the profitability of mining and discouraged them from expanding their slave gangs. The suggestion implicit in the appeal is that Indians sought to gain maximum profit from supplying Spaniards with foodstuffs.[131] It seems probable, therefore, that Indians had by this time moved beyond bartering for European goods, and begun to procure such goods as 'beads, lances and axes' directly from merchants. Though details are few, one report did indicate that the Chocó 'became crowded with merchants' following the Quevedo *entrada*.[132] Bishop Linán y Cisneros, writing in 1672, similarly indicated that since that *entrada*, many merchants had 'penetrated that territory'.[133]

Juan Bueso de Valdés' *entrada* to Citará province, 1676–77

It was Antioquia, rather than Popayán, that finally took measures to resolve the conflicts that threatened the continuation of the Franciscan mission. In 1676, Governor Miguel de Aguinaga instructed his predecessor, Juan Bueso de Valdés, to conduct an *entrada* to the provinces of Citará and Tatama, the first armed expedition to the area since Francisco de Quevedo's in 1669. In authorising the *entrada*, Governor Aguinaga signalled his intention to endorse the activities of the Franciscan missionaries and bolster their authority. But more significantly for the future of relations between Spaniards and Indians in the Chocó, the 1676 *entrada* signalled the governor's determination to strengthen Antioquia's control over the resources of Citará, still disputed by neighbouring Popayán, to extend the influence of his *gobernación* over unexplored areas further north, and to transform the frontier character of this region and finally incorporate its resources and its people into the colony. It was for this that the presence of the Franciscans was required. As Bueso de Valdés informed Aguinaga in June 1677, missionaries and settlements were needed, 'not only to achieve the principal aim [which is] the well-being of the souls of the natives [but also] so that they will become more docile and [willingly] provide maize for the maintenance of the mines which they [presently] lack because such order [has not been introduced]'.[134]

The 1676 *entrada* was privately financed to the tune of over 3000 pesos by Juan Bueso de Valdés,[135] since, in spite of continued encouragement from the Crown, no capital was forthcoming from official sources to finance new ventures into the region. By royal *cédula* of 6 June 1674, the Crown reaffirmed its intention to bring about the reduction and conversion of the native peoples of the Chocó and bordering areas, but, reiterating the provisions contained in the *cédula* of 1666, explicitly stated that this should be achieved without recourse to the royal treasury. The *audiencia* of Santa Fe was once again required to assist the endeavour to the best of its ability, but without capital to invest it was powerless to do more than guide and direct the initiatives of others.[136] In several important respects, however, this expedition was different from those which preceded it. First, the former governor had the full support of Miguel de Aguinaga, and of the *audiencia*, which in 1675 granted him the title of *Juez Auxiliador Superintendente* (Superintendent) of the Chocó mission, in which capacity he was entrusted with promoting the interests of the Franciscans who administered it.[137] Secondly, Bueso de Valdés could expect few privileges from the Crown for his efforts. No titles of nobility or positions of responsibility were offered in return for services rendered. Royal *cédulas* of 1666 and 1674 forbade the distribution of Indians in *encomiendas* and exempted newly pacified Indians from tribute payments for the first ten years of their subjection to Spanish rule – provisions that the former governor was charged not only with observing personally but also with implementing across the region. The best Governor Aguinaga could offer was a promise that he should 'inform His Majesty so that he might bear you in mind and reward you with the posts that you may expect from His Royal Hand'.[138] And thirdly, fifteen years of relatively peaceful coexistence between Indians and Spaniards in Citará province made this a far more confident expedition than any that had preceded it: no harm came to any of its members, and no major incident of armed resistance was reported.[139]

The party that left Antioquia on 31 August 1676 consisted of twenty armed soldiers, apart from the superintendent.[140] Two missionaries, Fray Esteban de Iruñela and Fray Bernardo Pascual Ramírez, also joined the expedition and returned to the Chocó, though four others chose to remain in Antioquia and Anserma.[141] The expedition followed the route taken on many previous occasions by Antonio de Guzmán: from Antioquia to the *sitio de* Urrao, and from there to Nuestra Señora de la Candelaria de Taita, the first Indian settlement in the province of Citará. From Taita, the expedition made its way to San Juan de Negua, Nuestra Señora de la Concepción de Lloró, and San Francisco de Atrato – settlements that were used by the Franciscans as their bases, but which were clearly not yet regarded as such by the Indians themselves. Each settlement was said, in 1676, to contain several dwellings – 10 each in Negua and Lloró; 19 in San Francisco de Atrato – but most were uninhabited. Each settlement also had its own chapel, but these were either in ruins or used for purposes other than those for which they were intended. The chapel of Negua was said to be a ruin; that of San Francisco de Atrato was considered to be virtually unusable; that of Lloró was described as too small, and was used as a workshop for making canoes.[142] In the final months of 1676, as was the case before Spaniards came to the Chocó, the peoples of Citará continued to inhabit small and widely dispersed communities, thereby rendering impossible, as Bernardo Ramírez and Esteban de Iruñela argued, effective Christian instruction.¹⁴³

As we have seen, however, the main objective of Bueso de Valdés in conducting this *entrada* was to balance the purposes of the friars and the requirements of an emerging mining industry. With this aim in mind, the superintendent summoned the peoples of the many small communities scattered across the territory to those places that were to become the main settlements of Citará province. Between September and December 1676, a total of 1597 Indians were systematically resettled in San Juan de Negua (474), Nuestra Señora de la Concepción de Lloró (430) and San Francisco de Atrato (693). The small community of Taita (total population of 66) was to remain in its existing location.¹⁴⁴ By the end of January 1677, a total of 29 Indian dwellings, a church and a sacristy had been erected in Negua. Twenty more had been erected in San Francisco de Atrato and a further five were nearing completion. In Lloró, ten new dwellings had been completed, and a further four were being constructed; its chapel was also being lengthened.¹⁴⁵ Once the process of resettlement was complete, Bueso de Valdés dealt next with the issues of religious instruction and material support for the friars. The censuses taken during the *entrada* showed that the Franciscans had proved unable to baptise more than a small proportion of the indigenous population of Citará province since the mission's establishment – a mere 51 Indians having received that sacrament between 1673 and 1676. With the superintendent's assistance, hundreds more received baptism in 1676–77: 117 in Lloró, 187 in San Francisco de Atrato.¹⁴⁶ Moreover, to help the missionaries overcome the problems of procuring food, Bueso introduced guidelines to ensure that each adult male made an equal contribution towards the upkeep of the priests. Each *gandul* (male over the age of 15) was to provide his *doctrinero* with half a *fanega* (one *colado*) of maize per year. This, he stated, should cause no difficulties to the peoples of a fertile land capable of producing two harvests annually.¹⁴⁷ On the issue of stipends, however – advocated by the friars to enable them to purchase tallow, wine and clothing – Bueso observed Aguinaga's instructions to the letter. Though he recognised that easily accessible mines enabled Indians to acquire gold with which to pay stipends, he turned down the Franciscans' request.¹⁴⁸

One of the superintendent's objectives, therefore, was to strengthen the authority of the missionaries, necessary to accomplish the task of conversion, and to enable them to remain in the region in relative comfort and safety. The second objective was to foster and facilitate the activities of Spanish miners in Citará province. As a miner himself, and like Antonio de Guzmán before him, Bueso de Valdés understood the problems that too drastic a campaign of resettlement posed to future mining operations.¹⁴⁹ While on the one hand he sought to advance the process of *reducción*, on the other he sought to ensure Indian access to the scattered plots that provided them, the miners and their slaves with a livelihood.¹⁵⁰ Thus, he instructed the Indians of Negua that henceforth they should keep large dwellings in their settlements, for habitation, and small ones alongside their plots, 'to keep the maize while they harvested it and brought it to the towns'. Similar instructions were issued in Lloró and San Francisco de Atrato.¹⁵¹ That Bueso de

Valdés was guided by the need to balance the interests of miners and missionaries becomes particularly clear in the case of the settlement of Taita. Lying halfway between Urrao, the departure point for expeditions to the Chocó from Antioquia, and the Citará settlement of Negua, Taita had a very small population (just 66) and does not appear to have had any particular attraction for the Spaniards other than its mid-way location. Described as 'abundant in the produce of the land', Taita was a necessary resting place for travellers moving in and out of the Chocó from Antioquia.[152] One further question engaged the superintendent's attention: that of the cost of Indian supplies. Responding to the recommendations of local miners, Bueso de Valdés set a fixed scale of prices for Indian produce which were considerably lower than those customarily charged: two gold pesos for a *fanega* of maize; two *tomines* for a hen; and between one and two *tomines* for a bunch of plantains, depending on its type. Weights and measures were also to be rationalised, in order to prevent 'fraud'.[153] And finally, following a further petition, from miners in Tatama, instructions were issued to the effect that Indians must in future harvest twice a year, since larger supplies of maize were now required to maintain the region's slave gangs.[154]

We do not know by what means Bueso de Valdés succeeded in transferring some 1600 Indians from small communities dispersed across Citará territory to the missionary *reducciones*, nor why Indians offered little or no resistance to his new instructions. The fact that this was an armed *entrada*, albeit small, may have been one important element in the success of the campaign, for rumours that preceded the arrival of the expeditionary force were said to have caused some fear and consternation among Indians. Don Pedro Daza, of Taita, informed Bueso de Valdés that it was rumoured that he was to be accompanied by 'many armed men'. The superintendent himself also reported 'the fear they had of my entrada'.[155] However, it is equally plausible that the native population had no desire for confrontation with Spaniards. Not only did Indians assist Bueso de Valdés materially during the *entrada* – five fully manned canoes accompanied him on a journey of exploration down the Atrato river – but it is to be noted that in his report, he stated that 'from experience I have come to recognise the goodwill of the Indians of these provinces [towards the Spaniards] ... [which is] based on the great benefits they enjoy [as a result]'.[156] Finally, it was the Spanish who constituted the only source of European products for the peoples of the Chocó, and Bueso de Valdés' expedition took ample supplies of goods to win over *capitanes* and appease local populations. The former governor thus spoke of 'the goods I need ... to gratify the Chocó Indians and [to] buy from them the foodstuffs we need so that they won't be displeased'. His list of supplies for the expedition significantly included, 'for gifts and as payment for supplies', 50 bunches of white beads ('not of any other colour as they are not liked by the Indians'), 2500 fishhooks and fishing lines, and 25 dozen *cascabeles* (bells).[157] Even in the face of increased demands for labour and produce, it seems, the lure of items of European manufacture persuaded the Citará of the advantages of accommodating Spanish colonists and assisting their search for wealth. Thus, as Bueso de Valdés reported, several small slave gangs were then engaged in exploiting mines in the vicinity of Negua to which Indians, in exchange for 'modest gifts', had led them.[158]

In the short term, then, the *entrada* of former governor Juan Bueso de Valdés was a great success. For the first time in over a century of efforts to pacify and reduce the population, the Spanish reported significant progress in the process of *congregación*, in the religious instruction of Indians, and in the willingness of the local population to supply both friars and settlers in accordance with instructions issued by the superintendent. The Franciscans stated that Indians attended Doctrina punctually – according to Joseph de Córdoba, with a readiness never before experienced.[159] The miners, too, reported considerable progress. Indians sold maize at 2 pesos per *fanega*, as instructed, and prices were fixed on all other produce.[160] Thereafter, an ever-growing number of Spaniards began to penetrate the region, taking advantage of the opportunities for profitable mining activity which the Bueso de Valdés *entrada* had made possible. However, over the course of the following years, as the confidence of the Spanish increased, settlers gradually lost the support of many Indians in Citará, including most of those who, since the end of the 1660s, had acknowledged the benefits of interacting with the Spanish. How and why this loss of support occurred, and what effect it had on relations between Indians and Spaniards over the decade that followed, are the questions to be considered in Chapter 5.

Notes

1. Sweet, 'The Ibero-American Frontier Mission in Native American History', pp. 9–10.
2. Lockhart and Schwartz, *Early Latin America*, p. 281.
3. Priests could, of course, prove useful to an *entrada*, in that they could serve as emissaries to hostile Indian settlements, and perhaps even persuade their inhabitants to receive the Spanish troops peacefully. For examples of clergy who fulfilled this function, see Jones, *Maya Resistance*, pp. 170–87.
4. Romoli, 'El Alto Chocó', p. 15.
5. Anserma, 14 September 1639, AGN, Caciques e indios, 68, fol. 350.
6. Antioquia, 22 March 1640, AGN, Caciques e indios, 68, fol. 488.
7. The Panamanian Jesuit Pedro de Cáceres began work among the Noanama in 1651, founding two settlements and providing each of these with a chapel. He left the region within a year, however, disillusioned by his inability to persuade the Noanama to live there. Juan de Santa Cruz's attempt to evangelise among the Noanama was equally unsuccessful and short-lived. For the activities of the priests mentioned, see Pacheco, *La consolidación de la iglesia*, p. 671, and *idem*, *Los Jesuitas*, II, p. 449. According to J.J. Borda, one other Jesuit, Francisco de Orta, served as a missionary among the Chocó. See J.J. Borda, *Historia de la Compañía de Jesús*, Paris, 1872, pp. 78–79.
8. AGI Quito 67, 'Testimonio de Autos (Audiencia)', La Sed de Cristo, 29 May 1669, fol. 14.
9. Antonio de Guzmán to Miguel de Castro Rivadeneyra, Antioquia, 29 April 1674, AGI Quito 67, 'Testimonio de Autos (Franciscans)', fol. 90.
10. In requesting that Pedro Gómez del Valle be rewarded with a prebend in the cathedral of Popayán, the bishop informed the Crown that this priest had remained in the Chocó for two years and seven months. AGI Quito 67, Melchor Liñán y Cisneros to Crown, Santa Fe, 3 July 1672. The documents mention another secular priest, Joseph Garreto, who served as *doctrinero* of the small settlement of Carrapa (or Chamí) in the early

1670s. He was said to have abandoned his parish because its population was too small to support him. Juan Tabuenca to Miguel de Castro Rivadeneyra, Negua, 28 November 1673, in AGI Quito 67, 'Testimonio de Autos (Franciscans)', fol. 75.
11 This undated document had been received by the *audiencia* by October 1674. AGI Quito 67, 'Testimonio de Autos (Franciscans)', fol. 44.
12 Negua, 25 October 1676, AGI Santa Fe 204, Ramo 1, fol. 169. Two years earlier the Spaniard had claimed that three 'ranchos' had been erected to serve as chapels under Guzmán's direction, and that all were used as workshops for making arrows and building canoes. AGI Quito 67, 'Testimonio de Autos (Franciscans)', Sitio y Real de Minas de Nuestra Señora de Belén de Nemota, 27 July 1674, fol. 57.
13 Carvajal and Marzal were both members of the same Jesuit expedition, which arrived in New Granada in 1662. Carvajal stayed in the Chocó for two years only. Struck by ill health, demoralised by the behaviour of the white settlers, and fearing for his safety after suffering an assault at the hands of an Indian, he left Noanama in 1674 and returned to Popayán. Marzal took over San José de Noanama from Carvajal after the Franciscans arrived in Citará, and then began work among the Noanama settled along the Raposo and Sipí rivers. In 1678, he was reported to be accompanied by fellow Jesuit Juan de Escuder. The Jesuits formally abandoned the Chocó in 1689, although no missionaries were present there after 1685. See Melchor Liñán y Cisneros to Miguel Castro Rivadeneyra, Popayán, 4 June 1674, in AGI Quito 67, 'Testimonio de Autos (Franciscans)', fol. 82, and Pacheco, *Los Jesuitas*, pp. 450–51, 453, 486.
14 Fray Miguel de Castro Rivadeneyra, who was to become *comisario* of the Chocó missionaries, travelled to Spain in person to recruit operatives for the mission in 1669. See Doblado, 'Misiones de la Santa Provincia de Santa Fe', in Mantilla Ruiz, *Actividad misionera*, pp. 69–70 n. 88; and Fr Gregorio Arcila Robledo, *Las misiones franciscanas en Colombia*, Bogotá, Imprenta Nacional, 1950, p. 37.
15 AGI Quito 67, 'Testimonio de Autos (Franciscans)', Royal Cédula, 30 October 1671, fols. 4–5.
16 Jackson, 'Introduction', in Langer and Jackson (eds.), *The New Latin American Mission History*, p. vii. See also Robert H. Jackson and Edward Castillo, *Indians, Franciscans, and Spanish Colonization: The Impact of the Mission System on California Indians*, Albuquerque, NM, University of New Mexico Press, 1995, p. 3. Writing about the northern frontier of Mexico, Jackson and Castillo point out that 'missionaries, assisted by soldiers, congregated Indians into communities organized along the lines of those in the core areas of Spanish America, where Indian converts were to be indoctrinated in Catholicism and taught European-style agriculture, leatherworking, textile production, and other skills deemed useful by the Spaniards. The converts would lend their labor to the construction of building complexes organized in the grid plan of the colonial American city.'
17 Merrill, 'Conversion and Colonialism', p. 129.
18 Quoted in George W. Lovell, *Conquest and Survival in Colonial Guatemala: A Historical Geography of the Cuchumatán Highlands, 1500–1821*, Kingston and Montreal, McGill-Queen's University Press, 1985, pp. 75–76. According to Lovell, the spiritual aspects of the policy were incorporated into the Laws of Burgos as early as 1512.
19 Castillero Calvo, *Conquista, evangelización y resistencia*, p. 24.
20 AGI Santa Fe 199, San Francisco de Atrato, 5 October 1648.
21 Francisco Diaz's statement, AGN, Caciques e indios, 68, fols. 285–88.
22 Vargas Sarmiento, 'La fundación de pueblos', pp. 59–60.
23 Guzmán, 'Descubrimiento', in Ortega Ricaurte (ed.), *Historia documental*, p. 112.
24 AGI Quito 67, 'Testimonio de Autos (Franciscans)', San Francisco de Atrato, 18 August 1674, fol. 124.
25 Lloró, 9 January 1677, AGI Santa Fe 204, Ramo 1, fol. 162.

26 Juan Bueso de Valdés to Miguel de Aguinaga, n.p., 31 December 1676, AGI Santa Fe 204, Ramo 1, fol. 197.
27 Isacsson, 'The Egalitarian Society', p. 99. See also G. Reichel-Dolmatoff, 'Notas etnográficas sobre los indios del Chocó', *Revista Colombiana de Antropología*, Vol. 9, 1960, pp. 82–83.
28 AGI Quito 16, Miguel García to Crown, Popayán, 22 November 1674.
29 Marzal, 'Informe', in Pacheco, *Los Jesuitas*, II, p. 494.
30 West, *The Pacific Lowlands*, p. 87.
31 Guzmán, 'Descubrimiento', in Ortega Ricaurte (ed.), *Historia documental*, p. 117.
32 Juan Bueso de Valdés to Miguel de Aguinaga, Taita, 21 September 1676, AGI Santa Fe 204, Ramo 1, fol. 194.
33 West, *The Pacific Lowlands*, p. 87.
34 Guzmán, 'Descubrimiento', in Ortega Ricaurte (ed.), *Historia documental*, p. 112.
35 Isacsson, 'The Egalitarian Society', p. 99. For a discussion of indigenous settlement, recorded by archaeologists G. Reichel-Dolmatoff and Alicia Dussán de Reichel in 1960, see Reichel-Dolmatoff, 'Notas etnográficas', pp. 79–81.
36 Quoted in Isacsson, 'Fray Matías Abad', p. 473 n. 33. See also AGI Santa Fe 199, for a letter, dated Cartagena, 12 June 1649, which, though unsigned, was clearly reporting information received from Abad to the effect that the peoples of the Chocó 'have no leaders among themselves, except some capitanes, and these are little respected'.
37 Marzal, 'Informe', in Pacheco, *Los Jesuitas*, II, p. 501. Everywhere the Spanish went, they hoped to identify a political structure that could be bent to their own purposes, and they therefore saw the absence of such a political system as a serious obstacle to colonisation. Writing to the king in 1593, for example, in a tone that bears striking similarity to that which characterised observations on the peoples of the Chocó, Governor Martín de Loyola reported of the Reche (Mapuche) peoples of south-central Chile that 'they have no leaders . . . to obey except in matters of war and these [are chosen] for their personal bravery [so that] if any is found wanting they choose another in his place'. Quoted in Boccara, 'Etnogénesis mapuche' p. 428.
38 AGI Quito 67, 'Testimonio de Autos (Franciscans)', n.p., n.d., fol. 140.
39 The Franciscans also advocated the creation of leadership roles. Fray Lucas de Villa Veces, for instance, argued that a 'superior leader' was necessary to enforce congregation and the administration of the sacraments. See AGI Quito 67, 'Testimonio de Autos (Franciscans)', n.p., n.d., fol. 16.
40 Quoted in Isacsson, 'Emberá', p. 26. 'Caciques' imposed by the Spanish on the Tatama also failed to command the respect of the local population. Franciscan Francisco Moreno, reporting on the Indian Don Jacinto Choagra, said that 'he is not cacique nor is he respected as such by the Indians'. AGI Santa Fe 204, Ramo 2, 4 December 1676, fol. 49. Similar moves were made, in the eighteenth century, to create leadership roles among the Wayuú peoples of the Guajira Peninsula, with equally unsuccessful results. See Barrera Monroy, *Mestizaje, comercio y resistencia*, p. 69.
41 In general, only where a centralised indigenous political structure already existed were the Spaniards successful in co-opting local leaders to act as intermediaries between themselves and local populations. For an example of successful co-option on the Spanish frontier, see Amy Turner Bushnell, 'Ruling "the Republic of Indians" in Seventeenth-Century Florida', in Peter H. Wood, Gregory A. Waselkov and M. Thomas Hatley (eds.), *Powhatan's Mantle: Indians in the Colonial Southeast*, Lincoln, NE, and London, University of Nebraska Press, 1989, pp. 134–50.
42 Sitio de Buenavista, 7 September 1639, AGN, Caciques e indios, 68, fol. 375.
43 Isacsson, 'Emberá', p. 24. According to Isacsson, only the role of war leader was acknowledged by indigenous communities. See also David B. Stout, 'The Chocó', in J.H. Steward (ed.), *Handbook of South American Indians*, Vol. IV, New York, Cooper Square Publishers, 1963, p. 273.

44 Block, *Mission Culture*, p. 78.
45 San Francisco de Atrato, 23 November 1672, Documento No. 3, in Zuluaga Gómez (ed.), *Documentos inéditos*, p. 16.
46 AGI Quito 67, 'Testimonio de Autos (Franciscans)', Madrid, 30 October 1671, fols. 2–5. This *cédula* followed procedures established in the Recopilación (lib. I, tit. 14, laws 4 and 6) for the sending of missionaries to the colonies. 'Friars selected by the Orders for missionary work in the colonies', Haring explained, 'were recommended by them to the Council of the Indies, which issued passports to the Casa de Contratación. Travel expenses from the monasteries to Seville were furnished by the crown, the cost of clothing and food for the voyage by the Casa, and the passage money by the royal treasury in the Indies after safe arrival.' Haring, *The Spanish Empire*, p. 172 n. 20.
47 For reasons that may have had to do with the potential wealth of the Chocó, the Franciscan mission contrasted markedly with those established by Jesuits in other parts of the empire. Mission stations established among the Guaycuruans of the Gran Chaco, for example, received subsidies not only from Jesuit *colegios* and missions among the Guaraní – a feature of the functioning of Jesuit missions everywhere in Spanish America – but also from the Spanish authorities of towns most likely to benefit from the more peaceful conditions that would result from the priests' activities. The Moxos missions of the upper Amazon similarly received financial support from a variety of sources, including Jesuit investments in the secular economy, contributions from the Crown, and substantial charitable donations from the laity. Even in the Chocó, Jesuits appear to have been earmarked for financial assistance that was not offered to their Franciscan counterparts. On 17 November 1673, for instance, the Crown issued a royal *cédula* ordering officials in Popayán to provide the Jesuits of the Chocó with an annual stipend of 50,000 *maravedís*, though it is not certain that they ever received these funds. See, respectively, Saeger, *The Chaco Mission Frontier*, pp. 32–33, 35; Block, *Mission Culture*, pp. 65–72; and Pacheco, *Los Jesuitas*, Vol. II, p. 451.
48 The purpose of these exemptions was to persuade native peoples that the Crown's principal concern was not its own well-being but that of its new subjects. Real Provisión, 29 April 1675, in AGI Santa Fe 204, Ramo 1, fol. 13–19.
49 Antioquia, 8 January 1676, AGI Santa Fe 204, Ramo 1, fols. 9–13.
50 Jackson, 'Introduction', in Langer and Jackson (eds.), *The New Latin American Mission History*, p. viii.
51 The following list includes the names, places of origin and ages of the Franciscan team initially recruited for the Chocó mission: Fray Miguel de Castro Rivadeneyra (Galicia, 37), Fray Joseph Marton (Zaragoza, 40), Fray Juan Tabuenca (Zaragoza, 27), Fray Francisco Moreno (Zaragoza, 25), Fray Cristóbal de Artiaga (Zaragoza, 26), Fray Bernardo Pascual Ramírez (Logroño, 31), Fray Juan Chaverri (Navarra, 27), Fray Agustín Navarro (Burgos, 26), Fray Francisco García (Logroño, 26), Fray Pedro Arbues (Zaragoza, 40), Fray Miguel de Vera (32), Fray Pablo Ruiz (Zaragoza, 25), Fray Francisco Garrido (Burgos, 32), Pedro de Villa Verde (15), Bartolomé García (15). AGI Quito 67, 'Testimonio de Autos (Franciscans)', fols. 6–8.
52 These were Agustín Navarro, Pedro Arbues and Francisco Garrido.
53 In Tatama province, Fray Cristóbal de Artiaga was sent to San Francisco Ytaguri, Fray Pablo Ruiz was to take responsibility for Nuestra Señora de la Paz de Pureto and San Pedro de Alcántara de Maygara, and Fray Francisco Moreno was given responsibility for Poya and Yragugu. In Citará province, Fray Francisco García was assigned to San Francisco de Atrato, Fray Joseph de Córdoba to Nuestra Señora de la Concepción de Lloró, Fray Juan Tabuenca to Nuestra Señora del Pilar de Zaragoza, on the Negua river, and Fray Bernardo Pascual Ramírez and Fray Miguel de Vera to the small 'sitio' of Taita.
54 Juan Tabuenca to Castro Rivadeneyra, Negua, 29 May 1674, AGI Quito 67, 'Testimonio de Autos (Franciscans)', fol. 79.

55 These figures are calculated from population counts carried out by Juan Bueso de Valdés in Nuestra Señora de la Candelaria de Tàita (18 September 1676), San Juan de Negua (24 October 1676 and 3 November 1676), Nuestra Señora de la Concepción de Lloró (21 December 1676), and San Francisco de Atrato (16 December 1676). See AGI Santa Fe 204, Ramo 1, fols. 63–65, 75–93, 95–96, 143–54, 122–42.
56 Juan Tabuenca to Castro Rivadeneyra, Negua, 28 November 1673, AGI Quito 67, 'Testimonio de Autos (Franciscans)', fol. 76.
57 Petición, n.p., n.d., AGI Quito 67, 'Testimonio de Autos (Franciscans)', fols. 47–48.
58 AGI Quito 67, 'Testimonio de Autos (Franciscans)', Sitio y Real de Minas de Nuestra Señora de Belén de Nemota, 23 July 1674, fols. 50–51.
59 Juan Tabuenca to Castro Rivadeneyra, Negua, 29 May 1674, AGI Quito 67, 'Testimonio de Autos (Franciscans)', fol. 79.
60 Antonio de Guzmán to Castro Rivadeneyra, Antioquia, 29 April 1674, AGI Quito 67, 'Testimonio de Autos (Franciscans)', fol. 89.
61 Petición (Juan de León Castellanos), n.p., n.d., AGI Quito 67, 'Testimonio de Autos (Franciscans)', fol. 86.
62 Ignacio de Guzmán to Castro Rivadeneyra, Mina del Señor Santo Domingo, 30 April 1674, AGI Quito 67, 'Testimonio de Autos (Franciscans)', fol. 70. See also Petición (Francisco Mayoral de Olivos et al.), 28 August 1674, fol. 33.
63 Lloró, 14 November 1676, and San Francisco de Atrato, 18 November 1676, AGI Santa Fe 204, Ramo 1, fols. 97, 98.
64 Negua, 22 October 1676, AGI Santa Fe 204, Ramo 1, fols. 73–74.
65 Negua, 5 October 1676, AGI Santa Fe 204, Ramo 1, fol. 66.
66 There are also suggestions, though details are scarce, that Indians may also have perceived the mission settlements as insecure for the further reason that these separated the communities from the *retiros* (retreats) that constituted one of their main defences against attack, by Spaniards or by enemy Indian groups. Certainly, there are indications that access to those retreats was another factor in the location of Indian settlements. In his account of the 1670 *entrada* to Citará province, Antonio de Guzmán described how Capitán Coabra, one of his closest collaborators, 'directed me to four retreats they had for ... their defense'. See Guzmán, 'Descubrimiento', in Ortega Ricaurte (ed.), *Historia documental*, p. 113.
67 AGI Quito 67, 'Testimonio de Autos (Franciscans)', n.p., n.d., fol. 23.
68 Biblioteca Nacional (Madrid) Ms 19699[31], 'Declaración que hizo el Padre Fray Jacinto Hurtado'.
69 For a discussion of the divergent views of Jesuits and Franciscans on instruction and baptism, see Gradie, *The Tepehuan Revolt*, pp. 129–31.
70 Marzal, 'Informe', in Pacheco, *Los Jesuitas*, II, pp. 500, 502.
71 See Fray Lucas de Villa's comments on this subject, AGI Quito 67, 'Testimonio de Autos (Franciscans)', n.p., n.d., fols. 14–15.
72 Juan Tabuenca to Castro Rivadeneyra, Negua, 28 November 1673, AGI Quito 67, 'Testimonio de Autos (Franciscans)', fol. 77, and Juan Tabuenca to Castro Rivadeneyra, Negua, 29 May 1674, fols. 79–80.
73 AGI Quito 67, 'Testimonio de Autos (Franciscans)', n.p., n.d., fols. 14–15.
74 Susan Deeds, for example, has shown that the early acceptance of missionaries by indigenous communities in Nueva Vizcaya (in northwestern Mexico) centred in part on the Indians' desire for material benefits that would accrue from new farming and irrigation techniques, an expanded diet, and other material artefacts introduced by the Spanish. Daniel Reff has argued, for the Jesuit missions of Paraguay as well as northwestern Mexico, that Indian peoples accepted 'baptism and missionization' in exchange not only for material benefits, but also for protection from settler exploitation and/or attacks from enemy groups. Charlotte Gradie, whose concern is specifically with the Tepehuan

peoples of Nueva Vizcaya, considered that only when Indians were driven out of their *rancherías* by famine or disease did missionaries – also Jesuits – successfully persuade Indians to congregate in mission villages. For James Saeger, early acceptance of mission settlements among some Guaycuruan peoples of the Gran Chaco was made possible by material rewards and the expectation that baptism could cure disease. Finally, David Block drew attention to the fact that the first *reducción* established by Jesuits among the Moxos peoples of the upper Amazon (Nuestra Señora de Loreto, founded in 1682), was hastened by a slaving expedition that made captives of Indians settled nearby. 'The approach of the dreaded slave raid', Block states, 'convinced the Arawaks that their only "salvation" lay with the Jesuits.' See, respectively, Deeds, 'Indigenous Responses to Mission Settlement', p. 83; Daniel T. Reff, 'The Jesuit Mission in Comparative Perspective: The Reductions of the Río de la Plata and the Missions of Northwestern Mexico, 1588–1700', in Guy and Sheridan (eds.), *Contested Ground*, pp. 17, 25–27; Gradie, *The Tepehuan Revolt*, pp. 139–40; Saeger, *The Chaco Mission Frontier*, pp. 21–25, 27–28; and Block, *Mission Culture*, pp. 37–38.

75 AGI Quito 67, 'Testimonio de Autos (Franciscans)', Lloró, 15 September 1674, fol. 113.
76 Negua, 20 October 1676, AGI Santa Fe 204, Ramo 1, fol. 73.
77 Petición (Fray Miguel de Castro Rivadeneyra), n.p., n.d., AGI Quito 67, 'Testimonio de Autos (Franciscans)', fol. 44. For Fray Lucas de Villa Veces' comments, see fol. 16.
78 Esteban de Iruñela to Miguel de Aguinaga, Taita, 20 September 1676, in AGI Santa Fe 204, Ramo 1, fol. 194.
79 San José, 28 September 1672, in Zuluaga Gómez (ed.), *Documentos inéditos*, p. 20.
80 Marzal, 'Informe', in Pacheco, *Los Jesuitas*, II, p. 502.
81 Juan Tabuenca to Miguel Castro Rivadeneyra, Negua, 29 May 1674, AGI Quito 67, 'Testimonio de Autos (Franciscans)', fol. 77.
82 Negua, 24 December 1676, AGI Santa Fe 204, Ramo 1, fols. 121–22; and AGI Quito 67, 'Testimonio de Autos (Franciscans)', Lloró, 15 September 1674, fols. 113–14.
83 Weber, *The Spanish Frontier*, pp. 122–33.
84 See, for example, Knaut, *The Pueblo Revolt*, pp. 88–90.
85 With the sole exception of Don Juan Bueso de Valdés, whose methods of pacification will be discussed in the context of the *entrada* of 1676–77, Spaniards in the Chocó did not pay the Jesuits or the Franciscans the kind of deference that was shown to missionaries of the former order when they established a mission among, for example, the Tepehuanes. Writing of their activities there at the beginning of the seventeenth century, Charlotte Gradie has indicated that 'Jesuit authority was also promoted and validated by Spanish deference, often presented with great pageantry, to individual missionaries'. Their prestige, she continues, 'was purposely enhanced by the respect all Spaniards traditionally showed members of the clergy and the ceremony and solemnity with which they celebrated the rituals of their religion', the purpose being 'to impress the Tepehuanes and . . . to effect a diminishment of the prestige of the Tepehuanes' own leaders'. Even 'the Spanish military consciously ceded power over the natives to the missionaries and staged elaborate rituals in which they acknowledged the authority of the missionaries to the natives and increase[d] Jesuit influence among them'. Gradie, *The Tepehuan Revolt*, pp. 132, 134.
86 Juan Tabuenca to Miguel de Castro Rivadeneyra, Negua, 28 November 1673, AGI Quito 67, 'Testimonio de Autos (Franciscans)', fol. 77.
87 Indeed, at the beginning of the seventeenth century, the Archbishop of Santa Fe was instructed, by royal *cédula*, to appoint to Indian *doctrinas* clergy knowledgeable of native languages. However, as *audiencia* president Don Juan de Borja replied, by letter of January 1606, that order was difficult to enforce in the New Kingdom, because clergy knowledgeable of Indian languages were invariably creoles, and thus ineligible to take holy orders. According to Mantilla Ruiz, it was at this time that the Franciscan Province of Santa Fe began recruiting creoles. See Mantilla Ruiz, *Actividad misionera*, pp. 27–28.

88 Gradie, *The Tepehuan Revolt*, p. 130. See also p. 100.
89 It was one of their number, Luis de Bolaños, who wrote, in or around 1586, the first catechism in the Guaraní language, which was published in Europe in 1607. See Juan Carlos Garavaglia, 'The Crises and Transformations of Invaded Societies: The La Plata Basin (1535–1650)', in Frank Salomon and Stuart B. Schwartz (eds.), *The Cambridge History of the Native Peoples of the Americas, Vol. III: South America, Part 2*, Cambridge, Cambridge University Press, 1999, pp. 18–19.
90 Jones, *Maya Resistance*, pp. 142–45. Jones gives other examples of Maya-speaking missionaries who undertook the task of pacifying indigenous peoples in colonial Yucatán. See, for example, pp. 179, 215.
91 Although, as David Weber has noted, the Franciscans' enthusiasm for language learning 'seems to have waned from a high point in the first half of the sixteenth century'. Weber, *The Spanish Frontier*, p. 110.
92 The Jesuit Fray Pedro Marbán, for instance, who began his activities among Indian groups in the upper Amazon in 1675, compiled an *Arte y vocabulario de la lengua Moxa*, which was published in Lima in 1701. Other Jesuits in this region, largely because of their interest in teaching in the vernacular, were to contribute grammars and religious tracts written in Moxo, Baure, Mobima, Kayubaba, Itonama, Sapibocona and other savanna languages. Among eighteenth-century compilations is Antonio Maggio's *Arte de la lengua de los indios Baures de la provincia de los Moxos* (1749). See Block, *Mission Culture*, pp. 36, 118. There are many other examples, for regions outside Peru and Mexico, to demonstrate missionary dedication to the compilation of dictionaries and grammars. Inga Clendinnen mentions one such case, the Franciscan Fray Luis de Villapando, who was sent to the Yucatan in the mid-1540s, and who 'settled to unravelling the complexities of the native language, striving to develop a dictionary and grammar so that essential translations could be made'. In later years, studies of Indian languages were also produced by Jesuits working among the Araucanians. See Inga Clendinnen, *Ambivalent Conquests: Maya and Spaniard in Yucatán, 1517–1570*, Cambridge and New York, Cambridge University Press, 1987, p. 52; and Villalobos, *La vida fronteriza*, pp. 347–48.
93 There was, however, nothing unusual about this phenomenon, as missionary desertions were common throughout Spanish America during the colonial period. Some missionaries died en route to the colonies. Others deserted their expeditions at various ports before arriving at their intended destinations. There were also those who preferred to opt for the easier life offered in some other area of the colony to which they had been sent. Another proportion did go to the missions to which they were assigned, only to abandon their respective territories after only a short spell of activity there. For an analysis of the phenomenon of missionary desertions during the colonial period, and the ways in which the Crown tried to prevent it, see Pedro Borges Morán, *El envío de misioneros a América durante la época española*, Salamanca, Universidad Pontificia, 1977, pp. 544–65. The Chocó mission was no exception. In December 1675, Governor Miguel de Aguinaga, of Antioquia, claimed that four of the group of Franciscans originally sent to the mission were then residing in the city of Antioquia, despite a serious shortage of priests in the Chocó. See AGI Santa Fe 204, Ramo 1, Antioquia, 30 December 1675, fols. 5–6.
94 AGI Quito 67, 'Testimonio de Autos (Franciscans)', fol. 99.
95 Petición (Francisco Mayoral de Olivos et al.), 28 August 1674, AGI Quito 67, 'Testimonio de Autos (Franciscans)', fol. 33.
96 AGI Quito 67, 'Testimonio de Autos (Franciscans)', Antioquia, 18 July 1674, fol. 22. See also fol. 23.
97 Juan Tabuenca to Castro Rivadeneyra, Negua, 29 May 1674, AGI Quito 67, 'Testimonio de Autos (Franciscans)', fol. 78.
98 AGI Quito 67, 'Testimonio de Autos (Franciscans)', Mina del Señor Santo Domingo, 15 July 1674, fol. 41.

99 Corporal punishment became a standard tool of instruction for missionaries in Spanish America from the very beginning of the sixteenth century. In Mexico, for example, according to Inga Clendinnen, corporal punishment became 'integrated into the standard repertoire of missionary strategies' as early as the 1520s. By 1539, Bishop Zumárraga and the heads of the three orders then active in that region – the Franciscans, Augustinians and Dominicans – officially laid down that 'light punishments' could be imposed by missionaries on their Indian charges. However, as Clendinnen and others have shown, there is also much evidence to show that punishments were frequently taken to excess, and that missionaries often abused their power over Indians, subjecting them to torture and even death. Perhaps the most famous example of cruelty and brutality on the part of one order – the Franciscans – took place in Maní, in Yucatán, in 1562, when approximately 4500 Indians were tortured when it was discovered that 'Christian' Indians continued to worship their idols in secret. But equally brutal punishments were also carried out elsewhere. In the mid-seventeenth century, one group of Pueblo Indians (Zuñi) were reportedly set alight by Fray Salvador de Guerra, allegedly for idolatry, but actually because they had complained to the governor, López de Mendizabal, about conditions in the missions. See, respectively, Inga Clendinnen, 'Disciplining the Indians: Franciscan Ideology and Missionary Violence in Sixteenth-Century Yucatán', *Past and Present*, No. 94, February 1982, pp. 27–48; idem, *Ambivalent Conquests*, pp. 72–92; and Knaut, *The Pueblo Revolt*, p. 107. On discipline and punishment under the mission regime in general, see Sweet, 'The Ibero-American Frontier Mission', pp. 21–22.

100 AGI Quito 67, 'Testimonio de Autos (Franciscans)', Lloró, 15 September 1674, fol. 113.

101 AGI Quito 67, 'Testimonio de Autos (Franciscans)', Noanama, 22 May 1674, fol. 80. For the reactions of Jesuits faced with Indians with similar systems of political organisation, see, for example, Sweet, 'Misioneros jesuitas', pp. 279–80.

102 AGI Quito 67, 'Testimonio de Autos (Franciscans)', Anserma, 10 December 1674, fol. 119. It was not just Indians, however, who claimed to have experienced unreasonable behaviour on the part of missionaries. In March 1675, the *corregidor* Lorenzo de Salamanca complained that Joseph de Córdoba had stolen money from him. Anserma, 4 March 1675, fols. 168–69.

103 Petición (Juan de León Castellanos), n.p., n.d., in AGI Quito 67, 'Testimonio de Autos (Franciscans)', fol. 87.

104 AGI Quito 67, 'Testimonio de Autos (Franciscans)', Anserma, 10 May 1675, fol. 167.

105 Pacheco, *La consolidación de la iglesia*, p. 673.

106 Juan Tabuenca to Castro Rivadeneyra, Río de Negua, 17 September 1673, AGI Quito 67, 'Testimonio de Autos (Franciscans)', fol. 74. See also Petición (Francisco Mayoral de Olivos et al.), 28 August 1674, fol. 33.

107 AGI Quito 67, 'Testimonio de Autos (Franciscans)', Noanama, 22 May 1674, fol. 80.

108 AGI Quito 67, 'Testimonio de Autos (Franciscans)', Lloró, 15 September 1674, fol. 113.

109 Antioquia, 3 January 1676, AGI Santa Fe 204, Ramo 1, fols. 6–8.

110 AGI Quito 67, 'Testimonio de Autos (Franciscans)', Lloró, 16 September 1674, fol. 112.

111 Antioquia, 3 January 1676, AGI Santa Fe 204, Ramo 1, fols. 6–8.

112 Castro Rivadeneyra even petitioned on behalf of his fellow friars for the appointment of a governor for the Chocó, independent of both Antioquia and Popayán, and for the dispatch of an armed escort to assist him. Petición, n.p., n.d., AGI Quito 67, 'Testimonio de Autos (Franciscans)', fol. 45.

113 Petición (Francisco Mayoral de Olivos et al.), 28 August 1674, AGI Quito 67, 'Testimonio de Autos (Franciscans)', fols. 34–35.

114 Petición (Antonio del Pino Villapadierna), AGI Quito 67, 'Testimonio de Autos (Franciscans)', fols. 36–37.
115 Petición (Francisco Mayoral de Olivos et al.), 28 August 1674, AGI Quito 67, 'Testimonio de Autos (Franciscans)', fols. 33–34.
116 Petición (Antonio del Pino Villapadierna), AGI Quito 67, 'Testimonio de Autos (Franciscans)', fols. 36–37.
117 Antonio de Guzmán to Castro Rivadeneyra, Antioquia, 29 April 1674, AGI Quito 67, 'Testimonio de Autos (Franciscans)', fol. 89.
118 Antioquia, 3 January 1676, AGI Santa Fe 204, Ramo 1, fols. 6–8.
119 AGI Quito 67, 'Testimonio de Autos (Franciscans)', n.p., n.d., fol. 16.
120 AGI Quito 67, Juan Luengo to Francisco Fernández Madrigal, 23 April 1676. For an account of the activities of all the orders in the Llanos region, see Rausch, *A Tropical Plains Frontier*.
121 AGI Quito 16, Miguel García to Crown, Popayán, 22 November 1674.
122 AGI Quito 67, Juan Bueso de Valdés to Crown, Antioquia, 12 July 1675.
123 AGI Quito 67, Melchor Liñán y Cisneros to Crown, 3 July 1672, and Melchor Liñán y Cisneros to Miguel de Castro Rivadeneyra, Popayán, 4 June 1674, in 'Testimonio de Autos (Franciscans)', fol. 83.
124 AGI Quito 67, Audiencia of Santa Fe to Crown, Santa Fe, 17 June 1675.
125 Antioquia, 3 January 1676, AGI Santa Fe 204, Ramo 1, fols. 6–8.
126 Colmenares, *Historia económica*, Tables 22 and 27, pp. 316, 327; Ann Twinam, *Miners, Merchants, and Farmers in Colonial Colombia*, Austin, TX, Institute of Latin American Studies, 1982, Table 1, p. 28; and McFarlane, *Colombia*, pp. 77–78.
127 The continuing independence of the Soruco was also thought to constitute the single most important obstacle to the development of an overland route linking the Chocó with Panama and Portobelo. See AGI Quito 16, Miguel García to Crown, Popayán, 22 November 1674; AGI Quito 67, Gabriel Díaz de la Cuesta to Crown, Popayán, 8 April 1669; and AGI Santa Fe 204, Ramo 1, Antioquia, 30 June 1677, fols. 189–90.
128 AGI Quito 67, Gabriel Díaz de la Cuesta to Crown, 20 July 1672. See also AGI Santa Fe 204, Ramo 2, Tadó, 4 December 1676, fol. 49.
129 It should be noted, however, that these observations referred only to the provinces of Citará and Tatama, and that much more mining activity was taking place, by 1678, in the province of Noanama. In that year, the Jesuit Antonio Marzal reported that two slave gangs (30 slaves in total) were exploiting gold deposits along the Raposo river; another two gangs (a total of 30 slaves) were employed in the mines of San Agustín, along the Sipí river; and five slave gangs (36 slaves) were employed in the mines of San Gerónimo de Nóvita and Sed de Cristo. Marzal also observed that some twenty slaves were employed in extracting gold from deposits along the Negua and other rivers, in the province of Citará. See 'Informe', in Pacheco, *Los Jesuitas*, II, p. 495.
130 Antioquia, 30 June 1677, AGI Santa Fe 204, Ramo 1, fol. 185.
131 Petición (Bartolomé de Borja et al.), Negua, 30 October 1676, AGI Santa Fe 204, Ramo 2, fol. 225.
132 Domingo Ruiz y Gamboa to Francisco de Quevedo, n.p., n.d., AGI Quito 67, 'Testimonio de Autos (Audiencia)', fol. 29.
133 AGI Quito 67, Melchor de Liñán y Cisneros to Crown, Santa Fe, 3 July 1672.
134 Antioquia, 30 June 1677, AGI Santa Fe 204, Ramo 1, fol. 186.
135 See Governor Aguinaga's report, dated Antioquia, 14 July 1677, in AGI Santa Fe 204, Ramo 1, fol. 208.
136 Royal Cédula, Madrid, 6 June 1674, AGI Santa Fe 204, Ramo 1, fols. 1–4.
137 AGI Quito 67, Juan Bueso de Valdés to Crown, Antioquia, 12 July 1675. See also Real Provisión, 1 April 1675, AGI Santa Fe 204, Ramo 1, fols. 58–59.
138 Antioquia, 8 January 1676, AGI Santa Fe 204, Ramo 1, fols. 9–13.

139 In October 1676, Bueso de Valdés reported that many communities in the vicinity of Negua had retreated towards the rivers Baberama, Ichó and Nemota to escape Spanish forces. Others, however, met the expedition laden with foodstuffs to offer in friendship. San Juan de Negua, 5 October 1676, and Taita, 21 September 1676, in AGI Santa Fe 204, Ramo 1, fols. 66, 192–93, respectively.
140 Antioquia, 30 June 1677, AGI Santa Fe 204, Ramo 1, fol. 183. The following list includes all the Spaniards who took part in the expedition: Juan Bueso de Valdés, Alexos Rodríguez, Joseph de Lescano, Cristóbal de Viñola, Juan Antonio Velásquez, Joseph Rodríguez, Jerónimo García, Juan de Muriel, Juan Ramírez Osorio, Laureano de Benalcázar, Francisco Antonio de la Cruz, Pedro Pablos Moreno, Francisco Degois, Alejandro de la Cruz, Gaspar Francisco de la Cruz, Pedro Ordoñes, Pablo Ordoñes, Roque Ordoñes, Gregorio Ordoñes, and Simón de Betancur. See fols. 60–63.
141 Negua, 24 December 1676, AGI Santa Fe 204, Ramo 1, fols. 120–21.
142 AGI Santa Fe 204, Ramo 1, Negua, 5 October 1676, fol. 66; Lloró, 15 November 1676, fol. 97; Negua, 24 October 1676, fol. 168; and Antioquia, 30 June 1677, fol. 184.
143 AGI Santa Fe 204, Ramo 1, Lloró, 14 November 1676, fol. 97; San Francisco de Atrato, 18 November 1676, fol. 98.
144 For details, see reports dated Taita, 18 September 1676; Negua, 24 October 1676 and 3 November 1676; San Francisco de Atrato, 16 and 19 December 1676; and Lloró, 21 December 1676, in AGI Santa Fe 204, Ramo 1, fols. 63–65, 75–93, 95–96, 122–43, 143–54.
145 AGI Santa Fe 204, Ramo 1, Negua, 7 October and 24 December 1676, fols. 68, 160; San Francisco de Atrato, 5 January 1677, fols. 160–61; Lloró, 9 January 1677, fols. 161–62; and Antioquia, 14 July 1676, fols. 206–207.
146 AGI Santa Fe 204, Ramo 1, San Francisco de Atrato, 5 January 1677, fols. 160–61; Lloró, 9 January 1677, fols. 161–62.
147 AGI Santa Fe 204, Ramo 1, Taita, 17 September 1676, fol. 63; Negua, 23 October 1676, fol. 75; Lloró, 15 November 1676, fol. 97; San Francisco de Atrato, 19 November 1676, fols. 98–99; and Antioquia, 30 June 1677, fols. 184–85.
148 Antioquia, 30 June 1677, AGI Santa Fe 204, Ramo 1, fols. 184–85.
149 By 1684, Bueso de Valdés had himself become an important mine- and slave-owner in the Chocó, holding a slave gang in partnership with Domingo de Veitia.
150 Writing on the Upper Tarahumara and Chínipas missions of northern Mexico, controlled by the Jesuits, William Merrill also noted the impracticality of permanently congregating populations in regions where arable plots were small and scattered. It seems that at least some Indians in the Upper Tarahumara missions adopted a modification to the congregation programme similar to that proposed by Bueso de Valdés, in that they lived at their farms during the growing season, and in the mission villages the rest of the year. Most, however, rejected even temporary congregation, continuing the traditional pattern of dispersed settlement. Merrill, 'Conversion and Colonialism', pp. 142–43.
151 AGI Santa Fe 204, Ramo 1, Negua, 7 October 1676, fol. 68; Lloró, 15 November 1676, fol. 97; San Francisco de Atrato, 19 November 1676, fols. 98–99.
152 Antioquia, 30 June 1677, AGI Santa Fe 204, Ramo 1, fol. 183.
153 AGI Santa Fe 204, Ramo 1, Negua, 12 October 1676, fols. 69–70; Lloró, 15 November 1676, fol. 97; and San Francisco de Atrato, 19 November 1676, fol. 99.
154 AGI Santa Fe 204, Ramo 1, Tadó, 27 November 1676, fols. 115–16, and 29 November 1676, fols. 101–102. According to the *oidor* of the *audiencia*, Vicente de Aramburu, writing in 1713, the land was 'capable of providing two equal crops each year'. See AGI Quito 143, Vicente de Aramburu to Crown, Santa Fe, 8 September 1713.
155 Negua, 6 October 1676, AGI Santa Fe 204, Ramo 1, fol. 67.
156 Antioquia, 30 June 1677, AGI Santa Fe 204, Ramo 1, fols. 186–87.
157 Juan Bueso de Valdés to Miguel de Aguinaga, 14 May 1676, AGI Santa Fe 204, Ramo 1, fols. 33–34, and 'Memorial de los géneros', fols. 34–35.

158 Antioquia, 30 June 1677, AGI Santa Fe 204, Ramo 1, fol. 185.
159 San Francisco de Atrato, 5 January 1677, AGI Santa Fe 204, Ramo 1, fols. 160–61.
160 Bartolomé de Borja et al. to Crown, Negua, 30 October 1676, AGI Santa Fe 204, Ramo 2, fols. 225–26.

CHAPTER FIVE

Protest and Rebellion, 1680–1684

On 15 January 1684 a mass Indian rebellion broke out in Citará province, marking the end of a prolonged period of tense but essentially peaceful Spanish–Indian interaction in this part of the Chocó. The uprising was timed to break out concurrently in the main settlements of Negua, Lloró and San Francisco de Atrato, from where it rapidly spread to the many small mining camps scattered across the province. Over the course of that day, Indians massacred all but a few of the Spanish residents of Citará territory, as well as black slaves, Indian servants and carriers from the interior, Spanish traders or *tratantes*, and even many women.[1] According to Governor Gerónimo de Berrio, of Popayán, a total of 126 'Spanish Christians' lost their lives in the uprising.[2] In addition to killing the Spaniards, Indians burned down settlements, desecrated chapels and took church ornaments.[3] In Negua, where the rebellion was first planned, all but one of the inhabitants were killed within minutes of the outbreak of violence.[4] Of the 11 bodies later found there, four had been decapitated and the Franciscan *comisario*'s body was burned. In this, as in all the other settlements and mining camps of the province, everything that could be carried away was taken by the rebels.[5] Hundreds fled from the main areas of Spanish settlement thereafter. Some retreated to inaccessible areas in the vicinity of Lloró; others, such as Don Pedro de Bolivar, Don Juan Chigri and Don Fernando Tajina, opted for the greater safety of more distant zones, escaping across the Atrato river to the Bojaya river, or northwards to the Murri river.[6]

Three separate expeditions were recruited in the immediate aftermath of the rebellion and sent to rescue the survivors who took refuge in Bueso de Valdés' mine of Naurita, to capture and punish the rebel leaders, and to return the remainder of the population to their settlements. One came from Antioquia; the other two from Popayán. From Antioquia, Juan Bueso de Valdés led a company of 40 armed soldiers, eight *aventureros*, and more than 40 Indians.[7] From Popayán, one expedition was sent under the command of Juan de Caicedo Salazar, consisting of more than 100 armed men and aided by 30 Tatama and 130 Noanama – the Indians having been promised a ten-year exemption from tribute payments in exchange for service, the soldiers, a share of the pillage.[8] A second, even larger force followed, led by Cristóbal de Caicedo and consisting of 200 Spaniards and 200 Indians.[9] Once in Citará territory, Spanish forces conducted *correrías* – expeditions to capture rebels – across the length and breadth of the region.[10] Hundreds of Indians were captured as a result, but many, including several believed to have been among the principal ringleaders, evaded capture and held out against the Spanish for three more years. At least seven *capitanes* escaped to a distance of many leagues from the occupied territory, from where they continued to attack Spaniards. It was not until 1687 that the head of the Indian Quirubira, apparently the most prominent of all the rebels, was sent to Spain as proof that the Citará had finally been defeated, after a conflict lasting from 15 January 1684 to 31 August 1687.[11]

The scale, speed and degree of organisation of the January uprising indicates that the purpose of the rebels was to clear the entire Citará region not just of Spaniards, lay and religious, but of all traces of their presence, hence the massacre of slaves, Indian carriers and servants, and some women. Indeed, twelve days after the rebellion occurred, an estimated 300 Indians returned to the Naurita mine to persuade the survivors to leave the Chocó. According to Don Juan Joseph Azcárate de Castillo, one of only six Spaniards who escaped with their lives, Indians offered food and transport to enable them to leave with their slaves, for they wanted no more war.[12] Among the many statements taken following the arrival of the Bueso de Valdés expedition, those of Azcárate de Castillo and Esteban Fernández de Rivera indicated other possible reasons for revolt, of a more specific kind. In their testimonies, Azcárate and Fernández both claimed that in the days following the rebellion the Indian Quirubira admitted to having killed Domingo de Veitia because he had threatened that the Indian *capitanes* of the province were themselves to be put to death. According to Azcárate, Quirubira also stated that another Spanish victim of Citará violence, Martín de Ardanza, was responsible for killing an Indian and wounding another.[13]

The statements of the Indians Miguel Baquera and Nicolás Yapeda, however, suggest that the uprising had less to do with specific incidents of abuse than it did with a more general and premeditated decision on the part of a small group of prominent *capitanes* to rid the region of outsiders. Giving evidence to Bueso de Valdés, Miguel Baquera related that days before rebellion broke out, Capitán Chevi and Don Fernando de Tajina travelled to San Juan de Negua for discussions with Don Pedro de Bolivar, Juan Chigri and Cecego. During their meeting, Tajina reportedly told Bolivar that he, Capitán Chuagra, Capitán Aucavira and Chaguera had all reached the decision that it was necessary to kill the Spaniards, and reminded him that Bolivar, too, had come to that same conclusion a few months before. According to the Indian Nicolás Yapeda (who, having been brought up among Spaniards, tried to warn them of the rebellion), a similar sequence of events took place in San Francisco de Atrato. He stated that Capitán Chuagra, Biva and Capitán Aucavira all travelled to San Francisco to invite the Indians who lived along the river bank to join the uprising, 'to kill the Spaniards'.[14] It is also entirely possible that rebellion was religiously motivated, for there were clear elements of anti-Catholicism in the actions of the rebels. In addition to the desecration of chapels, at least three Franciscan missionaries met particularly gruesome deaths. Esteban de Aviles was burned to death; Joseph Flores was tied to a pole and subsequently dismembered; Dionisio Palomino was so badly beaten that he died from his injuries.[15]

By no means all Indians participated in the rebellion, however, for divisions emerged between *capitanes* even before the outbreak of violence. Indeed, it appears that the action may even have been timed to coincide with the absence from the province of certain individuals whose loyalty to the indigenous community could not be counted upon. According to Juan Joseph Azcárate, neither Don Pedro Tegue nor Capitán Pancha was present in Citará territory on 15 January.[16] Don Rodrigo Pivi claimed to have been away from the province, in Antioquia in fact, when violence broke out.[17] Thereafter, Tegue, Pancha and Pivi – as well as Capitán Certegui, Capitán Taichama and Don Juan Mitiguirre, among others – continued to collaborate with Spaniards inside and outside the Chocó. Between January and July 1684, when two parties finally arrived to rescue the survivors at Naurita mine, the Spaniards, mestizos, mulattos and slaves who had taken refuge there depended entirely on the assistance offered by Indian allies. Not only did they provide essential food supplies, but they also gave advice on the fortification of the camp, and, by carrying letters in and out of the Chocó, made possible communication with the cities of Antioquia and Anserma.[18] No explanations were given, however, to indicate why some Indians remained loyal to the Spaniards, while others led the largest and most organised challenge to Spanish colonialism ever to take place in Citará territory.

How, then, should we understand the rebellion of 1684? If we look back to Spanish–Indian relations in Citará in the years leading up to 1684, the rebellion appears as an unexpected and shocking rupture. For as we shall see, in the years before 1680, interactions between the two groups remained essentially peaceful, and in many instances even amicable. Left largely to their own devices following the Bueso de Valdés *entrada* – its effects on *reducción* and evangelisation having been only temporary – Indians showed no desire to bring to an end their association with Spaniards. Even in 1680, in the face of severe provocation on the part of powerful Spanish colonists, Indians sought means other than rebellion for obtaining redress of grievances and protecting native interests, and in so doing, demonstrated their growing ability to exploit political divisions among Spaniards to their own advantage. When, in that year, conflict developed between the indigenous population on the one hand, and the Franciscan missionaries, supported by an official recently appointed *teniente de gobernador* by the governor of Popayán, on the other, Indians made common cause with Spaniards within the Chocó to appeal to the authorities in Antioquia for the replacement of the individuals concerned rather than taking action that could threaten the relatively peaceful coexistence which had been achieved in Citará province over the previous two decades.[19] Despite severe tension, no harm came to any Spaniard in Citará territory as a result of Indian action in 1680. Indeed, in describing Indian appeals for aid against the missionaries, Governor Radillo de Arce, of Antioquia, commented that their endeavours to reach an amicable resolution of their grievances were 'to be commended'.[20] Likewise, until 1680, the authorities in Antioquia, always mindful that colonisation in this part of the New Kingdom depended on Indian tolerance, if not co-operation, made serious efforts to propitiate prominent *capitanes*, placate indigenous peoples, and prevent abuse. However, while some Spaniards sought to insinuate their control over the region by peaceful means, others were more impatient. Their behaviour, and Indian protests against it, provide a context for understanding the onset of violent rebellion in 1684.

Indian protest, 1680

The first indications of mounting tension came in September 1679, when a party of seven or eight Indians, including the *capitanes* Don Rodrigo Pivi, Don Juan Chigri and Don Simón Amata, appeared in Antioquia before the governor, Don Diego Radillo de Arce. Communicating with him through their own *ladino* interpreters, Pivi, Chigri and Amata stated that they had come to the city specifically to protest of ill-treatment at the hands of Fray Joseph de Córdoba and Fray Pablo Ruiz, and to request that Radillo intervene to ensure that the friars behave 'charitably' towards their Indian charges.[21] In early April 1680, a second small party from the Chocó arrived in Antioquia, consisting of two Indians from the settlement of Taita, Gregorio Bogassaga and Esteban Opin, and the Spaniards Antonio Quintana and Sebastián Velásquez. Claiming to represent the native inhabitants of the two 'sitios' of Taita and Guebara, Bogassaga and Opin informed the governor of the 'disquiet' which had arisen in those communities as a result of a recent attempt on the part of the Franciscans, assisted by *teniente de gobernador* Lope de Cárdenas, to transfer their small populations to a larger settlement on the Atrato river, close to the border between Citará and Tatama territories – a distance of four days' travel from the maize fields and plantain groves essential to their survival.[22] Supported in their claims by Velásquez and Quintana, the Indians also protested the methods adopted by the friars to achieve their ends. 'People from Popayán', armed with 'rifles', were sent to remove the population of Taita and Guebara by force. They had orders to confiscate Indian tools, to kill livestock and to destroy crops, in order that, 'deprived of shelter . . . they would be reduced to life in a settlement'. Bogassaga further complained about the behaviour of Joseph de Córdoba, of whom he said that 'he has . . . a stick' for punishing Indians.[23] Then, at the end of April, a third party from Citará province came before the governor, consisting of nine Indians including Don Rodrigo Pivi and Don Pedro de Bolivar, a *ladino* and an ally of the Spaniards since the 1660s. This group of Indians, too, appealed for the governor's protection against the Franciscans.

Indians made no threats against the personal safety of the friars in late 1679 or early 1680, nor did they make any demands that the governor could not meet. No request was made, for example, to the effect that Spaniards in general, or even missionaries in particular, withdraw from Citará territory. Prepared to negotiate on all issues, including evangelisation, Bogassaga and Opin stated that Taita possessed its own chapel, and merely asked that a new *doctrinero* be dispatched for their settlement, whom they committed themselves to support in exchange for an assurance that their people should not be resettled.[24] According to Diego Radillo, writing to *audiencia* president Don Francisco de la Concha, the Indians only desired that 'they be assigned ... doctrineros to teach them [Christian doctrine] ... without threats or violence, for in what we have seen of them here, they are Christians in name only'.[25] Even in August 1680 – a time when tension between Indians and Franciscans had escalated to dangerously high levels – Indians sent to Antioquia on behalf of Don Pedro Tegue and Don Rodrigo Pivi for discussions with the governor demanded only that Fray Joseph de Córdoba and his colleagues be replaced by other missionaries 'who will live in peace and quiet'.[26]

Initially, the Indians' appeal to the governor of Antioquia for protection came to nothing because, after Bueso de Valdés completed his *entrada* in 1677, that *gobernación* did not have an official presence in Citará province.[27] The absence of an official representing Antioquia's interests effectively meant that the governor's appeals for calm were directed at the *teniente* and the missionaries whose provocative behaviour lay at the heart of Indian discontent. Hamstrung by the fact that the *audiencia* of Santa Fe had overall control of the Chocó region, the governor stated that he could do no more than report the matter to its president, and, claiming jurisdiction over the entire Citará area, require Lope de Cárdenas and all other representatives of Popayán to refrain from relocating Indians to new settlements until such time as Santa Fe sent further instructions. Significantly, he also requested the missionaries and the official concerned to endeavour to safeguard the peace and tranquillity in which 'said Indians ... have been constant for more than ten years'. Lope de Cárdenas was also instructed to return all confiscated tools and other property, and to pay the Indian communities the full value of the slaughtered livestock.[28]

The *teniente de gobernador* refused to comply with instructions, on the grounds that he could not accept Radillo's authority in the province. Stating, quite inaccurately, that the reduction of its peoples had been achieved through the efforts of the *gobernación* of Popayán alone, Cárdenas argued that it was Popayán's governor, rather than Antioquia's, who held jurisdiction over Citará. But in seeking to justify his actions before Radillo de Arce, Cárdenas provided confirmation that the protests of the Indians of Taita and Guebara were well-founded. First, Cárdenas claimed that he had 'done them no wrong', and denied the Indians' 'sinister' allegations of coercion and ill-treatment. But he then went on to admit that he had tried to move the population of Taita and three or four other 'sitios' nearby. Since none of these consisted of more than one or two households, they did not constitute proper settlements. Furthermore, 'these Indians who inhabit them devote themselves solely to killing as I know they did to a mulato slave of Captain Ignacio de Guzmán, who was on his way to Antioquia, in order to take his gold'.[29] The Franciscans also defended their position and denied all allegations made against them. But their response to the governor of Antioquia's entreaties, like that of Lope de Cárdenas, indicates that Indian discontent was widespread in Citará province in 1680, and that Indian anger had been aroused by the missionaries' conduct. Thus, Fray Cristóbal de Artiaga informed Radillo de Arce that the accusations made against the religious were 'sinister' and 'false', but blithely acknowledged that they had tried to 'correct' Indians for remaining in their retreats and 'failing to attend [Christian] Doctrine'. The governor was mistaken, he added, in his belief that the Indians had been at peace with the Spanish for many years: 'although said governor considers the Indians to be the meekest [of people] I have learned that it would be easier to tame the wildest of beasts'. Such obstinacy, Artiaga went on to argue, resulted not only from the Indians' ill-feeling towards the Franciscan clergy, but also, significantly, from their frequent 'visits to this city [Antioquia]'.[30]

An incident involving the same Fray Cristóbal also suggests that the Franciscans' frustration at the Indians' continuing resistance to their evangelisation efforts had almost certainly led them, by 1680, to resort to corporal punishment to achieve the aims of their mission. The incident occurred in Negua, when a few Indians were occupied in putting a roof on the Indian Batassa's house. According to Fray Cristóbal's account, the confrontation began when he called the Indians to Mass, but they ignored him and continued working on the roof. 'Irritated' by the situation, Fray Cristóbal lightly struck Batassa on the leg 'with a small stick', to which his son Garaupá, behaving 'like a wild beast' and helped by fellow Indians, reacted by throwing the friar on the ground and beating him. Had other Spaniards not come to his aid, Artiaga asserted, he should have died at the hands of 'those barbarians'.[31] The only punishment inflicted on the perpetrators of this act of violence against the friar, Lope de Cárdenas further informed Radillo, was 'to place each of them in irons for . . . an hour'.[32] The Indians' story is a different one. Gregorio Bogassaga, questioned about the affair in Antioquia, confirmed that the incident took place when the Indian Batassa, his son Garaupá, and several other Indians were occupied in building a roof for the former's house in Negua. Just as they were completing the job, Fray Cristóbal de Artiaga arrived, accompanied by 'many Spanish men', whereupon he ordered the Indians to Mass. To this Batassa responded that they would go in a moment as they had almost finished their task. For this reply, Bogassaga related, 'the said father beat him with a stick he carried'. When Batassa's son Garaupá protested, 'one of the Spanish men . . . beat Garaupá and [then] apprehended him and his father and kept them imprisoned'.[33] The differing accounts of the incident – Fray Cristóbal claimed that he was assaulted; Bogassaga claimed that no harm was done to the missionary and that it was the Indian Garaupá who was assaulted – make it impossible for us to determine exactly what occurred on this occasion. But it is to be noted that in his account of the incident, Lope de Cárdenas attributed the defiance of Batassa and his son to the fact that Don Rodrigo Pivi was at that time travelling to Antioquia to complain to the governor: 'it was Don Rodrigo Pivi, cacique, who was responsible for the Indians' insolence, for he gave orders that whilst he was absent . . . [from the Chocó] . . . they should neither attend . . . Mass nor prayers'.[34]

This dispute between Indians on one side and the missionaries and Lope de Cárdenas on the other had, by April 1680, escalated into a conflict that involved not just the authorities in Antioquia, but also Spanish settlers in the Chocó. We have few details to indicate who the friars' Spanish supporters were, but as we have seen, in his account of the confrontation between Artiaga and Garaupá, Bogassaga claimed that Fray Cristóbal was accompanied by 'many Spanish men'. And although the identity of the friars' allies is not recorded, the indications are that, in 1680, missionaries could count on the support and assistance of some colonists in the region. In justifying his actions to Radillo de Arce, for example, Cristóbal de Artiaga stated that the governor should 'seek the advice of Christian persons . . . in said province and you will discover that they [the Indians] have repeatedly taken up arms to kill others who live here [as well]'.[35] Because Antioquia is the source of the bulk of the documents, we know far more about the Spaniards who opposed the Franciscans, and about their identity. We know, for example, that between April and August 1680, at least 20 colonists, all of whom were engaged in mining in the Chocó, wrote letters, signed petitions, or travelled to Antioquia in person to report the 'apprehension and mistrust' provoked by the friars' methods, to request the dispatch of new missionaries who would limit themselves to instructing Indians in Christian doctrine, and to warn the governor of the possible consequences of official inaction.[36] Some, such as Antonio Quintana and Sebastián Velásquez, employed by *vecinos* of Antioquia to prospect for mineral deposits in Citará territory, were sufficiently fearful of Córdoba – of whom they reported 'the violence of his actions' – to abandon their activities in the Chocó. Others, such as Francisco de Borja, warned that unless *teniente* Lope de Cárdenas was replaced, all Spaniards would leave the region. Over a five-month period in 1680, in other words, a substantial group of Spanish settlers in the Chocó feared their fellow colonists more than they did the Indians.

The conflict that ensued in 1680, therefore, did not simply pit Indians against Spaniards in general. It was a more complicated dispute which set Indians and their Spanish allies against the friars, the *teniente* Cárdenas, and their Spanish supporters, whom the Citará generally described as 'people from Popayán', or, less frequently, as 'people from Popayán and Anserma'. Don Antonio de Legarda, for example, reportedly stated that the Citará were not prepared to allow Spaniards from either Popayán or Anserma in their territory, and that these should limit their activities to Noanama province.[37] The distinction the Indians made between Popayán and Anserma on the one hand, and Antioquia on the other, was probably not quite as clear-cut as the governor's reports suggest, for many of the Indians' allies, such as Jacinto Roque de Espinosa and Diego Díaz de Castro, were *vecinos* of Anserma, and Cristóbal de Viñola came from Mariquita.[38] On the whole, however, the groups involved in conflict in 1680 did divide along these lines. That this was the case may have had something to do with the respective records of the *gobernaciones* in the Chocó over the previous decade. Or it may have been the result of the fact that by 1680–81, the Franciscan missionaries, frustrated by years of failed efforts to convert native peoples, directed their requests for assistance to the authorities in Popayán rather than Antioquia. Lope de Cárdenas, for example, a Popayán appointee, was described in 1680 as 'on good terms with said doctrineros'.[39] When conflict turned into confrontation in the summer of that year, moreover, it was to

Popayán that Fray Joseph de Córdoba turned for military assistance, and it was from Noanama province, over which that *gobernación* held jurisdiction, that a force of 30 armed men and 30 Indians under the command of *teniente* Arce Camargo came to their aid.

It is also clear, however, that Indians, by now fully aware of the competition between the *gobernaciones* for control of the Chocó, understood that they could manipulate rivalries between Spanish groups to protect native interests. Certainly, Indians repeatedly indicated that their wish was to be administered by *tenientes* representing Antioquia, rather than Popayán. When Don Juan Mitiguirre appeared before Governor Radillo de Arce in October 1680, he requested not only a new *doctrinero* for the settlement of Negua and an assurance that henceforth missionaries would be forbidden to carry arms and to keep dogs, but also a new *teniente* appointed by Radillo de Arce himself.[40] Indians also sought to use Antioquia's interests in the Chocó as a lever to bring about the removal of individuals unacceptable to native peoples. For example, when Esteban Opin and Gregorio Bogassaga appealed to the governor in April 1680, they warned that if he did not protect the Indians of Taita and Guebara from the Franciscans, the communities would retreat into the *monte*, or backland. And even if they were unable to flee, and were forced to resettle against their will, Spaniards from Antioquia would in any case be deprived of material support from their native allies.[41] In October, Don Juan Mitiguirre issued a similar warning. Unless Indian demands were met, they would abandon Citará territory and retreat beyond Spanish reach to the lands of the Soruco, 'because they have made their peace with the said nation'.[42]

Whatever the motives underlying the distinction made by the Citará between Spanish groups inside and outside the Chocó, it is clear that Indians received the more sympathetic hearing in Antioquia, and that Cárdenas and the friars believed that Indian defiance was entirely attributable to the encouragement they received from that quarter. In responding to Radillo de Arce's entreaties on the matter of Indian ill-treatment, for example, Fray Cristóbal de Artiaga protested that the priests 'are reviled . . . because of the encouragement . . . the Indians receive in . . . Antioquia'.[43] Radillo de Arce's reports on the conflict indicate that such suspicions were not misplaced. For as he informed *audiencia* president Don Francisco Castillo de la Concha, 'I endeavoured to indulge . . . said Indians as I have done each time they have come . . . because of the inclination which I have recognised they feel towards this province and its people'.[44]

The more important feature of the events of 1680, however, is that, despite complaints and warnings, at no point did the indigenous population of Citará province show any sign that they wished to sever links with Spaniards, nor did they take any action to threaten the fragile coexistence that had been established between them. Certainly, by May 1680 Radillo de Arce's reluctance to do more than inform the *audiencia* of the situation, and require missionaries and *teniente* to avoid confrontation, had led to an escalation of tension, provoking fear among all colonists for their own safety. Cristóbal de Viñola, for example, reported that he had seen '15 canoes transporting 218 Indians with 18 capitanes', and that many 'war canoes' were preparing to confront Cárdenas and put an end to his bad government.⁴⁵ But no violence broke out at that stage. Even when matters came to a head in late June – by which time Cárdenas's 'extortions' were said to have brought 'altercations' to new levels – it was a group of Spaniards, rather than Indians, who made the first moves against the *teniente*. For when Lope de Cárdenas attempted, according to the settlers, to 'garrotte an Indian' without cause, the Spaniards prevented this action by depriving him of his staff of office, as much a weapon as a symbol of his authority, because 'this was what was demanded by the said Indians whose savagery and resolution they feared'.⁴⁶ Thereafter, they further reported, the Indians returned to 'peace and friendship with the Spaniards'.⁴⁷ *Teniente* Arce Camargo, of Noanama province, confirmed that Spaniards, not Indians, made the first move against the *teniente*. It was Diego Díaz de Castro, Sebastián García, Nicolás de Murcia and Cristóbal de Viñola who first 'pointed their loaded rifles', took Cárdenas' title and staff of office, and announced that his authority should no longer be recognised.⁴⁸ Similarly, when the Franciscan Joseph de Córdoba left the region for Popayán, ostensibly to seek help against Cárdenas's enemies, it was once again the Spaniards who took it upon themselves to persuade the friar not to return. According to the testimony of nine settlers, this was in response to a threat made by several *capitanes*, including Rodrigo Pivi and Pedro de Bolivar, that the friar would be killed if he returned – a threat that had to be taken seriously, they said, since few Indians were unarmed, their resolution was plain, and Pivi's people had been seen 'ready for war'.⁴⁹ This action, too, according to Salvador Vidal, had the effect of calming Indian unrest.⁵⁰

The developments that took place following the affray over the staff of office further show that this became as much a conflict among Spaniards as one between Indians and missionaries. For when, at the end of August, missionaries and *teniente* all returned to Negua, accompanied by Noanama's *teniente* Arce Camargo and an armed force 30 strong, Lope de Cárdenas charged the settlers with treason and acted ruthlessly against those most directly involved. Díaz de Castro was the first to suffer the consequences of allying with Indians against the Spanish official. In sentencing him to death, Cárdenas ordered that 'after he has been garrotted . . . he shall be quartered and [each quarter] shall be hung on the accustomed paths and his head shall be placed . . . in this town of San Sebastián de Negua for his own punishment and as an example to others'.⁵¹ Although a handful of Diego Díaz's co-conspirators succeeded in fleeing the region – Jacinto Roque and Francisco González left for Antioquia; Sebastián García and Nicolás de Murcia retreated 'to the protection of the Indians of Guebara' – many more paid a heavy price for co-operating with Indians. Juan Nuño de Sotomayor and Alonso de Baca were imprisoned and placed in irons. Others were first imprisoned and then exiled from the region. The silversmith Joseph Enrique was obliged to remain in Negua as Joseph de Córdoba's servant. All suffered sequestration of property. Diego Díaz de Castro's property and personal effects – clothing, a bed, two slaves – were taken and auctioned to the highest bidder, the proceeds used to pay Arce Camargo's men. Don Alonso de Baca lost 100 pesos and 'eight jars of wine from Peru'. Francisco González lost his clothing; Francisco Onofre, his clothing and his bed; Manuel Quintero Príncipe lost his clothes and 150 gold pesos. Mining operations were also taken over. According to Juan Nuño de Sotomayor, Lope de Cárdenas 'appropriated . . . Captain Juan de Guzmán's mine which he operates in partnership with Jacinto Roque and they appointed an administrator for the slaves'. Córdoba was alleged to have appropriated for himself the gold mined from this operation.[52] Even after implementing harsh penalties on all Spaniards who aided Indians in this dispute, Lope de Cárdenas did not abandon his efforts to seek revenge on the men directly involved in the confrontation over the staff of office. In November, Sebastián García and Nicolás de Murcia were found, charged with treason, and summarily executed.[53]

Spanish settlers, then, paid a high price for their alliance with Indians in the late summer of 1680. But several factors probably contributed to their decision to support the Citará against their fellow colonists. One was undoubtedly fear that inaction might provoke the wrath of the peoples among whom they lived and by whom they were vastly outnumbered. Another was perhaps the knowledge that during this transitional stage of colonisation in the Chocó, they all had to rely on Indian assistance to continue mining and prospecting in the region. Indians not only served as guides, but also built and manned canoes, and sold the foodstuffs on which Spaniards and slaves depended for their subsistence. We know, for example, that Jacinto Roque de Espinosa, whose mining operations were based around Negua, obtained maize supplies from Indians in Guebara.[54] Spanish–Indian collaboration on the question of the *teniente* may also have derived, however, from the fact that Lope de Cárdenas, who was the sole official representative of two *gobernaciones* in a region isolated from the centres of authority elsewhere in New Granada, acted with almost complete impunity against settlers as often as against Indians. Early on in the conflict, Don Francisco de Borja, a miner with several years' residence in the Chocó, warned Governor Radillo de Arce that unless action was taken against this official, who proceeded as unjustly against Spaniards as against Indians, neither he 'nor the other Spaniards who live here will remain'.[55]

These considerations, combined with the ruthlessness and recklessness with which Cárdenas proceeded against the colonists following his return to Citará, ensured that the alliance between Indians and Spaniards held fast despite severe tension. Indeed, even after the arrival of Arce Camargo and his men, who detained Don Pedro de Bolivar and appropriated Indian crops and livestock for their own use, the new wave of Indian unrest that such actions provoked was limited to the burning down of the settlements of San Francisco de Atrato and Lloró, and the blockading of the trails linking the Chocó to Popayán and Anserma.[56] Attacks against settlements and the closure of trails into the Chocó did take place, but these were not followed by instances of violence on the part of Indians against Spaniards. Instead, it was reported that Indians tried to protect their allies from Cárdenas and Arce Camargo. When Cristóbal de Viñola arrived in Negua, carrying instructions from the governor to the *teniente* and the missionaries, Indians in that settlement took up arms to protect him from Cárdenas, believing that otherwise he would be killed.[57] And when Francisco Onofre reported to Radillo on the situation in September 1680, he stated that Don Rodrigo Pivi remained in Negua to watch over Lope de Cárdenas's Spanish prisoners, 'so that if they did any harm to the Spaniards, to rescue them'.[58] Finally, when in October 1680, Bueso de Valdés, conducting a new *entrada* on orders of Radillo de Arce, requested a force of fifty men to protect him – from Cárdenas and his allies rather than from Indians – treasury officials in Antioquia replied that no such force would be needed, 'due to the assistance offered by the . . . natives of the said province'.[59]

The reasons for the Citará's continuing efforts to maintain their links with the Spanish during this period of severe tension are difficult to explain, for it is unlikely that the governor of Antioquia's conciliatory approach alone can account for Indian restraint. Indeed, as we have seen, Radillo de Arce at first did little more than send letters to the official and friars concerned, 'in which they are entrusted with the protection and calm of those natives and other people who reside there and the avoidance of the inevitable incident which is feared'.[60] It was not until October 1680, when the prospect became evident that the province would be deserted and that all that had been accomplished in terms of the pacification of its native population would be lost, that the governor sent Bueso de Valdés to the Chocó with instructions to remove the friars Córdoba and Ruiz to Santa Fe, to discipline Lope de Cárdenas and ensure that he compensate Indians for all the material damage suffered, and, more generally, to investigate and report on recent events.

It is probable, however, that the Indians were slow to rebel because they, or at least their *capitanes*, considered that sustaining satisfactory relations with Spanish settlers continued to be of advantage to native people. After all, as Bueso de Valdés commented later, they had received good treatment from Spaniards, obtained a variety of European products each time they travelled to the cities of the interior, and had also been honoured by the *audiencia*, the governors of Antioquia and even Popayán 'with titles of governors of their towns'.[61] Their readiness to enter into partnership with Spaniards is perhaps further signalled by the significant number of Indians who, by 1680, had adopted Spanish names and were addressed by the Spanish title of 'Don': Don Rodrigo Pivi, Don Juan Mitiguirre, Don Antonio Legarda and Don Simón Amata, among many others.

Whatever the motives underlying Indian attitudes, what is clear is that at least in 1680–81, co-operation and conciliation was the preferred option both for the Citará and for the authorities in Antioquia. Thus, when Bueso de Valdés finally arrived in the Chocó in November 1680, to discover that *teniente* Cárdenas had carried out two more executions (of Sebastián García and Nicolás de Murcia), he went further than instructed by Antioquia's governor. Not only did he order the arrest of the friars Córdoba, Moreno and Ruiz – they were to be sent to Santa Fe to appear before their Father Provincial – but also that of Lope de Cárdenas, who was to be placed under guard in Negua, from where he, too, was to be sent to Santa Fe.[62] Arce Camargo was also detained.[63] No further details were given about the reasons behind the conflict that broke out that year. However, in his report to the governor, Bueso de Valdés said of Lope de Cárdenas that 'it is difficult to explain the violence and harm he had done . . . and the clamourings of Indians and Spaniards'. As for the Franciscans, the new *comisario* Esteban Alvarez – heading a fresh team of four friars – merely reported that little progress had been made in converting the population, for Indians were unable even 'to cross themselves'.[64] Only the Indian Don Antonio de Legarda, giving evidence to Radillo de Arce, added to these general statements: 'the children do not know how to pray', he said, 'because the priests were occupied in collecting money for the clothing they sold'.[65]

The events of 1680 show, then, that the tensions caused by Spanish incursions could be resolved peacefully, thanks largely to the readiness of the Citará to use negotiation as a means of resolving a conflict that threatened to disrupt the peaceful coexistence that had been achieved between Indians and Spaniards in the province. Secondly, they show that in Antioquia at least, Spanish authorities were equally prepared to conciliate native peoples and to meet the conditions upon which their continuing co-operation depended – even when those conditions included the expulsion of a *teniente de gobernador* and the replacement of the entire membership of a Franciscan mission – in order to protect the advances that had been made in the pacification of a region rich in mineral resources. The reasons for Antioquia's decision to take prompt measures are, of course, self-evident. And in the short term at least, these were effective, for as Bueso de Valdés reported, Indians returned to their settlements as soon as Lope de Cárdenas was removed: 'the Indians with their families and the Spaniards have come out from the hills'.[66] In the longer term, however, Spanish colonisation in the Chocó was not to be based on compromise between Indians and Spaniards. As the confidence of the Spanish grew, their presence in the Chocó increased as well. By 1684, when rebellion broke out, Spanish miners, traders, slaves, servants and women had all made that presence felt, and the balance between Indians and Europeans had shifted decisively in favour of the latter.

Indian rebellion, 1684

Notwithstanding Governor Radillo de Arce's efforts, in 1680–81, to placate the Indians of Citará province, rebellion broke out just three years later. This time, however, the nature of the conflict was quite different. No warnings were given. No co-operation between Indians and Spaniards preceded the outbreak of violence. No distinction was made between acceptable and unacceptable Europeans. On the night of 15 January 1684, when the rebellion began, the Indians of Negua surrounded the houses of all colonists living in the settlement, killing them and the Franciscan *comisario*.[67] Spanish missionaries and settlers were also killed in Lloró and San Francisco de Atrato. The rebellion spread outside the main settlements as well. The accounts of the survivors, and the statements taken from Indians after capture, show that Spaniards were killed over a wide area.[68] The survivors listed 59 Spanish victims, but there were others, too: twelve slaves belonging to the Bueso de Valdés–Domingo de Veitia partnership; many Indian servants and 'pages'; Indian carriers from the interior; black slaves, mulatto slaves, female slaves, one child; others simply described as 'lads'. Apart from a handful of women, taken by prominent *capitanes*, only six Spaniards, and some 70 servants and slaves, escaped with their lives. They had been warned that the uprising had occurred and were able to take refuge in the mine of Naurita before they were reached by the rebels.[69] Even there, however, they were vulnerable to attack. According to Bueso de Valdés, writing in July 1684, 'the enemy ... has killed two men of the 80 who were here, as they went out to search for the palms on which they are surviving'.[70]

This was not, then, a spontaneous act of violence on the part of a few individuals, but a well-planned uprising that counted on widespread support and was timed to break out simultaneously in all the major settlements of the region, showing a degree of organisation that was, perhaps, only possible now that indigenous peoples came into more frequent contact in the centralised villages established by the Spanish.[71] Prominent Indian *capitanes* were responsible for planning the rebellion, organising their followers, and leading the assault on 15 January. Quirubira, Tajina, Manzano, Dechegama, Tavachi, Chuagra, Chuaru, Chevi, Aucavira, Gongera, Miarri, Devanado, Parimendo, Tevasa, Pidigara, Minguirri and Legarda are all mentioned in the statements made by Indians captured in the late summer and autumn of 1684 as playing key roles in the events of that day.[72] Even more significantly, Don Pedro de Bolivar, an ally of the Spaniards for many years, and Don Juan Chigri, 'one of the indios principales of this province' and an ally of such trustworthiness that he was appointed 'governor' of Citará by the president of the *audiencia*, both participated in the planning and execution of the rebellion.[73] Some of the rebel *capitanes* led the assault on Europeans in the settlements; others had responsibility for simultaneously eliminating Spaniards in outlying areas. Mateo, a mulatto slave belonging to Domingo de Veitia, a miner who was killed in the uprising, described how, when rebellion broke out on 15 January, the slave gang of which he formed part was working at the mine of Ingipurdú, where the Carrasco brothers were also present.[74] Four *capitanes* arrived, accompanied by a large Indian force, and proceeded to kill the Carrascos and twelve of their slaves, and to take others captive, including Mateo himself.[75]

This is not to say, however, that the rebellion enjoyed the support of the entire population of Citará province, or that all or even most Indians participated in the violence. In fact, a clear division emerged between those *capitanes* determined to recover Citará for its indigenous population and those keen to protect and strengthen their association with Europeans; as the evidence clearly shows, all moved to mobilise their peoples behind one cause or the other. The number of *capitanes* who threw their lot in with the European colonists was relatively small compared with the size of the rebel group, but they were, nevertheless, crucial both to the survivors and to the pacification campaign that followed. Don Rodrigo Pivi, perhaps the most important of all the Spaniards' allies, Don Juan Mitiguirre, Don Pedro Tegue and Capitán Taichama all carried letters to and from the mining camp of Naurita, the cities of Antioquia and Anserma, and Noanama province. Capitán Pancha supplied the survivors with food, and even returned to them some of the slaves taken captive by the rebels. Furthermore, Bueso de Valdés and the members of his expedition relied heavily on the assistance of their Citará allies once in Chocó territory. Don Rodrigo Pivi, once again, provided the canoes and the manpower that enabled Bueso to traverse the region in search of rebels.[76] He also accompanied the expedition on *correrías* directed against Indians in the Murri river region and, together with Don Juan Mitiguirre, provided Spanish expeditionary forces with detailed information regarding the whereabouts of many 'delinquents' and 'fugitives'. Both turned in at least two of their own people to the Spanish.[77] Pivi was also prominent in reducing Indians back to their settlements after capture.[78] Other *capitanes* also aided the pacification campaign. When, in early 1685, Bartolomé de Borja wrote to Bueso de Valdés to report the discovery of an Indian hide-out in Tatama province and to request the assistance of 24 Indians and two *capitanes* – the former to act as carriers and to man six canoes – Don Francisco Pancha and Capitán Certegui were selected to take charge of the Indians placed at his disposal.[79]

Many more Indians, however, participated actively in the violence, scouring settlements and mining camps for Spaniards to kill and property to take. The Indian Guaguirri, for instance, claimed that he was on the Bebará river when the rebellion broke out, and that he received orders from Quirubira, through Ubira, to kill all Spaniards settled along the Bebará. As the Indians of Guaguirri's community knew exactly who the outsiders were and where they could be found, they did the job in stages. First, they went to the house of one Francisco de la Carrera, where they found him and his servant Antonio. Then they went to a mine in search of two others, named as Bernardo and Bejarano. Finally they went to a ravine known by the name of Tabusido, where they discovered Juan de Guzmán and several of his companions. All were killed. Similarly, the Indian Noquia gave evidence that he was on the Andagueda river when Guagone arrived with news that the Spaniards were being killed. The Indian Masupi, he said, told him that if any Spaniards were nearby, each was to kill one. Noquia and a group of companions went after three people they knew to be in the vicinity – a mulatto, a mestizo and a mestiza. The two men were killed; the woman was captured. The Indian Juananui stated that he had been told by Yvagone that the uprising was taking place, and that he and his companions were to deal with the Spaniards who were due to arrive from Anserma. Juananui and a few others went to Dodubar, where the Spaniards were expected. All were killed, including four Indian carriers.[80]

News of the rebellion, then, spread rapidly and covertly. As Indians who lived along the banks of the many rivers that cut through the region heard of events in Negua and the other settlements, they quickly joined the uprising. Using machetes, axes, darts, and in some cases just their hands, they went in search of all outsiders scattered across Indian territory. Guaripua, for example, killed Francisco de la Carrera with an axe and Juan de Guzmán's son with a dart. Chaqueranvido killed an Indian by drowning. Soberano beat two black slaves to death.[81]

Widespread participation, combined with the covert nature of the entire operation, ensured the speedy elimination of well over one hundred people within a short time after the outbreak of violence. One group of Spaniards alone heard of the uprising in sufficient time to escape. There were no reports of casualties among the rebel group.

The uprising not only provided the opportunity to eliminate the Spanish, their servants and retainers, but also to take their property and personal effects. Indians captured slaves, mainly females, took church ornaments and the belongings of the victims. Ygaragaida gave testimony, for instance, that the Indian Dami took the Franciscan *comisario*'s cook and that Ybicua took a slave belonging to Captain Domingo de Veitia. Capitán Tajina gave testimony that four female slaves were taken from Domingo de Veitia's mining operation. The Indian Biramia claimed that his uncle, Umia, took a female slave from the mine of Yngipurdú. Ygaragaida stated that Don Juan Chigri took Fray Esteban's 'jewels' and ornaments, and that Pidigara took the chalice from the chapel in Negua. Ygaragaida was himself found to be in possession of a paten, clothing and salt when he was captured. Guaguirri stated that four Indians, including himself, divided between them the clothing and 'jewels' that they found in Francisco de la Carrera's house: he was still in possession of his share when he was captured. Noquia gave evidence that the Indian Natucama took a chest, while he and his father Pichorre took some articles of clothing. Guaripua, who admitted responsibility for the death of Francisco de la Carrera, informed Bueso de Valdés that he and the Indians who accompanied him divided among themselves the gold they found there. Guaripua's share amounted to 20 pesos, which he later used to buy axes.[82] And when Minguirri's family was captured in September 1684, they were found to be in possession of 16 axes, machetes, a relic on a chain, three pesos in gold dust, and old clothing, among other things.[83]

Many Indians who insisted that they had played no part in the massacres admitted that they took advantage of the opportunity afforded by the outbreak of violence to scour the area in search of Spanish goods to appropriate for themselves. Manigua, for example, stated that when the violence broke out he went to Negua to 'pick up utensils'. Umia said that he was at home on the Samugrado river when Meachama brought him news of the rebellion, and asked him to accompany him to the mine of Ingipurdú, for maybe 'they might get some effects'.[84] Ygaragaida gave evidence that although he had not taken up arms against the Spanish, he did go to Negua, 'as he saw that the Spaniards were to be killed and that they had a lot of salt which he came to take ... to eat'.[85] Anything that could be carried away was taken by the Indians. When, in August 1684, Bueso de Valdés' men captured a number of Indian canoes hidden along the Murri river, they recovered church ornaments, bedclothes, hammers, machetes, axes, steel and salt.[86]

Whether this was expediency on the part of Indians caught up in the violence, or a crucial explanation for the outbreak of rebellion, is impossible to ascertain on the basis of existing sources, since few attempts were made in the aftermath of the events of 15 January to determine the causes of rebellion. And when the

Spaniards sought to explain the Indians' widespread interest in taking, rather than destroying, the personal effects of Spaniards, their 'greed' and attraction to 'anything novel' were most often alluded to. When Diego de Galvis, appointed *defensor* by Bueso de Valdés, prepared his defence on behalf of the Indians Noquia and Manigua, for instance, he cited the 'covetousness' that characterised the peoples of Citará, which drove them eagerly to seek any means to acquire goods that 'smacked of novelty'.[87] There was nothing unusual in this assessment, as Galvis's language was in keeping with Spanish attitudes towards the character of native peoples across the Chocó. In August 1685, for example, one Alejo de la Cruz y Valencia, writing to Cristóbal de Caicedo, said of the Noanama who assisted the Spanish in quelling the rebellion that 'from the experience I have of the Noanamas, [I can say that] they are consummate thieves'.[88] At no point was any attempt made to draw parallels between this feature of the rebellion and the years of relative peace that Indians and Spaniards had enjoyed in Citará, which owed much to the native peoples' interest in obtaining items of European manufacture. The loyalty of many Indians who continued to collaborate with the Spanish throughout 1684 was probably also based largely on their desire to continue to benefit from the sale of goods and services to Europeans. Capitán Pancha – who was described as a friend to the Spaniards as early as 1674 – expected payment for all foodstuffs supplied and for all services rendered. In the words of Francisco Onofre, he 'never gave anything for nothing'. Indeed, Pancha was paid nine gold pesos for returning to the mining camp of Naurita an Indian woman servant and three female slaves who had belonged to Domingo de Veitia. Others apparently did the same. According to Fernández de Rivera, almost all Indians – the sole exception was Rodrigo Pivi – were paid for services rendered: 'they were always paid', as he put it.[89]

This, then, is one possible explanation for the factionalism that arose within the indigenous community over the most concerted challenge against Spanish colonialism ever to take place in the Chocó. It seems highly probable that commercial considerations – the opportunity to profit from exchange of goods and services with Europeans – had become a matter of priority to a substantial proportion of Citará *capitanes*. For others, trade and gain appear to have been far less crucial considerations, however. Don Rodrigo Pivi, in particular, showed no inclination to profit materially from the situation in which the survivors found themselves during the first half of 1684. All insisted that Pivi had provided a variety of vital services, including supplying essential foodstuffs, free of charge.[90] Pivi's motives are difficult to understand, not least because, in 1680, he had been directly involved in the conflict with the *teniente* Cárdenas and the friar Córdoba. It had been Pivi's followers who were said to be 'ready for war', and it was Pivi himself who threatened to kill Fray Joseph should he return to Negua.[91] And his decision, in 1684, to collaborate with Europeans was made at a price. Following the events of January, the rebel Quirubira declared Rodrigo Pivi – as well as Mitiguirre, Pancha and Tegue – to be an enemy to his people. Thereafter, attempts were made on his life, his wife was abducted, and his property was taken by rebels.[92] Why Pivi opted to support the Spanish against his own people remains unclear. It is to be noted, however, that he was later made hereditary cacique in recognition of his role in assisting the pacification process.[93]

While the sources suggest that the benefits of continued association with the Spanish weighed heavily on the minds of their Indian allies, too little was said during the investigation that followed the rebellion to indicate the factors that led others – including many of the Spaniards' most trusted erstwhile supporters – to seek to wipe out completely all traces of European colonisation. The Spaniards themselves gave no credence to the notion that the events of January 1684 were provoked by specific incidents of abuse. Juan de Azcárate, in discussing Quirubira's assertion that the uprising was precipitated by Martín de Ardanza's killing of an Indian and wounding of another, commented that he considered such claims 'sinister'.[94] Nor did the Spanish believe that the violence was caused by Spanish demands, for as Bueso de Valdés observed on passing sentence on Capitán Tajina, 'they lived . . . without taxes or tributes'.[95] Rather than seeking other ways of establishing exactly why Indians rebelled against the colonists, Bueso de Valdés and Diego de Galvis both focused instead on Indian character and the values of indigenous society as the keys to explaining the event. While their conclusions cannot be considered to have identified credible motives for revolt, they do nevertheless provide us with a rare glimpse of some of the values that underpinned indigenous society and the way in which the Spanish interpreted those values.[96]

Bueso and Galvis, for instance, both drew attention to one important feature of Indian society: the native peoples, they repeatedly asserted, were inherently truthful. 'They are so truthful', the *defensor* remarked, 'that none denies committing a crime knowing from experience that they are to be killed'.[97] In seeking to understand this feature of native culture, Bueso and the *defensor* identified a further crucial characteristic: the importance of warfare in general and prowess in warfare in particular. Thus, Bueso de Valdés explained that the Indians are 'so truthful in this regard that none denies what he has done out of vanity and because they consider it an honour [to be found responsible] for the crimes they commit'.[98] For his part, Diego de Galvis, arguing in the Indians' defence, explained what he termed their 'propensity' to participate in any kind of warfare, for 'they spend all their lives in this exercise, killing and capturing [Indians] of different provinces and nations situated among these hills'. In his defence of Udrapagui, the *defensor* argued that he should not be held responsible for the death of a blacksmith, because 'he was driven only by the curiosity of seeing people killed, a result of this nation's natural inclination towards anything related to war'. And, in making a case for leniency for the Indian Soberano, he further noted that native peoples 'spend most of their lives [at war] in different provinces, and do not consider the deaths they carry out to be a crime'.[99]

Such attitudes were probably shaped by the evidence of Indians such as Don Fernando Tajina, who claimed to be a *capitán* because 'he has killed five Cunacunas and Burgumias', or Guaguirri, who described his occupation as 'cultivating maize to maintain his children and go to war'.[100] Prowess in war was a feature of native culture identified by Spaniards long before 1684. The Jesuit Antonio Marzal, in discussing the absence of figures of authority in Citará society, observed that 'if they have capitanes it is not because they are obeyed in anything but because they are considered to be brave . . . they go to war out of vanity of being considered brave . . . for he who kills the most is considered the most brave'.[101] Perhaps because war was a crucial element of male identity in native culture here, *capitanes* readily admitted to the deaths for which they were responsible.[102] Minguirri, for instance, confessed to killing Francisco de la Carrera's servant, Antonio. Many others, who were not *capitanes*, were equally prepared to admit their involvement in the deaths of Spaniards, their slaves and retainers. Guaripua confessed to killing Francisco de la Carrera, and one of Juan de Guzmán's slaves. Tajina admitted to killing two people in Negua – one Leandro, and Perucho, a servant of Juan de Azcárate. Guatupua admitted to being responsible for the death of an Indian boy who accompanied Manuel de Borja. Dare confessed to killing a mulatto boy, while Soberano claimed that he had personally killed two slaves. As for the motives of those who were not directly involved in the planning of rebellion, two possible explanations emerge. While Dare claimed that Aucavira and Chuagra threatened that 'unless he killed the Spaniards they would be angry', Chaqueranvido, responsible for the death of an Indian in Martín de Ardanza's service, merely stated that 'as he saw that the other Indians . . . were killing, he killed as well'.[103]

While it might be argued that the interrogations of Indians were manipulated to make possible speedy punishments and a quick return to order – the Indians' own statements were, after all, to serve as the basis for sentencing – the evidence strongly suggests that this was not the case. Bueso de Valdés, who by 1684 had mining interests of his own to protect in Citará, had no intention of pursuing a policy of harsh retribution against Indian peoples. Shortage of men and difficulties of supply in this isolated but extremely rich region of New Granada, combined with the continuing and very real danger of attack by Indians who still evaded capture (900, out of a total population of approximately 1500, in October 1684), led him to the conclusion that such a policy was bound to be counterproductive to Spanish interests.[104] Thus, while he was aware that it was necessary to avenge the deaths of 'innocent' Spaniards, he was equally conscious that only 'the [heads of] ringleaders and instigators' should roll, for should the Spanish execute 'delinquents and accomplices', few Indians would remain in Citará, and many innocent people, caught up in the violence out of curiosity alone, would be punished unjustly.[105] And, writing to Popayán's governor Gerónimo de Berrio, he further insisted that it was imperative that the Spanish acknowledge the impossibility of imposing too strict a regime on the peoples of the Chocó, for as he perceptively pointed out, 'there are no gates or fences here, the Indians [have] no property to hold them back, the territory [is] vast, and in taking [no more than] an axe to cut down palm trees, they have enough to feed themselves in the wild'.[106]

Nor was this simple expediency on Bueso de Valdés' part, for in advocating a policy of moderation – he also advocated rewarding those who had remained loyal to the Spanish – he came into direct conflict with Juan de Caicedo, commander of one of the two punitive expeditions sent from Popayán. This conflict was provoked by what Bueso considered the latter's failure properly to differentiate between Indians responsible for the January massacres, Indians who had merely been caught up in a rebellion not of their own making, and Indians who positively assisted the survivors and the pacification campaigns. In a furious letter to Caicedo, dated 8 October 1684, Bueso de Valdés accused him of deliberately deceiving Indians who were widely known to have aided the Spanish in order first to imprison them, and then to pillage. Indians who had erected a fort for his protection and provided his men with food supplies, he wrote, were all unjustly captured. Not even those who, at great risk to themselves, had remained faithful to the king were spared, their homes pillaged of even the least valuable tools and possessions, 'so that today they find themselves without [the tools] they need to cultivate their fields'.[107] This was later repeated in another letter, this time to Governor Berrio, together with a further accusation to the effect that Caicedo was known to have unjustly executed Indians whose involvement in the events of January 1684 was not proved, and to have deprived them, prior to their deaths, of the spiritual comfort of their priests.[108]

No such methods were implemented by the men of Antioquia, who made as much effort in the closing months of 1684 to identify the innocent as the guilty. Those against whom no proof could be found were to be returned to their settlements. Those found guilty of taking the effects of the victims, or assisting the rebels in a small but not necessarily crucial way, were to be flogged, and their belongings sequestrated. They were also condemned to ten years of personal service to the Spaniards. The death penalty was limited only to those who were widely known to have played (or openly confessed to having played) a direct part in the deaths of the Spaniards or their servants. Thus, Don Fernando Tajina, one of the first *capitanes* to rebel, was to be publicly hanged; his property was to be distributed to the soldiers as pillage; his children were to be condemned to ten years of personal service. The same sentence was passed on Guaguirri, 'for his own punishment and as an example to others', as well as Guaripua, Minguirri, and many more. Others, however, suffered harsh, but far more lenient, penalties. Ygaragaida, Biramia, Umia and Manigua, to mention a few, were sentenced to be flogged and to serve the Spanish.[109]

It seems, then, that the men of Antioquia, after decades of experience of close contact with the Citará, had learned that extreme measures, even following a rebellion of the magnitude of that which took place in January 1684, were prejudicial to Spanish interests in the region. Yet despite what seems to have been a more humane approach to the question of pacification – even Juan de Caicedo, whose intention was certainly not to flatter his rival, claimed that Indians considered Bueso a 'better master' and 'defender of the ... criminals'[110] – it was in the end Don Carlos de Alcedo Lemus de Sotomayor, representing the *gobernación* of Popayán, who took control of the final stages of the pacification campaign. Faced with continuing disputes between the two *gobernaciones*, represented by Don Cristóbal de Caicedo (Don Juan de Caicedo having been killed by Indians) and Juan Bueso de Valdés, the *audiencia* finally made the decision to endorse the jurisdictional claims of Popayán over those of Antioquia, and to appoint Alcedo as 'governor of the conquest'.[111] His strategy for bringing to justice Indians who continued to attack Spanish forces consisted of extending assurances that all rebels who surrendered would be exonerated. Clearly intended to break the unity of the rebels, this measure created divisions among those who still held out against the Spaniards. Many, such as the followers of the Indian Anugama, turned themselves in. Others, led by Capitán Aucavira, apparently retreated to the safety of Soruco territory. Capitán Chuagra's followers moved north towards Cuna territory, where they were reported to have been killed. Sesego and Tabugara and their men split off from the main group, led by Quirubira, to set up their own fortified camp to defend themselves from Spanish attack. Once the Indians divided and disbanded, however, the process of defeating each individual band was completed swiftly. By 31 August 1687, Quirubira and Sanjua had been killed, while four other unidentified *capitanes* who continued to resist the Spanish advance were defeated and killed soon after.[112]

The rebellion of 1684 and the subsequent pacification campaign marked a turning point in the history of the Chocó. The *audiencia*'s endorsement of the jurisdictional claims of Popayán meant that, henceforth, all three provinces of Noanama, Tatama and Citará were to be administered by *tenientes* appointed by the governor of Popayán. Don Rodrigo de Mañosca, who replaced Gerónimo de Berrio as governor, took responsibility for these new appointments, thus finally introducing a system for the administration of the region that would remain in place until an independent governor was appointed to the Chocó in 1726. No further attempts were made to compromise or conciliate the indigenous peoples of Citará province. Indeed, when it was discovered, in 1690, that a small group of Indians planned a new conspiracy to kill the Spanish, the governor's *teniente* in Citará, Don Antonio Ruiz Calzado, proceeded ruthlessly against the suspects, detaining 80 Indians and sentencing four to death.[113] It was at this time that indigenous people in Citará province adopted flight as the most effective method of resistance to Spanish colonialism.

The pacification marked an important turning point in one other sense as well. From 1690, slave-owners from the province of Popayán became increasingly involved in mining activities in the region. In that year, for example, four of Popayán's largest slave-owners transferred slave gangs and administrators to the Chocó.[114] The number of miners and slaves in the Chocó grew gradually thereafter, and, over time, the Indians of Citará, just like those of the neighbouring province of Noanama, were drawn into the mining economy, as builders of dwellings and canoes, as transporters of goods, and as suppliers of foodstuffs to the growing local population. In spite of the complex ways in which Indians had for decades sought to resist, or at best control, the Spanish advance on their territory, in the 1700s the Chocó became a major mining region of late colonial New Granada.

Notes

1 See, for example, the testimony of Francisco Onofre, Río de Murri, 11 August 1684, and Lloró, 17 October 1684, in AGI Santa Fe 204, Ramo 6, fols. 2, 31. See also Esteban Fernández de Rivera's testimony, Lloró, 16 October 1684, fol. 27.
2 See AGI Quito 75, Gerónimo de Berrio to Crown, Popayán, 2 March 1689.

PROTEST AND REBELLION, 1680–1684   147

3   Cabeza de Proceso General, Río de Murri, 15 August 1684, in AGI Santa Fe 204, Ramo 6, fols. 8–9. See also Auto, 24 September 1685, in AGI Quito 15, 'Traslado de los autos del maestre de Campo Don Cristóbal de Caicedo Salazar . . . sobre los servicios hechos . . . en la Reducción y Pacificación de los Indios Rebeldes de la Provincia del Citará', fol. 245.
4   Only the mestizo Francisco Onofre, despite seven severe wounds, escaped with his life.
5   See the testimonies of Juan Joseph Azcárate de Castillo, Lloró, 14 October 1684; Esteban Fernández de Rivera, Lloró, 16 October 1684; and Francisco Onofre, Lloró, 17 October 1684, in AGI Santa Fe 204, Ramo 6, fols. 22–23, 27, 31.
6   Auto, Rio Bebará, 30 July 1684; Auto, Rio de Murri, 28 August 1684; Río de Murri, 17 August 1684, AGI Santa Fe 204, Ramo 5, fols. 30, 40, 37.
7   Auto, Antioquia, 9 May 1684, AGI Santa Fe 204, Ramo 5, fols. 1–2. See also the lists of members of the expedition, dated Antioquia, 14 May 1684, fols. 4–5.
8   Auto, Lloró, 7 October 1684; Auto, Lloró, 8 October 1684; Auto, Lloró, 12 November 1684. AGI Santa Fe 204, Ramo 7, fols. 1, 3, 11.
9   AGI Quito 75, Gerónimo de Berrio to Crown, Popayán, 2 March 1689. According to a petition presented by Bernabé Gregorio de Alarcón, representing Cristóbal de Caicedo, 150 Noanama Indians took part in the expedition. See Petición, in AGI Quito 15, 'Traslado de los autos del maestre de Campo Don Cristóbal de Caicedo Salazar', n.p., n.d., fol. 219.
10 Autos, Lloró, 7 and 8 October 1684, AGI Santa Fe 204, Ramo 7, fols. 1–3.
11 AGI Quito 75, Certificación, n.p., n.d.; Gerónimo de Berrio to Crown, Popayán, 2 March 1689.
12 See Juan Joseph Azcárate de Castillo's testimony, Lloró, 14 October 1684, in AGI Santa Fe 204, Ramo 6, fol. 23.
13 AGI Santa Fe 204, Ramo 6, fols. 23, 25. See also Esteban Fernández de Rivera's testimony, fol. 28.
14 See the statements of Miguel Baquera and Nicolás Yapeda, Lloró, 17 October 1684, AGI Santa Fe 204, Ramo 6, fols. 34–35.
15 The fourth friar, Juan de Llanos, was killed with a spear when trying to escape. See Doblado, 'Misiones de la Santa Provincia de Santa Fe', in Mantilla Ruiz, *Actividad misionera*, pp. 73–74.
16 See Juan Joseph Azcárate de Castillo's statement in AGI Santa Fe 204, Ramo 6, fols. 23–24, and Esteban Fernández de Rivera's, fol. 29. According to Bueso de Valdés, both Indians, and their followers, 'had gone to the wars they have with the Cunacuna'. See Bueso de Valdés to Gerónimo de Berrio, Lloró, 26 March 1685, in AGI Santa Fe 204, Ramo 7, fol. 38.
17 See Don Rodrigo Pivi's statement in AGI Santa Fe 204, Ramo 6, fols. 2–3.
18 See the testimonies of Juan Joseph Azcárate de Castillo, Francisco Onofre and Esteban Fernández de Rivera, in AGI Santa Fe 204, Ramo 6, fols. 23, 29, 31. The Spanish survivors were Juan Joseph Azcárate de Castillo, Juan Nuño de Sotomayor, Sargento Pedro Blandón, Francisco Rodríguez, Cristóbal Rodríguez and Esteban Fernández de Rivera.
19 In a 1685 letter to Governor Gerónimo de Berrio, Bueso de Valdés stated that it was the friar Córdoba who had appointed Cárdenas as *teniente*. See Bueso de Valdés to Gerónimo de Berrio, Lloró, 26 March 1685, in AGI Santa Fe 204, Ramo 7, fol. 35.
20 Antioquia, 6 April 1680, AGI Santa Fe 204, Ramo 3, fol. 8.
21 Auto, Antioquia, 7 August 1681, AGI Santa Fe 204, Ramo 3, fols. 1–2.
22 Auto, Antioquia, 5 April 1680, AGI Santa Fe 204, Ramo 3, fol. 4. See also Gregorio Bogassaga's statement, fol. 7. By 1680, Lope de Cárdenas had been active in the Chocó for nearly a decade. In 1674, he was described as a resident of the region and was said to

have arrived there in 1671. See AGI Quito 67, 'Testimonio de Autos (Franciscans)', Negua, 14 August 1674, fol. 154.
23 See the statements of Gregorio Bogassaga, Antonio Quintana and Sebastián Velásquez, in AGI Santa Fe 204, Ramo 3, fols. 4–7.
24 See Gregorio Bogassaga's evidence, AGI Santa Fe 204, Ramo 3, fol. 7.
25 Radillo de Arce to Francisco Castillo de la Concha, Antioquia, 28 April 1680, AGI Santa Fe 204, Ramo 3, fol. 12.
26 AGI Santa Fe 204, Ramo 3, fols. 24–25.
27 In 1679, Don Diego Radillo de Arce, who replaced Aguinaga as governor, commented that although the *audiencia* of Santa Fe appointed Bueso de Valdés 'Auxiliador Superintendente de la Reducción', there had not been an official representative of that *gobernación* in the Citará region for three years. Auto, 7 August 1681, AGI Santa Fe 204, Ramo 3, fol. 2.
28 N.p., n.d., AGI Santa Fe 204, Ramo 3, fol. 8.
29 Lope de Cárdenas to Radillo de Arce, Negua, 16 May 1680, AGI Santa Fe 204, Ramo 3, fol. 16.
30 Cristóbal de Artiaga to Radillo de Arce, Negua, 16 May 1680, AGI Santa Fe 204, Ramo 3, fols. 14–15.
31 Cristóbal de Artiaga to Radillo de Arce, Negua, 16 May 1680, AGI Santa Fe 204, Ramo 3, fol. 15.
32 Lope de Cárdenas to Radillo de Arce, Negua, 16 May 1680, AGI Santa Fe 204, Ramo 3, fol. 16.
33 1 June 1680, AGI Santa Fe 204, Ramo 3, fol. 17.
34 Lope de Cárdenas to Radillo de Arce, Negua, 16 May 1680, AGI Santa Fe 204, Ramo 3, fol. 17.
35 Cristóbal de Artiaga to Radillo de Arce, Negua, 16 May 1680, AGI Santa Fe 204, Ramo 3, fol. 15.
36 See, for example, Francisco de Borja to Radillo de Arce, n.p., n.d., and Cristóbal de Viñola y Villegas to Radillo de Arce, Taita, n.d., in AGI Santa Fe 204, Ramo 3, fol. 10. The following list includes all those who reported their complaints to the governor during 1680: Antonio Quintana, Sebastián Velásquez, Francisco de Borja, Cristóbal de Viñola y Villegas, Juan Nuño de Sotomayor, Sebastián García Benítez, Jacinto Roque de Espinosa, Diego Díaz de Castro, Francisco González Valdés, Bartolomé García, Nicolás de Murcia, Miguel Fernández, Rodrigo Blandón Jaramillo, Juan de Dios, Salvador Vidal, Francisco Onofre, Manuel Quintero Príncipe, Manuel de Burgos, Joseph Enrique and Alonso de Baca. See AGI Santa Fe 204, Ramo 3, fols. 4–7, 10, 13–14, 19–20, 22–24, 27–28, 31, 36–39, 45–46.
37 Antioquia, n.d., AGI Santa Fe 204, Ramo 3, fol. 44.
38 See Sebastián García et al. to Radillo de Arce, 21 July 1680, AGI Santa Fe 204, Ramo 3, fol. 22.
39 Auto, Antioquia, 7 August 1681, AGI Santa Fe 204, Ramo 3, fol. 2. Elsewhere, the *teniente* was described as 'a poor man, servant of the said father'. See Pacheco, *La consolidación de la iglesia*, p. 673.
40 Antioquia, 14 October 1680, AGI Santa Fe 204, Ramo 3, fols. 40–42.
41 AGI Santa Fe 204, Ramo 3, fols. 7–8.
42 Antioquia, 14 October 1680, AGI Santa Fe 204, Ramo 3, fols. 40–41.
43 Cristóbal de Artiaga to Radillo de Arce, Negua, 16 May 1680, AGI Santa Fe 204, Ramo 3, fol. 15.
44 Radillo de Arce to Francisco Castillo de la Concha, Antioquia, 28 April 1680, AGI Santa Fe 204, Ramo 3, fol. 12.
45 21 May 1680, AGI Santa Fe 204, Ramo 3, fol. 13.
46 Juan Nuño de Sotomayor et al. to Radillo de Arce, Negua, 25 June 1680, AGI Santa Fe 204, Ramo 3, fol. 19.

47 See the letters of Juan Nuño de Sotomayor, Sebastián García and Diego Díaz de Castro, Negua, 25 and 28 June 1680, AGI Santa Fe 204, Ramo 3, fol. 20.
48 Auto, 29 August 1680, AGI Santa Fe 204, Ramo 3, fol. 67.
49 Sebastián García, Juan Nuño de Sotomayor, Jacinto Roque de Espinosa, Rodrigo Blandón Jaramillo, Diego Díaz de Castro, Cristóbal de Viñola y Villegas, Francisco González, Joseph Enrique and Juan de Dios to Radillo de Arce, 21 July 1680, AGI Santa Fe 204, Ramo 3, fols. 22–24. See also Sebastián García to Radillo de Arce, Negua, 24 July 1680, fol. 24.
50 Santa Fe de Antioquia, 13 July 1680, AGI Santa Fe 204, Ramo 3, fol. 24.
51 Negua, 29 August 1680, AGI Santa Fe 204, Ramo 3, fol. 71.
52 See the statements in AGI Santa Fe 204, Ramo 3, fols. 27–28, 37–38, 39, 45, 46, 72. See also Certificación, Negua, 17 February 1681, fols. 109–10.
53 Auto, Negua, 14 January 1681, AGI Santa Fe 204, Ramo 3, fol. 59, and Bueso de Valdés to Radillo de Arce, Chaquinindo, 1 December 1680, fols. 57–58.
54 See Jacinto Roque de Espinosa's declaration, Antioquia, 15 September 1680, AGI Santa Fe 204, Ramo 3, fol. 27.
55 Francisco de Borja Montenegro to Radillo de Arce, n.p., n.d., AGI Santa Fe 204, Ramo 3, fol. 10.
56 See, for example, Sebastián Velásquez's declaration, Antioquia, 16 October 1680, AGI Santa Fe 204, Ramo 3, fol. 44. See also Don Antonio de Legarda's statement before the governor, fol. 44.
57 Cristóbal de Viñola to Radillo de Arce, n.p., 21 May 1680, AGI Santa Fe 204, Ramo 3, fol. 13.
58 See Francisco Onofre's statement, Antioquia, 30 September 1680, AGI Santa Fe 204, Ramo 3, fol. 37.
59 Auto, Antioquia, 17 October 1680, AGI Santa Fe 204, Ramo 3, fols. 47–48. See also Memorial, n.p., n.d., fol. 49, and the treasury officials' reply, n.p., n.d., fols. 49–50. In the event, Bueso de Valdés took a force of only nine men and 15 Indian carriers. See Memorial, fol. 54.
60 Antioquia, 20 September 1680, AGI Santa Fe 204, Ramo 3, fol. 32.
61 Cabeza de Proceso General, Río de Murri, 15 August 1684, AGI Santa Fe 204, Ramo 6, fol. 8.
62 Bueso de Valdés to Radillo de Arce, Negua, 11 June 1681, AGI Santa Fe 204, Ramo 3, fols. 117–18; Auto, Antioquia, 3 July 1681, fols. 116–17. Córdoba was later cleared of wrongdoing, and returned to the Chocó, as *comisario*, following the pacification. See Doblado, 'Misiones de la Santa Provincia de Santa Fe', in Mantilla Ruiz, *Actividad misionera*, p. 74 n. 93. See also Arcila Robledo, *Las misiones*, p. 37.
63 Bueso de Valdés to Gerónimo de Berrio, Lloró, 26 March 1685, AGI Santa Fe 204, Ramo 7, fol. 35.
64 As well as Alvarez, the team included Fray Dionisio Palomino, Fray Juan Llanos and the lay brother Joseph Flores. Esteban Alvarez de Aviles to Radillo de Arce, Anserma, 8 November 1680, AGI Santa Fe 204, Ramo 3, fols. 56–57. Fray Juan Llanos was mentioned in a contribution to a debate on the Chocó written by Fray Diego Barroso in 1719. See AGI Santa Fe 403, Santa Fe, 18 November 1719. For Alvarez's assessment of Indian understanding of Christianity, see AGI Santa Fe 204, Ramo 3, Negua, 14 January 1681, fol. 60.
65 AGI Santa Fe 204, Ramo 3, fol. 44.
66 Negua, 14 January 1681, AGI Santa Fe 204, Ramo 3, fol. 60.
67 Udrapagui's statement, Río de Murri, 15 August 1684, AGI Santa Fe 204, Ramo 6, fol. 9; Ygaragaida's statement, 11 August 1684, fols. 3–4.
68 The mining camps belonging to Joseph Díaz, Domingo de Veitia and Bueso de Valdés; in the mining camp of Ingipurdú; along the beach of Guacogo; by the mouths of the rivers Quito, Cavi and Bebará; along the Andaguda and Atrato rivers; at the port of Dodubar – wherever, that is, the Spaniards or their retainers could be found.

69 See the following statements in AGI Santa Fe 204, Ramo 6: Juan Joseph Azcárate de Castillo, fol. 25; Esteban Fernández de Rivera, fols. 30–31; Francisco Onofre, fols. 31–32; Ygaragaida, fols. 3–4; Udrapagui, fol. 9; Capitán Francisco Ignacio Betu, fol. 10; Capitán Tajina, fols. 11–12; Guaguirri, fols. 14–16; and Soberano, fol. 43.

70 Auto, Montes del Chocó, 16 July 1684, AGI Santa Fe 204, Ramo 5, fols. 26–27.

71 This point was also made by Susan Deeds in her analysis of a series of rebellions launched by the Tepehuanes, Conchos and Tarahumaras in Nueva Vizcaya. 'Paradoxically', Deeds argues, 'rebellions owed part of their organizational success to the coherence imposed by the mission system on previously disaggregated settlement patterns.' Deeds, 'Indigenous Responses to Mission Settlement', p. 88.

72 See the following statements in AGI Santa Fe 204, Ramo 6: Ygaragaida, fols. 3, 5–6; Udrapagui, fols. 9–10; Francisco Ignacio Betu, fol. 10; Tajina, fols. 11–12; Miguel Baquera, fol. 33; Don Pedro Paparra, fol. 41; Soberano, fols. 42–43.

73 Bueso said of Chigri that he was 'one of the principal caciques of this province [and] governor [of it], appointed by the current president of the [*audiencia*] . . . of Santa Fe'. See Bueso de Valdés' comments, Auto, Montes del Río de Bojaya, retiro y habitación del capitán Juan Chigri, 3 September 1684, AGI Santa Fe 204, Ramo 5, fol. 42.

74 Ambrosio, Mateo and Pedro.

75 The *capitanes* in charge of this attack were Manzano, Gongera, Tevasa and Chuagra. The slaves who were killed belonged to Bueso de Valdés and Domingo de Veitia. Lloró, 16 October 1684, AGI Santa Fe 204, Ramo 6, fol. 26.

76 Auto, Río de Bebará, 29 July 1684, AGI Santa Fe 204, Ramo 5, fol. 28. For other examples, see also Auto, Bartolomé de Borja, Montes del Río Murri, 31 August 1684, fol. 45.

77 See Auto, Río de Bebará, 30 July 1684, and Auto, Río de Murri, 11 August 1684, AGI Santa Fe 204, Ramo 5, fols. 30, 35, and the statements of Juananui and Sadragama, AGI Santa Fe 204, Ramo 6, fols. 46, 54.

78 Autos, Río de Murri, 30 August 1684, AGI Santa Fe 204, Ramo 5, fol. 41, and Río de Murri, 14 September 1684, fol. 49.

79 Bartolomé de Borja to Bueso de Valdés, 6 January 1685, and Auto, n.p., n.d., AGI Santa Fe 204, Ramo 7, fol. 26.

80 See the following statements in AGI Santa Fe 204, Ramo 6: Guaguirri, fols. 14–16; Noquia, fol. 44; and Juananui, fol. 47.

81 See the following statements in AGI Santa Fe 204, Ramo 6: Guaripua, fol. 19; Chaqueranvido, fol. 38; Soberano, fol. 43.

82 See the following statements, in AGI Santa Fe 204, Ramo 6: Ygaragaida, fols. 3–5; Capitán Tajina, fol. 12; Guaguirri, fols. 14–16; Guaripua, fol. 19; Biramia, fol. 41; Noquia, fol. 44.

83 Auto, Río de Bebará, 25 September 1684, AGI Santa Fe 204, Ramo 5, fols. 50–51.

84 See the following statements in AGI Santa Fe 204, Ramo 6: Manigua, fol. 45, and Umia, fol. 48.

85 See Ygaragaida's statement, AGI Santa Fe 204, Ramo 6, fol. 5.

86 Declaración, Rio de Murri, 9 August 1684, AGI Santa Fe 204, Ramo 5, fol. 34.

87 See Galvis' Petición, AGI Santa Fe 204, Ramo 6, fol. 50.

88 Alejo de la Cruz y Valencia to Cristóbal de Caicedo, n.p., 21 August 1685, in AGI Quito 15, 'Traslado', fol. 236.

89 See the statements of Juan Joseph Azcárate de Castillo, Esteban Fernández de Rivera and Francisco Onofre, in AGI Santa Fe 204, Ramo 6, fols. 23–24, 29, 32. See also Domingo de Veitia's evidence of 28 July 1674, in AGI Quito 67, 'Testimonio de Autos (Franciscans)', fol. 62.

90 See, for example, Esteban Fernández de Rivera's testimony, AGI Santa Fe 204, Ramo 6, fol. 27–28.

91 At least two other of the Spaniards' Indian allies of 1684 had also been involved in the

PROTEST AND REBELLION, 1680–1684 151

earlier conflict. Don Pedro Tegue was reported to have threatened to burn down the church of Lloró; Don Juan Mitiguirre had to be appeased by Governor Radillo with a promise that the Franciscans were to be replaced. See AGI Santa Fe 204, Ramo 3, fols. 22–24, 41–42, 43–44.
92 See the statements of Esteban Fernández de Rivera and Juan Joseph Azcárate de Castillo, in AGI Santa Fe 204, Ramo 6, fols. 28–29, 24.
93 Isacsson, 'Emberá', p. 31.
94 AGI Santa Fe 204, Ramo 6, fol. 25.
95 Culpa y Cargo, Río de Murri, 18 August 1684, AGI Santa Fe 204, Ramo 6, fols. 12–13.
96 On the difficulties of interpreting the content and meaning of confessions, frequently communicated by interpreters and recorded by notaries, see Eric Van Young, 'The Cuautla Lazarus: Double Subjectives in Reading Texts on Popular Collective Action', *Colonial Latin American Review*, Vol. 2, Nos. 1–2, 1993, pp. 8–14.
97 Joseph de Perianes acted as *defensor* between August and October 1684, when he was replaced by Diego de Galvis. See Auto, Río de Murri, 11 August 1684, and Auto, Lloró, 12 October 1684, in AGI Santa Fe 204, Ramo 6, fols. 3, 22. For Galvis's comments, see Petición, fol. 53.
98 Lloró, 10 November 1684, AGI Santa Fe 204, Ramo 6, fol. 37.
99 See Peticiones, AGI Santa Fe 204, Ramo 6, fols. 38–39, 49–50.
100 See the statements of Don Fernando Tajina and Guaguirri, in AGI Santa Fe 204, Ramo 6, fols. 11, 14.
101 Marzal, 'Informe', in Pacheco, *Los Jesuitas*, II, p. 501.
102 Charlotte Gradie makes this point – that 'war was an essential component of male identity in native culture' – in discussing the Tepehuanes of Nueva Vizcaya. See Gradie, *The Tepehuan Revolt*, p. 105.
103 See the following statements in AGI Santa Fe 204, Ramo 6: Tajina, fol. 11; Guaguirri, fols. 14–15; Guaripua, fol. 19; Minguirri, fol. 20; Guatupua, fol. 36; Dare, fol. 37; Chaqueranvido, fol. 38; Don Pedro Paparra, fol. 42; and Soberano, fol. 43.
104 For estimates of numbers still evading capture, see Auto, Lloró, 8 October 1684, AGI Santa Fe 204, Ramo 7, fol. 4.
105 Río de Atrato, 26 September 1684, AGI Santa Fe 204, Ramo 5, fol. 56.
106 Bueso de Valdés to Gerónimo de Berrio, Lloró, 26 March 1685, in AGI Santa Fe 204, Ramo 7, fol. 39. See also Antonio de Veroiz, 'Pacificación de la provincia del Citará. Su descripción. Tributos que pagaban los indios', 12 July 1688, in Ortega Ricaurte (ed.), *Historia documental*, p. 140. Veroiz also claimed that Caicedo put to death 30 Indians in the settlement of Lloró.
107 Bueso de Valdés to Juan de Caicedo Salazar, Lloró, 8 October 1684, AGI Santa Fe 204, Ramo 7, fol. 3.
108 Bueso de Valdés to Gerónimo de Berrio, Lloró, 26 March 1685, AGI Santa Fe 204, Ramo 7, fols. 37–38.
109 For the sentences passed see AGI Santa Fe 204, Ramo 6, fols. 7–8, 13–14, 17, 20–21, 40, 49, 51, 53, 56.
110 Auto de Exhorto, Lloró, 7 October 1684, AGI Santa Fe 204, Ramo 7, fols. 1–2.
111 AGI Quito 75, Rodrigo de Mañosca to Crown, Popayán, 16 May 1690.
112 AGI Quito 75, Gerónimo de Berrio to Crown, Popayán, 2 March 1689; and Certificación, n.p., n.d.
113 AGI Quito 75, Rodrigo de Mañosca to Crown, Popayán, 16 May 1690. See also Lorenzo de Salazar's evidence of 24 September 1711, in AGI Santa Fe 307, 'Cuaderno . . . sobre la entrada al río Murri y descubrimiento de nuevos minerales de oro', fols. 81–82.
114 AGI Quito 75, Rodrigo Roque de Mañosca to Crown, Popayán, 16 May 1690.

CHAPTER SIX

Government and Society on the Frontier

The aftermath of rebellion

The pacification of the Citará rebellion of 1684–87 did not immediately lead to a mass influx of miners intent on exploiting the new conditions on the frontier. The years of rebellion had been immensely destructive of both life and property, and the job of reconstruction was slow. Writing in 1688, Don Antonio de Veroiz y Alfaro, newly appointed *sargento mayor* and *corregidor* by Popayán's governor Gerónimo de Berrio, described how the years of warfare had not only brought agricultural activity to a standstill in Citará province, but had also brought in their wake famine and disease: 'there has been ferocious hunger [here], followed by its companion, disease'. The death toll had been high – half the population, according to Veroiz. Many of the survivors, fearful of Spanish reprisals, had gone to ground. Food was in short supply.[1] No more than 34 slaves – belonging to three small *cuadrillas* or slave gangs – remained in the region in 1688.[2] 'These, their overseers and four men to procure food', Veroiz stated, 'are the only Christians left in this miserable and wretched province, and one doctrinero, a secular priest who is very ill and longing to leave to recuperate'.[3] More than a decade passed before Indians were finally rounded up and resettled and some semblance of normality returned to this part of the Chocó frontier.[4]

With the exception of a handful of miners and a couple of officials, few Spaniards ventured to Citará province in the late 1680s and early 1690s. This does not mean, however, that they withdrew completely from the Chocó; rather, they concentrated their activities in those parts of the Pacific lowlands that were both more accessible to the cities of the *gobernación* of Popayán, and unaffected by the violence. Members of the leading families of the Cauca Valley, especially of Cali and Popayán itself, were already well entrenched in Raposo-Iscuandé and Noanama province before the outbreak of rebellion, since these were the areas over which that *gobernación* traditionally enjoyed jurisdiction. Some, such as the Caicedos of Cali, cautiously withdrew their slaves from Noanama when violence broke out in 1684, but, eager to prevent others moving in to exploit mining interests to which they had laid claim, they returned a few years later.[5] Other slave-owning Cauca Valley families were established in that region by the end of the decade, for in 1688 Veroiz y Alfaro reported that more than 100 slaves were employed in gold mining in Noanama; others whom he described as 'free people' were also actively involved in mining or in growing crops for the slaves.[6] The Arboleda Salazars, of Popayán, were among the slave-owners represented there by 1690: it has been estimated that over a six-month period in that year alone, Francisco de Arboleda's 18-strong slave gang produced for their owner a total of 4000 pesos.[7] Details of other Popayán families emerge by the beginning of the eighteenth century, among whom the Mosqueras (Cristóbal, Jacinto and Nicolás) and Bernardo Alfonso de Saa – owners of some of the largest slave gangs in the area – are the most prominent.[8]

By the turn of the eighteenth century, then, prominent slave-owning families from the cities of the *gobernación* of Popayán were well established in Noanama province. Far harder to determine is when they began to trickle back to Citará province, and what the nature of their activities was in that region in the early years of the century. The lack of official figures on gold production between 1690 and 1724, combined with a lively contraband trade and widespread tax evasion, means that there is a dearth of evidence to reconstruct the early development of gold-mining in that part of the Chocó. Sources dating from the decade of the 1710s show, however, that substantial mining and commercial activity was taking place by that time, and that those Spaniards who exploited the new opportunities available for mining and trade were profiting handsomely from their enterprises. In 1713, the *oidor* Vicente de Aramburu, back in Santa Fe after completing an official investigation into contraband in the Chocó, reported in the second of three informative *consultas* on the great wealth enjoyed by Spanish merchants and slave-owners in Citará province, which he attributed in large part to the freedom they enjoyed to evade taxes on mining and trade.[9] In 1718, Don Francisco de Alcantud y Gaona, appointed interim *teniente* of Citará with powers to detain and imprison the incumbent Don Luis de Acuña y Berrio on a charge of murder, confirmed the *oidor*'s findings. Writing in 1720, Alcantud y Gaona reported that the province was inhabited mainly by mine-owners, slave-owners, merchants and traders, and that the former two in particular were 'people who live with complete freedom in all their actions and way of life'. Alcantud y Gaona's reflections indicate that, by the second decade of the eighteenth century, Citará province was quite heavily populated by Spaniards, that mining operations were both extensive and profitable, that taxes in the form of *quintos* and *alcabalas* were rarely collected there, and that an 'illicit' contraband trade had developed between Spanish miners and French, Dutch and English traders based along the Portobelo coast. Over the course of a single year, this apparently conscientious official remitted to Santa Fe a total of 4000 pesos in *quintos*, corresponding to taxes on gold production in this section of the Chocó alone.[10]

While Spanish settlers and slave-owners from the cities of the interior gradually expanded their activities to the northern sections of Chocó territory, Noanama province remained the more important centre of gold production throughout these years. Only a comparatively small proportion of the region's slaves, for example, had been diverted to the alluvial deposits of Citará by the 1720s. Contemporary documents indicate that, by the middle of the decade, there were in the Chocó as a whole some 2000 slaves, belonging to some 50 to

60 *cuadrillas*, all of which were engaged in gold production.[11] Only about a quarter of these were employed in Citará. Giving evidence in 1720, Don Diego Maldonado de la Cerda, himself a miner and slave-owner, estimated that the 38 or 39 miners based in that province held between them no more than 500 slaves.[12] Numbers grew only marginally over the following decade. In 1729 Don Francisco de Ibero, first governor of the Chocó, estimated that 550 slaves were engaged in gold production in Citará, compared with more than 3000 in Nóvita.[13] The best deposits were concentrated along the banks of four main rivers – the Indipurdú, Nemota, Naurita and Puné – and it was here that the largest slave-owners concentrated their activities. These rivers, the Franciscan Manuel Caicedo informed the Consejo de Indias in 1724, 'are the best known and the richest in gold that have been discovered, [and] it is here ... where the majority of the slaves belonging to the miners of the Chocó are employed, as they yield high profits'.[14] Other slave-owners established operations along the Bebarama, Negua and Ichó rivers. And in all these areas there were also to be found many small-scale miners and prospectors, perhaps working alone or with a slave or two.[15]

Extant sources provide insufficient detail to identify more than a handful of miners and slave-owners active in this region at the beginning of the eighteenth century. The indications are, however, that those same families that were already entrenched in Raposo and/or Noanama were among the first to extend their mining and commercial interests northwards into Citará territory. The Caicedos of Cali are a good example. Active in Raposo and Noanama before the outbreak of rebellion, by the end of the 1680s they were among the largest slave-owners in Noanama, and by 1706–1709, they had also established their influence in government, several members of the family serving, at one time or other, as *tenientes de gobernador* in Raposo.[16] By 1711, the Caicedos – who had been particularly prominent in the pacification campaigns of the mid-1680s – were represented in two important capacities in Citará province as well. While Don Francisco Caicedo acted as *teniente general*, his uncle, Fray Manuel Caicedo, served as *doctrinero* of the settlement of Quibdó (formerly Negua). By the 1720s, another nephew of Fray Manuel's, the secular priest Roque de Caicedo, was based in the region as well.[17] The Mosqueras, a powerful slave-owning family with mining interests in Iró and Mungarra, in the vicinity of Tadó, also sought to extend their interests into Citará province early in the century, at least one member of the family – Don Jacinto – serving as *teniente* there before 1711.[18]

The wealthiest families of the Cauca and Popayán valleys, it seems, quickly sought to establish their influence over the entire Chocó frontier. Already the region's principal miners and slave-holders, they gradually extended their control over local government as well. Francisco Caicedo, Jacinto Mosquera, Francisco de Arboleda Salazar, Bernardo Alfonso de Saa, Miguel Gómez de la Asperilla, Agustín de Valencia and Antonio Ordoñez de Lara all served as delegates of the governor of Popayán in one or other of the provinces of the Chocó at the beginning of the 1700s.[19] And as the case of Fray Manuel Caicedo and his nephew Roque de Caicedo suggests, these families soon made their influence felt in a further role, that of *doctrineros* of Indian settlements. By 1720, the Arboledas and Hurtado del Aguilas were also represented in this capacity, Don Joseph Hurtado del Aguila and Dr Don Melchor Jacinto de Arboleda Salazar serving respectively as *doctrineros* of the settlements of Los Brazos and San Joseph de Noanama.[20] The Mosqueras, for their part, placed Nicolás de Inestrosa, a secular cleric with whom they were closely connected, as priest of the newly created parish of Iró and Mungarra, in Noanama province.[21] It was through their participation in secular and ecclesiastical government, as much as through their economic role, that these families came to exercise what Germán Colmenares described as 'incomparable power' in the Chocó.[22]

Historians have shown that it was mainly to these same large land- and slave-owning families of the *gobernación* of Popayán that the lion's share of the wealth derived from the exploitation of precious metal flowed. This is only partly attributable to their position as the Chocó's principal miners and to their control over local administration. It is also partly attributable to the trading activities that land-owning families developed on the frontier, supplying the mining camps with foodstuffs and other goods (dried and salted meat, tobacco, wheat, and sugar products) that could not be produced locally. As Anthony McFarlane explains, it was principally 'a small group of families in the cities of Popayán and Cali, most of whom linked their enterprises in Caloto and the Chocó with large agricultural holdings in the Cauca and Popayán valleys', who were enriched by new flows of gold coming from the Chocó.[23] It is not, however, the purpose of this chapter to analyse the impact of the incorporation of new alluvial deposits on the economy of the *gobernación* of Popayán, or to examine the development of the mining industry in the Chocó, since these are tasks that have already been undertaken. The purpose of this chapter is, rather, to examine the process whereby the Chocó was incorporated into the colony, and to provide a context for our discussion, in Chapter 7, of the impact of eighteenth-century colonisation on the native population of the region, and of the ways in which indigenous peoples, especially the Citará, reacted to the new conditions on the frontier. As all parties involved in the colonisation of this region played a part in determining the response of native peoples to Spanish occupation, this chapter will discuss the principal features of Spanish society in the Chocó, focusing on the structure and conduct of secular government, and the administration of Indian *doctrinas* by the Spanish priests who continued to play a leading role in the process of converting native peoples to the Christian faith.

This examination of colonial government on the Chocó frontier should be set in the context of the general decline in professional standards that affected all levels of the American bureaucracy during these years, for the closing decades of the seventeenth century and the opening decades of the eighteenth were years when standards of government everywhere in the Spanish empire were at their lowest ebb. By the late 1600s, the ideals of efficient, professional and impartial government for the Indies which the Habsburg state had envisaged and made provision for in the sixteenth century, while never fully living up to expectations, had largely been abandoned.[24] As respect for the strict rules and regulations drawn up to govern the behaviour of officials in the Indies – which were designed to prevent appointees from viceroys down to *corregidores* becoming corrupted by pressures of a financial, commercial or personal nature – steadily eroded, the quality of government at virtually all levels of Spanish administration deteriorated. A whole range of factors contributed to the general relaxation of standards during these years. Principal among these, because they led to a whole host of other problems, were the financial difficulties which the Crown itself faced during the seventeenth century, and which led it to the decision to raise revenue by means of the sale of offices in the American bureaucracy. The systematic sale of offices began in 1633, when a proposal was approved to sell high-ranking treasury appointments in the Indies; within a few years, provincial governorships and *corregimientos* were put up for sale; and in 1687, a still penurious monarchy extended the sale of bureaucratic appointments to include offices on the American *audiencias*, a policy that was continued intermittently, albeit with some reluctance and opposition, until 1750.

Sale of bureaucratic appointments had damaging long-term consequences for the quality of government across the empire. By making ability to pay more important than qualification for office, Spanish American administration from the most senior to the most junior levels was encumbered with appointees who in earlier times would have been considered unsuitable, or even undesirable, for office. By bringing into colonial government individuals whose primary loyalties were local rather than imperial, sale of office led to a shift in the balance of power within the empire and to a steady decline of royal authority. By converting government office into a kind of commercial investment, sale of bureaucratic appointments encouraged purchasers to seek to profit from their investments by using their positions for private gain rather than for the public good.[25] Gradually, sale of office, combined with ongoing financial difficulties, which frequently led the Spanish Crown to suspend payments on salaries that were already considered inadequate, led to an increasing disregard for rules of behaviour intended to ensure honest and disinterested government. As McFarlane argues in discussing the frequent contravention of regulations on trade and commerce in Spanish America, 'when regulations . . . were so often disregarded, they came into deeper disrepute, which in turn contributed to easing the consciences of those who contravened them'.[26]

The Chocó shared the same problems of corruption and maladministration identified in other parts of the empire, though on the frontier, this chapter will argue, the conduct and quality of government was further undermined by underdevelopment and isolation.[27] Unlike many other frontier territories of Spanish America, this region was not to become an ignored and neglected corner of the empire left largely to the control of the missionary orders. In the eighteenth century, as had been the case from the very beginning of the conquest period, gold continued to induce Spaniards to abandon the relative comfort of life in the towns and cities of the interior for the risks and discomfort of an existence in this hostile and forbidding environment. A combination of climate, topography and sheer distance from the towns of interior New Granada nevertheless ensured that Spanish colonisation here had less to do with long-term settlement and development than it did with the enrichment of individuals whose places of residence were Popayán, Cali, Buga or Cartago, rather than Quibdó or Nóvita. For all but a handful of small-scale miners and overseers, residence on the frontier, where it could not be avoided, was temporary. Whites were therefore never to comprise more than a small fraction of the Chocó's total population. No large urban centres were to develop there, nor did 'businessmen, farmers, educators, and pioneer families', as William Sharp commented, arrive in sufficient numbers 'to lend stability and further . . . social development'.[28] These conditions had important implications for all the aspects of life on the frontier that will be described and discussed in the pages that follow.

One final introductory comment is in order. In dealing with this remote and inaccessible area, where self-interest was for most colonists the sole motive for settlement, and where the potential for conflict between competing groups of Spaniards was ever-present, the utmost caution has to be applied to the interpretation of sources that are often contradictory, and commonly directed less at describing conditions on the frontier than at bringing before the attention of the authorities the behaviour of individuals – secular priests, Franciscan missionaries, colonial administrators, ordinary settlers – allegedly implicated in corrupt practices of one kind or another. As Don Francisco de Ibero, who was himself subject to charges of corruption that ended in his dismissal as governor, put it soon after taking up his post in 1729, Spaniards in the Chocó showed no hesitation in 'giving evidence [against a fellow Spaniard], even if it damages the reputation of an honourable man'.[29] Most reports were, of course, made by Spaniards, but Indian peoples were not averse to making repeated and robust allegations of corruption, injustice and ill-treatment on the part of colonial officials and Spanish *doctrineros*, especially the Franciscans. There can be little doubt that many such accusations were truthful, for laws designed to protect indigenous populations from the depredations of Spanish settlers were rarely, if ever, observed in this region where distance from the main centres of government in Santa Fe de Bogotá presented insurmountable problems of enforcement. However, it is also clear that native communities, with objectives and intentions of their own, frequently made claims against officials and priests, especially Franciscan missionaries, with the aim of furthering native interests and bringing about changes advantageous to themselves.[30] The biased and fragmented character of the sources constitutes a serious limitation for the historian seeking to reconstruct the early development of a frontier territory such as this.

Frontier government

Until 1719, when, as part of a major reform that resulted in the creation of the first Viceroyalty of New Granada, the Chocó was brought temporarily under the jurisdiction of a superintendent (and later converted into a *gobernación* in its own right), overall responsibility for the administration of this frontier territory lay with the governor of Popayán.[31] This was the direct result of the *audiencia*'s decision, following the rebellion of 1684, to endorse the jurisdictional claims of that *gobernación* over those of Antioquia. Until the 1730s, the Chocó remained subdivided, for administrative purposes, into three separate territories: Noanama (more commonly known as Nóvita by this time), Tatama or Chocó, and Citará.[32] Prior to the arrival, in 1729, of the first governor of the Chocó, and for reasons to do with distance from the city of Popayán, responsibility for day-to-day government lay with the *tenientes de gobernador* (lieutenant governors or deputy governors), of whom there were two: one in Noanama/Nóvita, and one in Citará. Below the *tenientes* came the *corregidores de indios*, whose main responsibilities, here as elsewhere, were to supervise the administration of the Indian settlements and to collect tributes. And in theory at least, a further layer, of native government, was to take its place alongside Spanish administration.

While responsibility for frontier government was placed in the hands of *tenientes* and *corregidores*, responsibility for the conversion of indigenous populations in the first half of the eighteenth century continued to be shared by Franciscan missionaries and the secular clergy. On arriving in the region in 1673, the Franciscans had taken control only of the 'provinces' of Tatama and Citará. Noanama was left under the control of secular priests, who had already established a presence there, and of the Jesuits, until their final withdrawal from the Chocó in 1689. The division of labour between the Franciscans and their secular counterparts effectively gave the former control over the conversion of the Emberá peoples, and the latter responsibility for the conversion of the Waunana. Thus, while nominally in charge of the provinces of Tatama and Citará alone, the Franciscans retained responsibility for the administration of the *doctrina* of Tadó, an Emberá settlement incorporated, in the eighteenth century, into the province of Noanama or Nóvita.

In theory, then, *tenientes de gobernador*, *corregidores*, Franciscan missionaries and secular priests were to share responsibility for governing the frontier, developing the mining economy, collecting taxes and tributes, enforcing Spanish laws, protecting native peoples from ill-treatment, reducing small and dispersed Indian communities to large and permanent settlements, and carrying out the process of evangelising and hispanicising indigenous populations. However, as successive senior officials and clergy in the colony acknowledged, existing methods for governing the frontier failed to create the conditions necessary to ensure either impartial administration of justice or the conversion of Indian peoples to the Christian faith. This was largely because the prospect of deriving wealth from the exploitation of alluvial deposits, or from the new commercial opportunities afforded by the expansion of the gold-mining industry, was the only incentive for service in government. Spanish administrators on the frontier were not recruited from the pool of career bureaucrats that filled higher-level posts in colonial government, but from a pool of Spaniards – mainly, though not exclusively, wealthy merchants and miners – who purchased a temporary posting in the Chocó not for the honour and prestige associated with government service but for the opportunities that residence in the region offered for quick and substantial earnings. Honest and disinterested government was unlikely to develop in these circumstances, the Franciscan Manuel Caicedo informed the Crown in 1724. Since neither *tenientes* nor *corregidores* expected their records in the Chocó to damage future prospects of employment or promotion in the royal service, they had no incentive to conduct themselves with integrity, and no reason to serve the king loyally, observe his laws, or collect his taxes.[33]

It was the *oidor* of the *audiencia*, Vicente de Aramburu, who first described in detail procedures for appointing the *tenientes* who served as deputies of the governors of Popayán. In setting out, in 1713, how the system of colonial administration functioned in the Chocó, Aramburu explained that the *tenientazgos* of Nóvita and Citará and the *corregimiento* of Tatama (which he described as 'a tenientazgo by another name') were all offered for sale by the governors, in whose power it was to make these appointments, for sums ranging from five to six thousand pesos. In exchange for a payment of this order – known as a *regalía* – purchasers obtained their own positions and gained patronage over the *corregimientos* within their districts. In the Chocó, the *oidor* continued, the main consequence of the practice of making appointments available for sale was an excess of officials, all of whom were 'directed to an unfortunate end, which is to manage Indians'. To prove his point, Aramburu observed that the province of Noanama, consisting of five settlements in 1713 (Tadó, Las Juntas, El Barranco, San Joseph de Noanama and San Agustín), was governed by one *teniente* and five *corregidores*. Citará province, composed at that time of three settlements (Quibdó, Lloró and Bebará), was governed by one *teniente* and three *corregidores*.[34] What the *oidor* was implying was that procedures for appointing *tenientes* had more to do with wealth and influence than with administrative requirements, and that, as a result, the ratio of administrators to population was far in excess of what would be expected elsewhere in the colony.

In 1720, Don Francisco de Alcantud y Gaona, back in Cartagena after completing a one-year stint as *teniente* of Citará province, also expressed concern about the effects of the sale of official posts on the quality of government in the Chocó. How likely was it, Alcantud y Gaona suggested, that *tenientes* would take seriously their duty to administer justice and collect taxes, given that their posts were not only not salaried but actually had to be purchased from the governor for prices that ranged from four thousand pesos to the eight thousand pesos which the *tenencia* of Nóvita had recently fetched? In a region as distant and isolated as this, where the cost of the most basic and necessary supplies was exorbitantly high, it was inevitable that the principal objective of officials was to recoup their investment and make a profit on that investment: 'a large sum of money was needed by these ministers [to purchase their posts], the consequence of which was that they had to recoup the sum paid, and a bit more, and double that as profit'.[35] And when Don Antonio de la Pedrosa returned to Spain after completing his commission to erect the first Viceroyalty, he made the further observation that an additional consequence of the sale of *tenientazgos* – the price of which, he too noted, was determined by 'the substance of the country' – was that it paralysed the ability of governors to exercise supervision over their deputies: 'because the governors sell the tenientazgos and other privileges, they have neither the courage nor the authority to curb misconduct'.[36] Similar problems were identified lower down the bureaucratic scale and for similar reasons. When in 1730 the Franciscan provincial, Dionisio de Camino, reported to the *oidor* Martínez Malo on various matters relating to secular and ecclesiastical administration in the Chocó, he discussed the recent sale of four *corregimientos*, whose purchase prices were likewise determined by the potential profits *corregidores* could expect to make from their terms of office. Camino indicated that the small *corregimiento* of Beté (consisting of 20 tributaries) had just sold for 500 pesos; that of Bebará (43 tributaries) had gone for 800 pesos; Bojaya was sold for 700 pesos, and Chamí for over 1000 pesos – all of which amounted, he said, to the formal sale of the villages and their inhabitants (see Map 6).[37]

Our sources describe in considerable detail the numerous ways in which Spanish functionaries in the Chocó, allegedly helped by a mutually beneficial relationship with successive governors in Popayán, contravened laws designed to regulate the behaviour of officials, and abused their offices for private gain.[38] At times these reports, in their concern to expose the corruption of colonial administration in this region, are strongly reminiscent of that famous eighteenth-century tract on corruption and misgovernment in the Spanish Indies, Jorge Juan and Antonio de Ulloa's 'Discourse and Political Reflections on the Kingdoms of Peru'.[39] Like Juan and Ulloa, our sources implicate governors, *tenientes*, *corregidores*, and frequently *doctrineros*, in a circle of corruption and misgovernment of which the Crown (through loss of revenue), and the Indians (through ill-treatment and injustice) were the victims. As Don Antonio de la Pedrosa y Guerrero reported in 1721, non-compliance with Spanish laws was tolerated and encouraged by all parties in the Chocó because all parties benefited – they all 'cover up for each other and give each other a hand'.[40]

Trading in contraband, evasion of taxes on mining and trade, and acceptance of bribes for turning a blind eye to frequent infringements of the law were among the principal targets of official concern. There is, indeed, considerable evidence to show that Spanish administrators in the Chocó, like other settlers, participated freely in a contraband trade conducted via the San Juan and Atrato rivers with foreign merchants based at Portobelo. There were strong incentives to trade in contraband in this region where all but the most basic supplies (plantains and maize) had to be imported and, for much of the route into the Chocó from the towns and cities of the coast and the interior, transported overland by Indian *cargueros*. The cost of basic supplies such as livestock, meat and salt, and of key inputs for the mining industry, was prohibitively high, increasing production costs considerably. According to Fray Manuel Caicedo, reporting to the Council of the Indies in 1724, the cost of such crucial inputs as iron and steel was significantly higher when transported overland than when imported by river from Cartagena.[41] It is no surprise to find, then, that repeated royal *cédulas* restricting navigation along the Chocó's two major arteries – the San Juan and Atrato – were largely ignored and that contraband trade flourished there.[42] To take one example, in September 1711, Lorenzo de Salazar, a resident of Citará province since 1691, commented that over the previous twenty years he had

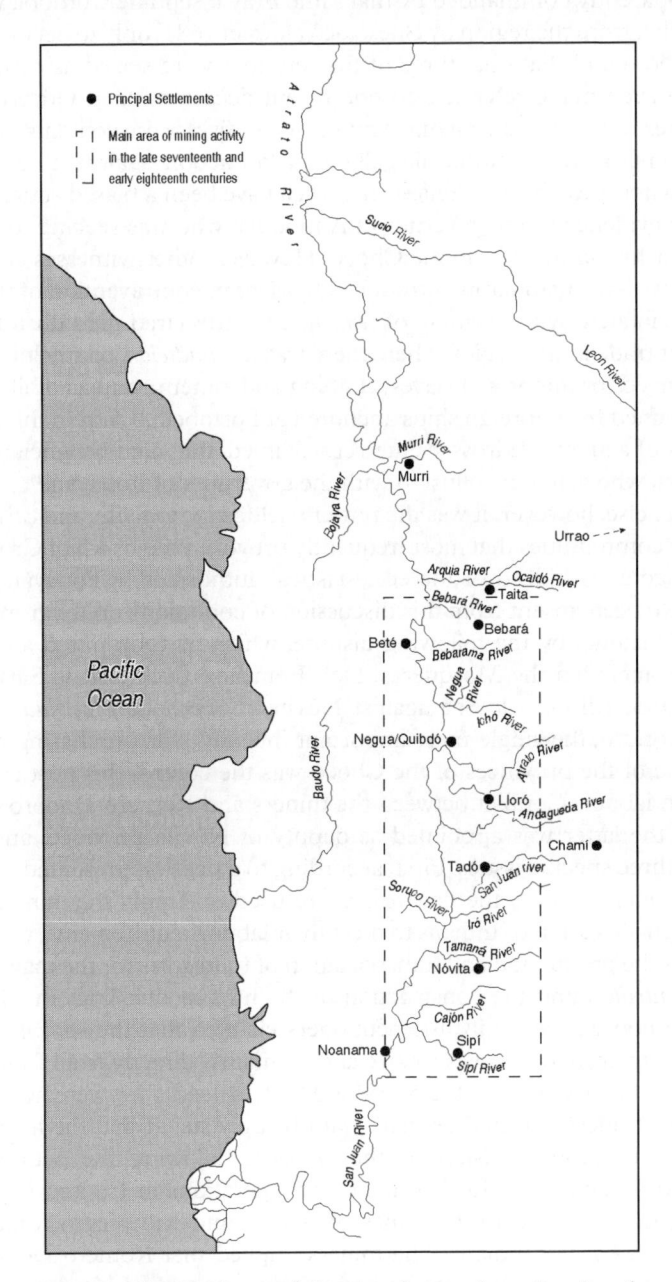

Map 6 *The Chocó: occupied area and approximate location of settlements (early eighteenth century).*

known of at least 18 to 20 vessels that had penetrated the Chocó in this way – the first apparently commanded by that same Fray Joseph de Córdoba who had been expelled from the region by Bueso de Valdés in 1681, only to become *comisario* by 1690 – and that only three of that number were seized as contraband. Indeed, he even made reference to one recent occasion when Governor Bartolomé Pérez de Vivero, having made moves to confiscate the contents of a vessel that had penetrated the Atrato illegally, took no action against its owners on receipt of a 400-peso bribe.[43] Salazar may well have been a biased source, for he was giving evidence to the governor of Antioquia, who was seeking to regain a foothold for his *gobernación* in the Chocó. However, other witnesses confirmed that imports were customarily introduced by river in contravention of the law, a practice facilitated by the bribing of *tenientes*.[44] Undeclared gold dust, the only currency of trade in this region where there was no *fundición*, or smelting house, was exchanged for imports of slaves, clothing and 'other products of illicit commerce' obtained from foreign ships anchored at Portobelo.[45] And in this, as in all other areas of activity, Pedrosa y Guerrero claimed, the main beneficiaries were the *tenientes*, who acted in collusion with the governors of Popayán.[46]

Above all else, however, it was the power wielded by *tenientes* and *corregidores* over native communities that most frequently provoked the wrath of Crown officials in Bogotá, as indeed of the ecclesiastical authorities in Popayán. So far, Indians have been absent from this discussion of conditions on the frontier, but as is clearly shown by the following dispute, which in 1709 pitted a clique of miners that included the Mosqueras, Don Francisco de Arboleda Salazar and Don Bernardo Alfonso de Saa against Nóvita's *teniente de gobernador*, Tomás Romero Donoro, the single most important incentive for purchasing a *tenientazgo* in one of the provinces of the Chocó was the control this post conferred over Indian labour. Conflict between the miners and Romero Donoro erupted soon after the latter was appointed as deputy of Nóvita province, and it was caused by three specific issues. First, according to a petition presented on behalf of the Mosquera faction, the new *teniente* refused to supply the miners with a large enough allocation of Indians to meet their labour requirements, which they specified as the production and transportation of foodstuffs for the maintenance of their *cuadrillas*, and the construction of the huts or dwellings in which the slaves were housed. Secondly, the petitioners claimed that the *teniente* forbade them to buy their food supplies (maize and plantains) directly from Indians – as they presumably had done in the past – and that, instead, they were now obliged to deal with 'traders and middlemen'. Thirdly, they stated that the *teniente* had overturned an earlier decision by the *audiencia* allowing the petitioners to employ 100 Indians from Tadó in their own operations in Iró and Mungarra, redirecting them instead to the mines of Nóvita and Río Negro, which were already served by 240 Indians. The miners implied that Romero Donoro had carried out these actions because he had mining interests of his own in Nóvita and Río Negro.[47]

Tomás Romero Donoro certainly seems to have been a miner in his own right, and to have represented a clique or faction of miners that included Don

Miguel de la Asperilla and Don Luis de Acuña y Berrio – the latter a former *teniente* of Noanama/Nóvita province, who was soon to become *teniente* of Citará.[48] It was he whom Don Francisco de Alcantud y Gaona attempted – unsuccessfully, as it turned out – to detain on a murder charge a decade later.[49] But it is not just the Mosquera petition that reveals the influence *tenientes* could bring to bear over the supply of labour. In passing judgement on the case in 1709, the *protector de naturales* commented on the impunity which that family had enjoyed when it had been represented in the office of *teniente* of Nóvita province. The *protector* clarified that the service of 100 Tadó Indians, which the Mosqueras claimed had been granted by the *audiencia*, had been granted only temporarily, and only in response to their request for assistance in the clearing, planting and irrigation of some land on which they intended to grow maize and plantains. While they certainly had been permitted to employ 100 Indians in the early stages, the *audiencia* specified that only six Indians would be allocated thereafter. That they had seen fit to ignore that instruction was entirely down to the autonomy they enjoyed as *tenientes* in that province.[50] Because these officials, the most senior representatives of royal authority in the region, played a key role in the allocation of labour (receiving a fee each time they allocated a group of Indians), they used their power and influence to favour their own mining or commercial enterprises, or those of their allies and collaborators, over others.[51]

Access to native labour was essential to the survival of the developing economy of the Chocó. However, it should be noted that with few exceptions, recorded at the very beginning of the eighteenth century, Indians were not to become the main labour force for the region's mining enterprises.[52] Instead, early in the century, black slaves began to be introduced in large and growing numbers, radically transforming the demographic structure of this frontier region. It was they who were to meet the labour requirements of the many mining camps scattered across the length and breadth of Nóvita and Citará provinces. Despite the high cost of procurement – approximately 500 pesos for a prime slave – the mining enterprises of the Chocó came increasingly to rely on imported slave labour.[53] According to William Sharp, in 1724 2000 slaves were employed in mining and related activities. By 1759, numbers had almost doubled, to 3918, and continued to rise steadily until 1782, when the slave population peaked at 7088. The total black population was considerably larger than this, however, for a large population of freedmen also emerged over the course of the eighteenth century, reaching 3899 by 1782.[54]

The Indian role in the emerging mining economy of the Chocó was to be a supporting, but equally critical one. As Vicente de Aramburu reported on returning to Santa Fe in 1713, 'although the Indians are not . . . employed in the . . . extraction of gold . . . they assist in and contribute to all [other] activities conducive to this end'.[55] Indians supplied the basic foodstuffs that constituted the staple diet of the slave labour force. At least during the early decades of the century, they built storehouses, slave huts, and dwellings for the Spaniards who inhabited mining camps and settlements established across the entire lowland area. Indians also supplied the canoes necessary for the transportation of goods, and, most importantly in this region where the streams and rivers constituted serious obstacles to the movement of men and materials, Indian males, by far the more proficient at river navigation, were drawn into the service of miners and merchants to introduce the supplies crucial to the continuance of Spanish settlement in the Chocó.[56] Tatama province was somewhat of an exception to this rule, in that Indians here fulfilled a far more limited role. This part of the Chocó contained fewer streams and rivers than Nóvita or Citará, and was poorer in alluvial deposits. It was also en route from the cities of the Cauca Valley, among the main sources of supplies for the region as a whole. It was, therefore, to the small population of the three settlements of Tatama province – Chamí, San Juan and Mombú, estimated to total 100 tributaries in 1720 (133 in 1729)[57] – that fell the task of carrying into the Chocó imports of foodstuffs, manufactures and other goods introduced by merchants and traders from Anserma, Cartago, Buga, Toro and other cities of the interior. This was said to be the most onerous labour service of all, for not only was much of the route overland, but the *cargueros* of Tatama were required to carry exceptionally heavy loads – three to four *arrobas* per man – for the duration of the eleven-day journey from Chamí to Dodubar, the point of embarkation on the Atrato from where supplies were later transported by river into Citará province.[58] The fact that children were usually taken along to ease the burden by carrying food supplies for the journey, and the low life expectancy of males in the province, attributed entirely to the physical strain caused by the heavy weights carried, were concerns brought before the attention of the Crown on two separate occasions in 1720 alone.[59]

The litany of abuses to which colonial officials subjected Indian peoples will undoubtedly be familiar to all historians of colonial Latin America, and for this reason, two further examples will suffice to illustrate the power wielded by *tenientes* and *corregidores* over native communities on the frontier. In 1713, Vicente de Aramburu drew attention to the process whereby *tenientes* were beginning to gain control over the supply of foodstuffs – a role previously assumed by the indigenous communities for profit – by appropriating agricultural lands, employing displaced Indians to cultivate and harvest maize, and selling on the product to the region's miners. This was a profitable operation indeed, for in displacing native communities from their lands, *tenientes* not only deprived Indians of income customarily earned from growing and selling maize to miners, but also cut off the latter's traditional source of supply, leading to the doubling of the cost of maize from one peso per *colado* to two.[60] That this phenomenon was taking place in Nóvita province by 1708 becomes clear from the documents relating to the Mosquera–Romero Donoro case, which show Jacinto and Nicolás de Mosquera and Bernardo de Saa (among others) as the owners of substantial agricultural holdings, from which other miners were obliged to purchase maize for the maintenance of their *cuadrillas*.[61] The same case also suggests, however, that merchants (perhaps allies or partners of the *teniente*) were beginning to assume the role of brokers between local Indian communities and Spanish miners, the Mosqueras referring to the 'traders and middlemen' from whom they now obtained foodstuffs sold by Indians. It would appear, in fact, that this latter practice was more widespread in the Chocó, for in 1711 Antioquia's *protector de indios*, Rafael de Oquendo, indicated that rather than appropriating land for their own use, *tenientes* and/or *corregidores* commonly purchased produce for re-sale at a higher price, depriving Indians in this way of a portion of their earnings.[62]

In all these activities, *tenientes* were assisted by the *corregidores*, whom Aramburu described as mere *factores*, or agents, of their seniors – swiftly replaced if seen to dedicate themselves too openly to their own interests: 'they appoint and remove [*corregidores*] . . . whenever it appears that they neglect [the *tenientes*'] business, applying themselves too energetically to their own [instead]'.[63] However, one way in which *corregidores* made a living in the Chocó, aside from the customary share of tributes collected, was through the *repartimiento de mercancías*, or forced sale of goods, a practice introduced in Spanish America in the late seventeenth century and finally legalised in 1756.[64] We have, in a long report submitted to the Council of the Indies in 1720 by the bishop of Popayán, Juan Gómez Frías, a good description of how the *repartimiento* functioned in the Chocó. According to information gathered by the ecclesiastical *visitadores* Nicolás de Inestrosa and Fray Manuel de Abastos y Castro, *corregidores* combined the forced distribution of goods with their role as labour brokers between Spanish merchants and Indian communities. In effect, the report claimed, when a merchant obtained the labour of a number of Indians to serve as *cargueros*, he paid the wages due not to the Indians but to the *corregidor*. This official in turn compensated Indians for their work, not in money, but in goods – principally clothing and *aguardiente* – which he had bought from that same merchant for re-sale locally. The value attached to the goods supplied to Indians was determined not by market value, but by the *corregidor* himself, with due regard for personal profit. According to the bishop, this was an extremely profitable operation for merchant and *corregidor* alike. The merchant maximised his profit. The *corregidor* appropriated for himself a share of the profits from trade.[65]

For the Indians, on the other hand, the *repartimiento de mercancías* was a particularly onerous imposition, for as the Franciscan provincial Dionisio de Camino informed *oidor* Martínez Malo, in order to purchase badly needed supplies, they were obliged to offer the goods received through the *repartimiento* at a fraction of the market value.[66] And this was not, moreover, the only way in which native communities served as a source of profit for administrators and merchants and as a market for European goods. In 1713, Vicente de Aramburu explained that Indians were also drawn into trade with merchants to obtain goods such as tools (knives, axes) and the glass beads with which they adorned various parts of their bodies. For all these goods, the *oidor* considered, Indians paid excessive prices: 'for a bunch of these glass beads, they are charged 10 to 12 gold pesos . . . prices for knives and axes are equally high . . . I was certainly astounded [to discover] that they were forced to pay four pesos for an axe'.[67]

This examination of the main features of frontier government in the early part of the eighteenth century illustrates the many and varied ways in which colonial administrators exploited short periods of political office in the Chocó to advance interests in mining or trade, and to amass great personal fortunes. This should not be interpreted to mean, however, that officials could act with complete impunity in this isolated region, distant as it was from the main centres of government elsewhere in the colony. For in spite of the coincidence of interest that led Spaniards to risk the danger and discomfort of a temporary sojourn in this inhospitable corner of the empire, relationships among Europeans were never free of strife. Conflict among Europeans – between individuals, factions, interest groups – was so common that the first governor of the Chocó, Don Francisco de Ibero, said of his fellow Spaniards that 'they do not know how to live without conflicts and quarrels'.[68] Many sources of dissension existed on the frontier, but no single issue caused greater friction than access to Indians, be this for the purpose of labour, tribute or conversion. Competition over Indians was a major source of conflict here because, far from accepting their assigned role in the developing economy of the region, native communities across the Pacific lowlands devised a variety of strategies to resist the impositions of Spanish colonisation, repeatedly deserting the villages to re-establish their communities in regions as yet unoccupied by the Spanish, and rejecting all efforts on the part of friars and other clergy to inculcate Christianity. These responses, common across the region but especially characteristic of the peoples of Citará, will be discussed in greater detail in Chapter 7. As the purpose of this chapter is to explain the main features of Spanish society on the frontier, the following section will introduce the clergy to the discussion, focusing specifically on the activities of Spanish *doctrineros* in the Chocó, their relationships with fellow Europeans, and the reasons why they seemingly failed to provide indigenous peoples with effective protection from the most exploitative aspects of Spanish colonisation.

Religious administration

Over the course of the first half of the eighteenth century, it was frequently alleged that far from dedicating themselves to the task of conversion and the administration of the sacraments, Spanish clergy in the Chocó (the Franciscans being singled out for particular criticism) rivalled *tenientes, corregidores* and other settlers in their exploitation of indigenous peoples. Writing in 1712 in the context of a recent mass migration from the settlements of Citará province to an uninhabited region in the vicinity of the Murri river, Antioquia's governor Don Joseph López de Carvajal commented that 'if . . . tenientes and corregidores are perceived as abhorrent by said natives . . . the friars are no less so . . . for they too have harassed and oppressed them . . . neglecting completely [their duty to provide] Christian instruction'.[69] Antioquia's *protector de indios*, Rafael de Oquendo, similarly reported the 'desperation' that 'the mere mention' of the Franciscans provoked in the Indians, to the extent that, as he put it, 'I can [truthfully] say that they view Christianity and the Gospel with hatred'.[70] To support their allegations, and thus justify their decision to offer protection to the Citará 'fugitives' and make permanent the new settlement at Murri, both governor and protector advanced evidence provided by prominent caciques and *capitanes* from the Citará villages of Quibdó and Bebará to the effect that the Franciscans, 'preferring . . . their own business to the teaching of Doctrine', attended only 'to the personal service of the chusma', and that 'they and their children . . . are . . . punished and oppressed by the priests'.[71] Other observers, more reliable witnesses than López de Carvajal and perhaps even Oquendo, also expressed profound reservations about the conduct of Spanish missionaries in the Chocó, reporting on numerous occasions the maltreatment of Indians subjected to 'Franciscan discipline', and the involvement of priests in commercial activities contrary to their religious ministry. In 1720, to give just one example, Don Francisco de Alcantud y Gaona claimed that it was the 'insupportable' nature of the abuses suffered by Indians at the hands of the friars that led them to escape to the *cimarronas* (remote and inaccessible communities), 'where they . . . [continue to] live in their idolatry'.[72]

Successive bishops in Popayán and senior members of the Franciscan order in Santa Fe, some of whom were more prepared than others to give credence to accusations of the general and non-specific kind that were most commonly made against priests on the frontier, nevertheless shared the concerns of Alcantud and other government ministers regarding the meagre achievements of the missionary programme in the Chocó.[73] As early as 1700, Bishop Fray Mateo de Villafañe wrote to the Franciscan *comisario* in Peru, Father Miguel Mora, to report that he considered unsatisfactory the quality of religious instruction provided by the missionaries.[74] In 1720, Bishop Juan Gómez Frías reported the Indians' 'total ignorance of Our Holy Catholic Faith and aversion towards everything relating to Christian Doctrine'.[75] Sixteen years later, Bishop Diego Fermín de Vergara, travelling through the region on the first leg of a pastoral visit that was to take him across a large part of his diocese, similarly considered the native population to be as 'heathen' as before their conquest. Not only were Indians extremely ignorant of Christian doctrine, but rarely participated in the sacraments of penitence or communion.[76] Even the Franciscan provincial Dionisio de Camino, writing in defence of the friars in 1731, recognised that despite the many years that had passed since their reduction, the Indians of the Chocó continued to practise many of their old customs, and that missionary instruction had been insufficient to implant Catholic practices among them.[77]

Among all the Spanish clergy based in the Chocó, it was the Franciscans who were most strongly criticised for their failure to advance Christianity among Indians long accustomed to Spanish colonisation. This was notwithstanding evidence that showed that the Franciscan record among the Emberá peoples was no poorer than that of the secular priests who administered the Waunana *doctrinas* of Nóvita province. Indeed, in informing the Crown in 1729 that the vast majority of native people in that province had no understanding whatsoever of even the most basic rudiments of Catholicism, the governor of Popayán commented that this deficiency was particularly marked in the *doctrinas* administered by the seculars.[78] And when Bishop Vergara reported on his 1736 visita to Nóvita, he too was most vehement in his criticism of the *doctrinas* administered by the secular clergy, reserving his fiercest words to describe the condition of the churches and chapels in their care. The chapel at Nóvita – principal town and residence of the governor – was infested with snakes, frogs and other 'filthy creatures', and since it served to keep livestock it could be said to be no more decent than a 'cattlepen'. The chapel at Noanama, built of straw and reeds, contained little more than a paper image of a saint. The chapel at Los Brazos was as 'indecent' as the others. In El Cajón a hut served as chapel, and in Iró no such building even existed. Conversely, the Franciscan-administered *doctrina* of Tadó the bishop considered the least 'indecent' of the province.[79] And in material terms at least, the Franciscan *doctrinas* of Citará were the best maintained of the entire Chocó region.[80]

All Spanish priests in the Chocó, regardless of the branch of the clergy to which they belonged, attributed the failures of Christian conversion not to lack of effort or commitment on their part, but to the autonomy and impunity of *corregidores*, and to the excessive powers which these officials and their superiors, the *tenientes*, enjoyed over native communities. In giving evidence in 1720 to two ecclesiastical *visitadores* acting on behalf of Bishop Gómez Frías, the secular priests Joseph Hurtado del Aguila (Los Brazos) and Melchor de Arboleda Salazar (Noanama) recognised that few advances had been made in converting the Chocó's Indians to Christianity. But, in their defence, both priests stated that this was because, with the exception of the Indian children, they had no jurisdiction over their parishioners beyond the doors of the church. According to Arboleda Salazar, all efforts on his part to require local officials to bring Indians out from their *retiros* (retreats) and subject them to the settlements where they might be instructed in the Catholic faith had been unsuccessful. Fray Marcos Camargo, *doctrinero* of Lloró, similarly gave evidence that local officials deliberately undermined the priests' authority over native peoples, and positively encouraged Indians to disobey their pastors: 'they absolutely expect the priest to be nothing more nor less than a statue', as he saw it.[81]

The arguments advanced by secular priests and Franciscan friars to account for the meagre results of the evangelisation effort were accepted by even the most vociferous of critics. Gómez Frías, for instance, whose period as bishop of Popayán was marked by a lengthy campaign to divest the Franciscan order of its mission in the Chocó, reported in 1720 that if Indians remained ignorant of the Catholic faith this was largely because, being continuously employed in the movement of goods across the region, they were denied the time to attend church and receive instruction in Christian doctrine.[82] In a similar vein, Bishop Diego Fermín de Vergara reported in 1736 that because Indians were permanently occupied in transporting goods on behalf of Spanish officials – he mentioned governors along with *corregidores* – they neither attended Mass nor fulfilled other Christian obligations. This bishop in fact described the *corregidores* as 'great thieves', whose houses were like warehouses stocked full of 'rotten clothing' and other 'ridiculous goods' with which they claimed to compensate Indians for their labour.[83] For his part, the Franciscan provincial, Fray Dionisio de Camino, focused on the practice of selling *corregimientos* to explain his order's failures in the region. Because the *corregidores* bought their posts they had no alternative but to keep the Indians employed throughout the year. Priests had no power to challenge *corregidores*. Not only was it made clear to them that their authority did not extend beyond the church, but even this authority was undermined when children were removed from the care of *doctrineros* whenever required to assist in the tending of maize fields. Furthermore, since it was in the church, or chapel, that the *corregidor* distributed tasks among Indians, it was not surprising that it was avoided at all costs.[84]

Conflict between priests and local administrators over access to Indians for the purpose of conversion was, then, a further notable feature of life on the frontier during the early part of the eighteenth century.[85] But for reasons explained at the beginning of this chapter, the real nature of relationships between officials and priests, many of whom were themselves members of the most prominent families of the region, were less clear-cut than the latter's justifications for poor performance would indicate. Contemporary documents certainly show that on occasion instances of serious conflict did erupt between Franciscan *doctrineros*, for example, and wealthy Spaniards who combined interests in mining and trade with official administrative posts. It was such a case that brought the friars into conflict with the Mosqueras in the early 1700s. Hostilities between the friars and the family first broke out in July 1704, when Fray Francisco Moreno, recently arrived to take control of the *doctrina* of Tadó, discovered that the vast majority of its Indian inhabitants lived not in that *doctrina*, but along the Iró river, where they were employed, on a rotational basis he described as a *mita*, in growing maize and plantains for the slaves of Jacinto Mosquera's mining camps. According to testimony dated March 1706, neither Fray Francisco nor the (unnamed) *corregidor* – who apparently assisted the friar in his efforts to return Tadó's Indians to their settlement, on feast days at least – could rival the power of Don Jacinto and his 'agents and servants'.[86] The control this miner exercised over native people was such, the Franciscan claimed, that he was able not only to appropriate extensive Indian lands in the area, but, through coercive means, to employ displaced Indians on those same lands for a mere three pesos (invariably paid in goods rather than cash) for three months of labour. The obvious implication of this state of affairs was that Father Moreno was powerless to carry out his religious duties among the Indians of Tadó, not least because in taking from native communities lands upon which they had traditionally relied for food, the Mosqueras obliged them to seek more remote and less fertile lands for their own use, thus placing ever greater distances between Indians and priest.[87]

The 'dominion' that the Mosqueras enjoyed over the Indian people of Tadó was not, however, the only, or even the main, issue that was to pit the Franciscan order against this important Popayán family. In 1707, undoubtedly in order to avoid further disruptive clashes with the missionaries, the Mosqueras succeeded in obtaining the agreement of Bishop Villafañe to erect a new parish in Noanama/Nóvita, which was to incorporate the Indian population transferred from Tadó to Iró and Mungarra, where the family's extensive lands and goldmines were located. They also persuaded the bishop to grant Don Nicolás de Mosquera, *teniente* and *corregidor* in the province by 1707, episcopal authorisation to appoint an interim priest (a secular), pending completion of the proper procedures for the erection of new parishes.[88] This dispute, which originated in an altercation between miners and missionaries over the latter's access to Indians for the purpose of indoctrination, became a far more serious and indeed long-running affair over the prerogatives of the Franciscans in this region – prerogatives that the order jealously guarded against encroachment by the secular church.

Further layers of complexity were added to the conflict in 1709, when Tomás Romero Donoro took up his post as *teniente* of Noanama/Nóvita province. We have already seen that this new appointment provoked further confrontations, two factions of miners colliding above all else over numbers of Indians allocated by the new *teniente* to the region's various enterprises. Two friars – Fray Manuel Caicedo and Fray José de Santa Teresa – were also involved in this affair on the side of Romero Donoro, and one secular priest – Nicolás de Inestrosa – in support of the Mosquera clique. As all three were then, or would later become, involved in mining enterprises of their own in the Chocó, their interests in the case were probably not confined to the purpose that supposedly brought Spanish clerics to the frontier – namely, Christian conversion. This is not to suggest, of course, that religious motives were entirely absent, but rather that these may also have been bound up with issues decidedly less lofty. This is shown most clearly in the case of Father Caicedo. As successor to Francisco Moreno in the *doctrina* of Tadó, Caicedo clashed repeatedly with the Mosquera brothers on a variety of matters that included his inability to provide Christian instruction to an indigenous population that was absent from its *doctrina* for much of the year, the derisory wages paid to Indian workers on the family's lands, and the widespread practice of compensating Indians for their labour in kind, which left them indebted to the Mosqueras and therefore unable to meet their tribute and stipend obligations. Conflict over the status of the new parish of Iró and Mungarra (Caicedo was to dedicate much time and effort over the following years to secure its restoration to the order) thus combined with more mundane concerns about the effects of the Mosqueras' actions on the priest's own livelihood. By 1708, Fray Manuel had been obliged to lay out 50 gold *castellanos* to purchase from one Antonio – a 'page' of Don Jacinto's – a tract of agricultural land, for his parishioners no longer possessed sufficient land of their own from which to supply their priest with food.[89] Caicedo was also, moreover, a member of a leading Cali family with extensive mining interests in the Chocó, and he was even related by marriage to that very same Mosquera family, his brother José (deceased) having been married to Doña Agustina, sister of Don Jacinto and Don Nicolás.[90] Furthermore, the Franciscan was personally involved in mining on his own account, for in 1724 he informed the Consejo de Indias that in 21 years of residence in the region he had not only administered several *doctrinas* but also engaged in goldmining, his reports demonstrating clearly the breadth of his experience in this field.[91] And when, in the mid-1720s, the Consejo discussed Father Caicedo, the *fiscal* noted that his nephew Roque de Caicedo – also a miner and priest – was at that time in charge of the administration of his uncle's ventures in the region.[92]

Fewer details emerge from the sources about the interests of the second friar, a lay brother, involved in the dispute over the Indians of Tadó, though the evidence certainly shows that Fray José de Santa Teresa also had mining interests of his own to advance. Fray José apparently travelled to New Granada at the turn of the century in the company of Mateo de Villafañe, bishop-elect of Popayán. Acting on behalf of his order, Nuestra Señora del Carmen de la Antigua, this lay brother came to the colony, with the permission of the Crown, for the specific purpose of collecting alms, the proceeds of which he was to use to purchase lands for the support of his monastery in Valladolid. According to testimony presented to the Consejo in the early 1720s by provincial Fray Francisco Montiel de Fuentenovilla, José de Santa Teresa did indeed purchase lands, comprising some gold-mines as well as plantain groves, on the banks of the Chocó's San Juan river, and administered the property in person from 1711 until he died (intestate) some time before 1723. The proceeds from the sale of the property – 896 pesos and 6 reales – were later forwarded to his order back in Spain.[93]

As for Nicolás de Inestrosa, he was just starting out on his clerical career when the Mosqueras and the Franciscans clashed over the new parish, and his support for the family at that time must surely be attributable to his appointment as priest of Iró and Mungarra in March 1707, a benefice he was to hold until the early 1730s.[94] Over the years that followed, Inestrosa's activities in the Chocó – like Manuel Caicedo's – expanded to include extensive interests in mining. In 1730 or 1731, following the promulgation of a royal *cédula* (June 1727) prohibiting clerics from owning or operating mines,[95] Inestrosa appealed to the Crown for permission to retain control of his own mine, in the discovery and operation of which he had invested a considerable sum of money, and in which he employed black slaves rather than Indian labour. He asked to be exempted from this ruling on the grounds that his sole purpose in operating the mine was to support his orphaned sisters, one of whom was a widow with five children. To add further weight to his case, Inestrosa clarified that he did not administer the property in person, but employed a 'third party' to do so on his behalf.[96] In November 1731, the Crown requested from the bishop of Popayán a report on Nicolás de Inestrosa's activities, and since witnesses favourable to him – including, ironically, his relative Nicolás de Caicedo Inestrosa – gave evidence that he properly fulfilled his priestly duties, did not reside in the mining camp, did not employ Indians in it or as suppliers of foodstuffs to it, and paid all *quintos* in full, we may assume that he was eventually granted the exemption requested.[97] Certainly, by the 1750s Inestrosa had become a prominent miner and slave-owner in his own right, a census dating from the middle of that decade listing him as the owner of the gold-mines of Santa Lucía del Calabozo, and of 78 working slaves (46 men and 32 women).[98] And, in a further twist of irony, when Don Nicolás died in 1759, he left a fortune in property and slaves, valued at 60,000 *patacones*, to the Franciscan College of Cali.[99] His early collaboration with the Mosqueras had clearly served him well.

While the cases of Manuel Caicedo and Nicolás de Inestrosa are the most conspicuous of all those found in the documents – largely because of the paperwork generated by the dispute over the status of Iró and Mungarra, which remained unresolved until 1748 – these priests were by no means exceptional in the Chocó in the first half of the eighteenth century. Participation in mining was prohibited by the Recopilación de Leyes de Indias – a prohibition frequently reiterated by royal *cédula* – but contemporary documents clearly show that this law, like so many others intended to regulate the behaviour of settlers in the colonies, was routinely violated by both branches of the clergy in the Chocó.[100] Late in the seventeenth century, for instance, Nóvita's secular priest, Don Nicolás Ordoñez de Lara, reportedly acted as overseer or administrator of a *cuadrilla* belonging to Agustín Ginés Fernández.[101] Don Agustín Roso de Villalba, who replaced Nicolás de Inestrosa as priest of Iró and Mungarra, was another secular to acquire a mining interest on the frontier, a census dating from the mid-1750s showing him as the owner of the mining camp of Piedra Piedra, and of 16 working slaves (11 men and 5 women).[102] Other examples emerge later in the century, such as Juan de Bonilla y Delgado, priest of Nóvita in the 1740s, who owned a mine in partnership with Francisco de Rivas.[103] According to William Sharp, in 1752 these two men formed a company to exploit gold deposits in Nóvita province, with costs and profits to be shared equally between both partners. Rivas and Bonilla y Delgado invested a total of 25,290 pesos in the venture. Half this sum was used to purchase a *cuadrilla* of 33 slaves; a proportion of the other half was invested in the purchase of equipment, the rest remaining as working capital. By 1759, Rivas and Bonilla y Delgado owned a total of 98 slaves; and by 1768, the year Rivas died, the property was valued at 78,980 pesos, the size of their *cuadrilla* having increased to 212 slaves.[104]

With the exception of Manuel Caicedo (who informed the Consejo in person of his mining interests in the Chocó) and Fray Juan Caballero (who was known to administer a gold-mine owned by his mother), the evidence of Franciscan involvement in the mining industry and/or other commercial ventures is indirect, no evidence having been found to link individual missionaries with specific enterprises.[105] In 1720, however, Bishop Gómez Frías reported to the Franciscan provincial, Fray Francisco Antonio Felices, on the 'disorderly' conduct of several friars in the Chocó, describing how their behaviour, participation in mining, and lifestyles that were at variance with their religious obligations and the poverty that they preached, had 'scandalised my flock'.[106] Although this bishop was a biased source, and his evidence perhaps unreliable, Fray Francisco clearly took his comments seriously and acted on that report, for when the Council of the Indies discussed the case a few years later, it was noted that the missionaries in question – Manuel Caicedo and Juan Caballero, both of whom we know to have operated businesses, and a third, Matías Méndez – had been withdrawn temporarily by their order, 'for their bad behaviour . . . [and their activities] as . . . miners, merchants and other vices'.[107] There are, in addition, suggestions that other friars may also have been guilty of infringing both the law and the strict vow of poverty that the Franciscan order demanded of its members. Certainly this was an opinion held by highly placed officials in the colony. When Don Antonio de la Pedrosa y Guerrero returned to Madrid after establishing the first Viceroyalty, for example, he advised the Crown that missionaries should not in future be permitted to operate mines in the Chocó, either on their own behalf *or through intermediaries*.[108] Furthermore, royal *cédulas* issued over the course of the 1720s and 1730s, intended to proscribe clerical involvement in mining and trade, reiterated time and again that that prohibition applied to both 'seculars and regulars'.[109]

One final phenomenon characteristic of the Chocó frontier during the first half of the eighteenth century should be mentioned here: namely, that in addition to the Spanish priests cited above, most of whom combined their priestly duties with ownership of substantial and profitable mining operations, many unbeneficed Popayán clergy made their way to the Chocó in the early decades of the eighteenth century in the expectation of deriving an income from mining or trade. In his study of seventeenth-century Popayán, Peter Marzhal showed that the number of unbeneficed clergy in the diocese was rising at the beginning of the eighteenth century, as opportunities for employment failed to keep pace with increasing numbers of ordained priests.[110] No information has been found to indicate whether this trend continued into the 1720s, but in a 1721 report to Bishop Gómez Frías, Miguel Chacón de la Enzina, *promotor fiscal* of the diocese, not only made reference to the large number of unbeneficed clergy who were known to live in the Chocó despite having no legitimate occupation to detain them there – which he specified as serving a parish *or administering a mine* – but also indicated that since the only other way to make a living was through 'trade and commerce', it was unsurprising that 'the common people should accuse them of being merchants and traders'.[111] In the mid-1720s, some five years after the bishop, following Chacón de la Enzina's recommendations, issued a decree to the effect that all priests not detained in the Chocó for a legitimate purpose should leave without delay,[112] Fray Dionisio de Camino informed the Crown of the 'disturbances' that unbeneficed priests continued to provoke in the Franciscan *doctrinas* of Citará province. Camino did not reveal the identity of the clergy in question, or provide details of the activities in which they were involved, but limited his complaint to the way in which they conspired 'with the inhabitants . . . to make reports against the religious', all in order, he claimed, to take over their Indian parishes.[113] In the short and medium term, the sources show, neither the bishop's decree nor repeated royal *cédulas* succeeded in bringing an end to the problem, for in 1743 Don Manuel Martínez de Escobar, governor of the Chocó, once again reported the 'pernicious' effects of the presence in the region of 'religious . . . [and] vagrant clergy'.[114]

Conflict between Spanish priests and colonial administrators over access to Indians; friction between different branches of the clergy over control of Indian parishes; participation of clerics in activities contrary to their religious ministry; the employment of Indians in mining, agriculture, transportation and other ventures for the benefit of local officials; the use of chapels for the purpose of distributing labour; and the general neglect of duty that characterised political and religious administration in the region: all these were features of frontier society in the Chocó during the first half of the eighteenth century, and all contributed to shaping indigenous responses to Spanish colonisation. This is not to imply, however, that the corruption that characterised frontier government, or the extent of exploitation to which native communities were subjected, were ignored by senior officials in the capital, or by ministers in Madrid. As the *fiscal* of the Council of the Indies commented in 1722, 'such complaints [regarding] the ... ill-treatment of Indians are well-known ... [and] the Council is not unaware [of them] ... on several occasions measures have been taken to contain the greed and ambition of those who govern [there]'.[115] At the local level, the first decades of the century were also marked by efforts on the part of senior ministers in Santa Fe and successive bishops in Popayán, most notably Juan Gómez Frías, to establish a greater degree of control over both frontier government and religious administration in the Chocó. These initiatives all failed to bring about anything more than some improvement in tax collection, as distance, isolation, and the haphazard and piecemeal nature of the Crown's policies for governing this frontier territory all combined to minimise the impact of reform and render ineffective official efforts to curb the worst excesses of Spanish colonisation. Nevertheless, as the measures taken during these years serve to illustrate further conditions on the Chocó frontier, they merit further consideration.

Political reform

In bringing before the attention of the Crown the irregularity of colonial administration on the frontier, senior officials in New Granada sought not only to bring about reform, but to explain the ways in which the region's characteristics contributed to its misgovernment. There was general agreement that existing methods of government failed to create the conditions necessary to ensure effective and impartial administration of justice, and that a combination of factors contributed to this state of affairs. First, the sale of *corregimientos* and *tenientazgos* not only rendered it inevitable that purchasers would seek to use their offices for private gain, but also prevented governors from exercising effective supervision over their deputies: 'royal laws and prerogatives are not recognised [here]', the *oidor* Aramburu commented in 1713.[116] Secondly, the numerous opportunities for personal enrichment that existed in this isolated territory constituted irresistible inducements to dishonesty at all levels of administration. Even the most senior representatives of royal authority in the *gobernación* were implicated in this circle of corruption, the autonomy and impunity of local officials being repeatedly attributed to mutually beneficial relationships with successive governors in Popayán. Giving evidence in 1711, for instance, Lorenzo de Salazar claimed that on a recent visit of inspection to the Chocó, the governor of Popayán (Pérez de Vivero) arrived laden with goods for sale. Fifteen Indian carriers, he said, were required to introduce the clothing which that official brought to sell to the miners and other residents.[117] The veracity of this particular allegation, like so many others made by Spaniards on the frontier, cannot be determined, but in reporting to the Crown on his findings in the colony, Don Antonio de la Pedrosa certainly considered that 'the only ... purpose' that took governors to the Chocó was to 'acquire wealth'. Pedrosa drew to the attention of the authorities in Spain the fact that these officials were known to complete their terms with savings far in excess of the sums they could be expected to accumulate from salaries alone. Thus it was possible for governors on a salary of 2750 *patacones* a year, which amounted to 13,750 *patacones* over a typical five-year term, to leave that *gobernación* with fortunes estimated to range between 150,000 and 200,000 pesos, depending on 'the industry and ability of each [individual]'. Such fortunes, Pedrosa said, could only be made by fraud or the 'sweat' of the king's vassals.[118]

Thirdly, the frontier character of the Chocó, by precluding social and political development, encouraged Spaniards to look on residence in the region as a temporary expedient, the sole purpose of which was to amass wealth. This was the conclusion of two *oidores* who conducted visits of inspection in the 1710s and early 1730s. The first, Vicente de Aramburu, attributed the 'disorder' of the Chocó largely to the absence, in the towns and villages, of 'such a properly organised community as Your Majesty has ordered be developed and maintained'.[119] The second, Martínez Malo, similarly drew attention to the fact that 'there are [in that territory] no long-term residents or persons such as might organise and form a community, since they are people without fixed abode there'. Order and *república* could not be expected in a region where the seat of the governor, the village of Nóvita, consisted of no more than 'twenty houses, made of wood and straw, as the nature of the territory allows nothing more', and where the Spanish inhabitants lived mainly in rustic encampments consisting of 'one or two houses, made of the same materials, scattered across an indescribably harsh and uncivilised land'.[120] All recognised the need to encourage social development. Alcantud y Gaona, for instance, recommended in 1720 that it was imperative that 'two cities or towns be founded, one in the province of Nóvita, and the other in Citará, and all mineowners and other settlers should be compelled to keep a house and home in the city or town of . . . [their respective] province, and no one should be allowed to exploit mines unless he keeps his family in the province, and his wife, if he is married'.[121]

The main thrust of reform during these years, however, was political, all observers focusing first and foremost on the desirability of segregating the entire Chocó from the *gobernación* of Popayán and appointing an independent governor with a salary generous enough to ensure that 'he should not have occasion, out of necessity, to allow himself to be bribed'.[122] But in 1719, Don Antonio de la Pedrosa, who while personally favouring complete segregation was reluctant to implement such a measure without royal authorisation, which was not in the short term forthcoming, took the decision to appoint not a governor, but a superintendent selected by, and answerable directly to, the *audiencia* in Santa Fe. Under the terms of the first *nombramiento*, of Don Luis de Espinosa, Popayán's governor retained his jurisdiction over this frontier territory, and the right to *confirm* all appointments other than that of superintendent. The duties of this official, in turn, were to be limited to collecting taxes and tributes, ensuring that the San Juan and Atrato rivers remained closed to navigation and illegal trade, and protecting indigenous populations from exploitation.[123] The creation of a new layer of government in the Chocó certainly brought some immediate improvements – Viceroy Villalonga reporting in 1723 that contributions to the royal treasury had increased significantly – but as Alcantud y Gaona argued, the only real change brought about by the appointment of a superintendent – 'with no income whatsoever to support himself' – was that patronage over the sale of official posts in the region was transferred from the governors to the new official.[124]

Despite initial reservations, the Crown finally accepted the advice of its senior representatives in the colony and, by royal *cédula* of 28 September 1726, segregated the Chocó from the jurisdiction of Popayán, created a new *gobernación*, and appointed Don Francisco de Ibero as its first governor, a post he took up in January 1729.[125] But even this appointment had minimal impact on standards of government on the frontier. For a start, it brought no change to the structure of government at lower levels: when he arrived in Nóvita in 1729, Don Francisco de Ibero proceeded to appoint his own *tenientes* and *corregidores*.[126] And since in 1730 Fray Dionisio de Camino reported on the recent sale of four *corregimientos* in Citará province, it is clear not only that sale of office continued, but that local administrators continued to enjoy the same autonomy and impunity as they had done under the management of Popayán. Nor did the segregation of the Chocó solve the problem of contraband in the short or medium term. By 1730, Francisco de Ibero had been dismissed from his post on the grounds of complicity with contrabandists, though it should be noted that in October 1729, just ten months after taking up the governorship, Ibero reported that allegations to the effect that he had permitted a vessel to sail up the Atrato in contravention of the law were false, resulting only from his efforts to curb 'the disorder' that characterised life on the frontier.[127] Nevertheless, as William Sharp observed, the sheer repetition of *cédulas* to prohibit navigation along the Chocó's two main river systems (1730, 1733, 1734, 1736) suggests ongoing problems of enforcement.[128] And it is clear from a much later petition presented to the Crown by the city of Buga in 1758 that even at this late stage supplies were customarily imported into the Chocó by vessels sailing up the San Juan from Buenaventura. According to the Buga petitioners, their trade with the region had virtually ceased, and unless measures were taken to stop the illegal introduction of supplies, not only that city but the entire *gobernación* of Popayán would face ruin.[129]

Religious reform

While ministers targeted the system of political administration, the ecclesiastical hierarchy, represented by the bishops of Popayán, targeted the region's religious administration. Their principal objective was to impose the authority and jurisdiction of the bishops over priests and parishes in this frontier territory. The Franciscans were seen as the single greatest obstacle to the achievement of this aim, and this was only partly the result of the poor reputation of the friars in the Chocó and their evident failure to convert Indians after decades of missionary endeavour.[130] It was also partly the result of the fact that diocesan bishops in New Granada, as in other parts of Spanish America during the first half of the eighteenth century, had begun to challenge the autonomy and independence of the regular orders in their mission territories.[131] There were good historical reasons for this move, for when in the sixteenth century the Crown placed responsibility for the pacification of border areas on the regular orders, it was envisaged that missionaries should assume control of unconquered Indian populations only for a limited period of ten years, after which the new converts would be handed over to the secular clergy, and a parochial and diocesan system of administration (parishes administered by secular priests under the direct control, jurisdiction and correction of the bishops) would be established. In practice, however, the conversion of Indians on the frontiers of the Spanish empire took a great deal longer, and in many areas, including the Chocó, the regulars continued to administer large territories and innumerable *doctrinas* long after their pioneering missionary work should have been completed.[132] As the zeal and moral integrity of the friars came into question, and as the number of ordained secular priests began to increase at a faster rate than the number of benefices available, it was inevitable that the privileges of the orders would clash with the jurisdictional claims of the bishops.

It is in this wider context that the vigorous campaign conducted by Bishop Juan Gómez Frías to divest the Franciscans of their mission in the Chocó must be interpreted. For in spite of overwhelming evidence to show that the efforts of the seculars to convert native peoples to Christianity were as ineffective as those of their regular counterparts, and that they were as guilty of routinely ignoring laws designed to prevent clergy participating in activities prejudicial to their religious ministry, the bishop not only singled out the friars for particular censure, but subjected them to a lengthy campaign intended to discredit them at court and curtail their influence in the colony. This is not to suggest, of course, that the bishop's evidence is invalid, but we must consider that other issues may also have motivated him repeatedly to bring conditions on the frontier before the attention of the Crown. Indeed, even at the highest levels of the Franciscan Province of Santa Fe, there was some acknowledgement that reports coming from the region might not be entirely reliable. Writing in 1719 in the context of a debate that took place within the order regarding the desirability of remaining in the Chocó, Provincial Francisco Felices stated that while he accepted that the friars were in danger of contravening their vow of poverty – 'who would deny . . . that a Franciscan would be in grave danger . . . where greed [and] self-interest . . . reign supreme' – he also doubted the veracity of some of the allegations made against the missionaries, which he attributed less to their conduct than to the general 'lawlessness' that characterised life on the frontier.[133]

Gómez Frías fought his campaign against the missionaries of the Chocó on two fronts. First, he sought to damage the reputation of the Franciscans by bringing before the attention of the authorities in Spain the profound divisions ('scandalous', in his words) that arose within the order in the run-up to the election, in 1723, of a new provincial to replace outgoing Francisco Felices. While these developments took place at a far higher level than that of the *doctrineros* on the frontier, they were nevertheless intimately connected with the Chocó in the sense that the candidates in this election – Manuel de la Prada, endorsed by Felices, and Dionisio de Camino, supported by one Fray Diego Barroso – divided over the future of the Franciscans' mission there. Whereas Camino and Barroso supported the order's continued presence in the Chocó, Felices represented a group within the Province of Santa Fe that favoured its withdrawal.[134] As provincial, Francisco Felices had certainly argued that, given the meagre achievements of the mission, no further progress could be expected among the Indians of the Chocó, whom he described as 'indomitable brutes involved in their idolatrous [practices]'. In discussing a communication from one Fray Juan Domingo Calderón to the effect that some sixty Indians had recently received the sacrament of penitence, and a handful of others that of communion, the provincial concluded that this was not much of an achievement after forty years of effort, and that a 'tree that bears no fruit is best cut down'.[135] According to Gómez Frías, Camino and Barroso opposed the election of Manuel de la Prada on precisely these grounds, but the important point in the context of our discussion is that the bishop used the debate as an opportunity to discredit both Diego Barroso – of whom he noted a long history of 'appointing favoured doctrineros, guardians, and other officers' – and Dionisio de Camino, whom he described as a man of 'no religious qualities'.[136] In 1721, in fact, it was even suggested that bishop and provincial had actually struck a bargain whereby the former would support the latter's candidate in exchange for his continuing efforts to convince the order of the desirability of transferring all the *doctrinas* of the Chocó to the secular clergy.[137] While neither candidate won the election on this occasion (the order chose Fray Buenaventura de Vega, a friar whom the viceroy considered sufficiently unconcerned about worldly matters to bring some unity back to the Province of Santa Fe), by the early 1730s Dionisio de Camino was in charge of the Franciscans in New Granada, his order having finally elected him as provincial.[138]

Of even greater impact at the local level were Gómez Frías's attempts to undermine the activities of the Franciscans, which he did by interpreting strictly the rights and privileges of the bishops under the terms of the Patronato Real.[139] Many examples are documented in government papers, but three will suffice to illustrate the ways in which this bishop sought to curtail the influence of the missionaries by, on the one hand, creating or confirming the creation of new secular-administered parishes and, on the other, refusing to erect new regular-administered *doctrinas*. The first case is that of Iró and Mungarra, the new parish that had been created in 1707 to incorporate the mines belonging to the Mosquera family. In 1719, Bishop Gómez Frías confirmed the appointment of Nicolás de Inestrosa as priest of the parish on the grounds that distance from Tadó prevented the Franciscan missionaries meeting the spiritual needs of the miners, slave gangs and other people who inhabited the camps, the basic premise being that since Iró and Mungarra had never formed part of Tadó and had thus never been administered by the Franciscans, it constituted a separate parish.[140] While in the medium term Gómez Frías lost the battle over Iró and Mungarra, the parish remained in the hands of seculars for the following thirty years: this was the time it took before the debate over its status at the highest levels of secular and ecclesiastical government in the colony and in Spain was finally resolved in favour of the Franciscans.[141]

The erection of a new parish for non-Indians in Citará province became the subject of another lengthy dispute between the bishop and the order. When, by royal *cédula* of 25 April 1722, the Crown acceded to the bishop's request for authorisation to erect a new parish for miners who claimed that their spiritual needs could not be met by the *doctrinero* of the distant settlement of Quibdó, Viceroy Villalonga, acting as vicepatron, refused to give consent to the appointment of a secular priest, on the grounds that if the new parish was deemed to fall within the jurisdiction of the Franciscan mission, then the order's right to present a candidate for appointment as its parish priest could not be waived. While this dispute was resolved far more quickly than that over Iró and Mungarra – a *cédula* of November 1724 authorised the Franciscans to present a candidate for appointment – by the end of the following year Fray Dionisio de Camino was reporting that the bishop had challenged the later *cédula* on the grounds that a secular priest had already been appointed, and that the implementation of the Crown's instruction would involve divesting the priest of his *curato*.[142]

While on the one hand Bishop Gómez Frías sought to curb the authority of the Franciscans by erecting new parishes for seculars, on the other he sought to prevent the order increasing its sphere of influence on the frontier by refusing to authorise the erection of new Indian *doctrinas*. When, in January 1720, Viceroy Villalonga presented Fray Juan de Ayala for appointment to the recently founded *doctrina* of Beté, Negua and Nemota, the bishop refused to confirm the appointment on two grounds. The first was a technical one: namely, that Beté had not been erected in accordance with canon law or the Patronato, under the terms of which the consent of the vicepatron followed, rather than preceded, the inspection and approval of the bishop. The second justification is more revealing. According to the bishop, a recent ecclesiastical *visita* conducted to the Chocó found that the settlement of Beté consisted of no more than three or four families captured in the Murri region, five or six dwellings, and a straw-covered chapel containing neither altar nor adornment. Moreover, Beté could not be established as a *doctrina* because the time granted by law to Indians to enjoy freedom from taxation while they settled in the new town had not yet passed, and therefore there was no source from which a priest's stipend might be paid. And besides, there was no evidence to indicate that the mining camps of the vicinity – which according to the Franciscans formed part of the new *doctrina* – were annexes of it and therefore required to contribute to its upkeep.[143] In this, as in the other cases, we may assume that the bishop's decision was overturned, for in the mid-1720s Fray Dionisio de Camino included Beté among the *doctrinas* administered by the Franciscans.[144]

Despite the vigorous campaign against the Franciscans conducted by Bishop Juan Gómez Frías, the order won a reprieve that lasted until the Bourbons finally introduced a major reform of the ecclesiastical establishment throughout the empire. This was largely because the Spanish Crown responded in an ambiguous and confused manner to the conflict between bishops and friars, supporting first one side and then the other. Despite the fact that the independence and autonomy of the friars continued to concern successive bishops – Diego Fermín de Vergara, for example, described the Franciscans in 1737 as a 'formidable regiment' of friars not subject to the vigilance and correction of the bishops but under the sole supervision of the prelates of their order – the missionaries did not begin their retreat until 1753.[145] In that year, Bishop Don Diego del Corro refused to appoint Fray Pedro Ramírez as *doctrinero* of Quibdó on the grounds that by royal *cédula*, of 1 February 1753, he was instructed to transfer all regular *doctrinas* in the Chocó to seculars as they became vacant.[146]

It is difficult to assess exactly what impact decades of conflict between bishops and friars over the status and administration of the region's *doctrinas* had on Indian populations in this frontier territory.[147] It is highly probable, however, that repeated disputes between the two branches of the Spanish clergy in the Chocó – as indeed between the religious and secular authorities – absorbed the energies of priests whose main duties were to protect native peoples from ill-treatment and convert them to the Christian faith; served further to discredit their religion before their Indian charges; and provided innumerable openings for Indians to continue to observe their own religious beliefs, and practise their traditional rituals.[148] As struggles for control over Indians dominated the activities of many clergy on the Chocó frontier over the first half of the eighteenth century, little attention was paid to the evangelisation and incorporation of indigenous peoples, severely limiting our understanding of the nature of Indian belief and ritual. Nevertheless, it is to the actions, if not the beliefs, of the indigenous population of the Chocó during these years that Chapter 7 now turns.

Notes

1 Antonio de Veroiz, 'Pacificación de la provincia del Citará. Su descripción. Tributos que pagaban los indios', 12 July 1688, in Ortega Ricaurte (ed.), *Historia documental*, pp. 139–40.

2 Antonio de Veroiz to Audiencia of Santa Fe, Lloró, 12 July 1688, in Ortega Ricaurte (ed.), *Historia documental*, p. 145. The 34 slaves Veroiz referred to belonged to the *cuadrillas* of Juan Bueso de Valdés (18), Miguel Benítez de la Serna (12) and Fabián Ramírez (4).

3 Veroiz, 'Pacificación', in Ortega Ricaurte (ed.), *Historia documental*, p. 141.

4 Even in the early 1690s, the process of discovering the location of Indian *retiros*, or retreats, was still taking place. In 1693, for instance, Antonio de Veroiz, now engaged in mining in Citará province with his own slave gang, founded a new settlement, Bebará, on the banks of the Bebará river, where he intended gradually to congregate Indians who had for many years lived dispersed in small groups in the vicinity of the river. See Antonio de Veroiz y Alfaro, 'Informe del sargento mayor D. Antonio de Veroiz y Alfaro sobre la fundación y reedificación del pueblo de Bebará, habitado por cincuenta y dos indios tributarios con sus familias. Sus gestiones al respecto', Citará, 30 November 1695, in Ortega Ricaurte (ed.), *Historia documental*, pp. 149–50.

5 Germán Colmenares, *Historia económica y social de Colombia, II. Popayán: una sociedad esclavista*, Bogotá, Editorial La Carreta, 1979, p. 144.

6 Veroiz, 'Pacificación', in Ortega Ricaurte (ed.), *Historia documental*, pp. 142–43.
7 William Frederick Sharp, *Slavery on the Spanish Frontier: The Colombian Chocó, 1680–1810*, Norman, OK, University of Oklahoma Press, 1976, pp. 179–80.
8 Colmenares, *Historia económica*, pp. 302–303; Zamira Díaz López, *Oro, sociedad y economía. El sistema colonial en la gobernación de Popayán: 1533–1733*, Bogotá, Banco de la República, 1994, pp. 263–67. See also AGI Santa Fe 411, Manuel Caicedo to Archbishop of Santa Fe, Tadó, 30 March 1707.
9 AGI Quito 143, Vicente de Aramburu to Crown, Santa Fe, 24 September 1713. Some years earlier, in 1694, the Bishop of Popayán had commented of the Chocó that it was inhabited by men 'with no fear of God stimulated [only] by greed and other vices'. AGI Quito 79, Pedro Díaz de Cienfuegos to Crown, Popayán, 7 June 1694.
10 Don Luis de Acuña y Berrio was accused of the murder of one Gaspar García Pizarro. No details of the incident have been found. AGI Santa Fe 362, Francisco de Alcantud y Gaona to Crown, Cartagena, 15 November 1720. It is to be noted that the terms 'contraband' and 'illicit' trade and/or commerce are used interchangeably in this chapter. According to Lance Grahn, however, 'more precise definitions existed in eighteenth-century Spanish jurisprudence'. The term 'illicit commerce' referred specifically to the direct and largely illegal trade of foreigners in Spanish America; where the term 'contraband' was used, it described cargo of Spanish or Spanish American origin, the carriage of which was forbidden to Spanish American ports; the term 'fraud' referred only to the movement between Spanish and Spanish American ports of products which, though part of legal trade, exceeded the amount allowed to be carried by a particular ship according to its licence. See Lance Grahn, *The Political Economy of Smuggling: Regional Informal Economies in Early Bourbon New Granada*, Dellplain Latin American Studies, Boulder, CO, and Oxford, Westview Press, 1997, p. 13.
11 AGI Santa Fe 362, Fray Manuel Caicedo, Madrid, 24 July 1724. According to Colmenares, the slaves working in the Chocó at the beginning of the century had been transferred there either from abandoned mining enterprises in Popayán, or from agricultural activities. See Colmenares, *Historia económica*, pp. 327–28. For figures on the Chocó's slave population see also Sharp, *Slavery*, pp. 199, 202.
12 Quibdó, 1 January 1720, in AGI Santa Fe 411, 'Testimonio de información recibida por . . . Don Nicolás de Inestrosa como visitador de las Provincias del Chocó', fol. 9. See also León Sánchez's testimony, fol. 10.
13 AGI Santa Fe 307, Francisco de Ibero to Crown, Nóvita, 29 October 1729.
14 AGI Santa Fe 362, Fray Manuel Caicedo, Madrid, 24 July 1724. See also the accompanying 'Relación y noticia individual de las ricas y abundantes Provincias del Chocó'. This document has no signature, but its content suggests that Fray Manuel Caicedo was its author.
15 See the testimonies of Captain Don Alejandro Casahus and León Sánchez, Quibdó, 1 January 1720, in AGI Santa Fe 411, 'Testimonio de información recibida por . . . Don Nicolás de Inestrosa', fols. 6, 10.
16 Colmenares, *Cali*, pp. 136, 142. According to Captain Don Alejandro Casahus, giving evidence before the ecclesiastical *visitador* Don Nicolás de Inestrosa, by January 1720 Francisco Caicedo employed slaves in Citará province as well. Casahus reported that Caicedo and the *ayudante* Manuel de Arriaga 'have about thirty slaves between them excluding chusma and . . . independent contractors'. This statement was dated Quibdó, 1 January 1720. AGI Santa Fe 405, 'Testimonio de autos pertenecientes al Convento de San Francisco sobre las doctrinas de las provincias del Chocó sobre la nueva erección que se hizo de parroquia en lo perteneciente a Quibdó, en virtud de real cédula', fols. 3–7.
17 See Lorenzo de Salazar's 'Declaración', Real de Minas de San Mateo, 24 September 1711, in AGI Santa Fe 307, 'Cuaderno . . . sobre la entrada al río Murri', fols. 81–82. For the family's role in the pacification campaigns of the mid-1680s, see AGI Santa Fe 204, Ramo

7, 'Autos obrados por ... Juan Bueso de Valdés sobre la retirada de Don Juan de Caicedo', and AGI Quito 15, 'Traslado de los Autos de ... Don Cristóbal de Caicedo Salazar ... sobre los servicios hechos ... en la reducción y pacificación de los indios rebeldes de la provincia de Citará'. For details of Roque de Caicedo's role in managing Fray Manuel's mining interests in the 1720s, see AGI Santa Fe 287, Fiscal to Consejo, n.p., n.d.

18 AGI Santa Fe 411, Manuel Caicedo to Archbishop of Santa Fe, Tadó, 30 March 1707. See also Lorenzo de Salazar's 'Declaración', Real de Minas de San Mateo, 24 September 1711, in AGI Santa Fe 307, 'Cuaderno ... sobre la entrada al río Murri', fols. 81–82.

19 See Colmenares, *Historia económica*, pp. 327–28. Antonio Ordoñez is mentioned in 'Declaración', Real de Minas de San Mateo, 24 September 1711, in AGI Santa Fe 307, 'Cuaderno ... sobre la entrada al río Murri', fol. 81.

20 See the 'Informes' of the *curas* of Los Brazos and San Joseph de Noanama, in AGI Quito 185, 'Autos sobre la opresión en que tienen los jueces seculares a los indios de las provincias del Chocó, que por testimonio se remite al Real y Supremo Consejo de las Indias por el ... Obispo de Popayán. Año de 1720'. Two Arboleda brothers – Fernando and Melchor – had served as *doctrineros* in Noanama by 1709. They were both nephews of the miner Don Francisco de Arboleda y Salazar. AGI Quito 185, Mateo de Villafañe to Crown, Popayán, 18 May 1709.

21 See AGI Santa Fe 411 for Bishop Villafañe's nomination of Inestrosa on 8 March 1707.
22 Colmenares, *Popayán*, pp. 20–21. See also Díaz López, *Oro, sociedad y economía*, pp. 267–68.
23 McFarlane, *Colombia*, pp. 74–75.
24 This discussion of colonial government in late-seventeenth- and early-eighteenth-century Spanish America is based on the following sources: John Phelan, *The Kingdom of Quito in the Seventeenth Century: Bureaucratic Politics in the Spanish Empire*, Madison, WI, University of Wisconsin Press, 1967, especially pp. 147–76; Leon G. Campbell, 'A Colonial Establishment: Creole Domination of the Audiencia of Lima During the Late Eighteenth Century', *Hispanic American Historical Review*, Vol. 52, 1972, pp. 1–25; Mark Burkholder and D.S. Chandler, 'Creole Appointments and the Sale of Audiencia Positions in the Spanish Empire under the Early Bourbons, 1701–1750', *Journal of Latin American Studies*, Vol. 4, 1972, pp. 545–79; idem, *From Impotence to Authority: The Spanish Crown and the American Audiencias, 1697–1808*, Columbia, MO, University of Missouri Press, 1977, especially, pp. 15–80; Kenneth J. Andrien, 'The Sale of Fiscal Offices and the Decline of Royal Authority in the Viceroyalty of Peru, 1633–1700', *Hispanic American Historical Review*, Vol. 62, No. 1, 1982, pp. 49–71; and Anthony McFarlane, 'Political Corruption and Reform in Bourbon Spanish America', in Walter Little and Eduardo Posada-Carbó (eds.), *Political Corruption in Europe and Latin America*, London, Institute of Latin American Studies, 1996, pp. 41–63.
25 McFarlane, 'Political Corruption', p. 52.
26 McFarlane, 'Political Corruption', p. 55.
27 John Phelan's work on Quito similarly suggested that misuse of office was far more prevalent at the lower levels of colonial administration – governorships and *corregimientos* – than it was in the upper echelons of the bureaucracy. In comparing the behaviour of functionaries on the Quito *audiencia* with that of officials in the *gobernaciones* of the kingdom, Phelan concluded that the kind of 'graft' practised by members of the higher institutions 'was mild compared to the corruption that prevailed in the provincial echelons of the imperial bureaucracy', where a combination of inadequate salaries and 'the ineffectiveness of the audiencia in supervising the magistrates in the provinces' resulted in a 'drift towards venality' and an 'almost total lack of professionalism'. Phelan, *The Kingdom of Quito*, pp. 165–69, 174.
28 Sharp, *Slavery*, p. 4. See also Bernardo Leal, '"Matar a los blancos bueno es, luego Chocó acabará": Cimarronaje de esclavos jamaiquinos en el Chocó (1728)', *Fronteras*, Vol. 2, No. 2, 1998, p. 148.

29 AGI Santa Fe 307, Francisco de Ibero to Crown, Nóvita, 29 October 1729.
30 Indians in other parts of the empire became equally adept at exploiting divisions between Spanish factions. Writing of the missions among the Moxos of the upper Amazon in the post-Jesuit years, for example, David Block states that one of the major strategies of indigenous peoples was precisely the petitioning of colonial authorities 'to rein in the curas'. See Block, *Mission Culture*, p. 145.
31 Colmenares, *Popayán*, p. 20. Colmenares dates the creation of a separate *gobernación* to 1720. This did not, however, take place until 1726. See AGI Santa Fe 307, Francisco de Ibero to Crown, Nóvita, 29 October 1729.
32 The sources frequently described Raposo as the fourth province of the Chocó. However, its status was less clearly defined, for it was considered to fall within the jurisdiction of the *audiencia* of Quito rather than that of Santa Fe. See AGI Santa Fe 307, Francisco de Ibero to Crown, Nóvita, 29 October 1729.
33 See Fray Manuel Caicedo's report, dated 24 July 1724, in AGI Santa Fe 362.
34 AGI Quito 143, Vicente de Aramburu to Crown, Santa Fe, 8 and 30 September 1713.
35 AGI Santa Fe 362, Francisco de Alcantud y Gaona to Crown, Cartagena, 15 November 1720.
36 AGI Santa Fe 362, Antonio de la Pedrosa y Guerrero to Francisco de Arana, Madrid, 8 March 1721.
37 Dionisio de Camino, 'Representación hecha por nuestro M.R.P. Fr. Dionisio de Camino, siendo provincial, al señor oidor don Josef Martínez Malo hallándose en las Provincias del Chocó, sobre lo que halló conveniente para el remedio del buen gobierno y aumento de aquellas misiones. Año de 1730', *Boletín de Historia y Antigüedades*, Vol. 43, 1956, p. 247.
38 As John Phelan pointed out, all officials in the Indies, from viceroys down to the *corregidores* who were on the lowest rung of the provincial bureaucracy, 'were specifically forbidden to engage in commerce either on their own or through intermediaries. Nor could they own in their names or in the names of others any kind of urban or rural real estate. They could not engage in either pastoral agriculture or any branch of mining.' See Phelan, *The Kingdom of Quito*, p. 151. See also p. 38.
39 For a summary and analysis of the contents of the 'Discourse', see McFarlane, 'Political Corruption', pp. 41–48.
40 AGI Santa Fe 362, Antonio de la Pedrosa y Guerrero to Francisco de Arana, Madrid, 8 March 1721. Pedrosa y Guerrero also noted that, in carrying out tours of inspection to the Chocó, the governors took merchandise to sell, on which duties were not paid. Nor were *quintos* paid on the gold obtained in exchange.
41 One *quintal* of iron fetched 131 silver pesos and one *quintal* of steel 210 silver pesos when transported overland; when brought in by river, costs fell to 20 and 30 pesos respectively. Caicedo also provided details of costs of foodstuffs on the frontier: an *arroba* of meat, he said, cost six gold pesos; an *arroba* of pork, 12 pesos; live cattle, 14 pesos per head; salt cost three gold pesos per *arroba* when there was a plentiful supply, but rose astronomically in times of shortage. The cost of sugar, tobacco, other essential foodstuffs and clothing was equally exorbitant. See AGI Santa Fe 362, Fray Manuel Caicedo, Madrid, 24 July 1724. The Chocó's first governor, Don Francisco de Ibero, similarly commented a few years later on the extent to which the price of supplies served as a disincentive to the establishment of new mining ventures. Were it not, he said, for the cost of basic items such as flour, wine, meat, wax and clothing, nine or ten thousand slaves might usefully be employed in mining in Citará province alone. See AGI Santa Fe 307, Francisco de Ibero to Crown, Nóvita, 29 October 1729.
42 Commerce via the Atrato was prohibited, but trade via the San Juan was restricted. See Sharp, *Slavery*, pp. 10, 172–77. Similar problems occurred along the entire Caribbean coast. On the extent and impact of smuggling in Riohacha, Santa Marta and Cartagena, see Grahn, *The Political Economy of Smuggling*.

43 See Lorenzo de Salazar's declaration, Real de Minas de San Mateo, 24 September 1711, in AGI Santa Fe 307, 'Cuaderno . . . sobre la entrada al rio Murri', fol. 89. Pérez de Vivero was certainly on a 'visita de gobierno' in December 1710, and was still present in the Chocó in February 1711. See Baltasar Carlos Pérez de Vivero to López de Carvajal, Quibdó, 15 February 1711, and Auto, 15 December 1710, fols. 38, 50. That Córdoba was in the region in the 1690s is confirmed by a royal *cédula* of 26 November 1696, which instructed the new bishop of Popayán, Mateo de Villafañe, to confer with the Franciscan order regarding whether Father Córdoba should remain in the Chocó. By the time Villafañe arrived in Popayán in February 1700, however, Joseph de Córdoba had died. See AGI Quito 185, Mateo de Villafañe to Crown, Popayán, 20 June 1712.

44 In addition to the evidence of Vicente de Aramburu and Francisco de Alcantud y Gaona, see AGI Santa Fe 362, Fray Manuel Caicedo, Madrid, 24 July 1724. See also AGI Quito 185, Mateo de Villafañe to Crown, Popayán, 20 June 1712.

45 It was in the *fundiciones* that gold was, according to the law, assayed and taxed. See McFarlane, *Colombia*, p. 73. The absence of a royal foundry in the Chocó clearly facilitated the illegal exchange of gold dust for imports.

46 AGI Santa Fe 362, Antonio de la Pedrosa y Guerrero to Francisco de Arana, Madrid, 8 March 1721. There are no figures to indicate even approximately what proportion of the output of the region's mines disappeared without trace. Colmenares cited one report, dated 1717, which suggested that as much as one million pesos was extracted annually from the Chocó – a figure that he acknowledged was exaggerated, but which nevertheless illustrated the extent of the fraud practised in the region. See Colmenares, *Historia económica*, p. 328.

47 'Miguel de Gerónimo González . . . representa sobre la necesidad de Indios para rocerías, cosechas y transporte de los mantenimientos', in Germán Colmenares et al. (eds.), *Fuentes coloniales para la historia del trabajo en Colombia*, Bogotá, Universidad de los Andes, 1969, pp. 130–33. See also 'El gobernador de Popayán ordena entregar los indios necesarios para el mantenimiento de minas en el Chocó', 4 August 1708, p. 134.

48 Nicolás de Inestrosa to Cristóbal de Mosquera, Iró, 11 October 1708, in Colmenares et al. (eds.), *Fuentes coloniales*, pp. 137–39.

49 See the testimony of Alférez Juan de Bustos, San Gerónimo de Nóvita, 26 March 1707, in AGI Santa Fe 411. See also AGI Santa Fe 362, Francisco de Alcantud y Gaona to Crown, Cartagena, 15 November 1720. Acuña y Berrio had extensive mining interests in the Chocó, owning a *cuadrilla* of 48 slaves by 1721. Sharp, *Slavery*, pp. 204–205.

50 'Solicitud del protector de naturales para que los mineros no exijan servicios que desarraigan a los naturales', in Colmenares et al. (eds.), *Fuentes coloniales*, pp. 141–46.

51 AGI Santa Fe 362, Fray Manuel Caicedo, Madrid, 24 July 1724.

52 When in 1711, for example, three Indians from Bebará and Lloró, in Citará province, informed the governor of Antioquia of their grievances against *teniente* Don Joseph de la Cuesta and Manuel de Vargas, *corregidor* of Bebará, they stated that when they were sent to work in the mines they were never provided with the necessary tools for the task, and that they received only a fraction of the wages paid by the miners for their labour, the *teniente* appropriating the remainder for himself. See the statement of Joseph Veragone, Antioquia, 10 March 1711, in AGI Santa Fe 307, 'Cuaderno . . . sobre la entrada al río Murri', fol. 57.

53 Sharp's figures indicate that prices fluctuated between 500 and 525 pesos between 1711 and 1761. See Sharp, *Slavery*, Table 10, p. 202.

54 Sharp, *Slavery*, Table 7, p. 199.

55 AGI Quito 143, Vicente de Aramburu to Crown, Santa Fe, 30 September 1713.

56 See, for example, the testimony of Don Domingo de la Romana, Quibdó, 30 December 1719, in AGI Santa Fe 411, 'Testimonio de la información recibida por . . . Dr Dn Nicolás de Inestrosa como visitador de las provincias del Chocó', fol. 2. See also the

comments of the *oidor* Martínez Malo, Quibdó, 2 October 1732, in Zuluaga Gómez (ed.), *Documentos inéditos*, Documento No. 8, p. 53.

57 For the 1720 figure, see AGI Santa Fe 362, Francisco de Alcantud y Gaona to Crown, Cartagena, 15 November 1720; for the figure for 1729, see AGI Santa Fe 307, Francisco de Ibero to Crown, Nóvita, 29 October 1729.

58 AGI Quito 143, Vicente de Aramburu to Crown, Santa Fe, 30 September 1713. See also Camino, 'Representación', pp. 242–43.

59 AGI Quito 185, 'Autos sobre la opresión', Certificación del notario de visita, Popayán, 9 July 1720; and AGI Santa Fe 362, Francisco de Alcantud y Gaona to Crown, Cartagena, 15 November 1720. By 1729, according to the first governor of the Chocó, Don Francisco de Ibero, the province comprised only two settlements: Chamí and San Juan. See AGI Santa Fe 307, Francisco de Ibero to Crown, Nóvita, 29 October 1729. See also Martínez Malo's comments, dated Quibdó, 2 October 1731, in Zuluaga Gómez (ed.), *Documentos inéditos*, Documento No. 8, p. 52.

60 AGI Quito 143, Vicente de Aramburu to Crown, Santa Fe, 8 September 1713. According to the *oidor*, it was the priests, as much as the *tenientes*, who profited from the resulting increase in maize prices.

61 'Declaración de Fray Manuel Caicedo', Tadó, 1708, in Colmenares et al. (eds.), *Fuentes coloniales*, p. 152. According to Caicedo, Don Luis de Acuña and Agustín de Valencia both relied on this source of supply.

62 See Petición, n.p., n.d., in AGI Santa Fe 307, 'Cuaderno . . . sobre la entrada al río Murri', fol. 25.

63 AGI Quito 143, Vicente de Aramburu to Crown, Santa Fe, 8 September 1713.

64 McFarlane, 'Political Corruption', p. 42.

65 According to the bishop, Indians were given tools and *aguardiente*; according to *oidor* Martínez Malo, however, Indians were given 'bayetas, argollas, chirichíes, Parumas, chaquiras, manillas' and other such goods 'which they use'. Auto, Bishop Juan Gómez Frías, Popayán, 8 July 1720, in AGI Quito 185, 'Autos sobre la opresión', and Juan Gómez Frías to Crown, Popayán, 6 November 1723. For Martínez Malo's remarks, dated Quibdó, 2 October 1732, see Zuluaga Gómez (ed.), *Documentos inéditos*, Documento No. 8, pp. 51–52, 58.

66 Camino, 'Representación', p. 243. Martínez Malo described the 'great repugnance' with which Indians received unwanted goods. Zuluaga Gómez (ed.), *Documentos inéditos*, Documento No. 8, Quibdó, 2 October 1732, pp. 51–52, 58.

67 See AGI Quito 143, Vicente de Aramburu to Crown, Santa Fe, 8 September 1713. Similar accusations of over-charging were made by Indians of Tadó in 1708. See Díaz López, *Oro, sociedad y economía*, pp. 268–69.

68 AGI Santa Fe 307, Francisco de Ibero to Crown, Nóvita, 29 October 1729.

69 Joseph López de Carvajal to Vicente de Aramburu, Antioquia, 14 August 1712, in AGI Santa Fe 362, 'Testimonio de Autos', fol. 23.

70 Petición, Rafael de Oquendo, n.p., n.d., in AGI Santa Fe 362, 'Testimonio de Autos', fols. 17–18. Elsewhere the protector reported the 'abhorrence and hatred . . . felt by the Indians towards the regular priests, because the ill-treatment they receive from them is outrageous'. See AGI Santa Fe 362, Rafael de Oquendo to Crown, Antioquia, 20 September 1712.

71 Petición, n.p., n.d., AGI Santa Fe 307, 'Cuaderno . . . sobre la entrada al río Murri', fol. 25.

72 AGI Santa Fe 362, Francisco de Alcantud y Gaona to Crown, Cartagena, 15 November 1720.

73 Four bishops served in Popayán over the period covered here. These were Mateo de Villafañe (of the Calced Carmelite order, who took possession of the diocese in 1699 and was promoted to the diocese of La Paz in 1714); Juan Gómez Frías (a secular, he took

possession of the diocese in May 1716 and was promoted to the diocese of Quito in 1726); Diego Fermín de Vergara (of the Augustinian order, who arrived in the city in 1735, and became Archbishop of Santa Fe in 1740); and Francisco José de Figueredo y Victoria (a secular priest born in Cali, who took possession of his diocese in 1743, and became Archbishop of Guatemala in 1752). See Manuel Bueno y Quijano, *Historia de la diócesis de Popayán*, Bogotá, ABC, 1945, pp. 155–59. For a discussion of the authority and duties of the bishops and of the apparatus of ecclesiastical government over which they presided, see Peter Marzahl, *Town in the Empire: Government, Politics, and Society in Seventeenth Century Popayán*, Austin, TX, University of Texas, 1978, pp. 137–41.

74 Juan Manuel Pacheco, *Historia eclesiástica, vol. 3: La iglesia bajo el regalismo de los Borbones*, Bogotá, Ediciones Lerner, 1986, pp. 357–58.
75 AGI Quito 185, Juan Gómez Frías to Crown, Popayán, 27 November 1720.
76 AGI Quito 185, Diego Fermín de Vergara to Miguel de Villanueba, Medellín, 30 February 1737, and Diego Fermín de Vergara to Crown, Popayán, 1 December 1737.
77 Camino, 'Representación', pp. 242, 245–47.
78 AGI Quito 137, Governor of Popayán to Crown, Popayán, 26 August 1729.
79 AGI Quito 185, 'Certificación de la visita de Nóvita', Tadó, 6 October 1736; and Diego Fermín de Vergara to Miguel de Villanueva, Medellín, 30 February 1737.
80 AGI Quito 185, 'Testimonio de la visita del Citará', Quibdó, 2 November 1736. See also the statements made before *visitador* Nicolás de Inestrosa by the following witnesses: Don Domingo de la Romana, Captain Don Diego de Montoya, Don Alejandro Casahus, and Don Diego Maldonado de la Cerda. All may be found in AGI Santa Fe 411, 'Testimonio de la información recibida por el Dr Dn Nicolás de Inestrosa como visitador de las provincias del Chocó' (1719), fols. 2–10.
81 AGI Quito 185, 'Informe del cura de Nóvita', in 'Autos sobre la opresión'; see also 'Informe del cura de Quibdó' and 'Informe del cura de Lloró'. Despite the poor record of Arboleda Salazar after more than a decade as priest of this *doctrina*, Bishop Juan Gómez Frías nevertheless included him, in a letter of 1719, among those 'worthy of being rewarded' with a prebend in the diocese. In May 1744, Bishop Francisco Joseph de Figueredo y Victoria similarly mentioned Don Melchor de Arboleda (formerly of the Chocó, and more recently of Cali) among those worthy of a prebend or other 'honourable occupations'. AGI Quito 185, Juan Gómez Frías to Crown, Popayán, 8 May 1719, and Francisco Joseph de Figueredo to Crown, Popayán, 26 November 1744.
82 AGI Quito 185, Auto, Popayán, 8 July 1720.
83 AGI Quito 185, Diego Fermín de Vergara to Crown, Popayán, 1 December 1737.
84 Camino, 'Representación', pp. 242–43, 247–48. Lorenzo de Salazar, giving evidence to Governor López de Carvajal in 1711, similarly claimed that Indians 'are not free [even on] feast days, for the Church only serves [as the place from where] they are taken to the house of the teniente or corregidor from which they are [in turn] hired out'. 'Declaración', Real de Minas de San Mateo, 24 September 1711, in AGI Santa Fe 307, 'Cuaderno . . . sobre la entrada al río Murri', fol. 83.
85 This was a feature of life on the frontier to which Isacsson has also drawn attention. 'We must keep in mind', he explained, 'that the incompatible interests of the Church and the state generated constant discord between their respective representatives in the native village. Typically the missionary priest serving indios de doctrina, on one hand, and the corregidor ruling tributarios, on the other, struggled acrimoniously, each one accusing the other of abuses that caused the Indians to desert and cease upholding both doctrina and the Royal tribute.' Isacsson, 'The Egalitarian Society', p. 108.
86 Evidence presented before the governor of Popayán in 1707 suggests that one Martín Damiano may have been the *corregidor* in question. See AGI Santa Fe 411, 'Información', San Gerónimo de Nóvita, 26 March 1707.

87 AGI Santa Fe 411, 'Certificación', Tadó, 16 March 1706.
88 AGI Santa Fe 411, Manuel de Caicedo to Pedro Bolaños y Mendoza, Tadó, March, 1707. According to Caicedo, the process was initiated by the 'provisor', a relative of the Mosqueras, prior to the arrival of the new bishop ('en sede vacante'), the intention being to secure the appointment of a secular more manipulable than the Franciscans.
89 'Testimonio de Fray Manuel Caicedo', Tadó, 1708, in Colmenares et al. (eds.), *Fuentes coloniales*, pp. 149–60.
90 See Mateo Vivas Sedán to Jacinto Mosquera, Iró, 12 October 1708; 'Solicitud del protector de naturales', Santa Fe, 9 January 1709; and 'Testimonio de Fray Manuel Caicedo', Tadó, 1708, all in Colmenares et al. (eds.), *Fuentes coloniales*, pp. 139–41, 142–43, 153–54, and 160.
91 AGI Santa Fe 362, Fray Manuel Caicedo, Madrid, 24 July 1724. See also 'Relación y noticia individual de las ricas y abundantes provincias del Chocó'.
92 AGI Santa Fe 287, Fiscal to Consejo, n.p., n.d.
93 Francisco Montiel de Fuentenovilla was reporting that the money had been held up by the Casa de Contratación in Cádiz, pending an investigation into the claims of another member of the order, from Andalucía, who claimed that the money belonged to him. The provincial requested the return of the money in question. See AGI Quito 190, Francisco Montiel de Fuentenovilla to Crown, n.p., n.d. The Consejo requested a report on the matter on 15 June 1723.
94 AGI Santa Fe 406, Agustín Roso de Villalba to Crown, n.p., n.d.
95 C.L. Osorio, 'Prohibición de los reyes españoles a los eclesiásticos sobre propiedad y beneficio de minas', *Boletín Histórico del Valle*, Vol. 31, 1936, p. 329. The royal *cédula* of 27 June 1727 may also be found in AGI Santa Fe 405.
96 AGI Quito 144, Nicolás de Inestrosa to Crown, n.p., n.d. The Consejo discussed this letter in October 1731.
97 The Cathedral Chapter dealt with this request. See Osorio, 'Prohibición ... a los eclesiásticos', pp. 329–35. One of the witnesses called to give evidence on Inestrosa's behalf, Don Ignacio de Piedrahita, stated that he had earlier owned another mine, El Bordo, but that this one had been abandoned because platinum had been found in the gold extracted.
98 AGI Santa Fe 733, 'Descripción del Gobierno del Chocó, en la jurisdicción del Nuevo Reino de Granada, que se presenta, con Memorial, a S.M. por Don Pedro Muñoz de Arjona, hijo del Coronel Don Alfonso de Arjona'. Although this document is undated, its contents suggest that it corresponds to the mid-1750s, for in 1753, Don Pedro's father, Don Alfonso de Arjona, sent the Crown a map of the Quibdó region.
99 Colmenares, *Cali*, pp. 138–39, 149.
100 AGI Santa Fe 405, Dionisio de Camino to Crown, n.p., n.d., and Dictamen del Fiscal, Madrid, 22 May 1727. See also Osorio, 'Prohibición ... a los eclesiásticos', p. 329.
101 AGI Santa Fe 411, 'Declaración', Silvestre Palomino, Quibdó, 16 October 1728.
102 AGI Santa Fe 733, 'Descripción del Gobierno del Chocó'.
103 Juan de Bonilla is mentioned in AGN Curas y obispos, 6, Auto, Nóvita, 26 November 1743, fol. 437. See also Juan de Bonilla y Delgado to Manuel Martínez de Escobar, Nóvita, 28 November 1743, fols. 442–43.
104 Sharp, *Slavery*, p. 182, and Table 5, pp. 204–205.
105 For details of Fray Juan Caballero, see AGI Santa Fe 286, Jorge de Villalonga to Crown, Cartagena, 15 March 1721.
106 AGI Santa Fe 287, Juan Gómez Frías to Crown, Popayán, 18 April 1720.
107 AGI Santa Fe 287, Fiscal to Consejo, n.p., n.d.
108 See AGI Santa Fe 362, Antonio de la Pedrosa y Guerrero to Francisco de Arana, Madrid, 8 March 1721.
109 See, for example, the royal *cédulas* dated 28 September 1726 and 3 June 1734, in AGN, Curas y obispos, 6, fols. 438–39, 440–41.

110 His figures show that whereas in 1701, 19 priests in the diocese remained without a benefice, by 1706, the number had risen to 25. Marzahl, *Town in the Empire*, p. 139.
111 Miguel Chacón de la Enzina to Juan Gómez Frías, Popayán, 9 June 1721, in AGI Santa Fe 405, 'Despacho Circular que se remite a las provincias del Citará y Chocó para que los Vicarios de ellas compelan a los clérigos y regulares salgan de aquellas provincias y ejecuten los demás de su contexto. Año de 1721'.
112 AGI Santa Fe 405, 'Despacho Circular'. Unbeneficed clergy were given fifteen days to leave the Chocó. Furthermore, the decree further stated that all priests without exception who remained thereafter without licence from the bishop should be denied the use of churches, chapels and altars for the celebration of the Mass. By royal *cédula* of 29 October 1722, the Crown confirmed the bishop's instructions. See AGI Santa Fe 404, 'Testimonio de Autos', Real Cédula, 29 October 1722.
113 AGI Santa Fe 405, Dionisio de Camino to Crown, n.p., n.d. The Consejo discussed the letter in May 1727. At that time the *fiscal* advised that the *cédula* should be reissued on the grounds that unbeneficed clergy could not be detained for any purpose other than the exploitation of gold mines, which was prohibited by law.
114 For the royal *cédulas* of 28 September 1726 and 3 June 1734, see AGN, Curas y obispos, 6, fols. 438–39, 440–41 For the royal *cédula* of 29 October 1722, see AGI Santa Fe 404, and for the royal *cédula* of 27 June 1727, see AGI Santa Fe 405. For Martínez de Escobar's comments, see AGN, Curas y obispos, 6, Auto, Nóvita, 26 November 1743, fols. 436–37.
115 See the *fiscal*'s remarks on the 'consulta' submitted by Bishop Gómez Frías in 1720, Madrid, 9 July 1722, in AGI Quito 185.
116 See, for example, AGI Quito 143, Vicente de Aramburu to Crown, Santa Fe, 24 and 30 September 1713. It is to be noted that in the early eighteenth century, the *audiencia* of Quito also acted to prevent the continued unchecked abuse of native peoples in Barbacoas, though in this case it was the *encomenderos* who were investigated, this being one of the few regions where the *encomienda* still survived. See Lane, 'Taming the Master', pp. 494–504.
117 See Lorenzo de Salazar's 'Declaración', Real de Minas de San Mateo, 24 September 1711, in AGI Santa Fe 307, 'Cuaderno . . . sobre la entrada al rio Murri', fol. 84.
118 See AGI Santa Fe 362, Antonio de la Pedrosa y Guerrero to Francisco de Arana, Madrid, 8 March 1721. Pedrosa y Guerrero's conclusions may have been influenced by the findings of Don Francisco de Alcantud y Gaona, whose stint as interim *teniente* of Citará province coincided with Pedrosa's years in the colony. Reporting from Cartagena in 1720, this latter official was to describe the visits of inspection conducted by the governors as neither more nor less than gambling expeditions, during which the abuses and excesses of officials went unpunished. See AGI Santa Fe 362, Francisco de Alcantud y Gaona to Crown, Cartagena, 15 November 1720. Senior clerics were also convinced of the dishonesty of governors. Following a report from Bishop Gómez Frías (of 8 July 1718), the Council of the Indies instructed Don Antonio de la Pedrosa to remove the Conde de las Lagunas from his post as governor of Popayán, though the order arrived in Santa Fe only after Pedrosa had returned to Spain. See the *fiscal*'s comments, dated 1 July 1724, in response to a letter from the bishop of Popayán, in AGI Quito 185, Juan Gómez Frías to Crown, 6 November 1723.
119 AGI Quito 143, Vicente de Aramburu to Crown, Santa Fe, 30 September 1713.
120 Quoted in Colmenares, *Popayán*, p. 21.
121 AGI Santa Fe 362, Francisco de Alcantud y Gaona to Crown, Cartagena, 15 November 1720.
122 AGI Santa Fe 362, Francisco de Alcantud y Gaona to Crown, Cartagena, 15 November 1720.
123 AGI Santa Fe 693, 'Nombramiento de Superintendente del Chocó hecho por el Dr. Don Antonio de la Pedrosa y Guerrero . . . en . . . Don Luis de Espinosa y Galarza', Santa Fe,

GOVERNMENT AND SOCIETY ON THE FRONTIER 189

14 November 1719. See also AGI Santa Fe 362, Antonio de la Pedrosa y Guerrero to Francisco de Arana, Madrid, 8 March 1721.
124 AGI Santa Fe 362, Viceroy Villalonga to Crown, Santa Fe, 19 May 1723, and Francisco de Alcantud y Gaona to Crown, Cartagena, 15 November 1720.
125 'Se segrega de la Gobernación de Popayán la provincia del Chocó', in Ortega Ricaurte (ed.), *Historia documental*, pp. 167–69; AGI Santa Fe 307, Francisco de Ibero to Crown, Nóvita, 29 October 1729; and British Library, Additional MSS, 15740, 'Descripción Histórica Geográfica Política Eclesiástica y Militar de la América Meridional . . . Ordenada por el Pe Fr Manuel Sobrevida Misionero de Ocopa. Año 1796'.
126 AGI Santa Fe 307, Francisco de Ibero to Crown, Nóvita, 29 October 1729.
127 Ibero was dismissed by the *oidor* Martínez Malo. See Colmenares, *Historia económica*, p. 331. See also Martínez Malo's comments to the effect that action was also taken against the governor's accomplices, 'as enemies of the crown'. Zuluaga Gómez (ed.), *Documentos inéditos*, Documento No. 8, Quibdó, 2 October 1732, p. 51. For Ibero's response to earlier allegations, see AGI Santa Fe 307, Francisco de Ibero to Crown, Nóvita, 29 October 1729.
128 Sharp, *Slavery*, p. 10.
129 AGI Quito 139, City of Buga to Crown, Buga, 20 January 1758.
130 Friars were accused of exploiting Indians, failing to administer sacraments, and leading Indians to escape to the hills without ever having received a single sacrament. See, for example, AGI Santa Fe 404, Francisco Seco to Crown, n.p., n.d., but dated by the Consejo in February 1724. See also AGI Quito 185, Diego Fermín de Vergara to Miguel de Villanueba, Medellín, 30 February 1737, and Diego Fermín de Vergara to Crown, Popayán, 1 December 1737.
131 The Franciscans found themselves challenged on many fronts, not only in New Granada but in many other parts of Spanish America. In Cartagena, for instance, the same Franciscan province of Santa Fe came into conflict with two bishops and the cathedral chapter over the appropriation by seculars of four *doctrinas* in the Urabá/Darién/Sinú area, during exactly the same period. AGI Santa Fe 405, Dionisio de Camino to Crown, n.p., n.d. The Consejo discussed the letter in August 1727 and concluded that the Franciscans were to be reinstated as *doctrineros* of the four settlements.
132 Boxer, *The Church Militant*, pp. 65–66, 71–72.
133 This debate was initiated by Fray Joseph Palos, Provincial of the Franciscan province of Chile and Visitor General of the Province of Santa Fe. See AGI Santa Fe 403, Fray Francisco Antonio Felices, Santa Fe, 13 November 1719.
134 Francisco Felices had already brought about two other changes which had a bearing on this election. First, he had withdrawn the friars Caicedo, Caballero and Méndez from the Chocó for reasons of alleged misconduct; secondly, he sought to abolish the contributions that the region's *doctrinas* made towards the upkeep of the Franciscan order, and which were considered to encourage the involvement of friars in commercial activities. AGI Santa Fe 287, Juan Gómez Frías to Crown, Popayán, 18 April 1720; and Fiscal to Consejo, n.p., n.d. In the early 1720s, Fray Francisco Seco confirmed that the order had, since 1702, taken whatever funds were left to the *doctrineros* after their own immediate needs had been met. These funds were applied to the Divine Cult, the promotion of studies, and used to meet the requirements of the monasteries. See AGI Santa Fe 404, Francisco Seco to Crown, n.p., n.d. For further discussion of the issue of contributions, see AGI Santa Fe 287, Juan Gómez Frías to Crown, Popayán, 18 April 1720, and AGI Quito 185, Diego Fermín de Vergara to Miguel de Villanueba, Medellín, 30 February 1737.
135 AGI Santa Fe 403, Fray Francisco Antonio Felices, Santa Fe, 13 November 1719. The arguments of the opposing faction were that the order would be failing in its duty to the king in the event of withdrawal, that the Chocó mission was the most honourable branch

of the Franciscan order in the New Kingdom, and that indigenous peoples would be deprived of the protection afforded by the friars. AGI Santa Fe 403, Fray Diego Barroso, Santa Fe, 18 November 1719.

136 AGI Santa Fe 287, Juan Gómez Frías to Crown, Popayán, 18 April 1720, and Fiscal to Consejo, n.p., n.d. An interesting twist in this story is that in 1722, the Viceroy reported the embargo at the port of Honda of ten boxes and two trunks containing contraband goods, allegedly imported by Fray Dionisio de Camino and Fray Diego Barroso. See AGI Santa Fe 286, Jorge de Villalonga to Crown, Santa Fe, 9 August 1722. It should be noted, however, that Diego Barroso was later cleared of wrongdoing by the Council of the Indies. See the Consejo's discussion of a letter from Fr Dionisio de Camino, n.p., n.d., in AGI Santa Fe 405. The Consejo's decision is recorded on 9 August 1727.

137 AGI Santa Fe 286, Jorge de Villalonga to Crown, Cartagena, 15 March 1721.

138 AGI Santa Fe 287, Jorge de Villalonga to Crown, Santa Fe, 8 February 1723. In the event, Francisco Antonio Felices was said to have gained the support of only one like-minded member of the order, Fray Tomás Guerrero. See AGI Santa Fe 404, Francisco Seco to Crown, n.p., n.d.. The *fiscal*'s 'dictamen' is dated 4 February 1724. Dionisio de Camino was later to be succeeded as provincial by his brother, Fray Jerónimo de Camino, who was to serve four terms between 1732 and 1764. See Mantilla Ruiz, *Actividad misionera*, pp. 41–44.

139 Under the terms of the Patronato, the Spanish Crown assumed responsibility for financing and administering the Catholic Church in the newly conquered territories, and for promoting the conversion of native populations to Catholicism. In exchange for promoting the Faith, the Crown was granted the right to collect and administer tithes, and to present candidates for ecclesiastical appointment. The Crown took upon itself the privilege of presenting candidates for higher-level ecclesiastical positions, its nominations for archbishops and bishops going directly to the Pope, who confirmed and instated the nominees. The Crown, or the Consejo, also nominated members of the cathedral chapters. Nominations for lesser benefices were taken care of at the local level: candidates were presented by local prelates for the approval of the viceroys, or the provincial governors, acting as vicepatrons, and the nominees were formally installed by the local bishops or archbishops. See Josep M. Barnadas, 'The Catholic Church in Colonial Spanish America', in Leslie Bethell (ed.), *The Cambridge History of Latin America*, Vol. I, Cambridge, Cambridge University Press, 1984, pp. 512–13, and John F. Schwaller, 'The Ordenanza del Patronazgo in New Spain, 1574–1660', in *idem* (ed.), *The Church in Colonial Latin America*, Wilmington, DE, Scholarly Resources, 2000, pp. 53–54.

140 AGI Santa Fe 411, 'Testimonio de información recibida por el Dr Dn Nicolás de Inestrosa', fols. 1–20.

141 Nicolás de Inestrosa was replaced in the early 1730s by Agustín Roso de Villalba. For further details, see AGI Santa Fe 408, Joseph Antonio de Oliva to Crown, n.p., n.d., and AGI Santa Fe 406, Agustín Roso de Villalba to Crown, n.p., n.d.

142 AGI Quito 185, Juan Gómez Frías to Crown, Popayán, 26 November 1720; AGI Santa Fe 405, Dionisio de Camino to Crown, n.p., n.d., and the *fiscal*'s discussion dated 22 May 1727. See also AGI Quito 127, Jorge de Villalonga to Crown, Santa Fe, 13 November 1723.

143 AGI Quito 185, 'Testimonio de los autos obrados sobre la erección de curato en el Citará Provincia de las del Chocó y informes de los curas sobre el maltratamiento que los indios reciben de los jueces seculares, de que hace remisión al Real y Supremo Consejo de las Indias el . . . Obispo de Popayán. Año de 1720'.

144 AGI Santa Fe 405, Dionisio de Camino to Crown, n.p., n.d., but discussed by the Council of the Indies in May 1727.

145 For the bishop's views on the Franciscans, see AGI Quito 185, Diego Fermín de Vergara to Miguel de Villanueba, Medellín, 30 February 1737.

146 Pacheco, *La iglesia*, pp. 368–69. It is to be noted, however, that in 1780, Capitán de Ingenieros Don Juan Jiménez Donoso observed of the parishes of the Chocó region, where he had recently completed a visit of inspection, that the mission remained under the control of the Franciscan order. 'Relación del Chocó . . . en que se manifiesta su actual estado y el en que parece se podrían poner conforme al reconocimiento del Capitán de Ingenieros don Juan Jiménez Donoso', in Ortega Ricaurte (ed.), *Historia documental*, p. 211.

147 It is instructive to compare the record of the Franciscans here, however, with that of their sixteenth-century counterparts in other regions of the empire. As Juan Carlos Garavaglia has argued, for instance, a key factor accounting for the early success of the Franciscans among the Guaraní 'was the example they set in their personal lives. They tried to be living antitheses to the greedy and often impious European colonists whom Indians knew so well.' Precisely because they were poor, he states, the Franciscans were able to present themselves 'as Christian people of dignity, worthy of native respect'. See Garavaglia, 'The Crises and Transformations of Invaded Societies', p. 19.

148 David Weber has drawn similar conclusions for the cases of Florida and New Mexico, which were engulfed, in the seventeenth century, by struggles among Spaniards. 'Through such behavior', he argues, 'Spaniards must have demeaned themselves in the eyes of natives and diminished their own prestige and authority'. Weber, *The Spanish Frontier*, p. 132.

CHAPTER SEVEN

Resistance and Adaptation under Spanish Rule: The Peoples of Citará, 1700–1750

So far, our discussion of conditions in the Chocó in the eighteenth century has concentrated mainly on the shape and conduct of secular and religious administration, and on the abuse and exploitation inflicted upon Indians by frontier officials and other settlers, both lay and religious. This is largely because, in their concern to expose the worst features of Spanish administration in this isolated corner of the empire, senior officials and ecclesiastics in the colony focused almost exclusively on the effects of corruption and misgovernment on native populations, rather than on the ways in which Indians adapted to the changed conditions of colonial rule during the early decades of the eighteenth century. This does not mean, however, that native peoples in the Chocó came passively to accept the efforts of Spaniards to incorporate Indians into the local economy as providers of labour and tribute and as a market for Spanish goods, or indeed to inculcate Christianity and European norms more generally. Far from resigning themselves to the 'fate the Spanish Crown designed for them',[1] Indian groups in the Chocó continued to seek ways to challenge Spanish domination and Christian evangelisation, and to protect their ethnic interests, identity and cohesion.

To escape Spanish retribution in the aftermath of the Citará rebellion, many Indians established runaway communities in distant and inaccessible parts of the region which remained undiscovered until the 1710s and 1720s.[2] Giving evidence in 1710, the Indian Joseph Veragone, of the community of Bebará, informed *protector* Rafael de Oquendo that many *cimarronas* had been in existence in the Chocó since the outbreak of rebellion in 1684. Pedro Hato de la Banda, a Spanish settler in Quibdó and Bebará, similarly reported that 'since the uprising many *cimarroneras* have been formed consisting of large numbers of Indians'.[3] Other natives in Citará province, rounded up and reduced to villages in the late 1680s and early 1690s, repeatedly deserted those villages in the decades that followed, also in order to establish independent communities in 'the remotest of places', well out of the reach of Spanish colonists.[4] Several such communities were discovered in the region to the north of the Murri river between 1711 and 1712: that of Candrumbida, an 'Indian of renown in his nation, with a large following', and a fugitive since 1684; that of Caraupe, an 'indio principal of the settlement of Quibdó, and greatly esteemed and respected by his many followers'; and that on the banks of the Dorroguigo river, which counted a population of at least 55 in November 1711: 'in said houses there are eleven men [and women] married according to their custom, twenty four girls and boys, four babies, three old women, two single men of tributary age'.[5]

Indians in the Chocó also continued to reject all efforts on the part of missionaries and other clergy to inculcate Christian teaching, and steadfastly refused to assimilate the language, customs and values of the colonisers. Reporting in 1736 on his recent pastoral visit to the Chocó, Bishop Diego Fermín de Vergara indicated that everywhere he travelled, he found Indians to be 'ignorant of Christian Doctrine and the mysteries of the Catholic Faith'.[6] Six years later his successor, Joseph de Figueredo y Victoria, conducting his own pastoral visit, commented of the Indians of the villages of San Joseph and San Agustín, in Nóvita province, that 'after so many years [since] their reduction and conversion [they] are as ignorant as they were in the beginning . . . persevering in the errors of their heathenism'.[7] Even as late as 1807, Governor Don Carlos de Ciaurriz was obliged to report that Indians in the Chocó remained 'possessed by superstition'. Although it was now customary for all Indians to be baptised in the Catholic Faith, they still referred to the 'God of the Christians', who formed no part of their own religious experience.[8] By the end of the colonial period, Ciaurriz's observation suggests, Indians had neither appropriated, nor reinterpreted for their own religious purposes, the beliefs, rituals or symbols of Catholic Christianity.

Thus, while violent rebellion of the kind that took place in the mid-1680s was not to be repeated in the Chocó,[9] less overt forms of resistance continued to pose serious obstacles to Spanish efforts fully to incorporate Indians into the society and economy of this distant frontier region. The implications of such responses for the Crown's long-term objective of converting Indians to Christianity, and for the survival of native beliefs and values, will be considered in due course. We begin, however, with an example of adaptation to the colonial regime on the part of Indians in Citará province. For although rejection of the 'God of the Christians', flight from the main villages of the region, and withdrawal from all but the most necessary contact with Europeans were the means to which many indigenous people resorted in the eighteenth century to resist the impositions of settler society and to protect their autonomy, these were not the only strategies pursued. From the very beginning of the century, individuals within the native community continued to develop strategies strongly reminiscent of those of earlier decades, not, it will be argued, in a now futile bid to break completely with Europeans, but to protect and advance native interests under colonial rule.

The case in question dates from the beginning of the 1710s, when prominent members of the Citará community, led by cacique Don Joseph Sagito, entered into negotiations with Don Joseph López de Carvajal, governor of Antioquia, for the purpose of bringing about the relocation of Indians from the existing villages of the province to new settlements in the vicinity of the Murri river, where they proposed to exchange government by Popayán for government by Antioquia.[10] The Indians' most obvious motives in manipulating and exploiting long-standing rivalries between the *gobernaciones* over access to the human and material resources of the Chocó were to improve conditions for native peoples and to protect indigenous traditions and ways of life. However, issues to do with the authority and privileges to be enjoyed by the native elite, and with the role that elite was to play in the administration of the villages, are also central to understanding the events that took place in Citará in 1710–13. Elsewhere we have seen that in the 1670s and 1680s, to facilitate control of a population whose political organisation at contact was decentralised, the Spanish sought to develop a system of native government drawn from an elite of friendly and co-operative caciques and *capitanes*, but that, because of the source from which their new authority emanated, and because of their collaboration with the colonisers, these caciques were neither respected nor perceived as legitimate by their peoples.[11] Of Don Pedro Tegue, upon whom the Spanish conferred the title of cacique of Citará province, it was said that 'he only enjoys the title of cacique'; Don Rodrigo Pivi, appointed hereditary cacique in the mid-1680s in recognition of his role in assisting the pacification campaign that followed the Citará rebellion, was not only declared an enemy to his people but suffered attempts on his life.[12] Under the changed conditions of the eighteenth century, however, the role of caciques and *gobernadores* as representatives and defenders of the native community seems to have acquired a legitimacy that was absent in earlier decades, and for this reason was now to be protected from encroachment by Spanish administrators on the frontier.

This is a phenomenon to which Sven-Erik Isacsson also drew attention in a study of the controversies surrounding a series of incidents that took place in the Emberá settlement of Tadó, in Nóvita province, between 1720 and 1793. The most significant of those controversies, dating from the early 1790s, related to an apparent dispute over the *cacicazgo* of Tadó between the current holder, Manuel Carampaima, and his cousin and rival for the post, Calixto de Cárdenas. The papers relating to the case seemed to indicate that competition between the cacique and his rival lay at the heart of the conflict: that because Cárdenas believed himself to have a stronger claim to the *cacicazgo*, he tried to manipulate the authorities in the Chocó and Santa Fe into transferring the hereditary title from his cousin to himself. However, in a perceptive interpretation of the case, Isacsson concluded that this apparent dispute over rights to the *cacicazgo* was a plot, hatched between the two men, to manipulate the authorities into appointing Cárdenas as new cacique, because he was the more knowledgeable in Spanish administration and legislation: 'the Indians of Tadó had agreed to make Cárdenas their cacique instead of the illiterate Carampaima, so as to obtain the proficient defender their difficult situation demanded'.[13] Of course, the Carampaima–Cárdenas case dates from a much later period than that covered by this study, but the events that took place in Citará province in 1710–13 strongly suggest that as early as the second decade of the eighteenth century, the Indians of the Chocó had adopted and adapted for their own purposes the 'alien institution' of the village cacique, leading to the emergence and consolidation, over the decades that followed, of a clearly defined political elite whose role was to defend and protect the interests of the indigenous community under Spanish colonialism. 'From this position as tribal chief and co-organizer of Spanish Indian administration', Isacsson argued, 'the cacique could change into a village chief and conspicuous deviser of native strategies for resistance and defense'.[14]

The resettlement at Murri

Negotiations became possible because, on taking office in 1708, Don Joseph López de Carvajal became interested in establishing a foothold for Antioquia in the region of the Murri river, a largely uninhabited zone stretching between Citará province and Cuna-controlled territory. This was in the expectation that the discovery of gold deposits in that area would revive the waning fortunes of the mining industry of a *gobernación* that he described, in 1708, as in a state of 'poverty and adversity . . . as in said places there are no longer mineral deposits to exploit'.[15] Figures on gold production, as measured by *fundición* entries, show that Antioquia's mining industry had entered a period of decline at the beginning of Joseph López's term of office. Whereas in 1706 gold production reached 25,583 gold pesos, by 1707, production figures had fallen to 21,673 pesos, and to just 16,643 pesos by 1708, when López took up his post. That downturn proved to be temporary – an example of the severe fluctuations to which the mining sector was subject during these years – and production began to recover by 1709 (28,748 gold pesos). However, the context remained one of decline. During the term of López's successor, Don Joseph de Yarza, Antioquia was to experience another, more serious downturn. Between 1713 and 1716, production figures for the *gobernación* fluctuated between 9746 pesos and 15,966 pesos – some of the lowest entries of the entire eighteenth century.[16] Indeed, on taking office in 1713, Yarza was to draw attention to the 'ruinous condition' to which the cities of his district had succumbed. Even the formerly prosperous cities of Zaragoza and Cáceres were now too poor (*aniquilados*), he informed the Crown, to pay for the services of a parish priest.[17]

This, then, was the context in which Joseph López de Carvajal proposed to conduct a new *entrada* to the Chocó, aimed at exploring the potential for the establishment of new mining ventures between the Murri and Sucio rivers. Explorations began in 1711, and they are of interest to us principally because rumours of the governor's intentions provoked – or precipitated – a major movement of people from the settlements of Citará towards the northernmost reaches of the region. By December 1710, only 10 or 12 of the 36 or 38 families normally resident in Bebará remained in the village. Similar movements were reported in Quibdó and Lloró. Indians, Spanish settlers claimed, were migrating en masse towards the Murri river.[18] Over the course of the following year, further movements took place, as Indians still remaining in the villages left to join *cimarronas* situated either in the vicinity of the Murri and Sucio rivers, or 'in many other parts . . . that fall within the jurisdiction of this province [Antioquia]'.[19] At the same time as Indians deserted their settlements in December 1710, prominent members of the village communities travelled to Antioquia in person, accompanied by their interpreters, to request the governor's assistance in making their resettlement legal and permanent.[20] Don Joseph Sagito was the first to appear before the governor, accompanied by Joseph Veragone, Agustín Bepa, and one Lorenzo, a *ladino* and Spanish-speaker.[21] Their arrival was followed, in January 1711, by that of Indians from Quibdó – in this case, Don Francisco Cuttibira and Nicolás Guacarama, sons-in-law, respectively, of the village cacique, and of the governor, Don Francisco Cumimbara.[22]

According to statements recorded by López de Carvajal, an interested and undoubtedly biased party in this affair, and Antioquia's *protector de indios*, Rafael de Oquendo, Indians all gave evidence of the oppression and exploitation suffered by their people under the harsh administration of *tenientes*, *corregidores* and priests. Cacique Don Joseph Sagito gave testimony that in his community of Bebará, Indians were oppressed and 'under a heavy yoke', the result of 'the ill-treatment and hostility which they suffer'. More specifically, he complained that Indians were not allowed the time to hunt, fish and plant crops for their own subsistence and that of their families; that they were deprived of the upbringing of, and authority over, their children; and that, to add insult to injury, their harvests were commonly purchased by Spaniards at extremely low prices and resold at much higher prices, thus depriving Indians of a portion of their profits.[23] In statements given a month later, Nicolás Guacarama and Don Francisco Cuttibira reported similar grievances, and indicated that it was due to 'the extortions and vexations which they suffer' that 'they and the caciques and governors [will] abandon that province'.[24]

To these general grievances to do with loss of control over land, labour and resources, the *indios principales* added grievances of a more personal kind. Don Joseph Sagito, who as cacique was the most senior member of Bebará's Indian community, claimed that he had only recently been released from the stocks and chains in which he had been held by one Manuel de Vargas, who was the village *corregidor*. No further details of Sagito's imprisonment were recorded on that occasion, *protector* Oquendo limiting himself to commenting that the official in question had exceeded his authority: 'Manuel de Vargas . . . misunderstands the extent of his jurisdiction [over the Indians], and even were his authority to extend over Don Joseph Sagito, which it does not, it would not be appropriate to carry out such a punishment on said cacique, as he is a natural lord'.[25] But in evidence to the governor in September of the following year, Lorenzo de Salazar, a settler in Citará for twenty years, described how, for demanding the *corregidor*'s dismissal, and threatening that should the official not be removed Sagito would appeal in person to the *audiencia* in Santa Fe, Vargas 'imprisoned him, and beat him, and [left him] covered in blood, which resulted in all the Indians leaving [the settlement], some heading for the mountains and others for the city of Antioquia'.[26] Similar incidents apparently took place in Quibdó in 1710. According to Nicolás Guacarama and Francisco Cuttibira, the caciques Cogayda and Don Juan Mitiguirre – the latter having once been among the most trusted of the Spaniards' allies in Citará province – received punishments of so violent a nature as to result in their deaths.[27] The fact that two of Don Juan Mitiguirre's sons, Don Sebastián Baquía (or Vaquira) and Don Juan Chaqueravia, were among the first Indians to join the new Murri settlement lends credence to the claims of the Indians from Quibdó.[28]

That issues to do with the power and privileges to be enjoyed by the native elite and the role that elite was to play in village government are crucial to explaining the Indians' actions was further confirmed by *oidor* Vicente de Aramburu, whose visit of inspection coincided with these events. In contravention of the Laws of the Indies, Aramburu reported to the Crown, which determined that Indian towns should be administered by their own caciques, governors, *alcaldes* and *capitanes*, no proper provision had been made in the Chocó to define the duties and responsibilities of native officials, or to safeguard their rights and privileges.[29] It was deeply regrettable, he wrote, that in none of the eight towns that comprised the provinces of Noanama and Citará did Indian officials play a role in their own administration, and that customary exemptions from labour services were routinely ignored in the Chocó, caciques, governors and *alcaldes* all being drawn into the service of *corregidores* much like the rest of the population.[30] Perhaps of even greater significance is that at the height of the crisis in 1712, by which time few Indians remained in the settlements of Citará, Aramburu not only offered assurances that their grievances would be dealt with – specifically those concerned with labour services – but that Indians should henceforth be entirely responsible for their own government, and that the privileges and prerogatives of native officials would in future be respected.[31]

This was a particularly favourable conjuncture, given Governor López de Carvajal's interest in staking a claim for Antioquia in a large and unexplored stretch of the Chocó, for the Indians of Citará to re-negotiate what might be called the 'terms and conditions' of Spanish rule. Indeed, there are indications that individuals acting on behalf of the governor in the months leading up to December 1710 exploited the Indians' discontent and actually encouraged them to desert their settlements with assurances of better conditions under Antioquia's administration. Certainly, lay and religious authorities in Citará were convinced that events in the province were attributable as much to the encouragement that Indians received from agents of the governor as to their long-standing resistance to settled living and Christian evangelisation. According to *teniente* Don Joseph de la Cuesta, Indians were 'incited' to desert their villages by one Juan Montaño and the mulatto Bernardo or Bernardino de Salazar, both of whom were engaged in assisting López de Carvajal in the arrangements for his forthcoming *entrada*, and were actually given assurances that in Murri they would neither be subject to government by Spanish officials, nor required 'to remain in their towns for instruction in Christian Doctrine'.[32] Fray Francisco Forero, *doctrinero* of Bebará, similarly attributed the Indians' actions to the inducements offered – namely, the freedom both to 'refuse instruction in Christian Doctrine' and to 'return to their former wars against the Cunacuna'.[33]

The governor's own reports confirm that Bernardino de Salazar was placed in charge of procuring supplies within the province to support explorations in Murri, and that he had close links with Indians there, for when he returned to Antioquia from the Chocó in September 1710, three months before Don Joseph

Sagito's arrival in the city, he was said to be accompanied by 'some Indian . . . friends [who are] fugitives from the province of Chocó'.[34] However, it is to be noted that Don Joseph de Yarza, López de Carvajal's successor, considered that it was the Indians who exploited the governor's interest in discovering new deposits of precious metals and increasing Antioquia's revenues. Their promises of future tributes, and most especially of discovery of 'very rich minerals' in a part of the Chocó where there was, in fact, no gold to speak of, was all in order, Yarza informed the king, 'to secure the Governor's protection in . . . Murri, to which they have retreated with their families to escape the doctrinas in the Province of Citará, the towns of which have [all] been deserted'.[35]

Perhaps the more important point is that the coincidence of interest between Don Joseph Sagito and Don Joseph López made both parties willing allies in the enterprise, and opened a new period of co-operation between Indians and Spaniards in this part of the Chocó. To regain a firm foothold for Antioquia in a region that was producing great wealth for miners and merchants from neighbouring Popayán, López intended to reduce and pacify so-called 'fugitives' rumoured to inhabit scattered *cimarronas* in the area between the Murri and Oromira (Sucio) rivers, and to create new settlements over which Antioquia, rather than Popayán, would exercise jurisdiction. The newly settled Indians, in their turn, would assist him in the reduction of unpacified groups (the Oromira) believed to inhabit territory to the south of the Gulf of Darién, where they were encircled by the Cuna.[36] The *indios principales* of Citará undoubtedly understood the implications of this development, and thus promised to 'provide information [about] and discover very rich mines located within the boundaries of this territory', to guide the governor to the lands of the 'infidel' Oromira, and to lead him to *cimarronas* scattered across the territory between the Murri and Sucio rivers. In this context, Indians mentioned a large *cimarrona* on the banks of the Sucio river, and a number of smaller ones in the vicinity of the Murri, inhabited by over 500 people.[37]

Over the course of 1711 and 1712, Governor López de Carvajal and his Citará allies co-operated in the process of opening a trail across the difficult terrain linking the city of Antioquia with the Murri river; in conducting explorations in the northern stretches of the Chocó region; in the establishment of a new mining camp, San Mateo; in the foundation of a new settlement, Nuestra Señora de Belén de Murri; and in reducing Indians from *cimarronas* scattered across a large expanse of territory between the Murri and Bojaya rivers. Between September and November 1711, for example, small parties of Indians, led by Don Joseph Sagito, Don Antonio Tribinoco and Martín Quiunape, among others, travelled from *cimarrona* to *cimarrona* in an effort to draw Indians to the new settlement of Murri, which had been formally founded, and a makeshift chapel erected, on 21 September 1711.[38] By mid-November, a total of 205 Indians, 142 of whom were women and children, had joined the settlement. The vast majority of this first group were recent fugitives from the villages of Citará, 33 of the 56 men having deserted their communities with their families within the previous year.[39] But some who joined the new settlement over the following year were members of long-standing *cimarronas*, and some, according to López, had never before encountered white men. Of 13 Indians who came to Murri in May 1712, three were children born in the *cimarrona*; seven of the remaining 10 (all originally from Quibdó) had lived in the vicinity of the river for 10 years, and one had lived there for eight.⁴⁰ A similar picture emerges from a group of 50 Indians who joined Murri between July and September 1713. Of the 14 men (36 were women and children), two, aged 25 and 26, had been born in the *cimarrona*; two others had lived there for 10 to 12 years; three had been there for eight years; and another three had been there for four. Unusually, one of the 14 men came from as far as Tadó, in Nóvita province, though the majority originated from Quibdó and Bebará.⁴¹ No details emerge, however, of the negotiations that must have preceded the decision of these previously isolated communities to establish contact with Spaniards at Murri.

The number of Indians living in Murri itself was still small in 1712, only a proportion of runaways opting for settlement there. But its very foundation in September 1711, under Antioquia's administration, nevertheless acted as a magnet for the peoples of the province, and precipitated further migrations from the established villages, despite the best efforts of the Spanish authorities to stem the flow. In December 1710, for example, Don Gregorio Chicaravia, *gobernador* of Bebará, was placed in chains, 'because it is understood that he, too, wishes to escape'. The same fate befell Francisco Peguegunra, '[an] Indian who has just returned from said place of Murri [to persuade others to leave]'.⁴² For fear that Don Joseph Sagito might seek to 'finish off this town and take with him the few Indians who are left', a watch was set up on the Arquía river, to await his return and/or that of his aide, Agustín Bepa.⁴³ And finally, in an attempt to forestall the inevitable escape of those Indians who still remained in the villages, *teniente* Joseph de la Cuesta instructed *corregidor* Pedro Rubio de Quesada to be particularly vigilant of their movements, and to punish 'severely' those 'who deserved to be punished'.⁴⁴ All of this was to no avail. When news of the foundation of Murri reached the province, more Indians abandoned their fields and homes and headed north, under the guise, Francisco Forero complained, of forming part of the original group of runaways, so as to guarantee for themselves the governor's protection: 'they have effected this retreat [by] passing themselves off as [the original] rebels'. Indeed, the Franciscan even claimed that the Indians who were already in Murri sent messengers to their old villages to encourage others to follow suit.⁴⁵ By mid-June 1712, Bebará was all but deserted, its population down to a total of three, according to *oidor* Aramburu.⁴⁶

As the indigenous population of Citará province steadily decreased between late 1710 and 1712, that of Murri steadily increased, so that by the latter year López de Carvajal was able to inform the king that the settlement now comprised approximately 500 Indians.⁴⁷ Hundreds made their way northwards, either to establish small communities somewhere between the Murri and Sucio rivers, or to join the new settlement, which not only offered some protection from reprisals but a promise of more favourable conditions for its indigenous population. The documents indicate that in addition to concessions on such matters as tributes and stipends – suspended for a year, while new dwellings were built, lands cleared and crops planted – Indians met two further objectives by their migration to Murri.[48] The first of these was self-government, acknowledged in the appointment of Don Joseph Sagito as cacique, Don Sebastián Baquía as *capitán*, and Pedro Anuada and Esteban Tovare as *alcaldes*, or judicial officials, 'in order that these natives may be . . . subject to legal process as well as government by their cacique'.[49] Agustín Bepa was appointed *fiscal*, or constable, entrusted with supervising attendance at Mass.[50] And, in accordance with Spanish law, all native officials were henceforth to be exempt from tribute obligations.[51]

The second objective was to regain the freedom to pursue traditional activities and protect the Indian way of life. This, it seems, included the freedom to engage in the long-established custom of making war on their old enemies, the Cuna. Not only did the census taken of one group of migrants from Lloró in September 1711 list three Cuna boys (aged 7, 10 and 13) as the property, respectively, of Esteban Tovare, Antonio Tribinoco and Martín Quiunape, but, in July 1712, Francisco Antonio de la Chica y Guzmán informed Governor López that 'twenty Indians went to fight the Cunacuna . . . they returned on the twenty-third of this month . . . they had good fortune [for] it is said that they brought back ten Indian women and five boys . . . they want to go off to fight again'.[52] One further piece of information, crucial, perhaps, to understanding the alliance between Indians and Spaniards in Murri, emerges from an 'Informe' submitted to the Crown by 11 *vecinos* of Antioquia in November 1716. According to this document, the purpose of which was to criticise López de Carvajal's record as governor and to bring his allegedly corrupt conduct to the Crown's attention, it was 'said Don Joseph López', as opposed to the royal treasury, who most profited from the Murri experiment, largely due to 'the illicit trade in which he has engaged with said Indians'.[53] Murri, perhaps, promised not only an alternative existence to that available in the settlements of Citará province, but a restoration of the mutually beneficial arrangements existing between Indians and Spaniards in Citará in the years before 1684.

Few details emerge from the documents to indicate what became of Murri after 1713, though it is clear that it failed to live up to expectations of rich deposits of precious metal to replace the exhausted mines of Antioquia, and that, partly for this reason, it did not survive in the medium term.[54] We do know that Indians resolutely refused to return to their settlements throughout 1710–13; that in 1712 they responded to *oidor* Aramburu's overtures by threatening that, unless they were allowed to remain in Murri, 'they will be obliged to retreat [beyond Spanish reach] . . . so that no vestiges of them will remain',[55] and that in 1719, the Council of the Indies, convinced by López de Carvajal's enthusiastic reports, urged him to continue his activities there.[56] However, the governor's experiment in colonising the northernmost reaches of the Chocó had come to an end five years earlier, in 1714. According to the 'Informe de Antioquia' cited above, López had by this time absconded to Cartagena, apparently to scupper an investigation (*residencia*) into his activities as governor.[57]

The fate of the population of Murri and surrounding *cimarronas* after that date is equally obscure. We know that the authorities eventually resorted to force to return the Citará to their villages, for when in 1723 Antioquia's governor Facundo Guerra Calderón made a new attempt to create settlements in the Murri district, he stated that the original foundation had been 'demolished' by the Spaniards.[58] We also know that *oidor* Aramburu had predicted all along that this would be the outcome of the Indians' actions, for as he informed the Crown in 1713, 'this is and has [always] been the method adopted in these situations, termed uprisings by tenientes and priests . . . which is then followed by the plunder and pillage of the fugitive Indians' fields and homes, as if they were enemies in a just war'.[59] Yet in spite of the use of forcible methods to resolve the problems posed by the establishment of Murri, the region had not returned to normality by the early 1720s, undoubtedly because the Spanish authorities continued to lack the means to enforce strict compliance with *reducción* policy. Many Indians remained dispersed in *cimarronas* across the Murri region, and of these, 60 to 70 were to make a fresh attempt to formalise settlement under Antioquia's administration in the early 1720s.[60] It was also at this time that one Don Agustín Morales y Mendoza submitted to the Crown a proposal – strikingly similar in tone and content to those of the seventeenth century – to undertake the reduction of the Indians of the Chocó, on the grounds that the population classified as *cimarrones* was, at that time, larger than that of village Indians.[61] And when, in 1747, Don Miguel de Santisteban reported on Viceroy Eslava's term of office, he described how, in 1743, Don Bartolomé de Montes, governor of the Chocó, rounded up 'an excessive number of Indians' (342) from *cimarronas* where many had been living for over twenty years, adding that in spite of the best efforts of his *teniente*, many escaped again within the year.[62]

In fact, by 1720, Spaniards in the Chocó had been obliged to create at least one new settlement, and perhaps two, to accommodate Indians who continued to evade *reducción*. In 1718 or 1719, Don Francisco de Alcantud y Gaona founded Nuestra Señora de Chiquinquirá de Beté, with some 50 tributaries and their families, 'the majority heathens and cimarrones who many years ago had retreated to the wilderness to escape the continuous vexations which they suffer'.[63] Within a year or two, however, no more than three to four families – all from the 'cimarrona de Murri' – remained.[64] A second settlement, San Juan de Bojaya, was founded for the same purpose some time between 1718 and 1729, when Don Francisco de Ibero took up his post as first governor of the Chocó.[65] Others were created later in the century, including a new town in the vicinity of the Sucio river, founded in the mid-1770s; Pabarandó, founded before 1780; and Cupica, situated some eight days' distance from Quibdó.[66]

As for Murri itself, it reappears in the records in 1736, as a Franciscan *doctrina* consisting of some 60 to 70 Indians.[67] However, far from becoming the place of safety envisaged by Indians fleeing the excesses of Spanish colonisation, Murri remained subject to the same problems that characterised other settlements of the Chocó. In 1745, Fray Juan Joseph Salazar informed Viceroy Eslava of his concern that excessive and unregulated labour demands would soon result in his *doctrina* being abandoned by its indigenous inhabitants.[68] Murri was, in fact, still in existence in 1782, although its population – Indian and black – was extremely small compared with those of other settlements. Only 279 Indians lived there, compared with 1533 in Quibdó, 1119 in Lloró, and a total for the province of 4545. The slave population reached a mere 20, out of a total for Citará of 2156.[69] Murri, it seems, turned out not to be as profitable as López de Carvajal anticipated.

For us, however, the significance of the events surrounding the establishment of the new settlement lies in the fact that they offer an important perspective on the ways in which Indians adapted to colonial rule during the early decades of the eighteenth century. Indian peoples everywhere, of course, underwent significant transformations in their political organisation as a result of their subjection to Spanish rule, leading sometimes to the enhancement, sometimes to the erosion, of the political authority of traditional elites.[70] But whereas in many areas (the Andean region being a good example) where a pre-existing elite survived the conquest, the role and legitimacy of the colonial cacique as spokesman for, and guardian of, the indigenous community had, by the eighteenth century, been severely weakened, among the Citará, where no such political leadership existed, a different process appears to have taken place.[71] Our sources indicate that this Indian group, characterised by a political organisation that was dispersed and decentralised, and for much of the seventeenth century apparently determined to resist the imposition of a strong, centralised political authority that would facilitate the consolidation of Spanish control, came, by the 1710s, to recognise the crucial role that could be played by a political elite that was itself, as Isacsson explained, 'an outcome of the colonial system'.[72] This was not, it must be emphasised, to assist the Spaniards, but to protect and promote the interests of native peoples under the new conditions of colonial rule: 'by virtue of the post he holds', Don Joseph Sagito was reported to have informed *protector* Oquendo in late 1710, 'he is obliged to seek ... redress of grievances and [insist] that Indian peoples be permitted to enjoy the privileges granted to them by His Majesty'.[73] Apparently fluent in the language of the colonists, increasingly knowledgeable of Spanish government and administration, and seemingly also fully cognisant of the rights and privileges accorded native peoples under Spanish law, this cacique became not only determined to insist on Spanish respect for the status, privileges and authority of the new elite itself, but extremely adept at developing strategies to exploit clashes of interest between Spanish groups, rivalries between agents of church and state, and competition between the various layers of Spanish government, to the advantage of the indigenous community he led.[74]

Failures of Christian conversion

However, in that other crucial aspect of colonisation – namely, Christian conversion – no such processes of adaptation appear to have taken place. At least for the first 70 to 80 years after the establishment of the mission, and despite nearly two centuries of wide-ranging contacts with Spanish settlers and priests – contacts that left their mark on native culture in numerous and varied ways – indigenous peoples in this part of the Spanish empire sought repeatedly to subvert the efforts of European missionaries to impose an alien religion and way of life. In reporting to the Crown in 1701, for example, Fray Mateo de Villafañe, bishop of Popayán, said of Indians in the Chocó that 'they observe that which pertains to our Christian religion more out of force than devotion or inclination'.[75] Ten years later, Francisco Solano de Salazar, recently appointed interim priest of Murri, commented of his early experiences there that 'having examined [the Indians] who have settled on the banks of the Murri River, starting with the cacique, I have found that neither he nor the other[s] . . . have been taught Christian Doctrine or . . . the principal mysteries of our Holy Catholic Faith [to the extent that] they do not know how to cross themselves and much less their daily prayers . . . many children have not been baptised and I have found that many are married according to their old customs . . . believing their women to be their legitimate wives without need for further ceremony'.[76] Writing in Santa Fe in 1719, where he had recently had opportunity to examine a group of Indians from the Chocó, Franciscan provincial Antonio Felices similarly concluded that 'they know nothing of Christian Doctrine'.[77] Even at the very end of the colonial period Spaniards were forced to acknowledge that Christianity had made few advances in the Chocó. While Francisco Silvestre made the observation that Indians instructed in Christian doctrine in childhood rejected those teachings on becoming adults, Governor Don Carlos de Ciaurriz considered that the peoples of the Chocó had not assimilated even the most basic rudiments of the Catholic faith.[78]

Eighteenth-century sources are, then, remarkably consistent in reporting the Indians' comprehensive rejection of missionary teaching and refusal to assimilate the religious practices of the colonisers. Their value to the historian seeking to reconstruct the main features of Indian religious belief is, however, far more limited. The apparent failure of generations of Spanish priests to learn native languages, or to investigate and record the beliefs of the Indian peoples with whose conversion they were entrusted – what we have is disparate, sporadic, and insufficient to build up a coherent picture of native religion – has resulted in an almost complete absence in the documents of this period of the kind of evidence that in recent years has permitted historians of other regions of Spanish America to assess the subtle ways in which Indians appropriated, assimilated and reinterpreted for their own religious purposes (often in ways that were not intended by Spanish missionaries) those elements of Catholic Christianity that were most meaningful and relevant to themselves.[79]

The pages that follow do not, therefore, purport to offer a comprehensive analysis of native religion, or to assess the ways in which native beliefs may or may not have been modified by decades of contact with Spanish missionaries.[80] In the absence of full and reliable data, my purpose is instead to explain the stiff and unwavering resistance with which Indians met every effort of the Spanish clergy to impose an alien religion, and the equally steadfast determination with which they acted to protect the practices and traditions that both continued to serve a purpose in their society and gave meaning to their lives. For the establishment of the mission was intended to bring about wholesale changes to Indian traditions and ways of life. The Franciscans aimed not only to replace native religion with Christianity, and to appropriate for themselves the role previously played by Indian shamans, but also to impose new norms of 'civilised' behaviour. In addition to the adoption of Christian marriage, European dress codes, and the Spanish language, Indians were required to relinquish traditional ceremonial practices such as dances, the consumption of alcohol, sexual practices described by Spaniards as promiscuous and incestuous, and the age-old practice of skirmishing with enemy groups, most especially the Cuna. Of equal importance for the semi-sedentary Citará, the requirement that Indians congregate in large, nucleated settlements involved the complete transformation of indigenous economic and social structures.

The many and varied ways in which Indians resisted the efforts of Spaniards to reduce populations to life in large, permanent village settlements have been fully discussed in this study, and no further examples need be presented here. Of greater relevance to this discussion are the persistence of native values and the survival of native practices long after the processes of conversion and assimilation should have been completed. Indeed, more than half a century after the Jesuit Antonio Marzal reported, in 1678, 'the horror with which they view Christian customs and their desire to observe and carry out their own rites and ceremonies',[81] the Spaniards Fray Dionisio de Camino and Don Pedro Muñoz de Arjona both confirmed that religious instruction had demonstrably failed to eradicate native religion, and that Indians continued to practise their old customs in defiance of Spanish missionaries. In 1730, Camino observed of the Indians of Citará that 'they still practice many rituals and ... customs [derived from their past] heathenism'; some twenty years later, Muñoz de Arjona described the local population as 'very attached to, and inclined towards, idolatry, observing and believing many customs [associated with their own religion]'.[82]

Central to the persistence of native belief were the practitioners of Indian religion, termed *mohanes, curanderos* or *brujos* by the Spaniards. First described by Antonio Marzal in 1678 as the community's intermediary with 'the devil', in whose honour he performed a variety of rituals 'to bring back to health he who is sick',[83] by the 1730s, the Indian shaman was more reliably reported to fulfil two key roles in Citará society. One of those roles consisted of casting spells on enemies, and carrying out curing rituals on the sick, involving leaves and incantations designed to defeat the disease in what can best be described as a battle between illness and healer: 'if the condition turned out not to be serious and the [patient] recovers', Dionisio de Camino informed *oidor* Martínez Malo, 'they say he is a good brujo ... and if [the patient] dies, they say the disease was very brave, and that a spell was cast upon him'. In addition to exercising their curative powers on behalf of their people, native shamans – at least some of whom also served as the moral and spiritual leaders of their communities – played an additional role in the preservation of indigenous beliefs and the rejection of those of the Christians: 'they preach that they should not abandon their ancient rites and customs, and that they should not believe the Christians (which is how they describe whites), and that these only teach their faith in order to make the Indians serve them and to turn them into slaves'.[84]

In this, no doubt, native shamans were aided by the Indians' experience of conquest and colonisation in the seventeenth century, and by their long record of interactions with Franciscan missionaries. Repeated outbreaks of disease during the seventeenth century, for example, may well have encouraged those Indians for whom the advent of Christianity coincided with these events to associate Catholic rites and rituals, such as baptism and penitence, with sickness and death. Such responses are known to have been common elsewhere in Spanish America. In Nueva Vizcaya, for instance, where the Jesuits conferred baptism only on the young, the willing when properly instructed, and, crucially, those who were in danger of dying, shamans could justifiably make the case 'that baptism brought sickness or death'.[85] Our sources provide only two examples to indicate that the peoples of the Chocó also made this connection. The first dates from the early 1670s, and it relates to an outbreak of smallpox in the Chocó, when the Jesuit Antonio Marzal travelled through Citará territory conferring baptism on a number of infants, several of whom subsequently died.[86] The second dates from the early 1730s, when Franciscan provincial Dionisio de Camino indicated that the sacrament of penitence, conferred on those nearing death, provoked similar fear among indigenous peoples. Indians did their utmost to avoid confession, Camino reflected, 'because they say that in doing so they die'.[87] Though our evidence is insufficient to draw definitive conclusions, it nevertheless suggests that Indians in the Chocó did not incorporate Christian rituals such as baptism into their own ritual systems to protect them against disease, nor ever appealed to their missionaries for spiritual comfort or material assistance to help them cope with the resulting suffering and death.[88]

Instead, following the establishment of the Franciscan mission, it was the religious above all other groups who came to be perceived as the greatest threat to the security and well-being of the indigenous community. Indeed, it seems that among the Citará, as among the Guajiros of Riohacha, on New Granada's Caribbean coast, the strategies developed by Indian peoples were intended first and foremost to protect themselves and their children from the influence and intervention of the friars.[89] Flight from the region's settlements, we have seen, remained an obstacle to *reducción* and conversion for the duration of the mission. But even where this was not a viable option, Indians resorted to a whole range of other tactics to distance themselves from the control exercised by the village priest. Despite an increase in grievances against all figures of authority as Spanish colonisation advanced in the eighteenth century, in the mid-1730s, the *doctrinero* of El Raposo informed Bishop Diego Fermín de Vergara that in his parish Indians positively preferred to be drafted into labour on behalf of colonial administrators rather than remaining in their villages subject to the vigilance of the priest. They 'are [always] greatly pleased to find themselves employed in ... transporting [goods] and working in the fields rather than [having to] remain in their towns subject to Christian Doctrine and the church bell', a state of affairs that was largely attributable, he said, to their 'hatred of that which is to the service of God and the keeping of his law towards which they are always fiercely resistant'.[90] El Raposo was, admittedly, a secular-administered *doctrina* of Nóvita province, rather than a Franciscan-administered *doctrina* of Citará province, but it is to be noted that in reporting to *oidor* Martínez Malo in 1730, Dionisio de Camino claimed of the Citará that their boys positively celebrated reaching the age at which they became tribute-paying adults, for this status absolved them of the obligation to attend catechism.[91] Rather than appeal to the religious for protection against the most exploitative aspects of Spanish colonisation, Indians in the Chocó saw in labour drafts that required them to absent themselves from the settlements a means of escape from the surveillance and control of the priests.

Similar defiance characterised native attitudes towards the missionaries' targeting of the young for intensive religious instruction. This was a feature of the encounter between Spanish priests and native communities even before the arrival of the Franciscans, the Jesuit Marzal describing how his 17-month evangelisation effort among the children of the Citará had proved in vain: 'what is the point in the priest endeavouring to ensure that the children . . . learn to be Christians', he wrote, 'for when the meetings of elders or drinking parties take place, they speak the exact opposite'.[92] In the 1710s and 1720s, it was further reported that the loss of control over the upbringing of children was a particular grievance of the Citará – Don Joseph Sagito, it will be recalled, objected specifically to his people's loss of authority over their children – and that Indians throughout the Chocó went to great lengths to protect their offspring from the influence of Spanish priests, one *doctrinero* noting the particular efforts he had made to 'bring the children out of the hideouts where they are secreted by their parents'.[93] Such attitudes may have reflected opposition to the disruption of generational relationships that missionary control over the young necessarily entailed, or perhaps more general hostility to the use of corporal punishment. A trend already evident by 1680 (when it was said of Fray Joseph de Córdoba that 'he has . . . a stick'), by the eighteenth century corporal punishment was used not only as a method of instruction, but to punish a whole range of other transgressions.[94] Thus, while in 1730 Fray Dionisio de Camino made specific reference to the striking of children for failure to memorise prayers,[95] in 1736, Bishop Vergara authorised the flogging of both men and women to punish drunkenness, incest and adultery.[96] Indian resistance to the control exercised by priests over the young, on the other hand, may have reflected opposition on purely ideological grounds. It is of significance that in 1807, Governor Ciaurriz commented that '[the children's] own parents [assume the role of] religious mentors [*dogmatizadores*]'.[97]

As a result of the long-standing success of the Citará in maintaining a safe distance from the friars, a wide range of indigenous social, religious and cultural practices – burial practices, marriage customs, ceremonial activities – proved exceptionally difficult to eradicate, while efforts to encourage participation in Catholic rituals, to introduce *cofradías*, and to enforce a rigorous regime of Sunday prayer proved entirely futile.[98] In these efforts, of course, Spanish clergy may also have been adversely affected by the absence in the Chocó of the large and ornate churches that so impressed indigenous populations in so many other, sometimes equally forbidding, parts of Spain's American empire.[99] For if, as David Block has argued for the Jesuit missions of the upper Amazon, the richness and ostentation of church interiors, with their statues, sacred images, candelabra, chalices and luxurious textiles, among other artefacts, 'underlined the superiority of the European religious system', then their absence in the Chocó must be considered to have contributed to the Indians' rejection of the religious system of the Spanish clergy that was so widely reported in seventeenth- and eighteenth-century sources.[100]

Indeed, the indications are that at least until the middle of the eighteenth century, indigenous peoples everywhere in the Chocó refused to relinquish traditional ceremonial practices which involved dancing and heavy drinking (hence the term *borracheras*), and which the Spaniards invariably attributed to the Indians' penchant for immoral customs and loathsome vices – incest, adultery and promiscuity. Giving evidence in 1720, for example, Melchor Jacinto de Arboleda Salazar said of the Indians of Noanama that they had a 'particular liking' for *aguardiente*, 'so that without being able to prevent it, they become intoxicated in order to commit incest, adultery and many other offences [contrary to the law of] God'.[101] Sixteen years later, the *doctrinero* of El Raposo attributed the Indians' refusal to be 'subject to Christian Doctrine and the church bell' to their 'innate propensity towards liberty and vices . . . drunkenness, sexual acts [of various sorts], incest at all levels [of consanguinity] towards which they are prone and [which] are occasioned by their . . . natural appetite for drunkenness'.[102] And, writing just after mid-century, Don Pedro Muñoz de Arjona said of the Indians of the Chocó that they desired 'only to live in the wilderness . . . to make use without hindrance of drink [and to take part in] lascivious [practices] towards which they are greatly inclined'.[103] The function and purpose of these ritual gatherings, and the occasions on which they took place, were not recorded by Spaniards.[104] We do know, however, that these were times when Indians came together in all their finery, their bodies painted and adorned with bells, beads and, in the case of women, garlands of flowers.[105]

The peoples of Citará also asserted their rejection of Christian teachings in many other important ways. Determined to resist the imposition of Christian morality as regards marriage, for instance, Indians persisted with their customary methods of selecting partners, and of contracting marital unions, despite the efforts of Spanish priests both to instil the values of monogamy and to prevent sexual unions which, due to the high degree of consanguinity between partners, were considered taboo in European society. In 1678 and 1730, respectively, Antonio Marzal and Dionisio de Camino both made reference to the survival of traditional practice in this facet of Indian life, and to the persistent refusal of indigenous peoples to legitimise their unions by availing themselves of the services of the village *doctrinero*.[106] 'They are so lascivious', Camino wrote of the women of Citará, 'that they pay no heed to family relationships, however close . . . they have such little regard for marriage that the men disavow the women and . . . [the women] openly take up with other men, all of whom have many concubines'.[107]

Because they conflicted with European values as regards marriage and sexuality, Spanish clergy detected in the apparent freedom that governed the sexual conduct of the Citará – pre-marital sexual relations, the taking of several partners (formal and informal) over the course of a lifetime, the men's acceptance as potential marriage partners of both females captured in warfare and the wives and concubines of deceased brothers and fathers – unequivocal evidence of native depravity.[108] In this, however, as in so many other observations on native conduct and custom, a note of caution is in order. In reporting in 1807 on the purpose of pre-marital relations (*amancebamiento*) among the Citará, Governor Carlos de Ciaurriz commented that cohabitation was specifically intended 'to test the qualities . . . and fidelity' of the woman chosen; that having proven herself satisfactory in this regard, 'they love each other mutually, treating [both] legitimate and illegitimate children with affection and kindness'; and that adultery was widely and generally 'abhorred . . . and rare the Indian who commits it'.[109] The extent to which Ciaurriz's assessment indicates changing attitudes towards marriage, as opposed to more sensitive and informed reporting, is, of course, uncertain.

Burial practices and attitudes towards the dead also remained, if not unchanged by decades of contact with Catholic missionaries, decidedly native in character. Writing in 1711 in the context of the recent resettlement of Indians in Murri, for example, secular cleric Francisco Solano de Salazar made the observation that, among the peoples he had encountered there, neither parent nor relative was ever mentioned by name after death, 'because they say that in mentioning [the person] who is dead, he [or she] will enter their mouths and extract their tongue, after which they perish'.[110] Twenty years later, Franciscan Dionisio de Camino not only confirmed that such attitudes persisted among Indians – 'once the deceased has been buried they neither remember nor refer to them again, because they say that [otherwise] he [or she] will harm their tongue and teeth' – but indicated that the Spaniards themselves had found ways of capitalising on this feature of native belief. If a Spaniard was owed money by the deceased, he referred to the person in question in front of his kin, 'and to stop them . . . [the Indians] quickly pay up'. Since such attitudes so clearly conflicted with those of Christians, who buried their dead in church grounds and said Masses for the repose of the souls of the departed, indigenous peoples opted to preserve their own methods (and associated rituals) for disposing of the bodies of the dead: 'when they die', Camino commented of the Citará, 'they believe that their souls pass on to another land where there is an abundance of food and drink, and for this reason . . . they inter [their dead] . . . with all their tools and other implements necessary to cultivate that land [awaiting them in the afterlife]'.[111]

One final and equally crucial way in which the Indians of Citará resisted Spanish efforts to impose new and alien cultural criteria was their refusal to relinquish the age-old practice of regular skirmishing with their Cuna neighbours.[112] A source of slaves for labour and, as we have seen, of additional marriage partners, warfare also played a crucial political role among the Citará, providing brave and successful males with the opportunity to acquire the status and authority that placed them in positions of leadership in times of conflict and conferred prestige in times of peace. Late-seventeenth-century sources make repeated reference to the fact that war played a role of central importance in this society. Antonio Marzal, it will be recalled, said of the Citará that 'they go to war out of vanity of being considered brave, for he who kills the most is considered the most brave'.[113] *Defensor* Diego de Galvis, commenting in the context of the 1684 rebellion, described how 'they spend all their lives in this exercise, killing and capturing [Indians]', which they 'do not consider . . . to be a crime'.[114] The value placed on male bravery within Indian culture was also clearly recognised by Dionisio de Camino in 1730, for in reflecting on native burial practices in this part of the Chocó, he drew attention to the fact that the chanting that took place on such occasions laid great stress on the courage of the deceased.[115] Citará incursions into enemy territory for the purpose of waging war thus continued unabated into the eighteenth century. In July 1712, Francisco de la Chica reported of the newly settled population of Murri that 'twenty Indians went to fight the Cunacuna . . . they want to go off to fight again'.[116] And in reporting, in the 1780s, on the establishment of a garrison on the Atrato river, one of the purposes of which was to prevent parties of Chocó and Cuna Indians raiding each other's communities, Juan Jiménez Donoso confessed that it had not sufficed to prevent the latter, at least, from making incursions into enemy territory.[117]

If the peoples of Citará were successful in resisting crucial elements of the programme of evangelisation and acculturation pursued by the Spanish Crown, they were undoubtedly aided by the particular conditions that characterised the colonial Chocó. As this study has shown, Spanish interest in this inhospitable frontier zone was limited to its potential for wealth, and few settlers – religious or secular – made more than half-hearted attempts to Christianise and acculturate native populations. Spanish indifference, combined with the reduced size of the white population, and the existence of large stretches of territory that remained largely unknown to Europeans until the end of the eighteenth century, all facilitated Indian resistance to the Christianising and 'civilising' project of the Franciscan missionaries, and perhaps even reinforced native values. This should not be interpreted to mean, however, that Indians responded to the advance of Spanish colonisation by rejecting outright all aspects of Spanish culture. Indians, we have seen, readily appropriated a whole range of items of European material culture (metal tools, cloth, beads and trinkets, even *aguardiente*), though these were invariably put to purposes that were both useful and familiar to native peoples themselves. Thus, whereas in the 1670s, a time when many Indians of the Chocó showed themselves open to closer and more frequent contact with Spaniards, the Citará were said to 'imitate the Spaniards . . . in . . . taking particular care in dressing to go to church', by the early 1750s, Pedro Muñoz de Arjona indicated that the beads and clothing that had for many years been so prized by Indians across the region had been adapted to suit not European sensibilities, but the practices and preferences of indigenous society: 'the men . . . wear no clothing other than that which nature gave them, [while] the women only wear a very short and ill-fitting covering of cloth [stretching] from the waist ... to the knees, and the greatest and most exquisite adornment ... [reserved for] feast days ... which is the custom of these peoples, is the body painted black to fake [the appearance of] clothing [with] ... some lines on the face; at other times they use for the purpose of adornment some small glass beads which are their greatest pride'.[118]

Far from Indians succumbing to the blandishments of Christianity, then, Christian teachings appear to have made no long-lasting impact on the religious lives of native peoples in the Chocó. And while it is true that the paucity of documentary evidence prevents us assessing whether subtle changes took place in the beliefs of indigenous peoples in this isolated corner of the Spanish empire as a result of decades of missionary labour, it seems unlikely, given the sheer repetition of the view that the peoples of Citará were 'incredulous', 'averse', 'very far from God' and 'very hostile', that Indians adapted elements of Catholic Christianity in ways that were meaningful and relevant to themselves.[119] This is not to suggest, of course, that Indians failed to understand the central importance of Christian chapels, priestly vestments, sacred images and holy vessels, for when rebellion against the inexorable advance of Spanish colonisation broke out in 1684, rebels specifically targeted priests, desecrated chapels, and took church ornaments. Neither at that time nor in later years, however, is there any evidence that Indians incorporated into their own religious beliefs and practices the objects and symbols of Catholic Christianity.[120] As Governor Ciaurriz sadly commented in 1807, 'in their houses they keep neither a Holy Cross, nor an image of a saint ... nor are they [ever] heard to invoke the sweet name of Jesus or his Holy Mother'.[121]

Notes

1. Isacsson, 'The Egalitarian Society', p. 97.
2. For reasons to do with the availability of uninhabited or sparsely inhabited land to the north of the Chocó, the settlements of Citará were most affected by Indian flight. However, settlements elsewhere in the region were not immune to mass desertions. In 1713, for example, Vicente de Aramburu informed the Crown that Nóvita province (especially the villages of San Joseph and San Agustín) was prone to be frequently deserted by its indigenous inhabitants, who retreated specifically to escape the Spanish. AGI Quito 143, Vicente de Aramburu to Crown, Santa Fe, 8 September 1713. Ten years later, in 1723, Bishop Juan Gómez Frías reported that the conduct of Noanama's *corregidor* Don Francisco de Laja, who diverted Indians to work on his own (extensive) lands, led Indians to flee their village for the refuge of their retreats. Of 148 tributaries who inhabited the settlement when the last *doctrinero* took up his post, only 60 remained. AGI Quito 185, Juan Gómez Frías to Crown, Popayán, 6 November 1723. The same phenomenon was reported in the Barbacoas region. In 1691, the governor of Popayán informed the Crown that the *encomiendas* of Barbacoas were unprofitable due to the large number of Indians who were absent from the province, whereabouts unknown. AGI Quito 75, Rodrigo Roque to Crown, Santa María del Puerto de Barbacoas, 16 March 1691.
3. AGI Santa Fe 307, 'Cuaderno ... sobre la entrada al río Murri'. See, in particular, Rafael de Oquendo's 'Petición', n.p., n.d., fols. 24–26; Joseph Veragone's statement to the governor, Antioquia, 10 March 1711, fol. 58; and Pedro Hato de la Banda's statement, also to the governor, Antioquia, 14 March 1711, fol. 61.

4 AGI Santa Fe 307, 'Cuaderno . . . sobre la entrada al río Murri', 'Petición', n.p., n.d., fol. 25.
5 AGI Santa Fe 307, 'Cuaderno . . . sobre la entrada al río Murri', 'Diligencia', Río de Murri, 1 October 1711, 'Diligencia', Río de Murri, 11 October 1711, and 'Diligencia', Rio de Murri, 12 November 1711, fols. 103, 115, 126–27.
6 AGI Quito 185, 'Certificación de la visita de Nóvita', Tadó, 6 October 1736; and 'Testimonio de la visita del Citará', Quibdó, 2 November 1736.
7 AGI Quito 185, Auto, Don Joseph de Figueredo y Victoria, San Gerónimo de Nóvita, 12 September 1742.
8 Carlos de Ciaurriz, 'Visita del Gobernador del Chocó, Don Carlos de Ciaurriz, practicada en el territorio de su mando en los años de 1804–1807', ed. Victor A. Bedoya, *Revista Colombiana de Antropología*, Vol. 11, 1962, p. 158.
9 Mentions of *planned* uprisings do recur in the historical record. See, for example, Isacsson, 'The Egalitarian Society', p. 123. See also Zuluaga Gómez (ed.), *Documentos inéditos*, Documento No. 12, pp. 85–86, in which Tomás Polo, *escribano público*, discusses an uprising planned to take place in Quibdó in Easter week, 1797, which was, apparently, thwarted. Slave rebellions did, however, occur in Tadó, in 1728 and again in 1737. See Leal, '"Matar a los blancos bueno es"', pp. 143–61. Unlike Barbacoas province, however, where Spaniards feared the possibility of Indian–slave alliances, in the Chocó indigenous peoples isolated themselves as much from blacks as they did from whites. On Barbacoas, see Lane, 'Taming the Master', p. 499.
10 For reasons that are not clear, but were perhaps to do with geographical proximity, in the early 1710s the northernmost stretches of Chocó territory were still considered to fall within the latter city's jurisdiction. See, for example, Joseph López de Carvajal to Vicente de Aramburu, Antioquia, 14 August 1712, in AGI Santa Fe 362, 'Testimonio de Autos', fol. 24.
11 The Franciscans of the Chocó, like other missionaries working among similar groups on the frontiers of the empire, favoured the creation of a political structure that was more useful to the programme of Christian conversion. As the procurator general stated in the early 1670s, soon after the establishment of the mission, if the friars were to make any progress in 'reducing' the native peoples of the Chocó, and converting them to Catholicism, then it was imperative that the Spanish should select a 'leader' with the authority to ensure that they remained in their settlements, under the vigilance of their priests. See AGI Quito 67, 'Testimonio de Autos (Franciscans)', fol. 16.
12 Isacsson, 'Emberá', p. 26. See also the statements of Esteban Fernández de Rivera and Juan Joseph Azcárate de Castillo, in AGI Santa Fe 204, Ramo 6, fols. 28–29, 24.
13 In this, however, they were unsuccessful: the *audiencia*'s judgement, in 1804, was that Carampaima's offspring could not be deprived of the *cacicazgo*. Isacsson, 'The Egalitarian Society', pp. 114–18.
14 Isacsson, 'The Egalitarian Society', p. 125. In a more recent study, Erick Werner Cantor also makes brief reference to the increasingly prominent role played by the cacique, over the course of the eighteenth century, as spokesman for and defender of the indigenous community. The developing role of caciques (or *mandones*) is not a central concern of this study. Nevertheless, the evidence presented, and Werner Cantor's interpretation of it, supports the argument presented here that the legitimacy and authority gained by the indigenous political elite derived from their position as intermediaries between their communities and the Spanish authorities. See Erick Werner Cantor, *Ni aniquilados ni vencidos: Los Emberá y la gente negra del Atrato bajo el dominio español. Siglo XVIII*, Bogotá, Instituto Colombiano de Antropología e Historia, 2000, pp. 70–72, 141–42.
15 AGI Santa Fe 362, Joseph López de Carvajal to Crown, Antioquia, 13 June 1708, and Joseph López de Carvajal to Audiencia of Santa Fe, Antioquia, 15 May 1708, in AGI Santa Fe 307, 'Cuaderno . . . sobre la entrada al Río Murri', fols. 1–2.

16 Twinam, *Miners, Merchants, and Farmers*, Table 1, p. 28.
17 AGI Santa Fe 307, Joseph de Yarza to Crown, Antioquia, 2 April 1713.
18 See, for example, the statements of Don Ignacio Bernardo de Quirós and Esteban Velásquez, in AGI Santa Fe 307, 'Cuaderno . . . sobre la entrada al río Murri', Bebará, 7 and 9 December 1710, fols. 47–48. See also the statement of Don Gregorio Chicarabia, Indian governor of Bebará, 5 December 1710, fol. 40. Don Gregorio claimed that a total of 18 families had left the village.
19 See the 'Declaración' of the Indian Esteban Fernández, of the settlement of Lloró, dated Antioquia, 10 March 1711, in AGI Santa Fe 307, 'Cuaderno . . . sobre la entrada al río Murri', fol. 56. See also Juan Amaro Meneses' 'Declaración' of 25 October 1711, fols. 122–24, and Baltasar Carlos Pérez de Vivero to Joseph de Carvajal, Quibdó, 15 February 1711, fol. 38.
20 AGI Santa Fe 307, 'Cuaderno . . . sobre la entrada al río Murri', 'Petición', n.p., n.d., fol. 24.
21 AGI Santa Fe 307, 'Cuaderno . . . sobre la entrada al río Murri', Auto, Antioquia, 24 December 1710, fol. 29, and Petición, n.p., n.d., fol. 24. See also AGI Santa Fe 362, Joseph López de Carvajal to Crown, Antioquia, 28 April 1712.
22 AGI Santa Fe 307, 'Cuaderno . . . sobre la entrada al río Murri', Petición, n.p., n.d., fols. 33–34, and Auto, 19 January 1711, fol. 31. The identity of Quibdó's cacique is not clear from the documents: Don Juan Mitiguirre and Cogayda are both mentioned in this petition. According to Governor López, the cacique of Lloró was one Capitán Cauche. See Diligencia, Murri River, 12 November 1711, fols. 126–27.
23 AGI Santa Fe 307, 'Cuaderno . . . sobre la entrada al río Murri', Petición, n.p., n.d., fols. 24–25. Rafael de Oquendo's *petición* on behalf of the Indians of Citará may also be found in Zuluaga Gómez (ed.), *Documentos inéditos*, Documento No. 5, pp. 29–37.
24 AGI Santa Fe 307, 'Cuaderno . . . sobre la entrada al río Murri', Petición, n.d., n.p., fols. 33–34.
25 AGI Santa Fe 307, 'Cuaderno . . . sobre la entrada al río Murri', Petitición, n.p., n.d., fol. 28. Exemption from corporal punishment, manual labour and taxation were among the legal privileges that the Spanish Crown everywhere bestowed on native leaders, in an effort to guarantee the loyalty of the Indian elite, and to secure their assimilation into the administrative system devised to control native populations. Exemption from control by the *corregidor* seems, however, to have been reserved to the native nobility, such as the *kurakas* of the Andean region. See, for example, Axtell, *The Indians' New South*, p. 29; Turner Bushnell, 'Ruling "the Republic of Indians"', pp. 138–43; and Spalding, *Huarochirí*, p. 221.
26 AGI Santa Fe 307, 'Cuaderno . . . sobre la entrada al río Murri', Declaración, Real de Minas de San Mateo, 24 September 1711, fol. 84.
27 AGI Santa Fe 307, 'Cuaderno . . . sobre la entrada al río Murri', Petición, n.d., n.p., fol. 34.
28 AGI Santa Fe 307, 'Cuaderno . . . sobre la entrada al río Murri', 'Lista, discreción, y matrícula de los indios', Río de Murri, 1 October 1711, fol. 99.
29 By the mid-eighteenth century, the key figures in Indian village government were the cacique, *capitán* and *alcalde*. In the early 1750s, all but one of 12 Indian settlements were headed by a cacique. The number of *capitanes* and *alcaldes* (between one and three) depended on the size of the indigenous populations. See AGI Santa Fe 733, 'Descripción del Gobierno del Chocó . . . que se presenta . . . por Don Pedro Muñoz de Arjona'.
30 AGI Quito 143, Vicente de Aramburu to Crown, Santa Fe, 8 September 1713, and 30 September 1713.
31 All that was required to prevent Indians fleeing their settlements, Aramburu insisted, was that the privileges accorded native peoples under Spanish law should be observed. For Aramburu's comments, dated Quibdó, 16 June 1712, see AGI Santa Fe 362, 'Testimonio de Autos', fols. 13–14, and AGI Quito 143, Vicente de Aramburu to Crown, Santa Fe, 8 September 1713.

32 See the statements taken by Joseph de la Cuesta in Bebará on 5 and 6 December 1710, in AGI Santa Fe 307, 'Cuaderno . . . sobre la entrada al río Murri', fols. 43–47. See also Baltasar Carlos Pérez deVivero to Joseph López de Carvajal, Quibdó, 15 February 1711, fols. 38–39, and Decreto, Bebará, 5 December 1710, fols. 39–40.
33 AGI Santa Fe 307, 'Cuaderno . . . sobre la entrada al río Murri', Petición, Antioquia, 5 January 1712, fols. 148–49.
34 AGI Santa Fe 307, 'Cuaderno . . . sobre la entrada al río Murri', Auto, Antioquia, 2 January 1710, and Auto, n.p., 8 September 1710, fols. 12, 18.
35 AGI Santa Fe 307, Joseph deYarza to Crown, Antioquia, 2 April 1713.
36 AGI Santa Fe 362, Joseph López de Carvajal to Crown, Antioquia, 13 June 1708. See also López de Carvajal's 'Autos' of 2 January and 27 September 1710, in AGI Santa Fe 307, 'Cuaderno . . . sobre la entrada al río Murri', fols. 11–12, 21. None of these objectives could be achieved without the assistance of Indian allies, for not only was the governor unfamiliar with the territory, but on the first *entrada*, López was accompanied only by two Spaniards (Don Joseph Matorel y Balvasil and the secular priest Don Francisco Solano de Salazar Beltrán) and four slaves. AGI Santa Fe 362, Joseph López de Carvajal to Crown, Antioquia, 28 April 1712.
37 AGI Santa Fe 307, 'Cuaderno . . . sobre la entrada al río Murri', Petición, n.p., n.d., fols. 26–28, and Petición, n.p., n.d, fol. 34.
38 For details, see AGI Santa Fe 307, Joseph de Yarza to Crown, Antioquia, 2 April 1713, and 'Cuaderno . . . sobre la entrada al río Murri', fols. 78–79, 93–95, 103, 115–16, and 124–27.
39 Of the total 205, 68 originated from Bebará; 42 came from Lloró; the largest number, 93, came from Quibdó. For the composition of this group, see AGI Santa Fe 307, 'Cuaderno . . . sobre la entrada al río Murri', fols. 97–102, 114–15, 119–20, 127–28.
40 Discreción de los indios, 28 May 1712, in AGI Santa Fe 362, 'Testimonio de Autos', fols. 6–7. See also Joseph López de Carvajal to Crown, n.p., 1 October 1713.
41 AGI Santa Fe 362, Lista, Discreción, y Matrícula de los indios, 16 July and 23 September 1713.
42 Decreto, Bebará, 5 December 1710, in AGI Santa Fe 307, 'Cuaderno . . . sobre la entrada al río Murri', fols. 39–40.
43 AGI Santa Fe 307, 'Cuaderno . . . sobre la entrada al río Murri', Auto, Bebará, 5 December 1710, fol. 41.
44 AGI Santa Fe 307, 'Cuaderno . . . sobre la entrada al río Murri', Auto, Bebará, 15 December 1710, fol. 51.
45 AGI Santa Fe 307, 'Cuaderno . . . sobre la entrada al río Murri', Petición, Antioquia, 5 January 1712, fols. 148–49.
46 These were Miguel Mateaso, Pablo Chever and Juan Bosoro. The *oidor*'s comments are dated Quibdó, 16 June 1712. See AGI Santa Fe 362, 'Testimonio de Autos', fols. 12–14.
47 AGI Santa Fe 362, Joseph López de Carvajal to Crown, n.p., 1 October 1713.
48 In June 1712, López de Carvajal issued instructions to the effect that all Indians recently arrived from the 'cimarrona grande' should be exempted from stipends and tributes for a year. See Auto, Antioquia, 17 June 1712, AGI Santa Fe 362, 'Testimonio de Autos', fol. 2, and Gregorio de Salazar y Santillana to Joseph López de Carvajal, Murri, 6 June 1712, fol. 7.
49 Esteban Tovare was a key figure in the negotiation and 'muy ladino en el idioma castellano'. See 'Diligencia', Río de Murri, 14 and 15 November 1711, in AGI Santa Fe 307, 'Cuaderno . . . sobre la entrada al río Murri', fols. 134–35. See also Auto, Antioquia, 18 June 1712 and Gregorio de Salazar y Santillana to López de Carvajal, Murri, 6 June 1712, in AGI Santa Fe 362, 'Testimonio de Autos', fols. 3, 8.
50 AGI Santa Fe 362, 'Testimonio de Autos', Petición, n.p., n.d., fol. 15. For the role of Indian lay assistants to the parish priests, see Spalding, *Huarochirí*, pp. 217–18.

51 For example, Capitán Baquía, according to *doctrinero* Gregorio de Salazar, 'does not pay tribute because he is capitán'. See Gregorio de Salazar y Santillana to López de Carvajal, Murri, 6 June 1712, AGI Santa Fe 362, 'Testimonio de Autos', fol. 8.

52 Lista, Discreción y Matrícula, Río de Murri, 1 October 1711, AGI Santa Fe 307, 'Cuaderno . . . sobre la entrada al río Murri', fol. 102, and Francisco Antonio de la Chica y Guzmán to Joseph López de Carvajal, Murri, 27 July 1712, in AGI Santa Fe 362, 'Testimonio de Autos', fol. 11.

53 AGI Santa Fe 403, 'Informe de la Provincia de Antioquia', Antioquia, 25 November 1716.

54 AGI Santa Fe 307, Joseph de Yarza to Crown, Antioquia, 2 April 1713. According to Yarza, little of profit had resulted from Spanish activities in Murri. Interestingly, however, in 1777 Murri was described as a gold-rich area. See Anónimo, 'Descripción de la provincia del Zitará y curso del río Atrato', *Boletín de la Sociedad de Geografía de Colombia*, Vol. 8, 1948, p. 38. This document may also be found in Antonio B. Cuervo (ed.), *Colección de documentos inéditos sobre la geografía y la historia de Colombia*, 4 vols., 1891–94, Vol. II, pp. 306–24.

55 AGI Santa Fe 362, Rafael de Oquendo to Crown, Antioquia, 20 September 1712. See also Aramburu's comments, dated Quibdó, 16 June 1712, and Petición del Protector, n.p., n.d., in AGI Santa Fe 362, 'Testimonio de Autos', fols. 13–14, 16. In this position, they were clearly supported by Governor López, who was equally resolute in his determination not to co-operate with the authorities by returning the Murri people to their original villages. See, for example, Baltasar Carlos Pérez de Vivero to Joseph López de Carvajal, Quibdó, 15 February 1711, in AGI Santa Fe 307, 'Cuaderno . . . sobre la entrada al río Murri', fol. 38. See also 'Noticia', Rancherías del Río Murri, 13 November 1711, fol. 129.

56 AGI Santa Fe 362, Joseph López de Carvajal to Crown, 1 October 1713. See also the decision of the *fiscal* and Council, dated 16 August 1719.

57 AGI Santa Fe 403, 'Informe de la Provincia de Antioquia', Antioquia, 25 November 1716. What became of Joseph López after 1714 is not known. However, when in 1724 the Consejo discussed Agustín de Morales y Mendoza's proposal to undertake a new *entrada* to the Chocó, it was stated that the former governor had by this time died. See AGI Santa Fe 362, Agustín de Morales y Mendoza to Crown, n.p., n.d. The *fiscal*'s comments on this proposal are dated 22 October 1724.

58 AGN Caciques e indios, 6, Facundo Guerra Calderón to Vicente Gaspar Rugero, Antioquia, 5 April 1723, fols. 347–48.

59 AGI Quito 143, Vicente de Aramburu to Crown, Santa Fe, 8 September 1713. Further evidence to suggest that, by 1720, at least a proportion of Indians had returned – willingly or unwillingly – to their settlements comes from a report, written in August of that year, to the effect that one Achuarra, a *capitán* or cacique of Quibdó, had travelled to Santa Fe specifically to protest of ill-treatment at the hands of Spanish officials there. See Isacsson, 'The Egalitarian Society', p. 111.

60 Significantly, on this occasion, Indians requested that the governor appoint Don Joseph López's son, Don Pablo de Carvajal, as their 'auxiliador y defensor'. Auto, Antioquia, 2 January 1726, in AGN Caciques e indios, 6, fols. 342–43.

61 The Council of the Indies discussed its contents, and gave it considerable attention, between May and November 1724. Morales y Mendoza proposed to undertake the 'reduction' at his own expense in exchange for the governorship for a period of ten years. See AGI Santa Fe 362, Agustín de Morales y Mendoza to Crown, n.p., n.d.

62 'Relación sobre el gobierno del Virrey Eslava', Santa Fe, 1 October 1747, in E.M. Posada and P.M. Ibáñez, *Relaciones de Mando: memorias presentadas por los gobernantes del Nuevo Reino de Granada*, Bogotá, Universidad Nacional de Colombia, 1910, pp. 30–31.

63 AGI Santa Fe 362, Francisco de Alcantud y Gaona to Crown, 15 November 1720. Francisco Forero similarly indicated in 1720 that Beté was a recent foundation, comprising

'the Indians that were captured in the cimarronas'. See AGI Quito 185, 'Testimonio de los autos obrados sobre la erección de curato en el Citará', especially the 'Certificación del Secretario', 11 September 1720.

64 See Certificación Fiscal, Popayán, 11 September 1720, in AGI Quito 185, 'Testimonio de los autos obrados sobre la erección de curato en el Citará'.

65 Ibero made no mention of Murri in his first report on the state of his *gobernación*. See AGI Santa Fe 307, Francisco de Ibero to Crown, Nóvita, 29 October 1729.

66 According to *ingeniero* Jiménez Donoso, reporting in 1780, one settlement was created in Pabarandó to incorporate 'fugitives' who lived in the vicinity; another was at that time being created, for the same purpose, in Cupica. See Jiménez Donoso, 'Relación del Chocó', in Ortega Ricaurte (ed.), *Historia documental*, p. 210. According to Governor Ciaurriz, Pabarandó was later abandoned, following an attack by the Cuna, which led to the death and capture of many of its residents. Quibdó, 2 August 1808, in Zuluaga Gómez (ed.), *Documentos inéditos*, Documento No. 13, p. 91. For details of the unnamed settlement founded in the vicinity of the Sucio River, see Anónimo, 'Descripción de la provincia del Zitará y curso del río Atrato', pp. 33–34.

67 See Fray Juan Calderón's statement, Quibdó, 26 October 1736, in AGI Quito 185, 'Testimonio de la visita del Citará'. It seems that the location of Murri did shift twice, however, between 1728 and 1740. See Jiménez Donoso, 'Relación del Chocó', in Ortega Ricaurte (ed.), *Historia documental*, p. 211.

68 Significantly, the *doctrinero* also reported that there were at that time many Indians, formerly inhabitants of Citará, who threatened to found a new community on the banks of the Giguamiando river which, he believed, would set a bad example and lead, in no time, to the complete depopulation of that province. AGI Santa Fe 290, 'Testimonio de la instancia movida en el Tribunal del Superior Gobierno . . . del Virrey de este Reino, por el R.P. Fray Juan Joseph de Salazar . . . sobre varias cosas conducentes al beneficio de los indios'.

69 Sharp, *Slavery*, pp. 197–99. By 1806, the indigenous population of Murri had declined to 115. See S. Henry Wassen, 'Etnohistoria chocoana y cinco cuentos waunana apuntados en 1955', *Etnologiska Studier*, Vol. 23, 1963, p. 38.

70 Indeed, even where the Spanish failed to establish control, such as among the Araucanians, Indians underwent significant changes in political organisation. Kristine Jones, for instance, has argued for the case of eighteenth-century Araucania that 'the prior century of political and military frontier negotiations with the Spanish had ultimately contributed to a militarization and political stratification within Araucanian society'. See Jones, 'Warfare, Reorganization, and Readaptation', p. 157.

71 As Susan Ramírez has noted for the case of the north coast of Peru, 'Spanish concepts of governing gradually changed the power structure and in the process subverted the original role of the curacas [caciques] as leaders of and spokesmen for the local indigenous peoples'. The erosion of the legitimacy of the colonial *curaca* began within decades of the conquest, and is explained by such factors as the increasing demands that led many to sacrifice the well-being of their own people, the temptations that led others to seek to increase their own wealth and power through the exploitation of their positions as agents of the colonial state, and the increasing tendency of the Spanish themselves to appoint as *curacas*, regardless of customary methods of selecting leaders, those Indians who were most willing to co-operate in the implementation of colonial demands. Susan Elizabeth Ramírez, *The World Upside Down: Cross-Cultural Contact and Conflict in Sixteenth-Century Peru*, Stanford, CA, Stanford University Press, 1996, pp. 7, 12–41; *idem*, 'The *"Dueño de Indios":* Thoughts on the Consequences of the Shifting Bases of Power of the *"Curaca de los Viejos Antiguos"* under the Spanish in Sixteenth-Century Peru', *Hispanic American Historical Review*, Vol. 67, No. 4, 1987, pp. 575–610. For further discussion, see also Steve Stern, 'The Rise and Fall of Indian–White Alliances: A Regional View of "Conquest" History', *Hispanic American Historical Review*, Vol. 61, No. 3, 1981,

pp. 461–91; Karen Spalding, 'Social Climbers: Changing Patterns of Mobility among the Indians of Colonial Peru', *Hispanic American Historical Review*, Vol. 50, No. 4, 1970, pp. 645–64; and *idem*, *Huarochirí*, pp. 209–38.

72 Isacsson, 'The Egalitarian Society', p. 125.

73 AGI Santa Fe 307, 'Cuaderno ... sobre la entrada al río Murri', Petición, n.p., n.d., fol. 26.

74 The records relating to the establishment of Murri show that, at the beginning of the 1710s, few Indians were described as 'ladinos' or 'lenguaraces'. Among those with knowledge of the Spanish language were Don Joseph Sagito, Agustín Bepa, Esteban Tovare and Joseph Veragone, all of whom played important roles in the negotiations and the resettlement that followed; Don Gregorio Chicaravia, appointed governor of Bebará by *teniente* Joseph de la Cuesta, also appears to have been a Spanish speaker. See Petición, n.p., n.d., Auto, Antioquia, 24 December 1710, and Auto, Bebará, 5 December 1710, in AGI Santa Fe 307, 'Cuaderno ... sobre la entrada al río Murri', fols. 28, 29, 40.

75 AGI Quito 185, Mateo de Villafañe to Crown, Popayán, 7 June 1701.

76 AGI Santa Fe 307, 'Cuaderno ... sobre la entrada al río Murri', Murri River, 1 October 1711, fols. 95–96.

77 Felices' opinion of the peoples of the Chocó was influenced by reports such as that of the Spaniard Bernardo Machado, who commented on returning from the region that even were Saint Augustine himself to come to the Chocó, 'he would not be able to teach them'. AGI Santa Fe 403, Fray Francisco Antonio Felices, Santa Fe, 13 November 1719.

78 Francisco Silvestre, *Descripción del Reyno de Santa Fe de Bogotá*, Bogotá, Universidad Nacional de Colombia, 1968, pp. 42, 74; Ciaurriz, 'Visita del Gobernador ... Don Carlos de Ciaurriz', p. 158.

79 Recent research on the 'encounter' between Christianity and native American religions has transformed the way in which historians approach the study of Spanish evangelisation during the colonial period. As Nicholas Griffiths has pointed out, these new perspectives reflect 'the current realization that in the past the loss and destruction involved in contact between Europeans and natives has been prioritized, in the religious sphere as elsewhere, at the expense of understanding the manifold strategies of adaptation on the part of indigenous communities'. Rather than assuming, as historians have done in the past, 'that the arrival of Christianity involved a one-way process whereby supine native religions were totally transformed by a more active, dynamic force', current research seeks to show not only that responses to Spanish efforts to convert indigenous populations were exceptionally complex and varied, but that interactions between Christianity and native American religions were characterised by 'reciprocal, albeit asymmetrical exchange' – that this was, in other words, a two-way process, 'in which there was less "conversion" than "conversation"'. See Nicholas Griffiths, 'Introduction', in Griffiths and Cervantes (eds.), *Spiritual Encounters*, pp. 1–2, 7.

80 It must be borne in mind, however, as Axtell has argued, that the presence among Indians of any European, regardless of his or her purpose for being there, 'could not fail to alter the behaviour and thinking of his [or her] native hosts'. Axtell, *The Indians' New South*, p. 3.

81 Marzal, 'Informe', in Pacheco, *Los Jesuitas*, II, p. 502.

82 Camino, 'Representación', p. 242, and AGI Santa Fe 733, 'Descripción del Gobierno del Chocó ... que se presenta ... por Don Pedro Muñoz de Arjona'.

83 Marzal added that 'if in reality they communicate ... with him [the devil] I do not know, but I do know they consult him and carry out certain ceremonies in his honour'. Marzal, 'Informe', in Pacheco, *Los Jesuitas*, II, pp. 500–501.

84 Camino, 'Representación', pp. 245–46. For an account of the continuing influence of 'medicine men' among twentieth-century Chocó Indians, see Erland Nordenskiold, 'The Chocó Indians of Colombia and Panama', *Discovery*, Vol. 8, 1927, pp. 347–50, and

Reichel-Dolmatoff, 'Notas etnográficas', pp. 122–25.
85 Charlotte Gradie makes the case, however, that outbreaks of disease could also serve to discredit native beliefs and religious leaders, thus paving 'the way for the acceptance of missionaries, who came equipped with a belief system that explained why natives but not Jesuits or other Spaniards were most affected by disease'. Gradie, *The Tepehuan Revolt*, pp. 131, 136, 139. For further examples of shamans who argued that baptism brought illness and death, see Cynthia Radding, 'Cultural Boundaries between Adaptation and Defiance:The Mission Communities of Northwestern New Spain', in Griffiths and Cervantes (eds.), *Spiritual Encounters*, p. 123; and Andrew Redden, 'The Enchanted Palace WhereWorlds Collide: Perceptions of Power, Struggle and Martyrdom in the Province of Paraguay', MA dissertation, Institute of Latin American Studies, University of Liverpool, 2000, pp. 10, 37, 88.
86 Marzal, 'Informe', in Pacheco, *Los Jesuitas*, II, p. 499. Records indicate that the region was affected by disease in 1666 and 1669–70. Luis Antonio de la Cueva reported that his first attempt to found a settlement in Noanama province, to which he arrived in July 1666, had to be abandoned 'because they all fell ill'; Francisco de Quevedo, reporting in May 1669, indicated that the settlement of Poya had recently been affected by an outbreak of smallpox, and that only two Indians remained there; Lorenzo de Salamanca reported 'an outbreak of . . . smallpox' in 1670. See, respectively, AGI Quito 67, Certificación, Sed de Cristo, 29 May 1669, in 'Testimonio de Autos (Audiencia)', fol. 14; Francisco de Quevedo's report, dated San Joseph de Noanama, 15 May 1669; and Declaración, 9 May 1672.
87 Camino, 'Representación', p. 245.
88 For examples of Indian groups that did, however temporarily, appeal to missionaries for aid and comfort, see Deeds, 'Indigenous Responses to Mission Settlement', pp. 77–108; Reff, 'The Jesuit Mission', pp. 16–31; Weber, 'Blood of Martyrs', pp. 429–48.
89 See Lance Grahn, '"Chicha in the Chalice": Spiritual Conflict in Spanish American Mission Culture', in Griffiths and Cervantes (eds.), *Spiritual Encounters*, pp. 264–66. According to Grahn, only a small proportion (2–3 per cent) of the Guajiro population accepted life in the Capuchin mission settlements, largely for 'what they perceived to be its relatively greater economic security and for the protection and prestige which it likely afforded headmen'. The vast majority, however, rejected 'Christianization and hispanization in favour of European contacts and adaptations that would promote and protect their cultural independence and political autonomy'.
90 AGI Quito 185, 'Certificación de la visita de Nóvita',Tadó, 6 October 1736.
91 Camino, 'Representación', pp. 246–47.
92 Marzal, 'Informe', in Pacheco, *Los Jesuitas*, II, p. 502.
93 See the evidence of Joseph Joaquín Hurtado del Aguila, *doctrinero* of the Noanama settlement of Nóvita, in AGI Quito 185, 'Autos sobre la opresión'.
94 For this accusation against Córdoba, see Gregorio Bogassaga's statement in AGI Santa Fe 204, Ramo 3, fol. 7.
95 Fray Dionisio also mentioned that the *corregidores*, for reasons he did not explain, objected to the friars striking the children. See Camino, 'Representación', p. 248. Perhaps he was referring to an incident, recorded in 1720, when the *corregidor* of Tadó, following an action of this kind on the part of Fray Salvador de Valenzuela, forbade the children to attend Christian instruction for two to three days. Certificación del notario de visita, Popayán, 9 July 1720, in AGI Quito 185, 'Autos sobre la opresión'.
96 Fray Juan Domingo Calderón, priest of Quibdó, was specifically instructed to administer 30 lashes on any Indian guilty of holding a *borrachera* in his own home; 12 lashes on those women who attended such ceremonies; and 12 lashes on Indians found to be guilty of adultery. AGI Quito 185, 'Testimonio de laVisita del Citará', Quibdó, 3 November 1736.
97 'Visita del Gobernador . . . Don Carlos de Ciaurriz', p. 158.

98 For the instructions of Bishop Vergara to the priests of Citará province, see AGI Quito 185, 'Testimonio de la visita del Citará', Quibdó, 2 November 1736.
99 For examples of church construction and ornamentation in the Jesuit missions among the Moxos and Guaraní peoples, see, for example, Block, *Mission Culture*, pp. 60–65, and Reiter, *They Built Utopia*, pp. 73–74. See also Saeger, *The Chaco Mission Frontier*, p. 151. It is to be noted, however, that at least during the early years of missionary activity, indigenous peoples did not necessarily respond positively to the churches of the priests. Charlotte Gradie, for example, found that when the Jesuits first congregated Tepehuanes at Santiago Papasquiaro (Nueva Vizcaya), their native charges proved unwilling to enter the church building, believing it to be 'the house of the dead'. Because the Tepehuanes destroyed the dwellings of Indians who had died, whereas the Spanish buried their dead under the church floor, they feared entering the church 'lest they die as well'. Gradie, *The Tepehuan Revolt*, p. 131.
100 The absence of large, richly decorated churches in the Chocó is only partly explained by climate and terrain, for here, unlike in the Moxos missions studied by Block, missionaries could not rely on the assistance and labour of neophytes, nor could they count on the skilled artisans who were so crucial to the building of churches in the latter area. See Block, *Mission Culture*, p. 65.
101 AGI Quito 185, 'Autos sobre la opresión'.
102 Even the bishop exhorted both priest and *corregidor* to put their best efforts into preventing drunkenness and the holding of dances that occasioned 'detestable acts'. See AGI Quito 185, 'Certificación de la visita de Nóvita', Tadó, 6 October 1736.
103 AGI Santa Fe 733, 'Descripción del Gobierno del Chocó . . . que se presenta . . . por Don Pedro Muñoz de Arjona'.
104 It is possible that rituals of this kind, as Susan Deeds proposed in discussing similar ceremonial practices among the indigenous population of Nueva Vizcaya, may have been intended to ensure good harvests or to promote health, or may have coincided with the coming together of a group to conduct business or co-operate in work, or may even have been associated with other ritual activities, such as the honouring of the dead. See Deeds, 'Indigenous Responses to Mission Settlement', p. 84.
105 Camino, 'Representación', p. 245. See also Stout, 'The Chocó', pp. 270–71.
106 The Jesuit, for instance, reported the Indians' insistence that they be allowed 'to marry according to their custom'. Marzal, 'Informe', in Pacheco, *Los Jesuitas*, II, pp. 501–502, and Camino, 'Representación', p. 245. It is to be noted, however, that in 1736 Bishop Vergara exhorted the *doctrineros* of Citará province not to administer the sacrament of marriage unless and until Indians were properly instructed in the Catholic faith, and had received the sacraments of communion and confession. AGI Quito 185, 'Testimonio de la visita del Citará', Quibdó, 2 November 1736.
107 Camino, 'Representación', pp. 242, 244–45.
108 It was Antonio Marzal who drew attention both to the taking of female captives as marriage partners and to the practice whereby indigenous males inherited (as their own) the wives and concubines of deceased brothers and fathers. Marzal, 'Informe', in Pacheco, *Los Jesuitas*, II, pp. 501–502. In 1711 it was further reported that the sisters of deceased wives were also taken as marriage partners. Murri, 1 October 1711, in AGI Santa Fe 307, 'Cuaderno . . . sobre la entrada al río Murri', fol. 96.
109 Ciaurriz, 'Visita del Gobernador . . . Don Carlos de Ciaurriz', pp. 158–59.
110 Murri River, 1 October 1711, in AGI Santa Fe 307, 'Cuaderno . . . sobre la entrada al río Murri', fol. 96.
111 Camino, 'Representación', p. 246.
112 According to *oidor* Vicente de Aramburu, the Citará observed a permanent 'declaration of war' against the Cuna. AGI Quito 143, Vicente de Aramburu to Crown, Santa Fe, 8 September 1713.

113 Marzal, 'Informe', in Pacheco, *Los Jesuitas*, II, p. 501.
114 AGI Santa Fe 204, Ramo 6, fols. 38–39, 49–50.
115 Camino, 'Representación', p. 246.
116 Francisco Antonio de la Chica y Guzmán to Joseph López de Carvajal, Murri, 27 July 1712, in AGI Santa Fe 362, 'Testimonio de Autos', fol. 11.
117 Jiménez Donoso, 'Relación del Chocó', in Ortega Ricaurte, *Historia documental*, p. 218. On Cuna incursions into Chocó territory in the 1770s, see also Francisco Antonio Moreno y Escandón, 'Estado del Virreinato de Santa Fe, Nuevo Reino de Granada', *Boletín de Historia y Antigüedades*, Vol. 23, 1935, pp. 568–69.
118 See Auto, Antioquia, 30 June 1677, in AGI Santa Fe 204, Ramo 1, fol. 187, and AGI Santa Fe 733, 'Descripción del Gobierno del Chocó . . . que se presenta . . . por Don Pedro Muñoz de Arjona'. Travelling through the Chocó on his pastoral visit of 1736–37, Bishop Vergara similarly despaired of the refusal of indigenous peoples to accept and adopt the dress codes of Europeans, and left strict instructions to the effect that local priests were to pay particular attention to ensuring that Indians covered their nakedness in church at least. See AGI Quito 185, Testimonio de la visita del Citará, Quibdó, 3 November 1736, and Certificación de la visita de Nóvita, Tadó, 6 October 1736. For a nineteenth-century description of Indian dress and adornment, see Gaspar Mollien, *Travels in the Republic of Colombia, in the Years 1822 and 1823*, London, 1824, p. 306. For a twentieth-century discussion, see Reichel-Dolmatoff, 'Notas etnográficas', pp. 90–92.
119 These terms were scattered throughout a report compiled during an ecclesiastical *visita* conducted in 1720 by Don Nicolás de Inestrosa and Fray Manuel de Abastos y Castro on behalf of Bishop Gómez Frías, but the impression they convey is repeated in countless documents of the period covered here. See AGI Quito 185, 'Autos sobre la opresión', and Juan Gómez Frías to Crown, Popayán, 27 November 1720.
120 For the purpose of comparison, see, for example, Radding, 'Cultural Boundaries', pp. 118–23.
121 Ciaurriz, 'Visita del Gobernador . . . Don Carlos de Ciaurriz', p. 158.

CHAPTER EIGHT

Conclusion

My principal aim in writing this study has been to throw further light on the evolution of inter-ethnic relations on a contested colonial frontier. These chapters, therefore, have focused on both the diversity of Spanish approaches towards, and strategies for, subduing, subordinating and governing the native inhabitants of this extremely important gold-producing territory, and the varied ways in which indigenous peoples, principally but not exclusively the Citará, sought to control and direct the nature and extent of contact with the world that lay beyond the boundaries of the Chocó itself. No rigid classification of action and reaction has been possible, of course, for this analysis has shown not only that Indian peoples – acting as individuals, communities or groups – responded in different ways, at different times, to the challenges and opportunities presented by the introduction of European ideas and artefacts and the imposition of European customs and institutions, but reserved to themselves the right to vary attitudes, as local needs and interests dictated, towards the range of new possibilities opened by the presence of outsiders in the native world.

Over the course of the seventeenth century, we have seen, many indigenous peoples made their peace with the Spaniards, in exchange for the metal tools and other items that facilitated food procurement and preparation, and made more efficient such necessary activities as the construction of dwellings and the manufacture of canoes. Others proved open to making ever greater concessions to protect their association with Europeans, along with the titles and rewards that enhanced their own status and set them apart from their fellow Indians. By the beginning of the eighteenth century, some individuals within indigenous society had also come to accept such aspects of Spanish rule as they could no longer change, but devised new ways to negotiate the conditions of their subjection to European domination, and to protect the rights and privileges accorded native peoples under colonial law. Others, however, while perhaps not rejecting all aspects of the material culture of the Europeans, remained consistently opposed to co-operating with the intruders, opting instead to exploit the advantages of a region that was of interest to Spaniards for its precious metal, rather than for settlement and development, in order to establish and re-establish their communities, according to traditional principles, alongside the many rivers that intersected this heavily forested and sparsely populated terrain. 'Aside from those who inhabit the villages', one official was to comment in 1749, Indians 'live along the [banks of the] rivers, without leaders, subject to no one, but each for himself, independent one from the other'.[1]

The particular responses of communities and individuals notwithstanding, it is clear that the decision to acknowledge the utility and value of European artefacts, to accept the titles and privileges that came from loyalty and collaboration, or even to participate actively in the political confrontations of the various Spanish factions that competed for control of the Chocó, did not invariably signify unconditional acceptance, or full assimilation, of the Europeans and their ways. For a key feature that emerges from this examination of inter-ethnic contact on the frontier relates to the ways in which indigenous peoples, while appropriating from Europeans what could usefully be incorporated into native practice, adopting for the purpose of communication with the Spaniards the names conferred on them at baptism,[2] and exploiting the political and economic rivalries between the various layers of Spanish government to the advantage of the indigenous community, also persistently rejected all efforts on the part of generations of Catholic clergy to inculcate Christian belief and practice, refused to assimilate the language and social customs of the colonisers, and strove to protect their ethnic identity from both the white population that dominated them, and the black population by whom they became increasingly outnumbered.[3]

Mindful of the paucity of documentary evidence to support further analysis, as of the fact that developments after 1753 are not central concerns of this study, no attempt will be made here to assess the longer-term significance of the apparent vitality of such 'critical symbols of cultural identity . . . as language, religion . . . and purity of blood'.[4] However, because they provide additional insights into the nature of resistance and adaptation on the Chocó frontier, I shall conclude my study with a brief survey of those facets of Indian life which late colonial officials were repeatedly to despair of ever seeing conform to their own cultural norms. Our sources suggest, for instance, that the Indians' persistent indifference to a Christian religion that, in inextricably linking doctrine and social behaviour,[5] compromised local customs and values, may eventually have persuaded the Spanish clergy of the futility of pursuing a process designed to impose a way of life that was rejected by native peoples themselves. By 1807, according to Governor Ciaurriz, the Noanama parish of El Cajón had been vacant for many years, no candidates having been presented to fill it. The priest of Nóvita, together with his auxiliary, shared responsibility for the spiritual well-being not only of the inhabitants of Nóvita itself, but of those of the widely dispersed villages of Los Brazos and Baudó, with predictable results. The Emberá villages of Tatama and Chamí, situated at a distance of two days' travel from each other, and comprising a combined total population of 1128, also shared the services of a solitary parish priest. Murri, too, had recently lost its *doctrinero*, leaving an additional 115 Indians free of even the most minimal pastoral intervention.[6] Carlos de Ciaurriz believed firmly in the potential of the region's native inhabitants to become fully Christian, but his observations regarding the still 'barbarous' and 'brutish' customs of otherwise 'rational' Indians confirm that, as the years of colonial rule drew to an end, 'not even the slightest signs of . . . Christianity and religion' were in evidence anywhere on the Chocó frontier.[7]

Native languages, it seems, proved equally difficult to supplant. Although our evidence in this, as in so many aspects of Indian existence, is severely limited by the Spaniards' failure systematically to record local practices, the indications are that by the turn of the nineteenth century, the language of empire remained limited to that elite – the caciques and *principales*, or *mandones* – that took upon itself the role of representing the interests of the indigenous community in negotiations with the colonial authorities. We know that in the 1790s, for example, Calixto de Cárdenas, cousin of Tadó's cacique Miguel Carampaima, 'wrote and signed his own letters and travelled far to see to his interests among the Spanish', skills that made him a strong contender to take over that *cacicazgo*.[8] But in 1789 and 1807 respectively, Antioquia's former governor Francisco Silvestre, and Don Carlos de Ciaurriz, both drew attention to the obstinacy with which Indian peoples of the Chocó clung to their native languages, thus precluding communication with the Spaniards. Their concern was to demonstrate that the failure of indigenous peoples to comprehend the principal precepts of the Christian religion, as indeed to participate in the sacraments of penitence and communion, was largely attributable to the fact that they remained 'inseparable from their language',[9] rather than to consider the wider implications of the Indians' continuing access to a means of communication that was barred to all but a handful of white settlers.[10] If, however, as has been argued for native groups elsewhere, 'a shared language and religion with its traditional rituals . . . were the means by which they defined themselves as a people',[11] then the evidence from the Chocó testifies to the remarkable tenacity with which indigenous peoples struggled to preserve such crucial areas of their lives outside the control and surveillance of the Spaniards.

One final feature of native life in the Chocó that colonial documents allow us to consider, albeit superficially, relates to the ways in which indigenous peoples responded to the potential threat to their 'purity of blood' presented by the gradual occupation of their territory by a small but powerful minority of white settlers, and a large and ever-growing population of black slaves. How are we to account for the fact that no new racially mixed populations were formed as a result of Indian contact with either group over the course of the eighteenth century,[12] when seventeenth-century records reported the practice, apparently widespread among the Citará, of incorporating into their society as potential marriage partners women captured in warfare against native enemy groups?[13] What fate befell those women, slave and white, taken captive during the 1638 attack on the Martín Bueno expedition, and the subsequent 1684 rebellion? The first manifestations of native attitudes derive from sources pertaining to the foundation of Murri, which provide clear indications that inter-racial mixing was widely condemned within indigenous society, and that abortion was one measure to which Indians commonly resorted to deal with the offspring of Indian–white unions. According to the Citará Baltasar Aripema, giving evidence to Governor López de Carvajal in 1711, 'females pregnant by those who are not Indians which they call Christians are made to deliver the child still-born, because they are greatly abhorred'.[14] No information was offered regarding the nature of these relationships, or the frequency with which they occurred. However, in discussing in 1713 the Cuna's widely reported alliances with English interlopers in the Darién region,[15] a matter of concern to the Spanish authorities throughout the eighteenth century, *oidor* Vicente de Aramburu was also to comment on the particular aversion the Citará were said to display towards the progeny of Indian–white relationships: 'they detest profoundly', he stated, those 'Cunacunas who are born white and fair'.[16]

Indigenous attitudes towards the region's black population, both slave and free, were also marked by such hostility as to preclude any possibility of social contact – or political alliance – between the two groups. In the early 1710s, for example, Antioquia's *protector* Rafael de Oquendo petitioned on the Indians' behalf that the gradual intrusion of slaves into Chocó territory was a cause of some distress to the local Citará population, and that the 'many slave gangs' then present there had contributed to the decision of many Indians to retreat towards the Murri river.[17] And it seems that no lessening of tension, or acknowledgement of shared interest in the face of exploitation and domination, came about over the decades that followed. For not only did Governor Ciaurriz describe indigenous peoples, in 1807, as 'friendly towards whites but enemies of the blacks',[18] but even the Frenchman Gaspar Mollien, travelling through the new republic of Colombia in 1822 and 1823, drew attention to the Indians' 'violent antipathy' towards blacks, whom they nevertheless addressed as 'amo' or master.[19]

The peoples of the Chocó were aided in their quest for an existence separate from those of the other groups with whom they came to share occupation of this distant and difficult terrain by the peculiar characteristics of the society the Spaniards created there following suppression of the 1684 rebellion. Although Indians did not succeed in turning back the Spanish advance into a territory that had become vital to the economic well-being of the viceroyalty of which it formed part, several factors particular to this frontier were nevertheless to contribute to their ability to maintain their physical and cultural distance from both colonisers and slaves. Principal among these were the numerical insignificance of the white population (359 in 1782, compared with an Indian total of 6552); the dispersed and temporary character of mining settlement and the strict *cuadrilla* regime to which slaves were subjected; the limited development to which gold-mining gave rise in this region that in all ways but one was entirely peripheral to Spanish interests; and perhaps even the discrimination that led many slaves, on becoming free, to retreat to the more inaccessible parts of the forest, where they survived by farming and small-scale mining.[20] In these circumstances, withdrawal from all but the most necessary contact was to continue to serve Indians as an effective mechanism to resist integration and assimilation until the very end of colonial rule. 'These Indians, fleeing their towns, hide in the ravines', *ingeniero* Juan Jiménez Donoso reported in 1780, 'which, as they are so sparsely populated, is extremely easy for them'.[21] And even as these movements brought about the unintended consequence of encouraging Spaniards to extend their control over larger and larger areas of the Chocó,[22] Indians were to seek out ever more distant and isolated refuges in the most northern and western sections of the Pacific lowlands region, beginning, by the late 1700s, a process of migration towards Panama and the Pacific coast that was to continue into the twentieth century.[23]

Given the extraordinary challenges the Spaniards faced in their efforts to dominate and transform the peoples of 'the richest [territory] in the world',[24] and the remarkable determination with which the latter strove to protect their communities from undesirable colonial influences, the observations of late colonial officials and early-nineteenth-century travellers, which convey the impression of an indigenous population that had become compliant and submissive to the demands of blacks and whites alike, are difficult to interpret. In reporting on a 1780 visit of inspection, for example, Don Juan Jiménez Donoso drew attention to the 'natural goodness' of the Chocó's native inhabitants, describing their demeanour, behaviour and form of expression as 'simple', 'docile' and 'unambitious'.[25] Gaspar Mollien, writing in 1823, similarly remarked on the pliant and submissive character of the region's indigenous peoples. Though indicating that they remained 'still little better than savages', he described the local inhabitants as 'very mild' and 'not brave', impressions the Frenchman apparently formed from the fearful attitudes Indians displayed on encountering strangers in their midst: they 'fly into the woods if a stranger enters their village', he stated, and their women 'weep and hide their faces with their hands, when spoken to'.[26] How and why this change occurred is beyond the scope of this study. I hope, however, that my raising a question that cannot yet be answered, given the many gaps that still exist in the historical literature on the Colombian Chocó, may encourage others to pick up the research at the point at which this study is brought to a close.

Notes

1 Quoted in Vargas Sarmiento, 'Los Emberá, los Waunana y los Cuna', p. 303.
2 This did not, of course, necessarily apply to Indians who chose repeatedly to flee their settlements to escape the clutches of the Spaniards, or who inhabited long-standing *cimarronas* that remained undiscovered into the eighteenth century, such as those, discovered in the region of the Murri river between 1710 and 1713, of the *indios principales* Doviga, Vianuado, Vagapuna and Udaño, 'whose Christian names are not known'. In the settlements, the situation was clearly different, however, for when, in December 1710, Joseph de la Cuesta questioned Don Gregorio Chicarabia on the whereabouts of the population that had recently deserted Bebará, the Indian gave 17 of 18 heads of family Christian first names; the eighteenth was referred to as 'Tenaure, whose Christian name he does not know'. See, respectively, Diligencia, Murri River, 12 December 1711, in AGI Santa Fe 307, 'Cuaderno . . . sobre la entrada al río Murri', fols. 126–27, and Bebará, 5 December 1710, fol. 40.
3 The distribution of population in 1782 was as follows: whites, 359; slaves, 7088; *libres*, 3899; Indians, 6552. Figures for 1808 are as follows: whites, 400; slaves, 4968; *libres*, 15,184; Indians, 4450. See Sharp, *Slavery*, Table 7, p. 199. Although the category of *libre*, as used in colonial censuses, included free blacks, mulattos, mestizos and *zambos* (those of Indian–black origin) as well as assimilated Indians, Peter Wade has shown that in the

Chocó, where the population has been and remains predominantly black, the *libre* group consisted largely, perhaps even entirely, of blacks and mulattos. See Peter Wade, 'Patterns of Race in Colombia', *Bulletin of Latin American Research*, Vol. 5, No. 2, 1986, pp. 4, 7, and *idem*, *Blackness and Race Mixture: The Dynamics of Racial Identity in Colombia*, Baltimore and London, Johns Hopkins University Press, 1993, p. 102.
4   Deeds, 'Legacies of Resistance', p. 45.
5   Weber, *The Spanish Frontier*, pp. 105–106.
6   Ciaurriz, 'Visita del Gobernador . . . Don Carlos de Ciaurriz', pp. 165–68. This represented a reduction in the size of an already inadequate clergy. In 1789, according to Francisco Silvestre, three missionaries and 16 secular priests alone shared responsibility for the religious instruction and pastoral care of a population of 15,286, divided among 15 towns, numerous mining camps and countless *cimarronas* dispersed across the length and breadth of the Pacific lowlands region. See Silvestre, *Descripción*, p. 42.
7   Don Carlos de Ciaurriz, 'Informe', Quibdó, 17 November 1803, in Ortega Ricaurte (ed.), *Historia documental*, p. 278.
8   Isacsson, 'The Egalitarian Society', p. 118.
9   Silvestre, *Descripción*, p. 42; Ciaurriz, 'Visita del Gobernador . . . Don Carlos de Ciaurriz', pp. 159–60; see also *idem*, 'Informe', in Ortega Ricaurte (ed.), *Historia Documental*, pp. 278–79.
10 As Isacsson pointed out, the Indians' 'tendency to use the native language in their internal discussions' not only offended the Spaniards, but also enabled native peoples, in the presence of Spanish officials, to consult and agree on the most suitable answers to a given question. Isacsson, 'The Egalitarian Society', p. 123.
11 Gradie, *The Tepehuan Revolt*, p. 146.
12 One of the most striking features of the Chocó, Wade has argued, is 'the fact that race mixture was not a pervasive process', and that Indian–white, Indian–black and black–white miscegenation were therefore not outcomes of inter-ethnic contact here. Wade, 'Patterns of Race', p. 7.
13 Marzal, 'Informe', in Pacheco, *Los Jesuitas*, II, pp. 501–502.
14 See the statement of Baltasar Aripema, 2 October 1711, in AGI Santa Fe 307, 'Cuaderno . . . sobre la entrada al río Murri', fol. 110.
15 The Darién region was, in fact, also a site of French activity during the early and middle decades of the eighteenth century, as it had been of the Scots between 1698 and 1700. See, for example, Francisco Martínez's report, dated Quibdó, 24 November 1752, AGN Caciques e indios, 6, fols. 36–42; and Ignacio Gallup-Díaz, '"Haven't We Come to Kill the Spaniards?" The Tule Upheaval in Eastern Panama, 1727–1728', *Colonial Latin American Review*, Vol. 10, No. 2, 2001, pp. 259–60. It is possible, however, that Aramburu was referring to the small number of albinos who lived among the Cuna, and who, Lionel Wafer had claimed, were regarded with distaste even by their own people. See John Prebble, *The Darien Disaster*, London, Secker and Warburg, 1968, p. 71.
16 AGI Quito 143, Vicente de Aramburu to Crown, Santa Fe, 8 September 1713.
17 Petición, n.p., n.d, 'Cuaderno . . . sobre la entrada al río Murri', fol. 26.
18 Ciaurriz, 'Visita del Gobernador . . . Don Carlos de Ciaurriz', p. 159.
19 Mollien, *Travels*, p. 306. Although this study does not review the anthropological literature, it is to be noted that this was a phenomenon frequently commented upon by anthropologists conducting fieldwork in the Chocó. In the 1920s, for example, Erland Nordenskiold described the way in which his Indian guide, 'the great medicine man' Selimo, 'was always superciliously and often insultingly treated by our more or less black servants', and how Selimo eventually asserted himself by deliberately placing a venomous snake among the clothing of the expedition's black steersman. In 1939, Robert Cushman Murphy similarly commented on the Chocó peoples' 'strong sentiment against miscegenation', to the extent that they 'become intolerant of association' with

blacks or mulattos. In the 1970s, Sven-Erik Isacsson and Nina Friedemann also drew attention to the fact that the region's indigenous inhabitants, reduced to a mere 7 per cent of the total population, had gradually pushed towards the headwaters and upper reaches of the Chocó's many rivers, separated from the black population, except for 'accidental commercial transactions'. See, respectively, Nordenskiold, 'The Chocó Indians', pp. 347, 349; Robert Cushman Murphy, 'Racial Succession in the Colombian Chocó', *The Geographical Review*, Vol. 29, 1939, p. 466; Nina S. de Friedemann, 'The Fiesta of the Indian in Quibdó, Colombia', in N.S. de Friedemann (ed.), *Tierra, Tradición y Poder en Colombia. Enfoques Antropológicos*, Bogotá, Biblioteca Básica Colombiana, 1976, p. 205; and Isacsson, 'Emberá', p. 22.

20 Wade, *Blackness and Race Mixture*, p. 101. See also Werner Cantor, *Ni aniquilados ni vencidos*, p. 155.

21 Jiménez Donoso, 'Relación del Chocó', in Ortega Ricaurte (ed.), *Historia Documental*, p. 210.

22 According to Silvestre, it was to those retreats that the *corregidores* travelled to employ Indians and collect tributes. Silvestre, *Descripción*, p. 42.

23 According to Robert West, in 1782, local officials in Quibdó 'complained bitterly that many of the ... Indian villages on the Atrato, such as Beté and Bebará, were rapidly declining in population because of such migrations'. West, *The Pacific Lowlands*, p. 91, and p. 224 n. 34. Such migrations, of course, largely explain the decline in the size of the Indian population from 6552 in 1782 to 4450 in 1808, although William Sharp has noted that an outbreak of smallpox between these dates also contributed to the decrease. Sharp, *Slavery*, pp. 21, 199.

24 These were the words used by Don Francisco de Quevedo to describe Noanama province in 1669. See AGI Quito 67, San Joseph de Noanama, 15 May 1669.

25 Jiménez Donoso, 'Relación del Chocó', in Ortega Ricaurte (ed.), *Historia documental*, p. 210.

26 Mollien, *Travels*, pp. 306–307.

APPENDIX

The Chocó: Towns and Mining Camps (c. 1753)

Taken from 'Descripción del Gobierno del Chocó, en la jurisdicción del Nuevo Reino de Granada, que se presenta, con memorial, a S.M., por Don Pedro Muñoz de Arjona, hijo del coronel Don Alfonso de Arjona', n.p., n.d., in AGI Santa Fe 733.

Towns: Province of Nóvita

San Gerónimo de Nóvita is the principal town of the province of Nóvita. It is here that the governor and his *teniente* reside. San Gerónimo contains a public jail, a church, and 65 dwellings – including the residence of the governor and *teniente*. The remaining dwellings are used by the merchants who come to the province to sell their wares. With the exception of four miners, there are no other residents in San Gerónimo de Nóvita. The Indian population inhabits the province's other five towns. The province's mining camps are divided into four *partidos*.

Town	Spanish Officials	Indian Officials	Clergy	Total Tributaries
Las Juntas	*Corregidor*	Cacique, *capitán*, alcalde	Served by the priest of Nóvita	28
Los Brazos	*Corregidor*	Cacique, *capitán*, alcalde	Served by the priest of Nóvita	25
Sipí	*Corregidor*	Cacique, *capitán*, 2 *alcaldes*	Served by its own priest	35
Tadó	*Corregidor*	Cacique, 2 *capitanes*, 2 *alcaldes*	Served by two priests	100
Noanama	*Corregidor*	Cacique, 2 *capitanes*, 2 *alcaldes*	Served by the priest of Sipí	108
Total for the province of Nóvita				296

Towns: Province of Citará

This province is composed of seven Indian towns, two of which formerly formed part of the province of Tatama/Chocó.

Town	Spanish Officials	Indian Officials	Total Clergy	Tributaries
Quibdó	Teniente	Cacique, 3 *capitanes*, 2 *alcaldes*	Served by its own priest	161
Lloró	Corregidor	Cacique, 3 *capitanes*, 3 *alcaldes*	Served by its own priest	220
Beté	Corregidor	Cacique, 2 *capitanes*, 1 *alcalde*	Served by its own priest	23
Bebará	Corregidor	*Capitán, alcalde*	Served by its own priest	24
Murri	Corregidor	Cacique, *capitán*	Served by its own priest	31
Chamí	Corregidor	Cacique, 2 *alcaldes*	Served by its own priest	97
Tatama	Corregidor	Cacique, *alcalde*	Served by its own priest	25
Total for the province of Citará				581

Mining Camps: Province of Nóvita

Mining Camp	Owner	Working Slaves – Male	Working Slaves – Female
La Concepción del Playón y San Antonio del Remolino	Don Salvador Gómez de la Asperilla y Novoa	151	63
La Concepción del Salto	Don Francisco Gómez de la Asperilla y Novoa	59	29
Santa Bárbara	Don Juan Bautista y Barguén	90	40
La Concepción del Salto	Don Tomás de Rivas	29	20
San Felipe de Tamaná	Don Felipe de Valencia y Estrada	32	11
Nuestra Señora del Socorro y Sitio del Milagro	Don Lucas de Estaio y Fortún	6	4
Nuestra Señora de la Soledad y Pie del Salto de Guarabal	Don Gerónimo Antonio de Cabrera	17	14
Sed de Cristo	Don Juan de Bonilla y Delgado	60	38
Nuestra Señora de Chiquinquirá del Caucho	Don Manuel Villa de Moros	5	3
San Antonio del Peñón y Aguaclara	Don Tomás Francisco de Urrutia	12	5

Mining Camps: Province of Nóvita *(continued)*

Mining Camp	Owner	Working Slaves – Male	Working Slaves – Female
Nuestra Señora de la Soledad de Opogodó	Don Cristóbal de Guzmán	46	20
Nuestra Señora de Chiquinquirá de Tajuatú	Agustín Leuro	13	6
Santa Rita	Don Bernardo García de la Granda	7	5
San Lorenzo de los Brazos	Don Joseph López García Aníbal	29	16
Total		*556*	*274*

Mining Camps: Province of Nóvita – Partido de Tadó

Mining Camp	Owner	Working Slaves – Male	Working Slaves – Female
San Antonio y Santa Lucía	Don Francisco Gómez de la Asperilla	25	13
Nuestra Señora de la Soledad	Don Santos de Obregón	24	6
Santa Lucía del Calabozo	Don Nicolás de Inestrosa	46	32
Papagayo	Miguel Durán	5	3
Santa Rosa de la Platina	Don Agustín de Perea y Salinas	16	5
Nuestra Señora de los Dolores	Don Marcos de Perea	6	3
San Joseph de Piedra Piedra	Don Agustín Roso de Villalba	11	5
Santa Bárbara de Iró	Don Cristóbal de Mosquera y Figueroa	46	30
Santa Rita de Iró	Don Joseph de Mosquera y Figueroa	34	19
Señor San Joaquín de Viró	Don Francisco Javier de Mosquera	30	15
San Miguel de Tadó	Pedro Salinas Becerra	11	5
Santa Rita de Ibordó	Francisco Perea y Salinas	8	5
San Miguel de Tadolito	Agustín Becerra y Salinas	4	2
Purdó Jondó	Joseph Perea Salinas	7	5
San Nicolás de El Salto	Don Fernando Martínez de Caso	30	10
Total		*303*	*158*

Mining Camps: Province of Nóvita – Partido de San Agustín

Mining Camp	Owner	Working Slaves – Male	Working Slaves – Female
Santa Rosa y Santa Lucía	Don Juan de Argomedo	28	8
Nuestra Señora de la Honda	Don Juan Antonio de Nieva y Arrabel	16	9
Señora Santa Ana	Belongs to the Holy Souls. Administered by Don Ignacio de Moia de Torres	36	19
San Antonio Bosiradó	Don Francisco Gerónimo Mondragón	57	27
San Antonio de las Cimarronas	Don Francisco Gómez de la Asperilla y Novoa	17	10
Total		154	73

Mining Camps: Province of Nóvita – Partido del Cajón

Mining Camp	Owner	Working Slaves – Male	Working Slaves – Female
San Joseph	Don Pedro de Arboleda	42	16
San Cayetano	Doña María Rosa de Vergara y Daza	29	25
Santa Bárbara de la Bola	Doña María Josepha de Arboleda	27	22
Santa Bárbara de Arriba	Manuel Morillo	23	5
San Antonio de Torrá	Doña Antonia Gómez de la Asperilla y Novoa	62	38
Jesús, María y Joseph de Taparal	Diego de Tovar (free black)	3	1
Total		186	107

Mining Camps: Province of Citará – Partido de Quibdó

Mining Camp	Owner	Working Slaves – Male	Working Slaves – Female
Ydipurdú Pequeño	Doña Josepha de la Cuesta	23	14
Dipurdú Grande	Doña Balthasara de la Cerda	9	5
Negua	Don Diego Palomeque	7	4
Negua de la Concepción	Doña María Clemencia de Caicedo	36	24
Quebrada de San Antonio	Miguel Velasco	4	2
Ychó	Don Carlos de Andrade	18	8
Ychó de Merodó	Don Francisco Javier de los Santos	15	11
San Bartolomé de Necodá	Don Vicente Becerra de la Serna	3	4
San Bartolomé de Necodá	Don Joseph de Tapia	8	4
Quebrada de Duata	José Leonardo de Córdoba y Velasco	54	26
Certiga	Francisco González de Tres Palacios	45	22
Total		*222*	*124*

Mining Camps: Province of Citará – Partido de Bebará

Mining Camp	Owner	Working Slaves – Male	Working Slaves – Female
Bebará	Don Miguel de la Cuesta	46	28
Bebará	Doña Ignacia de Borja	24	11
Bebará	Don Toribio Sánchez de Arroyo	13	8
Gualaza	Ignacio de Quesada	4	4
Baberama	Cristóbal de Torres	5	4
Total		*92*	*55*

Mining Camps: Province of Citará – Partido de Lloró

Mining Camp	Owner	Working Slaves – Male	Working Slaves – Female
La Llave	Don Antonio de la Torre	12	12
Andagueda	Don Francisco de Maturana	45	33
Andagueda	Don Antonio Patiño	8	5
Andagueda	Don Francisco Martínez	58	30
San Bartolomé de Andagueda	Don Francisco de la Torre	6	2
Total		*129*	*82*

Bibliography

Published Primary Sources

Anónimo, 'Descripción de la provincia del Zitará y curso del rio Atrato', *Boletín de la Sociedad de Geografia de Colombia*, Vol. 8, 1948.

Camino, Fr Dionisio, 'Representación hecha por nuestra M.R.P. Fr. Dionisio de Camino, siendro provincial, al señor oidor don Josef Martínex Malo hallándose en las Provincias del Chocó, sobre lo que halló conveniente para el remedio del buen gobierno y aumento de aquellas misiones. Año de 1730', *Boletín de Historia y Antigüedades*, Vol. 43, 1956, pp. 241–60.

Cochrane, Charles Stuart, *Journal of a Residence and Travel in Colombia during the Years 1823 and 1824*, 2 vols., London, 1825, reprinted New York, AMS Press, 1971.

Ciaurriz, Carlos, 'Visita del Gobernador del Chocó, Don Carlos de Ciaurriz, practicada en el territorio de su mando en los años de 1804–1807', ed. Victor A. Bedoya, *Revista Colombiana de Antropología*, Vol. 11, 1962, pp. 153–67.

Colmenares, Germán, M. de Melo, and D. Fajardo (eds.), *Fuentes coloniales para la historia del trabajo en Colombia*, Bogotá, Universidad de los Andes, 1969.

Cuervo, Antonio B. (ed.), *Colección de documentos inéditos sobre la geografía y la historia de Colombia*, 4 vols., 1891–94.

Doblado, Fr Juan, 'Misiones de la Santa Provincia de Santa Fe o del Nuevo Reino de Granada de la Orden de nuestro Padre San Francisco', in Luis Carlos Mantilla Ruiz OFM, *Actividad misionera de los Franciscanos en Colombia durante los siglos XVII y XVIII. Fuentes documentales*, Bogotá, Editorial Kelly, 1980.

Escobar, Fray Gerónimo, 'Relación de Fray Gerónimo Descobar, de la orden de San Agustín, sobrel carácter e costumbres de los indios de la provincia de Popayán', in Jacinto Jijón y Caamaño, *Sebastián de Benalcázar*, 2 vols., Quito, Editorial Ecuatoriana, 1936–38, Vol. II, pp. 149–81.

Konetzke, Richard, *Colección de documentos para la historia de la formación social de Hispanoamérica, 1493–1810*, 5 vols., Madrid, Consejo Superior de Investigaciones Cientificas, 1953–62.

Marzal, Antonio, 'Informe sobre el Chocó', in Juan Manuel Pacheco, *Los Jesuitas en Colombia*, 3 vols., Bogotá, n.p., 1959–89, II, pp. 493–506.

Mollien, Gaspar, *Travels in the Republic of Colombia, in the Years 1822 and 1823*, London, 1824.

Moreno y Escandón, Francisco Antonio, 'Estado del Virreinato de Santa Fe, Nuevo Reino de Granada', *Boletín de Historia y Antigüedades*, Vol. 23, 1935, pp. 547–616.

Ortega Ricaurte, Enrique (ed.), *Historia documental del Chocó*, Bogotá, Departmento de Biblioteca y Archivos Nacionales, 1954.
Osorio, C.L., 'Prohibición de los reyes españoles a los eclesiásticos sobre propiedad y beneficio de minas', *Boletín Histórico del Valle*, Vol. 31, 1936, pp. 328–26.
Parry, John H., and Robert G. Keith (eds.), *New Iberian World: A Documentary History of the Discovery and Settlement of Latin America to the Early 17th Century*, 5 vols., New York, Times Books, 1984.
Posada, E.M., and P.M. Ibáñez, *Relaciones de Mando: memorias presentadas por los gobernantes del Nuevo Reino de Granada* Bogotá, Universidad Nacional de Colombia, 1910.
Silvestre, Francisco, *Descripción del Reyno de Santa Fe de Bogotá*, Bogotá, 1968.
Simón, Fray Pedro, *Noticias historiales de las conquistas de Tierra Firme en las Indians Occidentales*, 6 vols., Bogotá, Banco Popular, 1981.
Zuluaga Gómez, Victor (ed.), *Documentos inéditos sobre la historia de Caldas, Chocó y Risaralda*, Pereira, Universidad Teconológica de Pereira, 1988.

Secondary Sources

Adelman, Jeremy, and Stephen Aron, 'From Borderlands to Borders: Empires, Nation-States, and the Peoples in between in North American History', *American Historical Review*, Vol. 104, 1999, pp. 814–41.
Arcila Robledo, Fr Gregorio OFM, *Las misiones franciscanas en Colombia*, Bogotá, Imprenta Nacional, 1950.
Andrien, Kenneth J., 'The Sale of Fiscal Offices and the Decline of Royal Authority in the Viceroyalty of Peru, 1633–1700', *Hispanic American Historical Review*, Vol. 62, No. 1, 1982, pp. 49–71.
Armond, Louis de, 'Frontier Warfare in Colonial Chile', *Pacific Historical Review*, Vol. 23, 1954, pp. 125–32.
Axtell, James, *After Columbus: Essays in the Ethnohistory of Colonial North America*, Oxford and New York, Oxford University Press, 1988.
Axtell, James, *The Indians' New South: Cultural Change in the Colonial Southeast*, Baton Rouge, LA, Louisiana State University Press, 1997.
Barnadas, Josep M., 'The Catholic Church in Colonial Spanish America', in Leslie Bethell (ed.), *The Cambridge History of Latin America*, Vol. I, Cambridge, Cambridge University Press, 1984.
Barrera Monroy, Eduardo, *Mestizaje, comercio y resistencia: La Guajira durante la segunda mitad del siglo XVIII*, Bogotá, Instituto Colombiano de Antropología e Historia, 2000.
Block, David, *Mission Culture on the Upper Amazon: Native Tradition, Jesuit Enterprise, and Secular Policy in Moxos, 1660–1880*, Lincoln, NE, and London, University of Nebraska Press, 1994.
Boccara, Guillaume, 'Etnogénesis mapuche: resistencia y restructuración entre los indígenas del centro-sur de Chile (siglos xvi–xviii)', *Hispanic American Historical Review*, Vol. 79, No. 3, 1999, pp. 425–61.
Bolton, Herbert E., 'The Mission as a Frontier Institution in the Spanish-American Colonies', *American Historical Review*, Vol. 23, 1917, pp. 42–61.
Borda, J.J., *Historia de la Compañía de Jesús en la Nueva Granada*, 2 vols., Paris, 1872.
Borges Morán, Pedro, *El envío de misioneros a América durante la época española*, Salamanca, Universidad Pontificia, 1977.
Boxer, C.R., *The Church Militant and Iberian Expansion, 1440–1770*, Baltimore, Johns Hopkins University Press, 1978.

Bueno y Quijano, Manuel, *Historia de la diócesis de Popayán*, Bogotá, ABC, 1945.
Burkhart, Louise, *The Slippery Earth: Nahua–Christian Moral Dialogue in Sixteenth-Century Mexico*, Tucson, AZ, University of Arizona Press, 1989.
Burkholder, Mark, and D.S. Chandler, 'Creole Appointments and the Sale of Audiencia Positions in the Spanish Empire under the Early Bourbons, 1701-1750', *Journal of Latin American Studies*, Vol. 4, 1972, pp. 545-79.
Burkholder, Mark and D.S. Chandler, *From Impotence to Authority: The Spanish Crown and the American Audiencias, 1697–1808*, Columbia, MO, University of Missouri, 1977.
Campbell, Leon G., 'A Colonial Establishment: Creole Domination of the Audiencia of Lima During the Late Eighteenth Century', *Hispanic American Historical Review*, Vol. 52, 1972, pp. 1–25.
Castillero Calvo, Alfredo, *Conquista, evangelización y resistencia. ¿Triunfo o fracaso de la política indigenista?*, Panama, Editorial Mariano Arosemena, 1995.
Clendinnen, Inga, 'Disciplining the Indians: Franciscan Ideology and Missionary Violence in Sixteenth-Century Yucatán', *Past and Present*, No. 94, February 1982, pp. 27–48.
Clendinnen, Inga, *Ambivalent Conquests: Maya and Spaniard in Yucatán, 1517–1570*, Cambridge and New York, Cambridge University Press, 1987.
Colmenares, Germán, *Historia económica y social de Colombia, 1537–1719*, Medellín, Editorial La Carreta, 1975.
Colmenares, Germán, *Cali: Terratenientes, mineros y comerciantes, siglo XVIII*, Cali, Universidad del Valle, 1975.
Colmenares, Germán, *Historia económica y social de Colombia, II. Popayán: una sociedad esclavista*, Bogotá, Editorial La Carreta, 1979.
Colmenares, Germán, 'La formación de la economía colonial (1500–1740)', in José Antonio Ocampo (ed.), *Historia económica de Colombia*, Bogotá, Siglo Veintiuno Editores, 1988, pp. 13–47.
Deeds, Susan M., 'Indigenous Responses to Mission Settlement in Nueva Vizcaya', in Erick Langer and Robert H. Jackson (eds.), *The New Latin American Mission History*, Lincoln, NE, and London, University of Nebraska Press, 1995, pp. 77–108.
Deeds, Susan M., 'Colonial Chihuahua: Peoples and Frontiers in Flux', in Robert H. Jackson (ed.), *New Views of Borderlands History*, Albuquerque, NM, University of New Mexico Press, 1998, pp. 21–40.
Deeds, Susan M., 'Indigenous Rebellions on the Northern Mexican Mission Frontier: From First-Generation to Later Colonial Responses', in Donna J. Guy and Thomas E. Sheridan (eds.), *Contested Ground: Comparative Frontiers on the Northern and Southern Edges of the Spanish Empire*, Tucson, AZ, University of Arizona Press, 1998, pp. 32–51.
Deeds, Susan M., 'First Generation Rebellions in Seventeenth-Century Nueva Vizcaya', in Susan Schroeder (ed.), *Native Resistance and the Pax Colonial in New Spain*, Lincoln, NE, and London, University of Nebraska Press, 1998, pp. 1–29.
Deeds, Susan M., 'Legacies of Resistance, Adaptation, and Tenacity: History of the Native Peoples of Northwestern Mexico', in Richard E.W. Adams and Murdo J. MacLeod (eds.), *The Cambridge History of the Native Peoples of the Americas, Vol. II: Mesoamerica, Part 2*, Cambridge, Cambridge University Press, 2000, pp. 44–88.
Díaz López, Zamira, *Oro, sociedad y economía. El sistema colonial en la gobernación de Popayán: 1533–1733*, Bogotá, Banco de la República, 1994.
Farriss, Nancy, *Maya Society Under Colonial Rule: The Collective Enterprise of Survival*, Princeton, NJ, Princeton University Press, 1984.

Friedemann, Nina S. de, 'The Fiesta of the Indian in Quibdó, Colombia', in N.S. de Friedemann (ed.), *Tierra, Tradición y Poder en Colombia. Enfoques Antropológicos*, Bogotá, Biblioteca Básica Colombiana, 1976, pp. 203–10.

Gallup-Díaz, Ignacio, '"Haven't We Come to Kill the Spaniards?" The Tule Upheaval in Eastern Panama, 1727–1728', *Colonial Latin American Review*, Vol. 10, No. 2, 2001, pp. 251–71.

Garavaglia, Juan Carlos, 'The Crises and Transformations of Invaded Societies: The La Plata Basin (1535–1650)', in Frank Salomon and Stuart B. Schwartz (eds.), *The Cambridge History of the Native Peoples of the Americas, Vol. III: South America, Part 2*, Cambridge and New York, Cambridge University Press, 1999, pp. 1–58.

Góngora, Mario, *Studies in the Colonial History of Latin America*, Cambridge, Cambridge University Press, 1975.

Gradie, Charlotte, *The Tepehuan Revolt of 1616: Militarism, Evangelism, and Colonialism in Seventeenth-Century Nueva Vizcaya*, Salt Lake City, UT, University of Utah Press, 2000.

Grahn, Lance, *The Political Economy of Smuggling: Regional Informal Economies in Early Bourbon New Granada*, Dellplain Latin American Studies, Boulder, CO, and Oxford, Westview Press, 1997.

Grahn, Lance, '"Chicha in the Chalice": Spiritual Conflict in Spanish American Mission Culture', in Nicholas Griffiths and Fernando Cervantes (eds.), *Spiritual Encounters: Interactions between Christianity and Native Religions in Colonial America*, Birmingham, University of Birmingham Press, 1999, pp. 255–75.

Griffiths, Nicholas, 'Introduction', in *idem* and Fernando Cervantes (eds.), *Spiritual Encounters: Interactions between Christianity and Native Religions in Colonial America*, Birmingham, University of Birmingham Press, 1999, pp. 1–42.

Guy, Donna J., and Thomas E. Sheridan, 'On Frontiers: The Northern and Southern Edges of the Spanish Empire in the Americas', in *idem* (eds.), *Contested Ground: Comparative Frontiers on the Northern and Southern Edges of the Spanish Empire*, Tucson, AZ, University of Arizona Press, 1998, pp. 3–15.

Hanke, Lewis, 'The Development of Regulations for Conquistadores', in *Contribuciones para el Estudio de la Historia de América. Homenaje al Dr. Emilio Ravignani*, Buenos Aires, Editorial Peuser, 1941, pp. 71–87.

Haring, C.H., *The Spanish Empire in America*, New York, Harcourt, Brace and Company, 1975.

Hennessy, Alistair, *The Frontier in Latin American History*, Albuquerque, NM, University of New Mexico Press, 1978.

Isacsson, Sven-Erik, 'Fray Matías Abad y su diario de viaje por el rio Atrato en 1649', *Boletín de Historia y Antigüedades*, Vol. 61, 1974, pp. 457–75.

Isacsson, Sven-Erik, 'Emberá: territorio y régimen agrario de una tribu selvática bajo la dominación española', in N.S. de Friedemann (ed.), *Tierra, Tradición y Poder en Colombia. Enfoques Antropológicos*, Bogotá, Biblioteca Básica Colombiana, 1976, pp. 21–38.

Isacsson, Sven-Erik, 'The Egalitarian Society in Colonial Retrospect: Emberá Leadership and Conflict Management under the Spanish, 1660–1810', in Harald O. Skar and Frank Salomon (eds.), *Natives and Neighbors in South America: Anthropological Essays*, Gothenburg, Göteborgs etnografiska museum, 1987, pp. 97–129.

Jackson, Robert H., 'Introduction', in Erick Langer and *idem* (eds.), *The New Latin American Mission History*, Lincoln, NE, and London, University of Nebraska Press, 1995, pp. vii–xviii.

Jackson, Robert H. (ed.), *New Views of Borderlands History*, Albuquerque, NM, University of New Mexico Press, 1998, pp. 1–8.

Jackson, Robert H., and Edward Castillo, *Indians, Franciscans, and Spanish Colonization: The Impact of the Mission System on California Indians*, Albuquerque, NM, University of New Mexico Press, 1995.

Jaramillo Uribe, Jaime, 'La economía del virreinato (1740–1810)', in José Antonio Ocampo (ed.), *Historia económica de Colombia*, Bogotá, Siglo Veintiuno Editores, 1988.

Jones, Grant D., *Maya Resistance to Spanish Rule: Time and History on a Colonial Frontier*, Albuquerque, NM, University of New Mexico Press, 1989.

Jones, Kristine L., 'Warfare, Reorganization, and Readaptation at the Margins of Spanish Rule: The Southern Margin (1573–1882)', Frank Salomon and Stuart B. Schwartz (eds.), *The Cambridge History of the Native Peoples of the Americas, Vol. III: South America, Part 2*, Cambridge and New York, Cambridge University Press, 1999, pp. 138–87.

Karasch, Mary, 'Interethnic Conflict and Resistance on the Brazilian Frontier of Goiás, 1750–1890', in Donna J. Guy and Thomas E. Sheridan (eds.), *Contested Ground: Comparative Frontiers on the Northern and Southern Edges of the Spanish Empire*, Tucson, AZ, University of Arizona Press, 1998, pp. 115–34.

Knaut, Andrew L., *The Pueblo Revolt of 1680: Conquest and Resistance in Seventeenth Century New Mexico*, Norman, OK, and London, University of Oklahoma Press, 1995.

Lamar, Howard, and Leonard Thompson (eds.), *The Frontier in History: North America and Southern Africa Compared*, New Haven and London, Yale University Press, 1981.

Lane, Kris, 'Taming the Master: *Brujería*, Slavery, and the *Encomienda* in Barbacoas at the Turn of the Eighteenth Century', *Ethnohistory*, Vol. 45, No. 3, 1998, pp. 477–507.

Leal, Bernardo, '"Matar a los blancos bueno es, luego Chocó acabará": Cimarronaje de esclavos jamaiquinos en el Chocó (1728)', *Fronteras*, Vol. 2, No. 2, 1998, pp. 143–61.

Lockhart, James, *The Nahuas after the Conquest: A Social and Cultural History of the Indians of Central Mexico, Sixteenth through Eighteenth Centuries*, Stanford, CA, Stanford University Press, 1992.

Lockhart, James, and Stuart B. Schwartz, *Early Latin America: A History of Colonial Spanish America and Brazil*, Cambridge, Cambridge University Press, 1983.

Lovell, W. George, *Conquest and Survival in Colonial Guatemala: A Historical Geography of the Cuchumatán Highlands, 1500–1821*, Kingston and Montreal, McGill-Queen's University Press, 1985.

Mantilla Ruiz, Luis Carlos, OFM, *Actividad misionera de los Franciscanos en Colombia durante los siglos XVII y XVIII. Fuentes documentales*, Bogotá, Editorial Kelly, 1980.

Marzahl, Peter, *Town in the Empire: Government, Politics, and Society in Seventeenth Century Popayán*, Austin, TX, University of Texas, 1978.

McFarlane, Anthony, *Colombia Before Independence: Economy, Society, and Politics under Bourbon Rule*, Cambridge, Cambridge University Press, 1993.

McFarlane, Anthony, 'Political Corruption and Reform in Bourbon Spanish America', in Walter Little and Eduardo Posada-Carbó (eds.), *Political Corruption in Europe and Latin America*, London, Institute of Latin American Studies, 1996, pp. 41–63.

Melo, Jorge Orlando, *Historia de Colombia: El establecimiento de la dominación española*, Bogotá, La Carreta, 1978.

Merrill, William L., 'Conversion and Colonialism in Northern Mexico: The Tarahumara Response to the Jesuit Mission Program, 1601–1767', in Robert W. Hefner (ed.), *Conversion to Christianity: Historical and Anthropological Perspectives on a Great Transformation*, Berkeley and Los Angeles, University of California Press, 1993, pp. 129–63.

Mills, Kenneth, *Idolatry and its Enemies: Colonial Andean Religion and Extirpation, 1640–1750*, Princeton, NJ, Princeton University Press, 1997.
Murphy, Robert Cushman, 'The Littoral of Pacific Colombia and Ecuador', *The Geographical Review*, Vol. 29, 1939, pp. 1–33.
Murphy, Robert Cushman, 'Racial Succession in the Colombian Chocó', *The Geographical Review*, Vol. 29, 1939, pp. 461–71.
Murphy, Robert Cushman, 'The Earliest Spanish Advances Southward from Panama along the West Coast of South America', *Hispanic American Historical Review*, Vol. 21, 1941, pp. 2–28.
Nordenskiold, Erland, 'The Chocó Indians of Colombia and Panama', *Discovery*, Vol. 8, 1927, pp. 347–50.
Pacheco, Juan Manuel, *Los Jesuitas en Colombia*, 3 vols., Bogotá, Editorial San Juan Eudes, 1959–89.
Pacheco, Juan Manuel, *Historia eclesiástica, vol. 2: La consolidación de la iglesia, siglo XVII*, Bogotá, Ediciones Lerner, 1975.
Pacheco, Juan Manuel, *Historia eclesiástica, vol. 3: La iglesia bajo el regalismo de los Borbones*, Bogotá, Ediciones Lerner 1986.
Padden, Robert Charles, 'Cultural Adaptation and Militant Autonomy among the Araucanians of Chile', in John E. Kicza (ed.), *The Indian in Latin American History: Resistance, Resilience, and Acculturation*, Wilmington, DE, Scholarly Resources, 1993, pp. 69–88.
Parry, John H., *The Spanish Seaborne Empire*, Berkeley and Los Angeles, University of California Press, 1990.
Phelan, John Leddy, *The Kingdom of Quito in the Seventeenth Century: Bureaucratic Politics in the Spanish Empire*, Madison, WI, University of Wisconsin Press, 1967.
Poole, Stafford, '"War by Fire and Blood": The Church and the Chichimecas', *The Americas*, Vol. 22, No. 2, 1965, pp. 115–37.
Prebble, John, *The Darien Disaster*, London, Secker and Warburg, 1968.
Radding, Cynthia, *Wandering Peoples: Colonialism, Ethnic Spaces, and Ecological Frontiers in Northwestern Mexico, 1700–1850*, Durham, NC, and London, Duke University Press, 1997.
Radding, Cynthia, 'Cultural Boundaries between Adaptation and Defiance: The Mission Communities of Northwestern New Spain', in Nicholas Griffiths and Fernando Cervantes (eds.), *Spiritual Encounters: Interactions between Christianity and Native Religions in Colonial America*, Birmingham, University of Birmingham Press, 1999, pp. 116–35.
Ramírez, Susan Elizabeth, 'The *"Dueño de Indios"*: Thoughts on the Consequences of the Shifting Bases of Power of the *"Curaca de los Viejos Antiguos"* under the Spanish in Sixteenth-Century Peru', *Hispanic American Historical Review*, Vol. 67, No. 4, 1987, pp. 575–610.
Ramírez, Susan Elizabeth, *The World Upside Down: Cross-Cultural Contact and Conflict in Sixteenth-Century Peru*, Stanford, CA, Stanford University Press, 1996.
Rausch, Jane M., *A Tropical Plains Frontier: The Llanos of Colombia, 1531–1831*, Albuquerque, NM, University of New Mexico Press, 1984.
Rausch, Jane M., *Colombia: Territorial Rule and the Llanos Frontier*, Gainesville, FL, University Press of Florida, 1999.
Redden, Andrew, 'The Enchanted Palace Where Worlds Collide: Perceptions of Power, Struggle and Martyrdom in the Province of Paraguay', MA dissertation, Institute of Latin American Studies, University of Liverpool, 2000.

Reff, Daniel T., 'The Jesuit Mission in Comparative Perspective: The Reductions of the Río de la Plata and the Missions of Northwestern Mexico, 1588–1700', in Donna J. Guy and Thomas E. Sheridan (eds.), *Contested Ground: Comparative Frontiers on the Northern and Southern Edges of the Spanish Empire*, Tucson, AZ, University of Arizona Press, 1998, pp. 16–31.
Reichel-Dolmatoff, G., 'Notas etnográficas sobre los indios del Chocó', *Revista Colombiana de Antropología*, Vol. 9, 1960, pp. 75–153.
Reichel-Dolmatoff, G., 'Contribuciones a la etnografia de los indios del Chocó', *Revista Colombiana de Antropología*, Vol. 11, 1962, pp. 169–85.
Reiter, Frederick J., *They Built Utopia: The Jesuit Missions in Paraguay, 1610–1768*, Potomac, MD, Scripta Humanistica, 1995.
Romoli, Kathleen, 'El descubrimiento y la primera fundación de Buenaventura', *Boletín de Historia y Antigüedades*, Vol. 49, 1962, pp. 113–22.
Romoli, Kathleen, 'Apuntes sobre los pueblos autóctonos del litoral colombiano del Pacífico en la época de la conquista española', *Revista Colombiana de Antropología*, Vol. 12, 1964, pp. 260–90.
Romoli, Kathleen, 'El Alto Chocó en el siglo XVI', *Revista Colombiana de Antropología*, Vol. 19, 1975, pp. 9–38.
Romoli, Kathleen, 'El Alto Chocó en el siglo XVI. Parte II: Las gentes', *Revista Colombiana de Antropología*, Vol. 20, 1976, pp. 25–67.
Romoli, Kathleen, *Los de la lengua de Cueva. Los grupos indígenas del istmo oriental en la época de la conquista española*, Bogotá, Ediciones Tercer Mundo, 1987.
Saeger, James Schofield, 'Another View of the Mission as a Frontier Institution: The Guaycuruan Missions of Santa Fe, 1743–1810', *Hispanic American Historical Review*, Vol. 65, 1985, pp. 493–517.
Saeger, James Schofield, *The Chaco Mission Frontier: The Guaycuruan Experience*, Tucson, AZ, University of Arizona Press, 2000.
Sauer, Carl, *The Early Spanish Main*, Berkeley and Los Angeles, University of California Press, 1992.
Schroeder, Susan, 'Introduction', in Susan Schroeder (ed.), *Native Resistance and the Pax Colonial in New Spain*, Lincoln, NE, and London, University of Nebraska Press, 1998, pp. xi–xxiii.
Schwaller, John F., 'The Ordenanza del Patronazgo in New Spain, 1574–1660', in *idem* (ed.), *The Church in Colonial Latin America*, Wilmington, DE, Scholarly Resources, 2000, pp. 49–69.
Scott, James C., *Weapons of the Weak: Everyday Forms of Peasant Resistance*, New Haven and London, Yale University Press, 1985.
Scott, James C., *Domination and the Arts of Resistance: Hidden Transcripts*, New Haven and London, Yale University Press, 1990.
Seed, Patricia, *Ceremonies of Possession in Europe's Conquest of the New World, 1492–1640*, Cambridge, Cambridge University Press, 1995.
Seed, Patricia, *American Pentimento: The Invention of Indians and the Pursuit of Riches*, Minneapolis, MN, and London, University of Minnesota Press, 2001.
Sharp, William Frederick, *Slavery on the Spanish Frontier: The Colombian Chocó, 1680–1810*, Norman, OK, University of Oklahoma Press, 1976.
Sheridan, Thomas E., 'The Limits of Power: The Political Ecology of the Spanish Empire in the Greater Southwest', *Antiquity*, Vol. 66, 1992, pp. 153–71.
Spalding, Karen, 'Social Climbers: Changing Patterns of Mobility among the Indians of Colonial Peru', *Hispanic American Historical Review*, Vol. 50, No. 4, 1970, pp. 645–64.

Spalding, Karen, *Huarochirí: An Andean Society under Inca and Spanish Rule*, Stanford, CA, Stanford University Press, 1984.

Stern, Steve J., 'The Rise and Fall of Indian–White Alliances: A Regional View of "Conquest" History', *Hispanic American Historical Review*, Vol. 61, No. 3, 1981, pp. 461–91.

Stern, Steve J., *Peru's Indian Peoples and the Challenge of Spanish Conquest: Huamanga to 1640*, Madison, WI, and London, University of Wisconsin Press, 1982.

Stern, Steve J., 'The Social Significance of Judicial Institutions in an Exploitative Society: Huamanga, Peru, 1570–1640', in George A. Collier, Renato I. Rosaldo and John D. Worth (eds.), *The Inca and Aztec States, 1400–1800: Anthropology and History*, New York and London, Academic Press, 1982, pp. 289–320.

Stern, Steve J., 'Paradigms of Conquest: History, Historiography, and Politics', *Journal of Latin American Studies*, Vol. 24, Quincentenary Supplement, 1992, pp. 1–34.

Storrs, Christopher, 'Disaster at Darien (1698–1700)? The Persistence of Spanish Imperial Power on the Eve of the Demise of the Spanish Habsburgs', *European History Quarterly*, Vol. 29, No. 1, 1999, pp. 5–38.

Stout, David B., 'The Chocó', in J.H. Steward (ed.), *Handbook of South American Indians*, Vol. IV, New York, Cooper Square Press, 1963.

Sweet, David, 'Misioneros Jesuitas e indios "recalcitrantes" en la Amazonia colonial', in M. León Portilla, M. Gutiérrez Estévez, G.H. Gossen and J.J. Klor de Alva (eds.), *De palabra y obra en el Nuevo Mundo*, Vol. I, *Imágenes interétnicas*, Madrid, Siglo XXI de España, 1992, pp. 265–92.

Sweet, David, 'The Ibero-American Frontier Mission in Native American History', in Erick Langer and Robert H. Jackson (eds.), *The New Latin American Mission History*, Lincoln, NE, and London, University of Nebraska Press, 1995, pp. 1–48.

Taylor, William B., and Franklin Pease (eds.), *Violence, Resistance, and Survival in the Americas: Native Americans and the Legacy of Conquest*, Washington and London, Smithsonian Institution Press, 1994.

Turner Bushnell, Amy, 'Ruling "the Republic of Indians" in Seventeenth-Century Florida', in Peter H. Wood, Gregory A. Waselkov and M. Thomas Hatley (eds.), *Powhatan's Mantle: Indians in the Colonial Southeast*, Lincoln, NE, and London, University of Nebraska Press, 1989, pp. 134–50.

Twinam, Ann, *Miners, Merchants, and Farmers in Colonial Colombia*, Austin, TX, Institute of Latin American Studies, 1982.

Van Young, Eric, 'The Cuautla Lazarus: Double Subjectives in Reading Texts on Popular Collective Action', *Colonial Latin American Review*, Vol. 2, Nos. 1–2, 1993, pp. 3–26.

Vargas Sarmiento, Patricia, 'La fundación de pueblos en la cuenca alta del Atrato. Siglo XVII', *Revista de Antropología*, Vol. 1, 1985, pp. 56–79.

Vargas Sarmiento, Patricia, 'Los Emberá, los Waunana y los Cuna: cinco siglos de transformaciones territoriales en la región del Chocó', in Pablo Leyva (ed.), *Colombia Pacífico*, Bogotá, Fondo José Celestino Mutis, FEN, Colombia, 1993, Vol. I, pp. 293–309.

Vargas Sarmiento, Patricia, *Los Emberá y los Cuna. Impacto y reacción ante la ocupación española. Siglos XVI y XVII*, Bogotá, Cerec, 1993.

Villalobos R., Sergio, *La vida fronteriza en Chile*, Madrid, Editorial Mapfre, 1992.

Wade, Peter, 'Patterns of Race in Colombia', *Bulletin of Latin American Research*, Vol. 5, No. 2, 1986, pp. 1–19.

Wade, Peter, *Blackness and Race Mixture: The Dynamics of Racial Identity in Colombia*, Baltimore and London, Johns Hopkins University Press, 1993.

Wassen, S. Henry, 'Apuntes etnohistóricos chocoanos', *Hombre y Cultura*, Vol. 1, No. 2, 1963, pp. 5–21.
Wassen, S. Henry, 'Etnohistoria chocoana y cinco cuentos waunana apuntados en 1955', *Etnologiska Studier*, Vol. 23, 1963, pp. 9–78.
Weber, David J., 'Blood of Martyrs, Blood of Indians: Towards a More Balanced View of Spanish Missions in Seventeenth-Century North America', in David Hurst Thomas (ed.), *Columbian Consequences Vol. 2: Archaeological and Historical Perspectives on the Spanish Borderlands East*, Washington and London, Smithsonian Institution Press, 1990, pp. 429–48.
Weber, David J., *The Spanish Frontier in North America*, New Haven and London, Yale University Press, 1992.
Weber, David J., and Jane M. Rausch, *Where Cultures Meet: Frontiers in Latin American History*, Wilmington, DE, Jaguar Books on Latin America, 1994.
Werner Cantor, Erick, *Ni aniquilados ni vencidos: Los Emberá y la gente negra del Atrato bajo el dominio español. Siglo XVIII*, Bogotá, Instituto Colombiano de Antropología e Historia, 2000.
West, Robert C., *Colonial Placer Mining in Colombia*, Baton Rouge, LA, Louisiana State University Press, 1952.
West, Robert C., *The Pacific Lowlands of Colombia: A Negroid Area of the American Tropics*, Baton Rouge, LA, Louisiana State University Press, 1957.
Whitehead, Neil L., 'Native Peoples Confront Colonial Regimes in Northeastern South America (c.1500–1900)', in Frank Salomon and Stuart B. Schwartz (eds.), *The Cambridge History of the Native Peoples of the Americas, Vol. III: South America, Part 2*, Cambridge, Cambridge University Press, 1999, pp. 382–442.
Williams, Caroline A, 'Resistance and Rebellion on the Spanish Frontier: Native Responses to Colonization in the Colombian Chocó, 1670–1690', *Hispanic American Historical Review*, Vol. 79, 1999, pp. 397–424.
Zavala, Silvio, *Las Instituciones jurídicas en la conquista de América*, 2nd edition, Mexico City, Editorial Porrúa, 1971.

Index

Abad, Fray Matías 76, 78, 88n. 16, 88n. 18, 95, 97, 99, 110
Abastos y Castro, Fray Manuel de 165
abortion 222–3
Acevedo Redes, Luis de 112
Acuña, Pedro de 29–30
Acuña y Berrio, Don Luis 153, 163
adelantado 43–4, 46
adelantado of Popayán 45, 50, 51, 52, 55, 58, 59, 61, 62, 63–4, 72, 95
    see also Guevara, Don Juan Vélez de
administration 155, 156, 158, 159, 197
Adoata 60
adultery 206, 207, 208
afterlife 208
agriculture 98, 164–5, 169, 170
Aguila, Don Joseph Hurtado del 155, 168
Aguinaga, Miguel de 112, 113, 114
Alaraz, Bartolomé de 102
Alarcón, Ruiz de 32
Alcantud y Gaona, Don Francisco de 153, 159, 163, 167, 175, 176, 188n. 118, 201
Alcedo Lemus de Sotomayor, Don Carlos de 145–6
Almagro, Diego de 12, 19, 20
Almaguer 17
Alvarez, Esteban 138
Amata, Don Simón 130, 137
Amazon 107, 207
Amigo, Simón 77, 78, 82, 95
Anchicayá river 15, 34, 76
Andagoya, Pascual de 15
Andagueda river 14, 15, 20, 85, 102, 140
Andean cordilleras 17

Andean region 96
Andrade, Diego de 50
Anserma 20, 27, 29, 30–1, 32, 47–8, 49, 50, 52, 55, 59, 60, 61, 63, 78, 108, 113, 129, 133, 136, 140, 164
Anserma-Cartago 17
Antioquia 46–52, 55, 57, 61, 62, 64–5, 72, 74–7, 81, 83, 86–7, 94–5, 98, 101, 103, 107–13, 115, 127, 129–35, 137–8, 140, 145, 162, 165, 166, 193, 195–201, 222–3
    see also Santa Fe de Antioquia
Antioquian region 14, 16, 29, 30, 31, 37
Anuada, Pedro 200
Anugama 146
Aramburu, Vicente de 153, 159, 163, 164, 165, 174, 175, 197, 199, 201, 223
Araucanian (Mapuche) people 69n. 65, 70–1n. 116, 92n. 79, 215n. 70
Arboleda Salazar, Don Francisco de 153, 154, 162
Arboleda Salazar, Don Melchor Jacinto de 155, 168, 207
Arboleda Salazar family 153, 155
Arce, Don Diego Radillo de 129, 130, 131, 132, 133, 134, 136, 137, 138
Ardanza, Martín de 128, 143, 144
Aricum 24, 27
Aripema, Baltasar 222–3
Arjona, Don Pedro Muñoz de 204, 207, 209–10
Arquía river 76, 199
Arrogoma 51
Artiaga, Fray Cristóbal de 131–3, 134
Atrato region 57, 99

Atrato (San Juan) river 10, 11–12, 15, 16,
    19, 20, 22, 29, 30, 32, 33, 34, 50, 51,
    58, 63, 64, 76, 81, 85, 97, 98, 102,
    103, 115, 127, 130, 160, 162, 164,
    175, 176, 209
  see also San Juan (Atrato) river
Aucavira, Capitán 103, 128, 139, 144, 146
audiencia 7
audiencia of Panama 74, 94
audiencia of Popayán 145–6, 157–8
audiencia of Santa Fe 57, 72, 73, 74, 77,
    79, 89n. 19, 91n. 60, 91n. 61, 96, 110,
    113, 131, 175, 196
Augustinians 44, 94
Aviles, Esteban de 129
Ayala, Fray Juan de 179
Aztecs 99

Baca, Alonso de 135–6
Balboa, Vasco Núñez de 11, 19
baptism 82, 90–1n. 52, 114, 203, 205, 221
Baquera, Miguel 128
Baquía, Don Sebastián 196–7, 200
Baquirura 55
barbacoas 32
Barbacoas region 35, 37, 42n. 93, 76
Barroso, Fray Diego 178
Bastidas, Rodrigo de 10
Batassa 132
Baudó 221
Baudó river 12, 34
Bauri 60
Bautista, San Juan 82
Bay of Buenaventura (Bahía de la Cruz)
    12
Bay of Solano 12
Bebará 159, 160, 166–7, 192, 195, 196,
    197, 199, 231
Bebará river 81, 102, 140
Bebarama river 61, 62, 154
Bejarano 140
Benalcázar, Sebastián de 14, 15
Benítez, Francisco 81
Bepa, Agustín 196, 199, 200
Bernardo 140
Berrio, Gerónimo de 127, 144, 145, 146,
    152
Berrio, Luis de 75, 79, 83
Betancur, Don Pedro Salazar 108

Beté 160, 179, 228
Biramia 141, 145
Biva, Capitán 128
black population 81, 139, 163, 221, 222,
    223, 224, 225–6n. 19
Block, David 207
bloodlines, purity of native 222–3
Bogassaga, Gregorio 130, 131–2, 134
Bogotá *see* Santa Fe de Bogotá
Bojaya, *corregimiento* of 160
Bojaya river 34, 127, 198
Bolivar, Don Pedro de 79, 82, 86, 127,
    128, 135, 136, 139
Bonilla y Delgado, Juan de 172
Borja, Bartolomé de 112
Borja, Don Francisco de 133, 136, 140
Borja, Don Gaspar de 48, 59, 61, 63
Borja, Don Juan de 51, 52
Borja, Manuel de 144
Botabirá peoples 24, 25–6, 27
Bourbons 179
bravery 143–4, 209
Buenaventura 15, 25, 26, 33, 34, 37, 77,
    176
Buenavista 49, 50, 51, 55, 56, 57, 58, 61,
    97
Buga 29, 30, 157, 164, 176
Burgos 11, 45
Burgumia (Boromea/Poromea/Burumia)
    19, 34, 111, 143
burials 14, 208

Caballero, Fray Juan 172
Cacajambres 37
Cáceres 17, 28, 195
Cáceres, Pedro de 95, 116n. 7
'cacicazgos' 26
caciques 99–100, 118n. 40, 194–5, 202,
    211n. 14, 212n. 29, 215n. 71, 222
Cádiz 101
Caicedo, Cristóbal de 127–8, 142, 145
Caicedo, Don Francisco 154, 181n. 16
Caicedo, Fray Manuel 154, 159, 160, 170,
    171–2
Caicedo, José 170
Caicedo, Juan de 144, 145
Caicedo (née Mosquera), Doña Agustina
    170
Caicedo, Roque de 154, 170

INDEX

Caicedo Salazar, Juan de 127
Caicedos family 152, 154
Cajón (Yarrama) river 23, 24
Calced Carmelites 94
Calderón, Facundo 201
Calderón, Fray Juan Domingo 178
Cali 14, 15, 16, 20, 29, 75, 76, 152, 154, 155, 157, 170
Calima river 20, 37
Caloto 155
Calvo, Alfredo Castillero 96
Calzado, Don Antonio Ruiz 146
Camargo, Arce 134, 135, 136, 137
Camargo, Fray Marcos 168
Camino, Fray Dionisio de 160, 165, 167, 168, 173, 176, 178, 179, 204, 205, 206, 207, 208, 209
Candrumbida 192
Cape Corrientes 19, 21, 22, 25, 33
capital punishment 145
capitánes 99–100, 194–5, 212n. 29
capitulaciónes 43–4, 45, 47, 53, 54, 65, 71n. 128, 72, 73
  1480 65n. 2
  1634 46, 50, 62
Capuchins 94
Carampaima, Manuel 194
Carampaima, Miguel 222
Caraupe 192–3
Cárdenas, Calixto de 194, 222
Cárdenas, Lope de 130, 131, 132, 133–5, 136–8, 142
Caro, Fray Francisco 109, 110
Carrasco brothers 139
Cartagena de Indias 14, 16, 29, 30, 64, 72, 74, 94, 101, 107, 159, 160, 200
Cartago 14, 20, 21, 29, 31, 32, 47, 48, 55, 60, 63, 78, 157, 164
Carvajal, Benito de (Jesuit) 85, 92n. 68, 99, 117n. 13
Carvajal, Don Joseph López de 166, 167, 193, 195, 196, 197, 198, 199, 200, 202, 213n. 48, 223
Carvajal, General Alfonso Rodas 47, 48
Casa de Contratación, Seville 43, 96, 100
Castilla del Oro 11, 20
Castillo, Don Juan Joseph Azcárate de 128, 129, 143, 144
Castro, Bermúdez de 45

Castro, Diego Díaz de 133, 135
Castro Rivadeneyra, Fray Miguel de 82, 87, 95, 101, 102, 105, 107–8, 109, 110
Catholicism 84, 97, 102, 167, 168, 193, 203, 205, 208, 210
Cauca river 14, 15, 17, 21, 24
Cauca Valley 14, 15, 20, 31, 33, 45, 152, 154, 155, 164
  Upper 16, 17
Cecego 128
cédula 74, 160, 172, 173, 176
  1666 79, 83, 94, 113
  1671 96, 100, 101, 119n. 46
  1674 110, 113
  1722 179, 188n. 112
  1724 179
  1726 176
  1727 171
  1753 180
Cerro de Buriticá 17
Certegui, Capitán 129, 140
Céspedes y Guzman, Gregorio 51–2, 54, 55, 61–2, 63–4, 72
Chaguera 103
Chamí 160, 164, 221, 228
Chanco people 20, 21, 22, 23, 25–6, 27, 28, 29, 33
Chancos river 21
Chaparro, Guillén 28
chapels 95–6, 113, 167–8
  see also churches
Chaqueranvido 140, 144
Chaqueravia, Don Juan 196–7
Chevi, Capitán 128, 139
Chibcha civilisation 16
Chicaravia, Don Gregorio 199
Chichimeca War 64
Chichiridó 97
Chigri, Don Juan 127, 128, 130, 139, 141
children, Indian 164, 206, 217n. 95
Chile 41n. 75, 94
Chiloma peoples 21, 22, 23, 25–6, 27, 29, 33
Chocoes 20–2, 23, 24, 25–7, 28, 31, 32, 34, 35
Christian doctrine 167, 193, 197, 203, 205, 207
Christianity 44, 46, 54, 76, 77–8, 82, 83, 89n. 31, 94–7, 100, 102–4, 106–7,

131, 158, 166–8, 170, 177, 180, 192, 193, 197, 202–10, 216n. 79, 221–2
  see also Catholicism; Dominicans; Franciscans; Jesuits; missionaries
Chuagarra 60
Chuagra, Capitán 128, 139, 144, 146
Chuaru 139
churches 207, 218n. 99, 218n. 100
  see also chapels
Churucupita (Gaspar de Luna) 49, 57, 58, 61
chusma (elderly Indians) 56, 58, 65
Ciaurriz, Don Carlos de 193, 203, 206, 208, 210, 221–2, 223
Cicerón, Jacome 31
Cifuentes, Mateo de 50, 52, 59, 60
Cirambirá peoples 25–6, 27
Citará 31, 32, 34, 35, 37, 45, 47, 48–51, 52, 53, 64–5, 74, 75, 76, 77, 79–83, 84–6, 87, 112, 166, 168, 173, 179, 206, 220, 222–3
  1700–1750 192–210, 228
  aftermath of the 1684 rebellion 152–7
  coercive missionary work 108, 109, 111
  government 158, 159, 160–2, 163, 164, 175, 176
  'guerra a sangre y fuego' against 55, 56, 57, 58–9, 60, 61–2, 63
  Juan Bueso de Valdés *entrada* 112–16
  mining camps 231–2
  obstacles to *reducción* 97–100
  peaceful missionary work 95, 96, 97, 101, 102, 103, 104, 105
  protest 1680–1684 130–8
  rebellion 1684 127–30, 138–46, 222
  territory 1669–1676 80
clothing, Indian 204, 209–10, 219n. 118
Coabra, Captain 81
Cobirá people 25–6
Cogayda 196
cohabitation 208
Colmenares 155
Colombia 12, 14, 223
colonial government 155–66
  reform 174–6
comisario 102
Comita 49, 50, 51, 55, 56, 57, 61, 97

congregación (reducción) 78–9, 82–3, 84–5, 86, 96, 97–108, 117n. 16, 120–1n. 74, 129
  changing strategies 108–12, 113, 114–16
  failure 97–108, 120n. 66, 125n. 150, 180n. 4, 192–3, 201, 204, 205
  obstacles to 97–100
conquistadores 44
Consejo de Indias 154, 170, 171
contraband 160–2, 176, 181n. 10, 190n. 136
conversion 74, 78, 84, 94, 96, 97, 100, 102, 108–12, 113, 114, 158, 168, 170, 177, 193, 202–10
  material benefits 120–1n. 74
  as reciprocal exchange 216n. 79
Coponama peoples 25–6
Cordillera Central 16, 17
Córdoba, Fray Joseph de 101, 103, 105, 106, 108–9, 116, 130, 131, 133, 134, 135, 136, 137, 142, 162, 206
corporal punishment 108, 123n. 99, 132, 206, 217n. 95, 217n. 96
correrías 128
Corro, Don Diego del 180
corruption 156, 157, 158–9, 160–2, 170–5, 176, 177, 180, 182n. 27, 182n. 38, 184n. 46, 188n. 118
Council of the Indies 43, 74, 160, 165, 172, 174, 200
creoles 121n. 87
Cruces Point 12
Cueva peoples 19, 20, 39n. 36
Cumimbara, Don Francisco 196
Cuna 19, 20, 39n. 36, 74, 76, 95, 111, 146, 195, 198, 200, 204, 208–9, 223
Cunacunas 143, 200, 209, 223
Cupamay 81, 103, 108
Cupica 201
customs, Indian 193, 204–5, 207, 208, 218n. 104
Cuttibira, Don Francisco 196

Dabeiba 11–12, 15
Dagua river 34, 76
Dami 141
Dare 144
Darién 74, 96, 97, 100, 110, 223

Darién river 56
Dávila, Miguel 28
Dávila, Pedrarias 11, 12, 20
Dávila, Pedro Martín 29
Daza, Don Pedro 79, 103, 115
dead, rituals of the 14, 208
decentralised societies 35, 42n. 89, 42n. 90, 81–2, 99–100, 118n. 37, 194, 202
Dechegama 139
demography 221, 223, 224–5n. 3
  demographic decline 19, 20, 27–9, 97
Devanado 139
Díaz, Francisco 54, 56, 57–8, 97
Dios, San Juan de 76
disease 12–14, 15, 20, 29, 105, 152, 204, 205, 217n. 85, 217n. 86
dispersed societies 62, 63, 70–1n. 116, 97–8, 113–14, 192, 201, 202, 210n. 2, 223–4, 224n. 2
Docio, Fernando 49, 54, 55–9, 60, 61, 63, 99
Dodubar 140
Dominicans 44, 94
Donoso, Juan Jiménez 209, 223, 224
Dorado 96, 100
Dorroguigo river 193
drunkenness 204, 206, 207

Ebirá peoples 25–6
Ecuador 15
Egües y Beaumont, Don Diego de 73, 74
El Barranco 159
El Cajón 168, 221, 230
El Raposo 205–6, 207
El Sarco (Omanbita) 49, 56, 57, 58, 99
Emberá 19, 35, 37, 158, 167, 194, 221
Emberá language group 34
English settlers 223
Enrique, Joseph 135
Eripedes Indians 24, 25–6
Escobar, Don Manuel Martínez de 173
Escobar, Fray Gerónimo de 28
Eslava, Viceroy 201
Espinosa, Don Luis de 175
Espinosa, Jacinto Roque de 112, 133, 135, 136
Espinosa Saravia, Lesmes de 28, 30, 31, 47–9

Esteba 57
Eulate, Juan de 86
extinction, of indigenous peoples 19, 20

factionalism 142–3
families, nuclear 97–8
famine 152
  see also hunger
Felices, Fray Francisco Antonio 172, 177–8, 189n. 134, 203
Fernández, Agustín Ginés 172
Fernández, Juan Gómez 48–9
Figueredo y Victoria, Joseph de 193
Figueroa y Barrantes, Don Benito de 74
Flores, Joseph 129
food supplies 47–8, 57, 98, 152, 160, 162, 169, 183n. 41, 196
  for the mining industry 112, 115, 136
  for missionaries 104–5, 114, 170
  price fixing by Indians 112
  price fixing by Spanish 114, 116
  shortages 53–4
  Spanish acquisition of 164–5, 169
Forero, Fray Francisco 197, 199
Franciscan College of Cali 171
Franciscans 44, 65, 75, 83, 86–7, 94–116, 119n. 51, 119n. 53, 127, 129, 130–8, 157, 158, 166–74, 189n. 131, 189–90n. 135, 191n. 146, 191n. 147, 204–6, 209, 211n. 11
  exploitative behaviour of 166–7, 177, 180, 189n. 130
  peaceful strategies 94–108
  reform 176–80
  violent strategies 108–10
  withdrawal 111
Franco, Luis 23
Frías, Bishop Juan Gómez 165, 167, 168, 172, 173, 174, 177, 178, 179, 185–6n. 73
Fuensalida, Fray Bartolomé de 107
Fuentenovilla, Fray Francisco Montiel de 171, 187n. 93
'fugitives' 198, 215n. 66

Galvis, Diego de 142, 143, 209
gandules (able-bodied Indian males) 56, 58, 60
Garaupá 132, 133

INDEX

Garcés, Santiago 76
García, Fray Francisco 109
García, Juan López 75, 77, 78–9, 84, 85, 89n. 25, 102, 105, 106, 109
García, Miguel 98, 110
García, Sebastián 86, 135, 136, 137
Garrapatas river 76, 77
Gaspar de Luna *see* Churucupita
Gerónimo de Nóvita 227
gift-giving 56, 57, 61, 77, 81, 115–16
gobernación of Antioquia 79, 82, 87, 111, 131, 162, 193–4, 195
gobernación of Chocó 46
gobernación of Popayán 15, 29, 47–8, 50, 76, 79, 87, 111, 131, 152, 155, 158, 174, 175, 176, 193–4
gobernación of San Juan 15, 38n. 20
gold
    dust 162
    treasures 12, 14, 22
gold miners 162–3, 164–5
    see also labour, Indian; slavery
gold-mining 11, 14, 16–17, 23–4, 30, 37, 45, 63, 74, 75, 78, 81, 82–3, 88n. 8, 89n. 25, 105–6, 111–12, 114, 115–16, 124n. 129, 136, 146, 152–4, 158, 169–70, 175, 198, 223
    corruption 184n. 46
    decline 195
    food supplies 112, 115, 136
    Franciscan interests 170–3
    recession 111
    tax (*quinto*) 46, 153
gold-mining camps 228–30
Gongera 139
Góngora 44
González, Francisco 135, 136
Gonzalo, Don 86
Gortisdiente, Gonzalo 31–2
government offices, sale of 156, 159–60, 168–9, 174, 176
Gradie, Charlotte 64
Guacarama, Nicolás 196
Guagone 140
Guaguirri 140, 141, 143, 144
Guajiro 205, 217n. 89
Guapama 51
Guaraní 86, 107, 191n. 147
Guaripua 140, 141, 144, 145

Guarra people 22, 23, 25–6, 27, 29, 33
Guatagoma 60
Guatupua 144
Guaycuruans 86
Guebara 130, 131, 134, 135, 136
'guerra a sangre y fuego' 52–64
Guerrero, García 24
Guerrero, Sebastian 31
Guevara, Don Juan Vélez de 37, 45–7, 49, 50, 51, 52–5, 58, 59, 61, 62, 63–4, 65, 72, 75–6, 84, 95
Guevara, Gabriel de 59
Gulf of Cupica 12
Gulf of Darién 198
Gulf of Urabá 10, 11, 19, 74
Guzmán, Antonio de 75, 79–83, 84, 85, 86–7, 91n. 60, 93n. 85, 95, 97, 98, 99, 100, 105, 106, 108, 109, 110, 111–12, 113, 114
Guzman, Francisco de 64–5
Guzmán, Gregorio de 81
Guzmán, Ignacio de 81, 82, 86–7, 91n. 60, 102, 103, 108, 109, 111–12, 131
Guzmán Jaramillo, Juan de 81
Guzmán, Juan de 136, 140, 144
Guzmán y Toledo, Luis Antonio de 77

Habsburg state 155
Heredia, Pedro de 15
Hernández, Gómez 14–15, 20, 27
Herrera y Castillo, Don Jorge de 56, 65
Hojeda, Alonso de 11
Honda 14, 101
hunger 12–14, 29
    see also famine; food supplies
Hurtado, Fray Jacinto 76, 78, 95, 104, 110

Ibagué 14, 17
Ibero, Don Francisco de 154, 157, 166, 176, 201
Icapá 81
Ichó river 103, 154
illicit trade 181n. 10
Inca 14, 16, 99
incest 204, 206, 207
Indipurdú river 154
Inestrosa, Nicolás de 155, 165, 170, 171–2, 178
Ingipurdú mine 139, 141

Iró 154, 155, 162, 168, 169, 170, 171–2, 178–9
Iró river 77
Iruñela, Fray Esteban de 101, 103, 113, 114
Isacsson, Sven-Erik 35, 98, 99–100, 194, 202
Iscuandé region 37
Iscuandé river 37
Itza-Maya 107

Jackson, Robert 101
Jesuits 44, 75, 85–6, 87, 92n. 79, 94, 96, 100, 101, 104, 107, 158, 207
'Jorge Juan' 160
Juananui 140
Junta de Propaganda Fide 73
Jurado, Martín Delgado 49

Knaut, Andrew 86

La Asperilla, Don Miguel Gómez de 154, 162–3
La Banda, Pedro Hato de 192
La Cámara, Joseph Ruiz de 60
La Candelaria, Fray Lucas de 50, 95
La Carrera, Francisco de 140, 141, 144
La Cerda, Don Diego Maldonado de 154
La Chica, Francisco de 209
La Chica y Guzmán, Antonio de 200
La Concha, Don Francisco Castillo de 131, 134
La Cosa, Juan de 10
La Cruz y Valencia, Alejo de 142
La Cuesta, Díaz de 34, 75, 77, 85
La Cuesta, Don Gabriel Díaz de 73, 82, 83–4, 91n. 61, 92n. 67, 111
La Cuesta, Don Joseph de 197, 199
La Cueva, Luis Antonio de 77, 78, 89n. 25, 95
La Enzina, Miguel Chacón de 173
La Losa, Rodrigo Río de 64
La Pedrosa y Guerrero, Don Antonio de 159, 160, 162, 172–3, 174–5, 188n. 118
La Pimienta 66–7n. 17
La Prada, Manuel de 178
La Sed de Cristo 48, 50, 52, 55, 59, 60, 61, 63, 77, 79, 85
La Serna, Francisco Ramírez de 37

labour, indigenous 17, 162–4, 168–70, 206
  exploitation 164, 168–9, 170, 196, 197
  native governors' inclusion in 197
  see also slavery
language 121n. 87, 122n. 92, 193, 203, 204, 222
Lara, Antonio Ordoñez 154
Lara, Don Nicolás Ordoñez de 172
Las Juntas 159, 227
Laws of the Indies 197
leaders, native 212n. 25, 222
  see also caciques; capitánes
Leandro 144
Legarda, Don Antonio de 133, 137, 138, 139
León Castellanos, Juan de 103
Lescano, Joseph 52
Liñán y Cisneros, Melchor 95, 110, 112, 116–17n. 10
Lira, Fray Bernardo de 76
Llanos 73, 74, 110
Lloró 85, 96, 98, 109, 113, 114, 127, 136, 138, 159, 168, 195, 200, 202, 228, 232
Lloró, Capitán 98
López García, Jorge 34, 109, 77
López García, Juan 75, 77, 78–9, 84, 85, 89n. 25, 102, 105, 106, 109
Lorenzo 196
Los Brazos 155, 168, 221, 227
'los frutas de la tierra' 101, 104, 105
Los Organos 56
Los Rios, Luis de 106
Lower Chocó 21
Lower Tarahumara 76
Luengo, Fray Juan 110

McFarlane, Anthony 14, 155, 156
Madrid 172, 174
Magdalena river 15, 16, 17
Magdalena Valley 17
Malo, Martínez 160, 165, 175, 204, 206
Manigua 141, 142, 145
Mañosca, Don Rodrigo de 146
Manzano 139
Mapuche (Araucanian) people 69n. 65, 70–1n. 116, 92n. 79, 215n. 70
Mariquita 14, 17, 133
marriage 204, 207–8, 218n. 106, 218n. 108, 222

Marton, Fray Joseph 107, 108
Marzal, Antonio (Jesuit) 35, 78, 82, 83, 85–6, 96, 98, 99, 100, 102, 104, 106, 108, 109, 117n. 13, 143–4, 204, 205, 206, 207, 209
Marzhal, Peter 173
Masupi 140
Mateo 139
Mayan 107
Meachama 141
Medrano, Fray Martín de 21, 22, 23
Membocana 33–4, 51, 76
Méndez, Matías 172
Mendoza, Don Antonio de 45
Mendoza, Don Pedro Carrillo de 48, 59, 62–3
Mercedarians 94
Merrill, William 86
Mesoamerica 96
Mexico 64, 86, 94, 99
Miarri 139
Micay river 37
middle-men 164–5
minas de la Montaña de Raposo 37
Minguirri 139, 141, 144, 145
missionaries 44, 45, 65, 73, 76, 77–8, 82–3, 85–7, 89n. 31, 92n. 79, 94–116, 129, 130–8, 157, 158, 166–74, 186n. 85, 189n. 131, 189–90n. 135, 191n. 146, 191n. 147, 197, 211n. 11
   coercive strategies 108–12
   corporal punishment 108, 123n. 99
   deference to 121n. 85
   desertions 122n. 93
   exploitative behaviour of 166–7, 177, 180, 189n. 130
   golden age 44
   peaceful strategies 94–108
   power of the Spanish Crown 190n. 139
   reciprocal exchanges 216n. 79
   reform 176–80
   resistance to 97, 192, 193, 202–10, 221–2, 225n. 6
   upkeep 100–1, 114, 119n. 47
   see also Franciscans; Jesuits
Mitiguirre, Don Juan 129, 134, 137, 139–40, 142, 196
mohanes 204
Mollien, Gaspar 223, 224

Mombú 164
Monguinera peoples 19
Montaño, Cristóbal 24
Montaño *entrada* 1593 29
Montaño, Juan 197
Montes, Don Bartolomé de 201
Montoya, Diego de 48, 50
Montoya family 48, 61
Montoya, Francisco de 48
Montoya, Ventura de 48
Montoya y Salazar, Don Francisco de 87, 101
Mora, Fray Miguel 167
Morales y Mendoza, Don Agustín 201
Moreno, Fray Francisco 137, 169, 170
Moriones, Pedro 22, 26
Morirama peoples 25–6
Mosquera, Don Nicholás de 164, 169, 170
Mosquera, Jacinto 154, 164, 169, 170
Mosquera-Romero Donoro case 164
Mosqueras family 154, 155, 162, 163, 168, 170, 171, 178
Moxos 86, 107, 183n. 30
Mungarra 154, 155, 162, 169, 170, 171–2, 178–9
Mungarra river 111
Murcia, Nicolás de 135, 136, 137
Murphy, Robert Cushman 12, 19
Murri 179, 195–202, 221, 222
Murri river 127, 140, 141, 166–7, 192, 193, 195–202, 203, 208, 209, 216n. 74, 223, 228

Nahuatl 107
national character, indigenous 224
Natucama 141
Naurita mine 127, 128, 129, 139, 140, 142
Naurita river 103, 154
Negro river 24, 76, 77
Negua 82, 85, 104, 107, 111, 113, 114, 115, 116, 127, 132, 134, 135, 136, 137, 139, 140, 141, 142, 144, 154, 179
   see also Quibdó
Negua river 81, 85, 102, 103, 154
Neiva 17
Nemota 179
Nemota river 154

New Granada 16, 17, 18, 20, 45, 46, 50, 73, 94, 136, 144, 146, 156–7, 171, 174, 176–7, 178, 205
New Mexico 86
Nicuesa, Diego de 11
Noanama (Nóvita) 23, 24, 25–6, 27, 28, 29, 33, 34, 35, 37, 48, 60, 74, 75, 76, 77, 78, 84, 127, 133, 134, 135, 140, 141, 146, 152, 153, 154, 155, 157, 164, 193, 194, 197, 199, 207, 221, 227, 228–30
  government 158, 159, 162, 163, 175, 176
  insignia 24
  missionaries 101, 108, 167–8, 169, 170, 172, 206
  obstacles to *congregación* 98, 99, 116n. 7
Noquia 140, 141, 142
Nóvita *see* Noanama
Nuestra Señora de Belén de Murri 198
Nuestra Señora de Chiquinquirá de Beté 201
Nuestra Señora de la Candelaria de Taita 113
Nuestra Señora de la Concepción de Lloró 103, 113, 114
Nuestra Señora de la Consolación de Toro 21, 23
Nuestra Señora de la Paz de Pureto 102
Nuestra Señora del Carmen de la Antigua 171
Nuestra Señora del Pilar de Zaragoza 102
Nueva Vizcaya 64, 205
Nuevo Reino de Granada 14, 73

Ocaidó river 97
Omanbita (El Sarco) 49, 56, 57, 58, 99
Onofre, Francisco 136, 137, 142
Opin, Esteban 130–1, 134
Oquendo, Rafael de 165, 166–7, 192, 196, 223
Ordenanzas para Descubrimientos (Ordinances for New Discoveries) 44, 94
1573 46
Orocubirá peoples 25–6, 27
Oromira (Sucio) river 29, 30, 33
Oviedo, Gonzalo Fernández de 10
Oycomea 99

Pabarandó 201
Pacific coast 19–20, 33, 224
Pacific lowlands 36, 224
Pacific Ocean 10, 11, 12, 16
pacification 20–1, 35, 44, 45, 46–7, 55, 65, 72, 74, 82, 94, 146, 177, 198
Palomino, Dionisio 129
Pamplona 17
Panama 12, 14, 15, 20, 22, 34, 64, 72, 96, 224
Pancha, Capitán Don Francisco 81, 129, 140, 142
Pani Pani river 49, 50, 56, 58, 61, 62, 97
Paparra 49
Paredes, Diego 23
Parimendo 139
Paripeso 26, 37
Pascual, Don 97
Pasto area 16, 37
Patía river 37
Patronato Real 178
Peco 86
Peguegunra, Francisco 199
Pereira, Juan Antonio 51, 54–5, 59–61, 62, 63, 74–5
Peru 14, 16, 99, 167
Perucho 144
Philip II, King of Spain 44, 94
Pichorre 141
Pidigara 139, 141
Piedra Piedra 172
Piles 37
Pino Villapadierna, Antonio del 109–10
Pivi, Don Rodrigo 129, 130, 131, 132, 135, 137, 139–40, 142–3, 194
Pizarro, Francisco 12–14, 19, 20
political organisation 118n. 37, 118n. 41
  of the Citará 99–100
  Indian 195–6, 201
  see also decentralised societies
Popayán 14–17, 20, 24, 29–31, 34, 37, 64, 72, 74–5, 77, 84–5, 94, 98, 110–12, 127, 129, 131, 133–6, 144–6, 152–5, 157–60, 162, 165, 167, 168, 171, 173, 174, 176, 193, 198, 203
  segregation of the Chocó from 176
  see also adelantado of Popayán; *gobernación* of Popayán
Portobelo 160, 162

Portocarrero, Antonio 76
Poya 31, 32, 33, 45, 47, 48, 50, 51, 52, 53, 74–5, 77
  and the 'guerra a sangre y fuego' 55, 59–60, 61, 62–3
  loyalty to the Spanish 59
pre-marital relations 208
Príncipe, Manuel Quintero 136
prowess, in warfare 143–4
Pueblo Quemado 12
Pueblos 86
Puerto de la Candelaria 12
Puerto de la Hambre 12
Puné river 154

Quesada, Pedro Rubio de 199
Quevedo, Don Francisco de 75, 83–5, 86, 95, 111, 112
Quibdó (formerly Negua) 11, 19, 154, 157, 159, 166–7, 179, 192, 195, 196–7, 199, 201, 202, 228, 231
Quintana, Antonio 130, 133
Quirubira 128, 139, 140, 142, 143, 146
Quito 14, 16, 182n. 27
Quiunape, Martin 198, 200

racial issues 222–3, 225n. 12, 225–6n. 19
Ramírez, Fray Bernardo Pascual 98, 103–4, 105, 107, 108, 113, 114
Ramírez, Fray Pedro 180
Ramírez, Gerónimo (Jesuit) 107
Ramón, Diego 76–7
Raposo 15, 154
Raposo mines 76–7
Raposo river 15, 34, 76, 104
Raposo-Iscuandé region 35, 76, 152
Recopilación de Leyes de Indias 172
Redondo, Francisco 63
reducción see congregación
regalia 159
religious administration 166–74
  reform 176–80
  see also missionaries
Remedios 17
Requerimiento 1512 54, 68n. 61
Río Negro 162
Riohacha 205
rituals, Indian 204–5, 207, 208, 218n. 104
Rivas, Francisco de 172

Rivera, Esteban Fernández de 95–6, 128, 142
riverine settlement patterns 98–9
Rodas, Juan de 56
Roldanillo 20, 21
Romero Donoro, Tomás 162–3, 170
Romero, Fray Miguel 76, 88n. 18, 95
Romoli, Kathleen 19, 20, 21, 26, 27, 28, 33
Rosas, Luis de 86
Royal Treasury 45, 50, 53, 73, 74, 176
Ruiz, Bartolomé 12, 14
Ruiz, Fray Pablo 102, 105, 108–9, 130, 137
Ruiz, Miguel 81
Ruje, Francisco 37

Saa, Don Bernardo Alfonso de 154, 162, 164
Sagito, Don Joseph 193, 196, 197–8, 199, 200, 202, 206
Saijá river 16, 37
Salamanca de los Reyes 50, 52, 55, 59
Salamanca, Joseph de 85, 97–8, 106
Salamanca, Lorenzo de 34, 85
Salamanca, Pedro García de 63
Salazar, Bernardo/Bernardino de 197–8
Salazar, Fernando Docio 47, 48
Salazar, Francisco Solano de 203, 208
Salazar, Fray Juan Joseph 201
Salazar, Lorenzo de 160–2, 174, 196
Salazar, Melchior de 23, 24, 27, 30
Samugrado river 102, 141
San Agustín 104, 159, 193, 230
San Francisco de Atrato 76, 85, 97–8, 100, 103, 113, 114, 127, 128, 136, 138
San Francisco de Atrato (second township) 102
San Gabriel 85
San Jorge river 14
San Joseph de Noanama 79, 84, 104, 155, 159, 193
San Juan (Atrato) river 15, 20, 21, 23, 24, 33, 34, 76, 79, 84, 160, 171, 175, 176
  see also Atrato (San Juan) river
San Juan Bautista, Fray Nicolás de 50, 95
San Juan de Bojaya 201
San Juan De Castro 49
San Juan de los Llanos 14

San Juan de Micay river 12, 16
San Juan de Negua 103, 113, 114, 128, 164
San Juan delta 12
San Mateo mining camp 198
San Miguel 85
San Pedro de Tacoda 85
San Sebastián de Buenavista 15
San Sebastián de Negua 85, 135
San Sebastián de Urabá 11
Sánchez, Simón 23
Sancho, Martin Bueno de 32, 49, 50, 51, 52–3, 57, 58, 59, 60, 64, 95, 222
Sangarra, Gaspar 60
Sanjua 146
Sanlúcar de Barrameda 101
Santa Ana de los Caballeros (Anserma) 14
Santa Bárbara 37
Santa Cruz, Juan de 95
Santa Fe de Antioquia 17, 29
Santa Fe de Bogotá 14, 16, 30, 45, 46, 50, 65, 72, 73, 108–9, 110, 137, 153, 157, 162, 163, 167, 174, 177, 178, 194, 203
see also audiencia of Santa Fe
Santa Lucia del Calabozo 171
Santa María del Puerto 37
Santa María la Antigua de Darién 10, 11, 12, 16, 30
Santa Marta 14, 16
Santa Teresa, Fray José de 170, 171
Santiago 23
Santisteban, Don Miguel de 201
Santo Domingo mine 81
Sara (Indian) 28
Sarco 56
Sarmiento, Patricia Vargas 19, 97
Sauer 10, 11, 19
See of Trujillo 50
Seed, Patricia 54
Serranía de Baudó 34
Sesego 146
sexual relationships 204, 206, 207–8
shaman 204–5
Sharp, William 157, 163, 172, 176
Siguma 81
Silva, Don Gerónimo de 20
Silvestre, Francisco 203, 222
Sima peoples 25–6

Simón, Fray Pedro 15, 21, 27, 29, 30, 40n. 41
Sinú region 14
Sinú river 29
Sipí 227
Sipí river 76
Sitio de Ocumita 61
slavery 78, 81, 111–12, 115–16, 146, 152–4, 163, 172, 181n. 11, 181n. 16, 222, 223
  Indian 52–3, 54, 55, 57, 60, 61, 63
  massacres 138–9, 140, 144
smallpox 29, 205, 217n. 86
Soberano 140, 143, 144
Sorrito, Andrés 47
Soruco 19, 34, 111, 134, 146
Soto, Pedro de 109
Sotomayor, Juan Nuño de 81, 112, 135, 136
Spain 10, 17, 159, 175, 177, 178, 179
Spanish Crown 43, 44, 45, 46, 53, 54, 65, 72–3, 74, 75, 76, 78, 83, 84, 85, 86, 112–13, 195, 197, 200, 201, 209
  colonial government 156, 159, 160, 162, 164, 174, 176
  Indian resistance to 192, 193
  and missionary work 94–5, 96, 100, 101, 105, 167, 171, 172–3, 177, 179–80, 190n. 139, 203
  tributes to 85
spell casting 204
Sucio (Oromira) river 195, 198, 199, 201
supplies 183n. 41
see also food supplies

Tabuenca, Fray Juan 101, 102–3, 104, 106, 107, 108, 109
Tabugara 146
Tabusido 140
Tacoda, San Pedro de 85
Tadó 111, 154, 159, 162, 163, 168, 169, 170, 178, 194, 199, 222, 227, 229
Tah Itza 107
Taichama, Capitán 129, 139–40
Taita 50, 51, 62, 63, 64, 79, 97, 98–9, 101, 103, 105, 107, 113, 114, 115, 130–1, 134
Taita river 62
Tajina 139, 141, 143, 144

Tajina, Don Fernando de 128, 143, 145
Tamaná river 76
Tamata 130, 140, 146
Tano 86
Tarascan 107
Tatama 25–6, 31, 32, 34, 35, 37, 45, 47, 48–9, 50, 51, 52, 53, 74, 75, 77, 78, 84, 85, 115, 127, 164, 221, 228
  colonial government 158, 159
  'guerra a sangre y fuego' against 55, 58, 59, 60
  Juan Bueso de Valdés *entrada* 112
  missionary work 101, 102, 105, 111
  obstacles to *congregación* (*reducción*) 99
Tatape people 25–6
Tavachi 139
Tavira, Juan de 11–12
taxation 46, 153, 159
Tebue 57, 58, 99
Tego 57, 58, 99
Tegue, Don Pedro 81, 82, 99, 103, 129, 131, 139–40, 142, 194
Teguerre 60
Telembí river 37
Tepehuan 107
Tequia 81
Tevasa 139
Tilimbí 37
Timbas 37
Timbiquí river 37
Tocama 50, 51, 63
Tootuma people 21, 22–3, 25–6, 27, 28–9, 33
Toro 23, 24, 25, 26, 27, 28, 29, 32–3, 33, 49, 50, 52, 53, 59, 63, 77, 164
  mines of 45, 46, 48, 53, 55, 61, 62
Toro Zapata, Fernando de 30, 64, 72
torture 58, 61
Tovare, Esteban 200
trade 67n. 23
  contraband 160–2, 176, 181n. 10, 190n. 136
  illicit 181n. 10
  Indian-Spanish 30–2, 41n. 75, 45, 47–8, 57, 75, 77, 78, 82, 89n. 31, 104–5, 115, 142, 165, 209, 220, 221
  middle-men 164–5
transportation 163–4
Tribinoco, Don Antonio 198, 200

tribute payments 158, 198
  exemptions 113
Troyano, Fray Juan 76
truthfulness 143–4
Tulua 84
Tunja 14, 16
Tutunendo river 103

Ubira 140
Udrapagui 143
Ulloa, Antonio de 160
Umia 141, 145
Urabá 10, 16, 19–20, 29, 33
Urrao 75, 79, 115

Valdés, Juan Bueso de 98, 103, 110, 127, 128, 140, 141, 142, 143, 144–5, 162
  entrada 112–16, 125n. 139, 125n. 140, 129, 131
  second *entrada* 137–8
Valdés-Domingo de Veitia, Bueso de 139
Valencia, Agustín de 154
Valladolid 171
Valle, Don Pedro Gómez del 84, 95, 116n. 10
values 193, 208
Vargas, Manuel de 196
Vargas, Patricia 76
Vega, Fray Buenaventura de 178
Veitia y Gamboa, Domingo de 85, 86, 90–1n. 52, 106, 109, 111, 128, 139, 141, 142
Velásquez, Melchor 17, 20–1, 22, 23, 24, 26, 28, 29, 95
Velásquez, Sebastián 130, 133
Vélez 14
Vera, Miguel de 103–4, 105, 107, 108
Veragone, Joseph 192, 196
Veragua 11
Vergara, Diego Fermín de 167, 168, 180, 185–6n. 73, 193, 205–6, 219n. 118
Veroiz y Alfaro, Don Antonio de 152
Vidal, Salvador 135
Villa Veces, Fray Lucas de 87, 105, 110
Villafañe, Fray Mateo de 167, 169, 171, 185n. 73, 203
Villalba, Don Agustín Roso de 172
Villalonga, Viceroy 176, 179
Villaquirán, Don Lorenzo de 52

Viñola, Cristóbal de 133, 134–5, 136–7
Vivero, Bartolomé Pérez de 162, 174

warfare, Indian attitudes to 208–9
water supplies 14
Waunana 158, 167
wealth acquisition 174–5
West, Robert 98
White-Indian relationships (sexual) 222–3

Yacos Indians 24, 25–6
Yaguare 26

Yapeda, Nicolás 128
Yarrama (Cajón) river 23, 24
Yarrami 60
Yarza, Don Joseph de 195, 198
Ybicua 141
Ygaragaida 141, 145
Yngará people 22–3, 25–6, 27, 28, 29, 33
Yngipurdú 141
Yvagone 140

Zaragoza 17, 195
Zavala, Juan Leyva 48, 63